Forging New Conventional Wisdom Beyond International Policing

Forging New Conventional Wisdom Beyond International Policing

Learning from Complex, Political Realities

By

Bryn Hughes, Charles T. Hunt, and Jodie Curth-Bibb

MARTINUS NIJHOFF PUBLISHERS

LEIDEN • BOSTON
2013

Library of Congress Cataloging-in-Publication Data

Hughes, Bryn
Forging new conventional wisdom beyond international policing : learning from complex, political realities / by Bryn Hughes, Charles T. Hunt, and Jodie Curth-Bibb.
pages cm
Includes index.
ISBN 978-90-04-24322-4 (hbk. : alk. paper)—ISBN 978-90-04-24482-5 (ebk.) (print)
1. Police—International cooperation. 2. Law enforcement—International cooperation. 3. Crime prevention—International cooperation. I. Hunt, Charles T. II. Curth-Bibb, Jodie. III. Title.

HV7921.H834 2013
363.2'3—dc23

2012040807

On the cover: The cover images NICA 21099, 317598, 425924, 426849, 442740, 473428, and 516063 are reprinted with permission from the United Nations Photo Library.

This publication has been typeset in the multilingual "Brill" typeface. With over 5,100 characters covering Latin, IPA, Greek, and Cyrillic, this typeface is especially suitable for use in the humanities. For more information, please see www.brill.com/brill-typeface.

ISBN 978-90-04-24322-4 (hardback)
ISBN 978-90-04-24482-5 (e-book)

This book is printed on acid-free paper.

FSC www.fsc.org MIX Paper from responsible sources FSC® C109576

Printed by Printforce, the Netherlands

CONTENTS

PART TWO

RECASTING KEY ONTOLOGICAL AND EPISTEMOLOGICAL ASPECTS

PART THREE

PUSHING BACK ON CONVENTIONAL MONITORING AND EVALUATION

PART FOUR

EVIDENCE FROM THE FIELD FOR AN UNCONVENTIONAL WISDOM

ACKNOWLEDGEMENTS

As with any body of work of the magnitude that follows, there are many to thank for enabling its completion. The research project from which this book's thinking derived would not have been possible without the generosity and support—both financial and intellectual—of two organisations: The Australia Federal Police (AFP) and the Institute for Social Science Research within the University of Queensland (ISSR). Practitioner organisations such as the AFP must continue to show vision and a willingness to embrace new ways of thinking if progress toward more effective and sustainable peace and development endeavours is to be made. The AFP's Andie Hider and Sue-Ellen Crawford were particularly helpful, having understood early on the fundamental shifts we were advocating, and then matching our determination to have such insights ultimately disseminated in order to make a difference. Paul Boreham, from ISSR, deserves special thanks for his steadfast facilitation of the many project outcomes that inform the content herein; and so too does Danielle Pratt, whose contributions and collaboration along the way proved invaluable. Members of the original project team, Thaddeus Lin, Sarah Evans, Alex Pound, Dominique Pomfret, Amy Bonshek, Marianna Duce, Patrick Law, and not least the person who started it all—Alex Bellamy—deserve our sincere gratitude for the ideas and camaraderie they extended over the years. Finally, let us not forget that it takes the broader community of practitioners, policymakers, academics—as well as the myriad voices within recipient countries—to build the knowledge needed for resilient peace and development solutions. We are accordingly indebted to the many who offered input over the years, because without it our thinking would have been far less representative of the diverse perspectives that make up this space.

INTRODUCTION

After years of substantial international community involvement to ensure Timor-Leste's peace and "self-sufficiency", the United Nations (UN) had begun the requisite draw down.[1] It was early in 2006, and the nascent country's progress was being hailed as a one of the most successful cases to date of externally led democratic nation-building.[2] The UN Office in Timor-Leste mission had been given until May 2006 to support "the development of critical State institutions and the police, and provided training in observance of democratic governance and human rights."[3] This latest permutation followed the 'successful completion' of the United Nations Mission of Support in East Timor to reform the security sector, with significant emphasis on the police.[4] With the egress well underway, all indicators pointed to the continued consolidation of previous achievements. Ticks could be given to all the important boxes: the institutions of a constitutional democracy had been established; public pronouncements of buy-in from the major stakeholders had been made; and considerable efforts in security sector reform had seen the delivery of countless hours of national police and military

---

1 United Nations Peacekeeping Operations in Timor-Leste Fact Sheet (2008), http://unmit.unmissions.org/Portals/UNMIT/Factsheets/Peacekeeping%20Operations%20in%20Timor%20Leste.English.pdf.

2 Myrttinen, Henri, "Timor-Leste A Relapsing 'Success' Story", *Taiwan Journal of Democracy*, 5 no. 1 (2009): 219–239.

3 The United Nations Mission of Support in East Timor, Website, http://www.un.org/en/peacekeeping/missions/past/unmiset/.

4 Specifically, "The new Office was to continue to support the development of critical State institutions by providing up to 45 civilian advisers; support further development of the police through the provision of up to 40 police advisers; and bolster the development of the Border Patrol Unit (BPU) by providing upt to 35 additional advisers. It was also to provide training in observance of democratic governance and human rights by providing up to 10 rights officers; and review progress on those fronts." The United Nations Mission of Support in East Timor (website, available at, http://www.un.org/en/peacekeeping/missions/past/unmiset/background.html).

training.[5] The conventional wisdom of how to conduct international peace and policing operations was thankfully delivering.

Until late April, that is. Seemingly out of nowhere, a national crisis erupted, described by the UN as "'a political, humanitarian and security crisis of major dimensions".[6] At the heart of the crisis was fighting between the police and army—the same security sector that was the focal point of international reform activities during the preceding years. By June 2006, the Timorese government was not only urging the UN Security Council for a UN police force to maintain law and order in the near term, but also arguing for the national police to undergo a major reorganisation in the longer term.[7]

The experiences of Timor-Leste raise grave questions not only about the intervention but its assessment instruments as well. In the first place, what had gone wrong with the best efforts of the international community to set the platform for sustainable peace? Why did the intervention programs apparently fail so resoundingly? Similarly, how could those in charge not have seen this coming? How did the monitoring and evaluation mechanisms fail to eliminate the blind spots? Put succinctly, how are the approaches and lenses that comprise conventional wisdom flawed?[8]

It is this puzzle which makes the Timor-Leste example the ideal springboard for the exploration undertaken throughout this book. The investigation that follows responds to questions about how to improve both the approaches to sustainable peace and the monitoring and evaluation that strives to tell us what is happening along the way in order that intervention footprints can be adjusted. Timor-Leste, we would contend, is merely emblematic of the broader forces at play regarding the construction and consequences of the present day's conventional wisdom: namely, it illustrates how the mutually reinforcing relationship between power

---

[5] Myrttinen, Henri, "Timor-Leste A Relapsing 'Success' Story", *Taiwan Journal of Democracy*, 5 no. 1 (2009): 219–239. See, as representative example, the 'UN Security Council Report, 12 May 2005' End of Mandate Report of the Secretary-General on the United Nations Mission of Support in East Timor', http://www.laohamutuk.org/reports/UN/UNDocs/2005/SGRept05_310.pdf; Also see the indicative foci on UN missions in Timor-Leste in UNMIT's 'Medium Term Strategy' document, http://unmit.unmissions.org/Portals/UNMIT/latest_docs/Medium_Term_Strategy-En.pdf.

[6] United Nations Peacekeeping Operations in Timor-Leste Fact Sheet, http://unmit.unmissions.org/Portals/UNMIT/Factsheets/Peacekeeping%20Operations%20in%20Timor%20Leste.English.pdf.

[7] United Nations Peacekeeping Operations in Timor-Leste Fact Sheet, http://unmit.unmissions.org/Portals/UNMIT/Factsheets/Peacekeeping%20Operations%20in%20Timor%20Leste.English.pdf.

[8] Interestingly, basically the same assessment criteria used then in Timor-Leste are used today. For UN missions in Timor-Leste (UNMIT) examples, see United Nations Peacekeeping Operations in Timor-Leste http://www.un.org/en/peacekeeping/missions/unmit/mandate.shtml and http://unmit.unmissions.org/.

and knowledge, which informs how humans interpret our worlds, can sanction spurious conclusions, built from false assumptions.[9] The power-knowledge nexus in this specific context has to do with the (re)production of notions about how to prosecute international assistance by lynchpin actors such as the UN, The European Union, various national policing bodies as well as their myriad sources of support (e.g. consultants or academics). The book's scope therefore extends to the broad ambit of peace and development operations while at the same time affording special attention to international policing. After all, international policing cannot be removed from the broader context of peace and capacity development operations if one is serious about its understanding. To be clear, the main concern herein is not to scour the technical minutiae of policing praxis in an attempt to redress what may warrant improvement at that level. The challenge we take up comes back to the main conceptual and philosophical building blocks that inform this broad space—because it is from there that seismic shifts in the day-to-day interactions will emanate.

The magnitude of this task to dramatically recast the dominant views of international policing has not, however, deterred a growing number who proffer alternative realities. Like them, we too have been unable to ignore the telltale evidence that has steadily revealed itself to us throughout the course of the research that has gone into this book. The insights gleaned from a critical analysis of this space have made it increasingly clear that, despite useful offerings from many experienced persons and concerned organisations over the years, there is a sizeable gulf between today's dominant thinking and the realities that do indeed exist on the ground, including, most pressingly, the courses of action that would contribute to sustainable peace and capacity building. That realisation has supplied the motivation to share these alternative views as widely as possible in order that future peace and development efforts may be better guided.

While our conclusion that the international community (broadly construed) is yet to gain an accurate grasp of what it takes to realise lasting, positive change in the societies they seek to assist may sound like a naysayer 'glass half empty' outlook to some, we would argue that the lack of refreshingly open and honest appraisal is one of the factors most responsible for the current state of affairs. Hence we maintain that one can be optimistic while at the same time aware of what needs to be improved and how far there is to go. The ethos should shift from a tussle over blame or conversely attempts to garner credit for achievements to one about developing *collaborative* solutions with given resources. Furthermore, we are heartened by the fact that the overarching field of peace operations is still quite young in historical terms, which allows us to envisage a day when the kinds

[9] See Michel Foucault, *Power/Knowledge: Selected Writing and Other Writings 1972–1977*, ed. Colin Gordon (New York: Pantheon Books, 1980).

of alternative thinking contained herein form the basis for a lasting conventional wisdom. The publication of this particular interrogation of international policing may assist in some small way toward bringing us closer to that future.

Given that introduction, it would be clear that the authors of this book are under no illusion as to the level of scepticism facing accounts that fundamentally diverge from today's conventional wisdom. The alternative ideas put forward within have been informed by the many iconoclasts before us who dared to question entrenched assumptions, even though such claims remain (for now) at the margins. These ideas present stark contrasts to many of the core ontological, epistemological, and methodological stances that currently characterise the mainstream lens.

Importantly, this critique not only renders pictures of reality that differ a great deal from the mainstream beliefs and corresponding practices, but also presents alternate sources of legitimate knowledge and processes needed to garner and interpret the incisive information used for future program learning. As an example, one of the key departures propagated herein is that recipient societies scarcely fit the ideal whereby the state either does or could in the foreseeable future provide the lion's share of security and public services.[10] Furthermore, the various forces which, together, make up today's circumstances do not exist independently of each other but rather continually emerge as a collective stew, so to speak, based upon how they combine and adapt.[11] Yet another point of departure is that, unlike the mainstream account which unwittingly presumes local societies share Western ideals, it has become clear to us that socio-cultural beliefs not only differ dramatically but that their unique content matters integrally to what unfolds during the interactions that comprise peace and development programs, and therefore to what courses of action are best suited to each context.

These ontological departures have far reaching consequences for how we understand and approach international policing endeavours. For instance, the current epistemological reliance on state-based sources of information to tell us what 'reality' looks like begins to appear decidedly problematic when state biases and blind spots are revealed and acknowledged. Similarly, methodological approaches that fail to enlist the opinions of a wide array of societal groups prove problematic not just for their lack of accurately relaying what is indeed happening but also for the way in which they exclude many of whom are needed to realise the end goal of sustainable peace and development itself.

Ultimately our thinking has arrived at the need for an understanding that is based on 'complex', 'political' realities, which, in short, means that the environ-

---

10 Saskia Sassen, "Cities and New Wars: After Mumbai", (2008), http://www.opendemocracy.net/article/the-new wars-and-cities-after-mumbai-0.

11 Margaret Wheatley, *Turning to One Another*, (San Francisco: Barrett-Koehler, 2002).

ments in which international policing operate are continually emerging according to how the specific belief systems of each of myriad actors influence how they interact with one another and how they adapt their behaviour accordingly.[12] The heretofore common remedy of 'technical' solutions, based on an ideal Western state model whereby activities are conceived of as somehow transpiring in isolation, therefore proves not only unfounded but, more to the point, ill-suited to help deliver appropriate programming analysis and guidance, because it ignores the centrality of the dynamism of interactions and adaptations as well as the fact these interconnected dynamics are informed by socio-cultural belief systems not typically grounded in either state-centrism or Western ideals.

Impediments to Effective Interventions

In specific terms, there are numerous and often daunting impediments that stand in the way of accurate analysis and thus sound programming advice. Many obstructions are truly daunting because they stem from shortcomings in broader societal thinking. Their remedy thus entails near seismic changes in our overarching thinking, not simply on issues pertaining only to policing. In other instances, improvements require a narrower scope concerned with reorienting the practices of international policing itself. These multi-level challenges are further hampered by the lack of common vocabulary, conceptual frameworks, and of course philosophical outlooks. To attain the requisite understanding would be an impressive achievement indeed.

Perhaps the principal barrier is that international policing largely fails to recognise the limits and impacts of its current ethnocentric and state-centric paradigms. As with the broader field of peace and capacity development operations, much of its practices echo the centuries' old 'mission civilisatrice' mindset, whereby Europeans deemed local cultures as backwards and thus in need of remaking in a European image. A related problem for international policing is that it is troubled by entirely unrealistic expectations of what it can achieve and the timeframes in which such improvements could in fact occur. Put otherwise, the dominant viewpoint seems to have forgotten how long it took Western societies to undergo some of the more seismic changes in their own histories.

More specific extant blind spots include:

- Programs overlook local forms of policing and instead pour resources into what are often the least appropriate and effective forms of policing.

---

12 Diane Hendrick, "Complexity Theory and Conflict Transformation: An Exploration of Potential and Implications," Working Paper 17 (Bradford: Centre for Conflict Resolution, Department of Peace Studies, University of Bradford, 2009), 5.

- International policing lacks local ownership, in that key decisions are seldom made by local actors.
- This lack of local ownership extends to missed opportunities to build local capacity, preferring instead to have external persons do the heavy lifting.
- The 'complex systems' comprising mission environments do not lend themselves to rigid or predictive planning; rather constant adaptation and learning should be used to determine which activities and modalities of assistance are best suited.

Hence, in spite of considerable effort and resources, and arguably some successes, international policing endeavours have yet to realise their potential.[13] The impediments however have considerably less to do with resourcing or intentions and instead the manner in which these programs have been approached. Put succinctly, there is a need to rethink international policing while at the same time to reorient the way in which programming informs monitoring and evaluation (M&E), and vice versa.

These contemporaneous characteristics of international policing are, unsurprisingly, shared with the monitoring and evaluation industry from which, crucially, we are meant to advance our understanding of how policing programs affect the local environment. When done well, that is, M&E can provide capacity building for significant elements of endogenous as well as exogenous actors, with the learning able to lead to better outcomes, helping to span the policy-praxis divide.[14]

Unfortunately, similar to many of the above international policing obstacles, M&E largely fails to recognise the limits and impacts of its current ethnocentric and state-centric paradigms. Misguided faith is put in sources that do not generate legitimate knowledge and processes that reinforce rather than help eliminate blind spots. As a result the 'learning' which occurs merely corroborates fallacies in the status quo thinking. The production of flawed realities is furthered by the ingrained practice of equating outputs, such as persons put through training courses or physical objects delivered, with success. Embraced largely because it is comparatively easy to account for, a reliance on outputs however ignores the fact that what matters most is how the particular outputs mix with the countless other forces surrounding security and development programs to affect mindsets and ultimately behaviours. Indeed, outputs have not uncommonly been linked to highly negative consequences; yet given the current M&E practices could nevertheless be claimed as accomplishments.

---

[13] Gordon Peake and Kaysie Studdard-Brown, "Policebuilding: The International Deployment Group in the Solomon Islands," *International Peacekeeping* 12, no. 4 (2005): 530.

[14] David H. Bayley, *Community Policing: Evaluation Programs* (New York: Civilian Police Division, DPKO, United Nations, 2005), 3.

Listed below are what we believe to be the main impediments currently to incisive *and* productive M&E.

- Complicated and lengthy reports are not only costly and time consuming to produce but largely inaccessible to those who matter most (i.e. practitioners and local actors).
- Highly flawed data (usually from sources traditionally sanctioned by the West such as government-generated statistics, but also context-specific surveys) passes as legitimate, ultimately populating reports with erroneous findings that lead to misguided advice.
- A heavy reliance on external 'experts' means that the opportunity to build the capacity of local actors gets squandered, robbing future generations of skills and knowledge to conduct their own M&E, and devise their own programs.
- M&E takes people away from doing their core business when in fact it could avoid this opportunity cost and be a part of normal program activities and program management, further enhancing both efficiency and efficacy through continual learning.
- Antagonistic relationships are engendered by the punitive nature of dominant approaches, pitting police practitioners and local actors against M&E experts and donor governments, thereby eroding mission buy-in from these key actors.
- The resistance engendered from this antagonism typically manifests in the manipulation of reporting data in order to please various masters, often resulting in a failure to reflect circumstances on the ground.
- Moreover, the traditional approach leads to perverse incentives to conduct ill-advised activities with scarce resources because of the 'what gets measured gets done' phenomenon, while at once maintaining a short-term focus on tangible items rather than a longer term eye to changing patterns of behaviour.
- The pervading mindset is informed by a traditional social science lens which wrongly presumes a linear reality in which social outcomes are attributed to program activities; when in actual fact we live in 'complex systems' where multiple relationships effect outcomes that are forever evolving, and which retain the multiple perspectives of the various societal segments. It is these complex realities that should be reflected in M&E findings.

The above discussion enumerates the topics examined throughout this book. Collectively these issues comprise the dimensions that need to shift in order for the conventional wisdom to yield an accurate reflection of this space. The examination herein has been generated with an Australian focus due to the position of the Australian Federal Police (AFP) at the cutting edge of international policing evolution. While the interrogation shines the spotlight on many of today's embedded myths and malpractices, vitally it also offers well-developed and innovative alternatives.

The Examination's Scope and Structure

Since our notion of this space requires that policing be conceived as part of a greater, complex whole, and appreciated in a setting of competing political understandings and aims, the scope of the book is necessarily wide-reaching. It examines not only policing practices but incorporates the broad spectrum of peace operation components, such as development programs and military operations since, consistent with complexity theory, policing does not occur in a vacuum. Against this backdrop, M&E is explored in depth. As aforementioned, the nexus between the advice emanating from M&E and the views of the broader peace and development industry is profound insofar as M&E can serve either to reinforce flawed accounts or facilitate their demise—in the quest to advance conventional wisdom.

The book is structured into the four comprising parts of (1) setting the context, (2) recasting core ontological and epistemological elements, (3) pushing back on conventional M&E, and (4) employing field work to demonstrate how the alternative thinking herein improves our capacity to assist vulnerable places. Hence, in the first part comprising two chapters, the context for international policing as well as its monitoring and evaluation is set out. This section concentrates on cutting-edge policing developments within Australia mainly, but also the United Nations (UN).

Chapter 1 looks at the global context, tracing the historical evolution of police in peace operations, starting from when the United Nations police (UNPOL) were first deployed in the Congo in 1960. It examines the role of UNPOL, both its downfalls and successes and asks us to consider what the future holds for international policing as police undertake roles in peacebuilding, development and as part of capacity building operations. In the process, it highlights how policing is integral to the success of peace missions—needing to be at the core rather than bolted-on as had been the early thinking. It finishes on a forward looking note by recounting the experiences of Australia's innovative developments in this space.

Chapter 2 brings M&E into the picture, putting forward an historical overview of M&E in police peace operations. This inclusion, as mentioned previously, is due to the importance of M&E in providing the information upon which to base our learning and understandings. Attaining a meaningful evaluation of UNPOL and other policing groups throughout their deployments is essential to developing an understanding of how these groups can be effectively utilised. The attention focuses on the immense challenges surrounding M&E's key objective of establishing causation toward broader societal changes, and how M&E and capacity building are necessarily linked. Having established that link, the exploration unpacks the notions of capacity and then capacity development vis-à-vis M&E. As a consequence it asks 'what are the conditions which allow an organisation to evolve into a self sustaining system?' This is an area which has received significant attention in more recent times, and for good reason, because enhancing local capacity should be an indispensible part of peace and capacity development operations.

The next part of the book probes the main ontological and epistemological contentions at the heart of this space. In so doing, it identifies the key conceptual issues that underpin a considered examination of international policing, and upon which the conventional wisdom falters. What forces and actors actually comprise mission environments? How, and by whom, are security and other public services being provided? What is, what could be, and what should be the role of the formal state? How do changes come about? How should interventions be approached? These questions frame some of the many the important foci to engage. The discussions centre on the role and capacity of the state, conversely the role of non-state actors, and the importance of the 'political' (referring to the socio-cultural belief systems which underpin recipients' societies and intervening actors alike). Throughout the investigation not only are the salient issues explored but innovative alternatives are developed where current imaginations are left wanting. What is more, these conceptions inform the innovative M&E framework recently developed for the AFP, and included in its entirety in the Appendix, which enables practitioners to pick up on key dynamics and actors that would remain invisible to conventional lenses.

Chapter 3 rethinks the important 'state of the state' debate invoked some years back by OECD. In so doing, it strives to overcome the initial impediment to successful peace support interventions, which is that international assistance continues to misunderstand the nature[15] of recipient societies by viewing conflict-affected societies through a self-image lens which wrongly presumes the Weberian state ideal. In nearly all cases this idealised Western construct is far from the truth, causing mission decisions to be misguided from their inception. The upshot is that security and development programs risk missing the mark.

Chapter 4 continues the critique of the dominant view with a focus on the highly consequential notion of Rule of Law (RoL). RoL is at the centre of discussions for how peace as well as development missions are conducted, being considered as the Holy Grail. Yet there are several critical blind spots and missteps in how it is conceived—beyond the mere fact that it remains a contested and under-conceptualised term. This chapter devotes time to the state-centric and formalist nature of its current conception, while ending up with a delineation which is both clear and lacking in the normal Western ethno-centricity.

---

[15] Importantly, the use of the term 'nature' (or 'true' further below) are not to be confused with essentialising environments. To the contrary, our arguments consistently decry the prospect of reducing any facet of any mission environment to one, and only one, truth or essential quality, and instead insist that there will forever be many perspectives on what constitutes the 'realworld'. This means we consider the environment to be contested, fluid, and multi-perspective—inexorably; that is its true nature.

By doing so, it provides the international community with a conception that can be operationalised in any setting so as not to continue the imposition of poor fit institutions and the many attendant problems that has created to date.

Chapter 5 aims to redress the core stumbling block vis-à-vis how actors have engaged during peace and capacity development operations so far: namely, there has been a focus on technical solutions when in fact the key to successful operations lies in navigating adroitly among the socio-cultural systems that comprise mission environments. We call this the need to engage with the 'political', and the chapter builds a compelling case why organisations such as the AFP need, first and foremost, to work on getting right the political encounter. Political lenses are how all sides of these engagements interpret actions, and thus when each group's preferences begin to be known, the chances for harmonious negotiations and solutions becomes markedly better.

The book's next part moves on from interrogating the underpinning realities of conventional wisdom into a specific exploration of extant M&E. Given our view that when M&E is conducted adroitly it can prove an enormous force in shifting the underlying thinking and practices that it strives to capture and make sense of, the need to devote considerable space unpacking and developing M&E facets cannot be overstated. Hence, chapters 6–8 push back on conventional M&E across a multitude of core areas. The ultimate aim of this section is to provide practical guidance by which to model future M&E. The approach taken is to first develop vital aspects that are commonly skimmed over to our peril (e.g. complex social systems characteristics or incorporating an awareness of emotion) and then provide the unconventional guidance that can be used to produce the kind of M&E that not only gives accurate assessments of complex political realities but also fosters both local capacity and ownership. These alternative views have been cohered into a framework manual (contained in its entirety in the Appendix) which is ready and capable to employ towards the M&E of any peace or development operations because of how its particular processes engender only context-specific content from diverse perspectives.

Chapter 6 retraces the key aspects of mainstream M&E in order not only to critique the conventional approach but, crucially, to make clear the points of departure for what we term 'Democratising' M&E. In so doing, the chapter articulates the inability of conventional M&E to accurately reflect the complex situations on the ground in peace policing operations while encouraging the consideration of new and improved practices to better address these issues. This includes providing a summary of a framework methodology developed by the authors, contained in detail in the appendices, which aims to illustrate what M&E could look like in a post-conventional wisdom era.

Chapter 7 builds on the discussion of M&E undertaken in Chapter 2. An innovative yet integral extension of this discussion pertains to how complex social systems affect capacity in an M&E context. The underlying contention is that our social worlds are complex social systems, and therefore attempts to understand or evaluate peace and capacity development operations must be informed by complexity thinking. Accordingly, a comprehensive summary of complex systems theory is put forward. Importantly, this chapter's exploration opens space to consider the ways in which the international community may begin to contemplate its role in future programs.

Chapter 8 fixes its gaze on the little acknowledged assumptions that underpin international missions and the corresponding M&E. By taking on conventional social science approaches in terms of what is considered legitimate versus illegitimate forms of knowledge, as well as the mythical construct of 'rational' behaviour, it further destabilises conventional wisdom by problematising its core. Its underlying premise is that humans make decisions based on emotions rather than logic *per se*, and therefore the chapter's purpose is to begin to see how we can use an understanding of emotion to inform assessment of peace operations—and thus ultimately peace and capacity building operations themselves. A key benefit of this shift in approach is that overlaying emotions and more conventional approaches produces an ideal way to eliminate the blind spots that normally trouble M&E. While embryonic, the exploration nevertheless points to ways that we could further develop such multi-disciplinary frameworks.

Chapter 8 completes the conceptual part of the book. Having built the logical case for a wholesale reimagining of the space of international policing, the question turns to whether or not evidence from the field suggests these proposed shifts in thinking are indeed both valid and warranted. It is one matter to construct an alternative picture but quite another to compile credible evidence in its support. Accordingly, the final part of the book is dedicated to seeing what above looks like on the ground, through actual case studies of peace and capacity development missions. A principal challenge is the amount of time needed to develop a longitudinal study. A generation, at minimum, would be the ideal. There are however ways to begin to gain a sense in the near term—one of which is to re-interpret raw and observational data through an alternative lens; another, which we have strived to do for this project, is to approach an analysis from the new perspectives, thus directly challenging their traction.

Three forays into contemporary interventions were added to this exploration, each according to how it adds a crucial vantage point and insights to the empirical case for our conceptual contentions. The first of these analyses, in Chapter 9, is the Republic of Marshall Islands (RMI), and more specifically ongoing police reform assistance from the AFP. This analysis, in a nutshell, shows how a heightened awareness of complex, political realities would lead to starkly different conclusions and thus recommendations for mission management and programming. The main message is to ensure that the socio-cultural perspectives, from which each stakeholder group inescapably views ongoing developments, are brought front and centre when making decisions. Albeit quite brief by comparison to the two detailed case studies that follow, it works nicely as an entrée by how it sets a platform for bringing the conceptual into the concrete.

Chapter 10 fixes its gaze on a regional, multilateral mission in Solomon Islands, undertaken by international community members from countries such as Australia and New Zealand. It looks closely at an unfolding community policing program in order to facilitate learning of a different kind. While reinforcing the main points established above pertaining to the need for a complex, political lens, the focus is hybridity in terms of how to grapple with the messy interaction between formal and informal institutions. In so doing, the examination underscores how interpreting mission environments through a complex, political lens—driven rather than garnished by local perspectives—will point to starkly unorthodox programming design and implementation.

Chapter 11 moves to an African milieu, exploring the UN mission in Liberia. The chapter brings together a truly extraordinary compilation of recent interviews from those in and around the UN mission, including UNPOL in particular, the Liberian government, and equally important—others from outside these powerful institutions. Its purpose is to ask how the cross-section of stakeholders feel about the current M&E practices, with the view to testing their opinions against notions from our alternative framework. In the final analysis it proves a clear endorsement of the notions to which we subscribe, having articulated a tacit consensus for the need to change significant facets of mainstream M&E convention.

In its entirety, this manuscript delivers not only a contemporary take on international policing and its M&E but one in which the conceptual moves are highly innovative. While its lengthiness violates one of our own cardinal rules—that of being accessible to the widest possible argument—its audience was never intended to be the widest possible array of coal-face practitioners as well as research-orientated persons (either in academe or those straddling the research/practice divide), whereas the M&E developed from its journey is. Its comprehensiveness is essential to capture the many involved debates that should inform a genuinely holistic framework. The vital outcome in this sense is the straightforward and practical framework represented in the Collaborative Policing Operational Manuals. It is these documents that have the capacity to reorientate the way international policing is monitored and evaluated.

Finally, on that last point of reorientating practices—both in headquarters and on the ground—there is the all-important question of how today's conventional wisdom can be supplanted by view and approaches that track accurately to the forces and conditions that comprise operations and their environs. Though the thorny space that encompasses that debate is (thankfully) beyond the scope of this book, we do finish with some thoughts about how to move forward on that quest. Dramatically reimagining entrenched ideas and practices has never been an easy road, and neither will it be for any who dare to push the agenda of reforging today's international policing conventional wisdom.

PART ONE

SETTING THE CONTEXT

CHAPTER ONE

THE GLOBAL CONTEXT: THE HISTORICAL EVOLUTION OF POLICE IN PEACE OPERATIONS

Police in Peace Operations

Given the book's emphasis, this first chapter provides the historical foundation for an examination of international policing by tracing its origins and evolution. Much has changed over the years and thus an awareness of whence policing has come enables us not only to appreciate how far the field has come since its inception, but also how nascent—in terms of how long it can take for human understanding to develop—the industry still is; such recognition offers hope concerning the eventual attainment of truly deep and therefore productive understanding. To do this important stage-setting task justice, the chapter is of significant length. The focus is the United Nations police (UNPOL) for the rather obvious reason that it has been the flagship organisation in this area. Considerable discussion is also given to the groundbreaking developments undertaken by Australia in recent years in order to sharpen the view to the future of policing.

Traditionally, international (also referred to as 'civilian') police components were treated by mission architects and member states as a 'bolt-on' capacity—an addendum to military-dominated mission structures.[16] However, this tendency has diminished over time as police components have become increasingly recognised as mission-critical.[17] Many now argue that 'getting policing right' is at the core of successful peace operations.[18]

---

16 Joshua G. Smith, Victoria K. Holt, and William J. Durch, *Enhancing United Nations Capacity for Post-Conflict Policing and Rule of Law*, Report from The Project on Rule of Law in Post-Conflict Settings (Washington DC: The Henry L. Stimson Center, 2007), 15.

17 Annika S. Hansen, "From Congo to Kosovo: Civilian Police in Peace Operations," *Adelphi Papers* 41, no. 343 (2002): 108.

18 Gordon Peake and Kaysie Studdard-Brown, "Policebuilding: The International Deployment Group in the Solomon Islands," *International Peacekeeping* 12, no. 4 (2005): 530;

UNPOL has been present in UN peacekeeping since they were first deployed in the ONUC mission in Congo Leopoldville in 1960. In the intervening years, UN civilian police from more than 100 police contributing member states have been part of more than 30 missions on 4 continents.[19] More accurately, the number of police deployed in UN peace operations has burgeoned since the end of the Cold War. In 1994, there were only 1,677 UN police serving in peacekeeping operations whereas by 2009, this number had increased to 11,000 and in 2010, UNPOL was authorised to deploy over 17,500 police.[20]

However, reflecting general trends in the peacekeeping system, the UN is far from the only actor operating in this realm. In parallel, the European Union (EU), Organisation for Security Cooperation in Europe (OSCE), and increasingly the African Union (AU), have developed their capacities and deployed police in their own operations both within and beyond their respective regions.[21] In 2004, Australia established a police group for international deployment that was the first of its kind in the world, and for this reason we dedicate appreciable analysis at the end of the chapter to recount their path forward. The Australian Federal Police's (AFP) International Development Group (IDG) is tasked to deploy overseas to assist with building policing capacity and to respond to emergencies. It is not the first of Australia's contributions to UN policing; it supplied police to the United Nations mission in Cyprus (UNFCYP) in 1964, but it was the first national policing group in the world solely committed to offshore policing and has contributed to major regional missions in East Timor (UNMIT) and the Solomon Islands (RAMSI).

Despite the increased number of providers, the quantity of UNPOL authorised increased by 500% in the past decade and doubled in real terms between 2006 and 2008.[22] See figure 1 below. For example, in 2006 when the Security Council mandated the UN-AU peace operation in Darfur it specified that UNPOL would be represented by over 6,000 officers. As of June 2010 there are over 13,700 police, from over 80 countries deployed in 12 peacekeeping missions; making the UN the biggest provider of support to police in post-conflict environments.[23]

Alex J. Bellamy, "The International Deployment Group," in *Policing in Context: An Introduction to Police Work in Australia*, ed. Roderic G. Broadhurst and Sara E. Davies (South Melbourne, Vic.: Oxford University Press Australia & New Zealand, 2009), 195.

19 UN Police Division, *UN Police Magazine* 5 (2010): 14–15, 28, http://www.un.org/Depts/dpko/police/division.shtml.

20 UN Police Division, *UN Police Magazine* 5 (2010): 14–15, 28, http://www.un.org/Depts/dpko/police/division.shtml.

21 For example, see European Police (EUPOL) in Democratic Republic of Congo.

22 United Nations, *Report on the Comprehensive Analysis of the Police Division, Office of Rule of Law and Security Institutions, Department of Peacekeeping Operations* (New York: UN, 2008), 8.

23 Ylber Bajraktari, Arthur Boutellis, Fatema Gunja, Daniel Harris, James Kapsis, Eva Kaye and Jane Rhee, *The PRIME System: Measuring the Success of Post-Conflict Police Reform*,

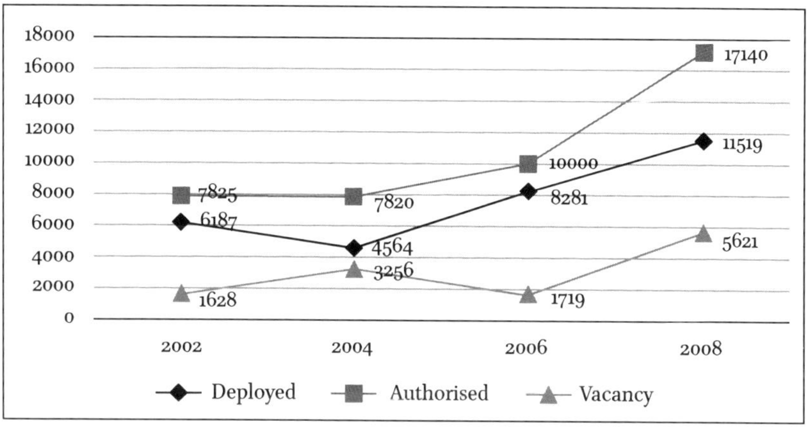

Figure 1: Authorised and deployed strength of United Nations police.[24]

This phenomenon has meant that the most recent conceptualisations of peacekeeping reflect a "more blue, less green" approach.[25]

Furthermore, not only does this play out numerically, but the negative consequences of coalition-led interventions assuming executive mandates and/or conducting intrusive reform processes (with dubious legal foundation),[26] have re-emphasised that the UN's representative nature, political legitimacy, and vast experience working in post-conflict societies—whether in an interim law enforcement function or as a driver of reform—render it well-placed to act as an arbiter and coordinator in 'post-conflict' societies. Therefore, the UN retains an unparalleled, if imperfect, international legitimacy compared to some other organisations mounting peace operations and deploying police.[27] In reaching its current manifestation, UN policing has gone through a number of metamorphoses,

(Princeton: Princeton University, 2006), 103; Joshua G. Smith, Victoria K. Holt, and William J. Durch, *Enhancing United Nations Capacity for Post-Conflict Policing and Rule of Law*, Report from The Project on Rule of Law in Post-Conflict Settings (Washington DC: The Henry L. Stimson Center, 2007), 15; UN Police Division, *UN Police Magazine* 5 (2010): 14–15, 28, http://www.un.org/Depts/dpko/police/division.shtml.

24 United Nations, *Report on the Comprehensive Analysis of the Police Division, Office of Rule of Law and Security Institutions, Department of Peacekeeping Operations* (New York: UN, 2008), 6.

25 Author Interview, Joshua Smith, Stimson Center—February 2009.

26 For example, Iraq.

27 United Nations, *Report on the Comprehensive Analysis of the Police Division, Office of Rule of Law and Security Institutions, Department of Peacekeeping Operations* (New York: UN, 2008), 7.

both 'in the field' and 'in the office'.[28] The next section examines its evolution in the field from its functional perspective.

'In the Field'

The role and posture of UNPOL has changed dramatically since their inaugural deployment. Functional expansion has often transpired out of necessity—'piloted' through 'mission-creep' in one case to be refined and reapplied in subsequent ones. However, despite this *ad hoc* ism, one can trace an approximately sequential development in their character.[29] In essence, the role of police in peace operations has evolved from passive observation of local police services to a more intrusive reform function and, on occasion, even assumed full law enforcement responsibilities.

As mentioned above, the first deployment of civilian police was in the Congo in 1960–4, closely followed by the UN Temporary Executive Authority (UNTEA) in West New Guinea/West Irian in 1962–3, and the UNFCYP mission in Cyprus, first deployed in 1964 but which continues today.[30] These and other UNPOL deployments during the Cold War were characterised by intermittency and *ad hoc*-ism, ultimately limited to providing support to military observers or conducting unobtrusive monitoring roles.[31] However, despite a significant time-lag, these policing mandates laid the foundations for the eventual evolution of civilian police activities to what is implemented by UNPOL in contemporary peace operations.

---

28 Nina M. Serafino, *Policing in Peacekeeping and Related Stability Operations: Problems and Proposed Solutions*, CRS Report for Congress (Congressional Research Service: The Library of Congress, 2004); Annika S. Hansen, "From Congo to Kosovo: Civilian Police in Peace Operations," *Adelphi Papers* 41, no. 343 (2002): 15–31; Eirin Mobekk, "Identifying Lessons in United Nations International Policing Missions," *Policy Paper* 9 (Geneva: Geneva Centre for the Democratic Control of Armed Forces (DCAF), 2005), 1–3.

29 Nina M. Serafino, *Policing in Peacekeeping and Related Stability Operations: Problems and Proposed Solutions*, CRS Report for Congress (Congressional Research Service: The Library of Congress, 2004), 6; Halvor Hartz, "Civpol: The Un Instrument for Police Reform," *International Peacekeeping* 6, no. 4 (1999): 27.

30 For in depth account of these missions, see: Nassrine Azimi, *The Role and Functions of Civilian Police in United Nations Peacekeeping Operations: Debriefing and Lessons*, Report and Recommendations of the International Conference, Singapore (London: Kluwer Law International and United Nations Institute for Training and Research, 1996), 11–23; Duncan Chappell and John Evans, "The Role, Preparation and Performance of Civilian Police in United Nations Peacekeeping Operations," *Criminal Law Forum* 10, no. 2 (1999): 179–90; Erwin A. Schmidl, "Police Functions in Peace Operations: An Historical Overview," in *Policing the New World Disorder: Peace Operations and Public Security* ed. Robert B. Oakley, Michael J. Dziedzic, and Eliot M. Goldberg (Washington DC: National Defense University, 1998).

31 Annika S. Hansen, "From Congo to Kosovo: Civilian Police in Peace Operations," *Adelphi Papers* 41, no. 343 (2002): 9; Roxane D.V. Sismandis, *Police Functions in Peace Operations*, Workshop Report (Washington DC: United States Institute of Peace, 1997), 2.

International policing operations began to take more coherent form, were assigned a specific role and were deployed strategically in the pursuit of overall goals of the mission as a whole following the end of the Cold War.

Monitoring and Advising

Police peacekeepers operated under the military component until 1989 when, with the inception of the UN Transitional Assistance Group in Namibia (UNTAG), the police component became an independent entity. This mission also represented a rebirth of policing deployments, as missions of increasing frequency were mandated to monitor, observe and report upon the conduct of local police services in relation to their obligations under cease-fire and peace agreements. The UN operation in Mozambique (ONUMOZ) followed in a similar vein as did the UNAVEM II and III missions in Angola.

Capacity-building and Institutional Development

Mandates for international police began to expand in the early 1990s and UNPOL were required to engage in an inflated set of tasks. The most significant augmentation was the move toward building the capacity of indigenous police services. It is an area of utmost importance to the discussions herein—not just UNPOL—and accordingly it warrants being further unpacked (at the end of Chapter 7). UNPOL's shift towards capacity building occurred in two phases. The first development was in the provision of training, first part of *ad hoc* arrangements in the UNTAC mission in Cambodia but more formally incorporated into UN missions in Somalia and Rwanda in the mid-90s. These missions required UNPOL to support, train and mentor with the aim of professionalizing domestic police services. Collectively, these functions came to be known as 'SMART' policing—an acronym for: *S*upport for human rights, *M*onitoring, *A*dvising, *R*eporting, and *T*raining. This model was instituted as the basic framework for international policing in 1995.[32] UNTAC highlighted the limits of SMART policing in complex operations as despite the deployment of 3600 international police observers, its Civpol sector failed to acquire the local knowledge necessary for good policing and failed to assert the authority needed to arrest and detain. It was granted the power of arrest in January 1993, in the first example of its kind, but did not bring any human rights cases to prosecution.[33]

---

[32] Nina M. Serafino, *Policing in Peacekeeping and Related Stability Operations: Problems and Proposed Solutions*, CRS Report for Congress (Congressional Research Service: The Library of Congress, 2004), 6; Annika S. Hansen, "From Congo to Kosovo: Civilian Police in Peace Operations," *Adelphi Papers* 41, no. 343 (2002): 22.

[33] Alex J. Bellamy, "The International Deployment Group," in *Policing in Context: An Introduction to Police Work in Australia*, ed. Roderic G. Broadhurst and Sara E. Davies (South Melbourne, Vic.: Oxford University Press Australia & New Zealand, 2009), 196.

The second and more intrusive development was into the realm of reforming, restructuring and (re-)building domestic police institutions. This programming had its antecedents in the missions in ONUSAL in El Salvador[34] and UNMIH in Haiti, but was most prevalent in the work of the International Police Task Force (IPTF) that made up the bulk of the UN Mission in Bosnia and Herzegovina (UNMIBH), beginning its operations in 1995. Under these mandates, UNPOL officers were involved in vetting, recruiting and selecting officers for reconstituted police services in addition to developing and teaching on curricula at policing academies and providing field training. The IPTF was charged under the Dayton peace agreement to carry out 'executive policing', that is to physically police Bosnia by, in addition to the above, performing the entirety of normal policing operations until such time that the Bosnian police could take them on and aiding the construction a new Bosnian justice system. Similar to other missions with a central policing role in ensuring security and building peace, the IPTF policing component was less than one-twentieth the size of the military one.[35]

Executive Policing

The most ambitious functional expansion came in 1999 as new UNPOL missions in Kosovo and East Timor were mandated with complete executive authority for law enforcement activities. That is, as the UN peace operations established civil administrations over both territories and embarked on nation-building, UNPOL assumed full responsibility for the interim maintenance of law and order, including the right to bear arms and execute powers of arrest and detention.[36] In addition, officers and units were required to perform a disparate array of tasks including *inter alia*: conducting investigations; directing traffic; providing border security; collecting, analysing and utilizing criminal intelligence as well as forensic evidence; training local police; and managing the organisation and administration of the police force.[37] In both of these cases processes of reconstituting the indigenous police service were conducted in parallel.

---

[34] Gino Costa, "The United Nations and Reform of the Police in El Salvador," *International Peacekeeping* 2, no. 3 (1995).

[35] Alex J. Bellamy, "The International Deployment Group," in *Policing in Context: An Introduction to Police Work in Australia*, ed. Roderic G. Broadhurst and Sara E. Davies (South Melbourne, Vic.: Oxford University Press Australia & New Zealand, 2009), 196.

[36] Renata Dwan, "Introduction," in *Executive Policing: Enforcing the Law in Peace Operations*, ed. Renata Dwan (Stockholm: Stockholm International Peace Research Institute (SIPRI), 2002), 3–4; Nina M. Serafino, *Policing in Peacekeeping and Related Stability Operations: Problems and Proposed Solutions*, CRS Report for Congress (Congressional Research Service: The Library of Congress, 2004), 7.

[37] Annika S. Hansen, "From Congo to Kosovo: Civilian Police in Peace Operations," *Adelphi Papers* 41, no. 343 (2002): 28.

Although this type of mandate had a forerunner in the UN Transitional Authority in Eastern Slavonia, Baranja and Western Sirmium (UNTAES) and the IPTF in Bosnia, UNMIK and UNTAET cemented this paradigmatic shift.[38] However, despite the critical role envisaged for UNPOL in plugging the public security gap in the short-term and building self-sustaining police service in the longer-term, the number of police in these missions continued to be dwarfed by the military component.[39] The UN's civil administrations in Kosovo and East Timor induced much debate around international transitional authority and the Department of Peacekeeping Operation's (DPKO) capacity to reproduce such executive policing functions in future operations. However, these mandates have not been replicated since and it seems that such executive authority remains an anomaly, not the rule.[40]

Multidimensional Policing

The emergence of multidimensional and integrated missions has had a significant effect on the operational objectives of UNPOL. Under these mandates, UNPOL has assisted host governments in all policing functions necessary for the restoration and maintenance of the RoL, public safety and order; and delivered comprehensive capacity-building measures to develop professional, democratic, self-sustaining local police services. The important distinction between this and executive policing is that, in this posture, UNPOL officers are not considered law enforcement officials under the legislation of the host government.

Policing tasks such as 'SMART', outlined previously, were very much in line with Westphalian conceptions of peace operations, which saw the primary goals as maintaining peace between states or strengthening the territorial integrity of a state. Policing components of even the largest missions continually deferred to the sovereignty of their host state, lacking in size, authority and, on principle, arms. However, the changing nature of peace operations saw the role of policing change during the 1990s, as peacekeeping operations became responsible for overseeing the implementation of complex peace agreements and ensuring

---

38 For further details of precursor missions UNEF I, ONUC and UNTAES, see Renata Dwan, *Executive Policing: Enforcing the Law in Peace Operations* (Stockholm: Stockholm International Peace Research Institute (SIPRI), 2002), 2–3.

39 Alex J. Bellamy, "The International Deployment Group," in *Policing in Context: An Introduction to Police Work in Australia*, ed. Roderic G. Broadhurst and Sara E. Davies (South Melbourne, Vic.: Oxford University Press Australia & New Zealand, 2009), 196.

40 Renata Dwan, "Conclusions," in *Executive Policing: Enforcing the Law in Peace Operations*, ed. Renata Dwan (Stockholm: Stockholm International Peace Research Institute (SIPRI), 2002), 123.

physical security immediately after a conflict. Thus, UNPOL has gradually been required to carry out a wider range of tasks to ensure these aims are met.[41]

In practice, multidimensional policing has seen UNPOL increasingly involved in many cross-cutting objectives, including: supervision of cease-fires; facilitating safe returnee programmes; combating organised crime in support of economic reconstruction; as well as provision of civilian protection.[42] Furthermore, UNPOL are also expected to play a central role in protecting UN personnel and facilities.[43] Missions in Liberia (UNMIL) and the DRC (MONUC) embody this *modus operandi*.

Aside from the ongoing observer missions in the Middle East and south Asia, practically all UN operations are now furnished with a significant police component. Moreover, UNPOL missions such as the one in Haiti (MINUSTAH) have been integral in tackling the gangs of Port-au-Prince and combating organised crime, reflecting its primary tasking to maintain law and order.

Formed Police Units

Despite the escalating technicality of UNPOL activities, the upsurge in demand for police since 1999 has primarily been met through the deployment of Formed Police Units (FPUs).[44] FPUs are national contingents, typically 125–140 in number, drawn from member state paramilitary/gendarmerie forces.[45] Their major benefits are that FPUs deploy rapidly and as a 'ready-made' law enforcement

41 P. D. Williams and A. J. Bellamy, "Contemporary Peace Operations: The Four Challenges to the Brahimi Paradigm," in *International Peacekeeping: The Yearbook of International Peace Operations*, ed. Harvey Langholz, Boris Kondoch, and Alan Wells (Koninklijke: Brill, 2007), 20.

42 See: Joshua G. Smith, Victoria K. Holt, and William J. Durch, *Enhancing United Nations Capacity for Post-Conflict Policing and Rule of Law*, Report from The Project on Rule of Law in Post-Conflict Settings (Washington DC: The Henry L. Stimson Center, 2007), 81–3, Table A1.2. for full list of UNPOL activities, 1999–2007. See also: Rick Linden, David Last, and Christopher Murphy, "Obstacles on the Road to Peace and Justice: The Role of Civilian Police in Peacekeeping," in *Crafting Transnational Policing: Police Capacity-Building and Global Policing Reform*, ed. Andrew Goldsmith and James Sheptycki (Oxford: Hart Publishing, 2007), 151; James Cockayne and Adam Lupel, "Introduction: Rethinking the Relationship between Peace Operations and Organized Crime," *International Peacekeeping* 16, no. 1 (2009).

43 United Nations, *Report on the Comprehensive Analysis of the Police Division, Office of Rule of Law and Security Institutions, Department of Peacekeeping Operations* (New York: UN, 2008), 9.

44 First deployed in UNMIBH (IPTF) in Bosnia; since present in UNMIK in Kosovo, UNMIT in Timor-Leste, ONUCI in Cote d'Ivoire, UNMIL in Liberia, and MINUSTAH Haiti.

45 Known more generally as *Stability Police Units* (SPUs). See: Michael Dziedzic and Col. Christine Stark, *Bridging the Public Security Gap: The Role of the Center of Excellence for Stability Police Units in Contemporary Peace Operations*, USIP Briefing (Washington DC: United States Institute of Peace, 2006).

unit, demonstrating a clear chain of command and history of joint training and functional coherence.[46] They are usually armed and trained for more volatile situations than patrolling officers, such as riot control, and have the flexibility to calibrate their use of force, as circumstances dictate. Senior UNPOL management has played a pivotal role in encouraging and enabling the use of FPUs, in large part due to their effective response to riots in Timor-Leste in 2006 and 2007. First deployed in the Balkans,[47] only two FPUs were present in the field in 2000 compared with 38 by mid-2008.[48] As of 2010, there are 60 FPUs consisting of more than 6000 of UNPOL's currently deployed police officers.[49]

The UN's penchant for FPUs has provoked both positive and negative consequences in the field. First and foremost, their use has helped to constrict the 'public security gap' in a way that has mitigated the pitfalls of employing military to deal with public disorder.[50] As a general rule, the military is not well adapted to and prefers to avoid civilian police functions.[51] Furthermore, societies emerging from conflict have often suffered at the hands of corrupt and abusive (para-)militaries. Therefore, the use of FPUs ensures a clear distinction between military actors and the civilian police in developing legitimate and accountable law enforcement institutions.[52] In essence, they constitute the proverbial 'velvet

---

[46] Benjamin Kwasi Agordzo, "Filling the 'Security Gap' in Post-Conflict Situations: Could Formed Police Units Make a Difference?," *International Peacekeeping* 16, no. 2 (2009): 288–90.

[47] Halvor Hartz, Laura Mercean, and Clint Williamson, "Safeguarding a Viable Peace: Institutionalizing the Rule of Law," in *The Quest for a Viable Peace: International Intervention and Strategies for Conflict Transformation*, ed. Jack Covey, Michael J. Dziedzic, and Leonard R. Hawley (Washington DC: United States Institute of Peace Press, 2005), 160.

[48] United Nations, *Report on the Comprehensive Analysis of the Police Division, Office of Rule of Law and Security Institutions, Department of Peacekeeping Operations* (New York: UN, 2008), 8.

[49] UN Police Division, Website, http://www.un.org/en/peacekeeping/sites/police/units.shtml.

[50] Benjamin Kwasi Agordzo, "Filling the 'Security Gap' in Post-Conflict Situations: Could Formed Police Units Make a Difference?," *International Peacekeeping* 16, no. 2 (2009): 287–8; Alice Hills, "The Inherent Limits of Military Police Forces in Policing Peace Operations," *International Peacekeeping* 8, no. 3 (2003); Eirin Mobekk, "Identifying Lessons in United Nations International Policing Missions," *Policy Paper* 9 (Geneva: Geneva Centre for the Democratic Control of Armed Forces (DCAF), 2005), 5–6; Peter Viggo Jakobsen, "Military Forces and Public Security Challenges," in *The United Nations and Regional Security: Europe and Beyond*, ed. Michael Pugh and Waheguru Pal Singh Sidhu (London/Boulder: Lynne Rienner Publishers, 2003).

[51] Erwin A. Schmidl, "Police Functions in Peace Operations: An Historical Overview," in *Policing the New World Disorder: Peace Operations and Public Security* ed. Robert B. Oakley, Michael J. Dziedzic, and Eliot M. Goldberg (Washington DC: National Defense University, 1998).

[52] United Nations Department of Peacekeeping Operations, *Handbook on UN Multidimensional Peacekeeping Operations* (New York: PBPU, 2003), 88.

gloved iron fist'.[53] Furthermore, FPUs eventuate to be approximately 50% cheaper than individual UNPOL officers to deploy.[54] However, these units continue to attract controversy. Despite their comparative advantage over military law enforcement alternatives, these stability policing teams still resemble paramilitaries in image and at times in conduct. There have been a number of accusations of FPUs being overly heavy-handed and over-stepping/jettisoning their rules of engagement.[55] A 2009 evaluation of FPUs found that only approximately one third could be labelled as operational.[56]

As a member of senior management in the Police Division at DPKO put it, "The United Nations police officer is no longer a passive onlooker but an active partner in consolidating peace and building democratic institutions that underpin the long-term stability and prosperity in peaceful societies."[57] In light of evolving UNPOL functions in the field, there have been a number of reforms at headquarters and within DPKO to facilitate and institutionalise these developments (i.e. 'in the office'), as the next section details.

'In the Office'

UN policing was managed through the UN Military Division,[58] until a dedicated *Civilian Police Unit* was created within the Office of the Military Advisor in May 1993, consisting of one staff member and three seconded police officers.[59] A Police Adviser was later appointed in 1997.

---

53 Alice Hills, "International Peace Support Operations and Civpol: Should There Be a Permanent Global Gendarmerie?," *International Peacekeeping* 5, no. 3 (1998).

54 Michael Dziedzic and Col. Christine Stark, *Bridging the Public Security Gap: The Role of the Center of Excellence for Stability Police Units in Contemporary Peace Operations*, USIP Briefing (Washington DC: United States Institute of Peace, 2006).

55 Benjamin Kwasi Agordzo, "Filling the 'Security Gap' in Post-Conflict Situations: Could Formed Police Units Make a Difference?," *International Peacekeeping* 16, no. 2 (2009): 288.

56 William J. Durch and Madeline L. England eds. (2010) *Enhancing United Nations Capacity to Support Post-Conflict Policing and Rule of Law, Revised and Updated*, Report from The Project on Rule of Law in Post-Conflict Settings (Washington D.C.: The Henry L. Stimson Center, 2010), 18.

57 Interview: Special Assistant to the Police Advisor, Police Division, DPKO, New York, February 2009; United Nations, *Report on the Comprehensive Analysis of the Police Division, Office of Rule of Law and Security Institutions, Department of Peacekeeping Operations* (New York: UN, 2008), 5.

58 Now the 'Office of Military Affairs' (OMA).

59 H. Broer and M. Emery, "Civilian Police in Un Peacekeeping Operations," in *Policing the New World Disorder: Peace Operations and Public Security*, ed. Robert B. Oakley, Michael J. Dziedzic, and Eliot M. Goldberg (Washington D.C.: National Defense University 1998); United Nations, *Report on the Comprehensive Analysis of the Police Division, Office of Rule of Law and Security Institutions, Department of Peacekeeping Operations* (New York: UN, 2008), 5.

In response to increasing demands upon the UNPOL apparatus, the 'Brahimi Report', recommended the establishment of an independent *Police Division*. Furthermore, the report advocated a 'doctrinal shift', such that the utilisation of police in peace operations should: "... focus primarily on the reform and restructuring of local police forces in addition to traditional advisory, training and monitoring tasks"[60]—whilst maintaining and developing its capacity to respond effectively to civil disorder and for self-defence.[61]

The *Civilian Police Unit* was reconstituted as the *UN Police Division* in 2001 with the division head promoted to the same echelon as the Military Advisor to the Under-Secretary-General (USG) for Peacekeeping Operations. Made-up of experienced officers from police contributing countries (PCCs), the division was to be responsible for planning and managing operations in accordance with mandates promulgated by the Security Council. By December 2008, the division consisted of 27 professional personnel with additional officers seconded to other parts of DPKO,[62] staffing three sections: the Office of the Police Advisor; the Mission Management and Support Section (MMSS); and the Strategic Policy and Development Section (SPDS).

The Police Advisor heads the division, providing leadership and strategic direction to its functions in addition to advising and supporting the USG for Peacekeeping Operations. The main function of the MMSS is to supply strategic guidance to police components of peacekeeping operations and special political missions. It manages the selection, deployment and rotation of UNPOL officers and units and provides a clearing house for documenting and reporting on mission-specific and thematic issues. The SPDS is responsible for developing, reviewing and updating policies, doctrine and standard operating procedures for headquarters and field missions. Furthermore, this section is tasked with analysing and assessing experiences of UNPOL in the field.

In more recent times, the Secretary-General has designated the Police Division as the focal point within the UN system and global lead on all matters relating to international law enforcement.[63] This coordination role reflects the expansive remit of the Police Division and its importance as the centre of gravity for what is an industry experiencing exponential growth.

60 United Nations High-Level Panel on United Nations Peace Operations, *Report of the Panel on United Nations Peace Operations* (New York: United Nations, 2000), 20.

61 United Nations High-Level Panel on United Nations Peace Operations, *Report of the Panel on United Nations Peace Operations* (New York: United Nations, 2000), 20.

62 For example, officers are regularly seconded to the Integrated Operational Teams (IOTs).

63 See: Decision of the Secretary-General, *Rule of Law*, No. 2006/47, 24 November 2006; Decision of the Secretary-General, *Security Sector Reform*, No. 2007/11, 16 February 2007.

Standing Police Capacity

First proposed in the Secretary-General's 2004 'High Level Panel on Threats, Challenges and Change',[64] in September 2005, the World Summit sanctioned the formation of the *Standing Police Capacity* (SPC) within the UN Police Division to provide operational capacity to field operations.[65] DPKO issued a policy directive on in May 2006 and the SPC reached initial operating capacity by October 2007.[66] The SPC constitutes a standby contingent of highly-trained, rapidly deployable, police officers.[67] Its aim is to decrease the much-maligned gaps associated with rapid and efficient deployment as well as improve management structures and recruitment processes. The core functions of the unit are two-fold. 1) To assist in the planning and establishment of a command structure for new UN police missions;[68] and 2) to support on-going UNPOL operations in the field through the provision of advice and expertise as tasked by the USG DPKO. In addition, it is envisaged that the SPC will take some responsibility for designing and conducting assessments of extant UNPOL missions.[69] Initially based within the Police Division, it is intended that the SPC will eventually be housed at the UN Logistics Base in Brindisi.[70] It is slated to be deployed as much as two-thirds of the time, on shorter cycles of four months on, two months off.[71]

The SPC's maiden expedition was as the start-up for MINURCAT in Central African Republic and Chad in Autumn 2007, where it provided the leadership of the police component for the first 9 months. It has since provided advice, expertise and assistance to existing police components in the policebuilding activities in Timor-Leste (UNMIT), Liberia (UNMIL) and Kosovo (UNMIK).[72]

---

[64] United Nations, *Report of the High-level Panel on Threats, Challenges and Change* (New Yorkl: UN 2004), 70–1.

[65] United Nations, *Report on the Comprehensive Analysis of the Police Division, Office of Rule of Law and Security Institutions, Department of Peacekeeping Operations* (New York: UN, 2008), 10.

[66] United Nations, *Report of the Panel of Experts on the Standing Police Capacity's First Year of Operation*, (New York: UN, 2008), 4.

[67] United Nations, *Report of the Panel of Experts on the Standing Police Capacity's First Year of Operation*, (New York: UN, 2008), 4. Original proposal was for 50–100—continued upscaling will be performance related.

[68] For further breakdown and detail of different dimensions to 'mission start-up process', see United Nations Department of Peacekeeping Operations, *Capstone Doctrine: United Nations Peacekeeping Operations: Principles and Guidelines* (New York: UN DPKO, 2008), 62–5. SPC fits into "functional component and field office start-up".

[69] Interview: Walter Wolf, Chief of SPC—New York, February 2009

[70] United Nations, *Report of the Panel of Experts on the Standing Police Capacity's First Year of Operation*, (New York: UN, 2008), 7.

[71] Joshua G. Smith, Victoria K. Holt, and William J. Durch, *Enhancing United Nations Capacity for Post-Conflict Policing and Rule of Law*, Report from The Project on Rule of Law in Post-Conflict Settings (Washington DC: The Henry L. Stimson Center, 2007), 57.

[72] United Nations, *Report of the Panel of Experts on the Standing Police Capacity's First Year of Operation*, (New York: UN, 2008), 5–7.

Policing War and Police as Peacebuilders

What do UNPOL do and need to do better?

Contemporary international policing missions are "tools both of immediate crisis management and of development assistance and democratisation."[73] Each mission environment is unique and displays idiosyncratic political circumstances that inevitably dictate the scope of the mandate and the rules of engagement in the field. However, at present, UNPOL activities can be summarised and split into two functionally distinct but interdependent areas: 1) provision of public security in immediate 'post-conflict' period—i.e. restoration of the RoL; and 2) supporting the development of a state's capacity to sustain fair and just law and order—i.e. policebuilding. B. K. Greener expands on this by arguing that the 'new international policing' reflects the increased willingness and capabilities of states to carry out international policing activities that include roles in humanitarian aid, risk management and the preservation of order. This necessarily enhances the role of international police to meet complex contemporary security dilemmas in fragile environments as well as bridge the gaps in both state and international level security operations.[74]

Restoration of the Rule of Law

Rather than signify a return to the RoL, the cessation of hostilities tends to usher in a period of lawlessness. Societies emerging from war often experience minimal public security, a breakdown in law and order and increased levels of criminality—ranging from opportunistic petty transgressions to pervasive organised crime—all of which contributes to the public's lack of faith in or willingness to adhere to the RoL and its associated institutions.[75] That is, the collapse of the RoL can be both a cause and consequence of conflict.[76] As noted by the Secretary-General in his 2004 report on the RoL: "... the heightened vulnerability of minorities, women, children, prisoners and detainees, displaced persons, refugees and others, which is evident in all conflict and post-conflict situations,

---

73 Annika S. Hansen, "From Congo to Kosovo: Civilian Police in Peace Operations," *Adelphi Papers* 41, no. 343 (2002): 108.

74 B.K. Greener, *The New International Policing* (Basingstoke, England: Palgrave Macmillan, 2009), 109.

75 James Cockayne and Adam Lupel, "Introduction: Rethinking the Relationship between Peace Operations and Organized Crime," *International Peacekeeping* 16, no. 1 (2009); Kirsti Samuels, "Rule of Law Reform in Post-Conflict Countries: Operational Initiatives and Lessons Learnt," *Social Development Papers: Conflict Prevention and Reconstruction* 37 (2006), 7; James Cockayne and Adam Lupel, "Conclusion: From Iron Fist to Invisible Hand—Peace Operations, Organized Crime and Intelligent International Law Enforcement," *International Peacekeeping* 16, no. 1 (2009).

76 Annika S. Hansen and Sharon Wiharta, *The Transition to a Just Order: Establishing Local Ownership after Conflict*, (Stockholm, Sweden: Folke Bernadotte Academy, 2007), 1.

brings an element of urgency to the imperative of restoration of the RoL."[77] This was the scenario that UNPOL faced in El Salvador, Mozambique, Kosovo, Liberia and Haiti.

There are two main reasons for this. First, and somewhat counter-intuitively, this can occur as a result of peace agreement. Incomplete disarmament programmes render communities awash with small arms and light weapons (SALW), whilst insufficiently designed and resourced sibling demobilisation and reintegration initiatives have left ex-combatants without the necessary skills and/or employment opportunities such that the resort to criminality becomes incentive compatible.[78] This transition from 'fighters' to 'felons'[79] is facilitated by the relative ease with which paramilitary activities can be transformed into criminal enterprises, particularly if deterrence is low and impunity high.[80] These maladies are often exacerbated by the psychological impact of war in desensitizing former militia-men and women to violence and danger.[81] In addition, if residual social divisions, ethnic tensions and justice issues are not sufficiently addressed, this can lead to conflict over privilege to political power, rights to land and access to scarce resources. In this context, without tangible preventive strategies, upsurges in criminality and challenges to the RoL are a predictable consequence of a peace agreement.[82]

Second, and more logically, the destructive and divisive nature of conflict can mean that the capacity of the state to tackle criminal activity and enforce law and order is severely reduced in the immediate post-violence phase. Public security and criminal justice institutions such as the police service are often politicised,

---

77 Kofi Annan, *The Rule of Law and Transitional Justice in Conflict and Post-Conflict Societies*, Report of the Secretary-General (New York: United Nations, 2004), 3.

78 Annika S. Hansen, "From Congo to Kosovo: Civilian Police in Peace Operations," *Adelphi Papers* 41, no. 343 (2002): 31.

79 For more detailed discussion of these dynamics, see Cockayne & Lupel's framework depicting *predatory*, *parasitic* and *symbiotic* organised criminal elements and the transition between groups: James Cockayne and Adam Lupel, "Introduction: Rethinking the Relationship between Peace Operations and Organized Crime," *International Peacekeeping* 16, no. 1 (2009), 11.

80 William J. Durch and Madeline L. England eds. (2010) *Enhancing United Nations Capacity to Support Post-Conflict Policing and Rule of Law, Revised and Updated*, Report from The Project on Rule of Law in Post-Conflict Settings (Washington D.C.: The Henry L. Stimson Center, 2010); Jaremey McMullin, "Reintegration of Combatants: Were the Right Lessons Learned in Mozambique?," *International Peacekeeping* 11, no. 4 (2004): 626.

81 Chrissie Steenkamp, "The Legacy of War: Conceptualizing a Culture of Violence to Explain Violence after Peace Accords," *The Round Table* 94, no. 379 (2005): 264.

82 T. Charles Call and William Stanley, "Protecting the People: Public Security Choices after Civil Wars," *Global Governance* 7, no. 2 (2001).

corrupted and co-opted during conflict as part the pursuit of political power.[83] It is common that sections of the justice and security apparatus are implicated in abuses or indeed that the country in question has no historical legacy of providing public security to the population *per se*.[84] In addition, the neglect, degradation and erosion of these institutions that can occur during periods of instability render the state unable to respond to breaches of law and further exacerbate a volatile post-conflict environment.

In reality, "Criminal violence may peak at precisely the time that a national government is least able to fight it."[85] The lack of capacity leads to what has been referred to as the 'institutional gap'[86]—a deficit which threatens to undercut peacebuilding initiatives[87] and allows the space for pernicious elements to operate and for organised criminality to flourish and gain a foothold which becomes increasingly hard to dislodge.[88] As Linden *et al.* explain: "Securing order for governance is central to international police mandate."[89] Hansen goes further to

---

83 Rick Linden, David Last, and Christopher Murphy, "Obstacles on the Road to Peace and Justice: The Role of Civilian Police in Peacekeeping," in *Crafting Transnational Policing: Police Capacity-Building and Global Policing Reform*, ed. Andrew Goldsmith and James Sheptycki (Oxford: Hart Publishing, 2007), 150; Halvor Hartz, Laura Mercean, and Clint Williamson, "Safeguarding a Viable Peace: Institutionalizing the Rule of Law," in *The Quest for a Viable Peace: International Intervention and Strategies for Conflict Transformation*, ed. Jack Covey, Michael J. Dziedzic, and Leonard R. Hawley (Washington DC: United States Institute of Peace Press, 2005), 157–60.

84 Eirin Mobekk, "Identifying Lessons in United Nations International Policing Missions," *Policy Paper* 9 (Geneva: Geneva Centre for the Democratic Control of Armed Forces (DCAF), 2005), 6.

85 Joshua G. Smith, Victoria K. Holt, and William J. Durch, *Enhancing United Nations Capacity for Post-Conflict Policing and Rule of Law*, Report from The Project on Rule of Law in Post-Conflict Settings (Washington DC: The Henry L. Stimson Center, 2007), 11.

86 M. J. Dziedzic, "Introduction," in *Policing the New World Disorder*, ed. Robert B. Oakley, Michael J. Dziedzic, and Eliot M. Goldberg (Washington D.C.: National Defense University, 1998).

87 Seth G. Jones, Jeremy M. Wilson, Andrew Rathmell and K. Jack Riley, *Establishing Law and Order after Conflict*, vol. 1 (Santa Monica, CA: RAND Corporation, 2005), 8–12.

88 Colette Rausch, ed. *Combating Serious Crimes in Postconflict Societies: A Handbook for Policymakers and Practitioners* (Washington D.C.: US Institute for Peace Press, 2006); Rick Linden, David Last, and Christopher Murphy, "Obstacles on the Road to Peace and Justice: The Role of Civilian Police in Peacekeeping," in *Crafting Transnational Policing: Police Capacity-Building and Global Policing Reform*, ed. Andrew Goldsmith and James Sheptycki (Oxford: Hart Publishing, 2007), 150; James Cockayne and Adam Lupel, "Introduction: Rethinking the Relationship between Peace Operations and Organized Crime," *International Peacekeeping* 16, no. 1 (2009).

89 Rick Linden, David Last, and Christopher Murphy, "Obstacles on the Road to Peace and Justice: The Role of Civilian Police in Peacekeeping," in *Crafting Transnational Policing: Police Capacity-Building and Global Policing Reform*, ed. Andrew Goldsmith and James Sheptycki (Oxford: Hart Publishing, 2007), 154.

suggest that, "security is the key to a 'new social contract' between the population and its government or society in which the population is willing to surrender the responsibility for its physical safety into government hands."[90]

For these reasons, international police can play a pivotal role in plugging the institutional civil law enforcement gap.[91] As described above, on occasion, this has been manifest in executive authority missions where UNPOL officers and units are directly responsible for all law enforcement functions. More commonly, the multidimensional non-executive mandates dictate that UNPOL support national law enforcement agencies in the execution of their functions in this regard.

This temporary restoration function meets an immediate and short-term, crisis-management requirement. However, the durability of a stable and secure environment depends upon self-sustaining RoL. UNPOL therefore engage in strategies to target this outcome.

Police as Peacebuilders

The first few years following the cessation of violent conflict are commonly believed to be the time when the platform for durable peace and stability can be laid. In addition to maintaining hard-won peace, building peace through support to the security sector, RoL, economic recovery (inter alia) from the earliest opportunity is now deemed to be best practice.[92]

As mentioned above: "In countries emerging from violent conflict, local police capacity is often non-existent and what does exist is frequently ineffective, highly politicized and/or abusive."[93] However, the democratic policing ideal holds that domestic police services "... play a crucial role in maintaining public security and order and in legitimizing the state's monopoly on the use of force through a commitment to the RoL. The nexus between good governance, RoL, and public security makes effective policing an important component of well-functioning, modern societies."[94]

In 'post-conflict' settings, where there is a peace agreement and perhaps political transition, there is both a need and an opportunity to (re-)establish the RoL as

---

90 Annika S. Hansen, "From Congo to Kosovo: Civilian Police in Peace Operations," *Adelphi Papers* 41, no. 343 (2002): 35.

91 See section on FPUs above for discussion of comparative advantage of police officers and units bridging this gap rather than military (police).

92 Ellie B. Hearne, *From New York to the Field: A Dialogue on UN Peace Operations* (New York: International Peace Institute, 2010), 4.

93 Joshua G. Smith, Victoria K. Holt, and William J. Durch, *Enhancing United Nations Capacity for Post-Conflict Policing and Rule of Law*, Report from The Project on Rule of Law in Post-Conflict Settings (Washington DC: The Henry L. Stimson Center, 2007), 10.

94 Joshua G. Smith, Victoria K. Holt, and William J. Durch, *Enhancing United Nations Capacity for Post-Conflict Policing and Rule of Law*, Report from The Project on Rule of Law in Post-Conflict Settings (Washington DC: The Henry L. Stimson Center, 2007), 10.

well as begin a process of transformation in the security sector and criminal justice system, thereby strengthening law and order, guaranteeing peoples human rights and providing a solid platform for recovery, development and sustainable peace.[95] Indeed, there is widespread consensus that a semblance of stability and public security is a prerequisite to peacebuilding in other social, political and economic domains[96] and that effective security sector reform can be a major factor in preventing relapse to conflict.[97]

As the UN itself declares: "The timely recovery of local capacities to enforce the law in accordance with international human rights standards and codes of conduct is vital for any post-conflict society to progress on its arduous path to a lasting peace. The functioning of police institutions within a RoL and rights-based framework ushers the prospects for secure and fair elections, the return of refugees and internally displaced persons, economic growth, good governance and civic trust and reconciliation."[98]

'Policebuilding' is therefore the longer-term process of building the capacity of local police services such that they are capable of creating and sustaining law, order and public trust;[99] ensuring that local law enforcement officers and institutions are respecting international human rights standards and protecting fundamental freedoms in the medium to long term.[100] UNPOL engage in this

---

95 Eirin Mobekk, "Identifying Lessons in United Nations International Policing Missions," *Policy Paper* 9 (Geneva: Geneva Centre for the Democratic Control of Armed Forces (DCAF), 2005), 6.

96 William J. Durch and Madeline L. England eds. (2010) *Enhancing United Nations Capacity to Support Post-Conflict Policing and Rule of Law, Revised and Updated*, Report from The Project on Rule of Law in Post-Conflict Settings (Washington D.C.: The Henry L. Stimson Center, 2010).

97 Annika S. Hansen and Sharon Wiharta, *The Transition to a Just Order: Establishing Local Ownership after Conflict*, (Stockholm, Sweden: Folke Bernadotte Academy, 2007), 1; Eirin Mobekk, "Identifying Lessons in United Nations International Policing Missions," *Policy Paper* 9 (Geneva: Geneva Centre for the Democratic Control of Armed Forces (DCAF), 2005), 6.; Annika S. Hansen, "From Congo to Kosovo: Civilian Police in Peace Operations," *Adelphi Papers* 41, no. 343 (2002): 25.

98 United Nations, *Report on the Comprehensive Analysis of the Police Division, Office of Rule of Law and Security Institutions, Department of Peacekeeping Operations* (New York: UN, 2008), 26.

99 William J. Durch and Madeline L. England eds. (2010) *Enhancing United Nations Capacity to Support Post-Conflict Policing and Rule of Law, Revised and Updated*, Report from The Project on Rule of Law in Post-Conflict Settings (Washington D.C.: The Henry L. Stimson Center, 2010).

100 H. Broer and M. Emery, "Civilian Police in Un Peacekeeping Operations," in *Policing the New World Disorder: Peace Operations and Public Security*, ed. Robert B. Oakley, Michael J. Dziedzic, and Eliot M. Goldberg (Washington D.C.: National Defense University 1998); Gordon Peake and Kaysie Studdard-Brown, "Policebuilding: The International Deployment Group in the Solomon Islands, *International Peacekeeping* 12, no. 4 (2005): 520.

policebuilding, enacting and supporting the reform, restructuring and rebuilding of national police and other law enforcement agencies with their explicit aim to ensure observance of principles of democratic policing.[101]

There is a growing emphasis on referring to this process as capacity development rather than capacity building for several often contradictory reasons. Some believe the term capacity development reflects the institutional focus of this work whereas capacity building represents a more community based focus. Others, including the IDG, see capacity development as recognition of the existing local capacity and collaborative action to enhance it. In fact, the IDG uses this term to deliberately acknowledge local capacity and avoid charges of paternalism against the work it does with other police forces. Capacity development is gaining currency in development policy however, this is not represented in development theory and argument still stands that good capacity building already acknowledges local capacity; if problems exist, changes should be made to actions rather than terms.[102]

In every case, UNPOL are just one of myriad international, regional and non-governmental organisations who manage, support and fund these processes. The protracted timelines associated with policebuilding diminish the role of UN peace operations in the longer term. However, in the short-term, they play an integral role in setting the wheels in motion in these capacity-building endeavours.

Summary

It is in this context that the police in UN peace operations typically operate and play a central role. The two types of tasks require different strategies and capabilities but are interdependent and often mutually reinforcing. It is evident that civil societies, and domestic police services, are likely to resist change if they fail to experience sufficient levels of stability first.[103] This seems to symbolise a logical

---

101 For detailed discussion and definition of democratic policing, see: David Bayley, *Changing the Guard: Developing Democratic Police Abroad* (New York: Oxford University Press, 2006); Bruce David and Rachel Neild, The Police That We Want: A Handbook for Oversight of the Police in South Africa (Johannesburg: Centre for the Study of Violence and Reconciliation, 2005); Joshua G. Smith, Victoria K. Holt, and William J. Durch, *Enhancing United Nations Capacity for Post-Conflict Policing and Rule of Law*, Report from The Project on Rule of Law in Post-Conflict Settings (Washington DC: The Henry L. Stimson Center, 2007), 13, Sidebar 3.

102 Vandra Harris, "Building on Sand? Australian Police Involvement in International Police Capacity Building," *Policing and Society: An International Journal of Research and Policy* 20, no. 1 (2010): 79–98, 81.

103 David H. Bayley, *Democratizing the Police Abroad: What to Do and How to Do It* (Washington D.C.: US Dept. of Justice, Office of Justice Programs, National Institute of Justice, 2001), 25; William G. O'Neill, *Police Reform in Post-Conflict Societies: What We Know and What We Still Need to Know*, The Security-Development Nexus Program Policy Paper (New York: International Peace Academy, 2005), 2–3.

progression such that things usually work best when the cart follows the horse. However, reform is regularly fast-tracked onto the agenda when it is deemed of benefit to the mission. For example, peace agreements often include DDR programmes where, as has been the case in a number of missions, ex-combatants have been integrated into reconstituted police services.[104] It has also been the case that, restructuring and training processes are necessary to meet the immediate security demands of the population, as was the case with UNPOL mandate in MINURCAT. Ultimately, the endeavours of international police are "cumulative rather than consecutive."[105] That is, irrespective of how far-reaching the rest of its mandate may be or how activities are sequenced, effective capacity-building remains the exit strategy for UNPOL. The sooner this process begins, the sooner dependencies can be disentangled and local institutions become self-sustaining.

Predicting UNPOL Future

UN peace operations continue to present a relatively inexpensive provider of post-conflict security and the demand for its on-going application is unlikely to wane.[106] There can be no doubt that police are now an integral component of contemporary peace operations. Despite the inherent uncertainty and evolutionary nature of UN peace operations, it appears that international police will continue to play an important role. Smith *et al.* suggest that: "Demand for highly-trained UN police with diverse expertise shows no signs of abating in the foreseeable future."[107] Hansen concurs, claiming that "civilian police deployment in UN peacekeeping [is here] to stay"[108] and the Police Division itself declared that: "... the demand for [UN] policing services remains high and is rising."[109] Linden

104 For example, ONUSAL in Alex J. Bellamy, "The International Deployment Group," in *Policing in Context: An Introduction to Police Work in Australia*, ed. Roderic G. Broadhurst and Sara E. Davies (South Melbourne, Vic.: Oxford University Press Australia & New Zealand, 2009).

105 Annika S. Hansen, "From Congo to Kosovo: Civilian Police in Peace Operations," *Adelphi Papers* 41, no. 343 (2002): 30.

106 United Nations Department of Peacekeeping Operations and Department of Field Support, *A New Partnership Agenda: Charting a New Horizon for UN Peacekeeping* (New York: UN DPKO and DFS, 2009), v, 27.

107 Joshua G. Smith, Victoria K. Holt, and William J. Durch, *Enhancing United Nations Capacity for Post-Conflict Policing and Rule of Law*, Report from The Project on Rule of Law in Post-Conflict Settings (Washington DC: The Henry L. Stimson Center, 2007), 38.

108 Annika S. Hansen, "From Congo to Kosovo: Civilian Police in Peace Operations," *Adelphi Papers* 41, no. 343 (2002): 21.

109 United Nations, *Report on the Comprehensive Analysis of the Police Division, Office of Rule of Law and Security Institutions, Department of Peacekeeping Operations* (New York: UN, 2008), 26.

et al. go further, declaring that: "... it is clear that police are going to play an increased role in future United Nations operations."[110]

In a global context, it is also apparent that UNPOL will remain a significant, if not preeminent, player in the field of international policing. Smith *et al.* declare that, despite devolved military command in peace operations and the expansion of some regional policing activities:

> *... the UN is still the dominant global provider of immediate post-conflict support to societies and governments attempting the difficult transition from often long-running war to lasting peace. No other entity is so frequently called upon to provide law and order support and, in particular, to provide direct assistance to local police forces in their law enforcement tasks, while seeking at the same time to transform them into successful and accountable providers of public safety who also enjoy the public's trust.*[111]

If UNPOL are to live up to this billing and meet these grand expectations, its headquarters apparatus and field operations will need to overcome a number of chronic challenges.

The Next Step in the Evolution: Australia's International Deployment Group

Despite its central importance, the evolution of international policing is of course not limited to UNPOL. The contributions and influences of nation-states have been vital as well. In recent times, arguably no state sits further atop the list of global innovators of international policing practice than Australia. In 2004, the Australian Government took the unprecedented step of creating a police group specifically for international deployment. The Australian Federal Police's (AFP) International Deployment Group (IDG) was spawned. Informed by the 2000 "Brahimi Report' on UN peace operations which, inter alia, recommended that the UN create a permanent stand-by pool of civilian police to ensure rapid deployment and enhance international collaboration on training, it was the first of its kind anywhere in the world to be tasked with overseas deployment to help build policing capacity and respond to emergencies.[112] This initiative came during

110 Rick Linden, David Last, and Christopher Murphy, "Obstacles on the Road to Peace and Justice: The Role of Civilian Police in Peacekeeping," in *Crafting Transnational Policing: Police Capacity-Building and Global Policing Reform*, ed. Andrew Goldsmith and James Sheptycki (Oxford: Hart Publishing, 2007), 152.

111 Joshua G. Smith, Victoria K. Holt, and William J. Durch, *Enhancing United Nations Capacity for Post-Conflict Policing and Rule of Law*, Report from The Project on Rule of Law in Post-Conflict Settings (Washington DC: The Henry L. Stimson Center, 2007), 67.

112 The IDG was established in February 2004 and granted a sizeable budget of A$1 billion over five years. Since then both its size and budget have increased significantly. In 2006, the Federal Government announced that it was to expand the IDG's staffing

a period where world leaders were increasingly recognising the importance of international policing for the prevention of armed conflict and state failure,[113] and more specifically, against a backdrop of the Australian Government's 2000 Defence White Paper, which placed policing at the forefront on national security.[114]

Created to respond to this increased demand for international policing in a more effective and professional manner, IDG officers have been deployed to the Solomon Islands, Timor-Leste, Papua New Guinea, Jordan, Tonga, Nauru, Sudan, Cyprus, Indonesia and the Philippines, doing everything from executive policing and institution building, to UN peacekeeping, to wide-ranging capacity building, and counter-terrorism capacity building. The IDG has identified two principal purposes: contributing to offshore law enforcement initiatives and participating in international 'capacity development programmes'.[115] Although the 'law enforcement' operations in places such as the Solomon Islands and Timor-Leste have attracted the most public attention, the bulk of the IDG's work is actually in the capacity-building arena, helping police forces overseas develop the capacity to provide law and order for themselves. Indeed, around 80 percent of the group's operational budget is spent on capacity building. Of this, only part of the IDG's capacity-building activities are directly related to post-crisis reconstruction, or the strengthening of fragile states. A significant part of its capacity-building activities is directly connected to combating transnational crime and terrorism. The IDG's international operations can be divided into two sets of activities: 1) those designed to build police capacity across a broad spectrum of areas and, 2) those associated with the Law-Enforcement Cooperation Program (LECP), which involves more focused cooperation and capacity-building measures relating in particular to transnational crime, drug trafficking and counter-terrorism.

As an entirely novel enterprise, predictably the IDG confronts many challenges—some to do with practical matters such as long term operational sustainability

levels to around 1200. See Australian Federal Police (AFP), *IDG Fact Sheet*, (Canberra: Commonwealth of Australia, 2007a).

113 Alex J. Bellamy, "The International Deployment Group," in *Policing in Context: An Introduction to Police Work in Australia*, ed. Roderic G. Broadhurst and Sara E. Davies (South Melbourne, Vic.: Oxford University Press Australia & New Zealand, 2009).

114 "Defence 2000—Our Future Defence Force" is the Defence White Paper released in 2000 under the Howard government. Commonwealth of Australia, *Defending Australia in the Asia Pacific Century: Force 2030, Defence White Paper 2009*, (Canberra: Department of Defence, 2009). Of note, this way of strategising Australia's security interests focuses on the unpredictability of the Asia-Pacific region and the risks this instability inflicts on Australia, concluding that efforts towards peace and security in the region are paramount to securing Australia against these possible regional threats, hence giving police a strong purview in the foreign policy space. [See Martin Clewes, "Australia's new defence white paper", *Military Technology* 25, no. 2 (2000): 10–18.]

115 Australian Federal Police (AFP), *IDG Fact Sheet*, (Canberra: Commonwealth of Australia, 2007a), 55.

while others stem from the need to work through doctrinal dilemmas. In terms of operational issues, there is a need for greater interoperability between the IDG and the Australian Defence Force, especially in relation to command and control relationships, intelligence and information sharing, the compatibility of systems (i.e. Communication and IT networks), and compatibility of planning strategies.[116]

Beyond these delicate issues there is a core challenge to long term sustainability pertaining to the requirements for 'standing capacity' vis-à-vis the need for rapid response. On the one hand, in recognition of the need for rapid deployment, the UN has set a benchmark of ninety days from the authorisation of a mission to the deployment of its policing component and even this modest goal has proved difficult to attain. The UN Mission to Sudan, for example, was still not fully deployed a full year after its authorisation. In an emergency situation, of course, even ninety days is far too long. For example, it is doubtful that the Timorese government would have survived, and civil war been averted, if Australia's intervention in 2006 had waited as long as ninety days before deploying. To enhance its ability to deploy rapidly, the IDG has created an Operational Response Group that provides fully formed policing units of around forty members equipped with vehicles, communications and other necessary equipment. Many of IDG's missions, especially those in Timor-Leste and Tonga, began life as rapid responses to emergencies, even though they then developed into broader capacity-building programs.

On the other hand, a rapid response capacity poses particular problems. Most critically, police officers who are not on active deployment are typically being used for other policing duties; and this characteristic, unsurprisingly, makes it difficult to deploy police rapidly because members have to be taken out of their domestic roles at short notice. Concerns arise about the long-term sustainability of a policing group specifically designed for overseas deployment. The existing problem of international policing missions struggling to recruit adequate numbers of suitably skilled officers is further exacerbated because domestic forces incur a net loss to their own operating capabilities when their officers are deployed overseas. The ripple effect creates the difficulty of recruitment and retention, and for the IDG that will need to be adroitly handled.

Regarding doctrinal conundrums, while capacity building may at first glance seem politically unproblematic, there are some lurking pitfalls. How should one proceed when dealing with non-democratic governments or governments with questionable human rights records? Can these sorts of regimes be reformed from

---

116 Australian Federal Police (AFP), *Australian Federal Police Submission to the Senate Standing Committee on Foreign Affairs, Defence and Trade: Inquiry into Australia's Involvement in Peacekeeping Operations* (Canberra: Commonwealth of Australia, 2007b), 15.

within by policing missions such as the IDG engaging with the indigenous police, thereby professionalising the local force from within to make it a powerful advocate of democracy and human rights? As a worst case, is there a danger that international police might help authoritarian regimes develop the capacity to repress their own people? These questions have arisen in relation to two of the IDG's missions in particular. The IDG's dealings with Indonesia's security devices are undoubtedly necessary from a counter-terrorism perspective, but they raise a host of troubling questions about assisting individuals and institutions that might be implicated in the commission of gross human rights abuses. Similarly, in Tonga, the IDG was effectively assisting an authoritarian government to investigate crimes committed (in part) during pro-democracy demonstrations. For the Australian Government, it raises questions about the guidance that it gives to the IDG and the jobs it asks the group to fulfil. Indeed, on occasion the IDG has been instructed to deploy to a country without clear instructions as to what it is to do. Second, although the IDG has begun to think systematically about the relationship between conflict prevention, peacekeeping and capacity building, and has committed to assisting the development of UN policing doctrine through the attachment of a police adviser within Australia's permanent mission to the UN, it has not yet developed a specific doctrine to guide its activities in these areas.

As a world leader experimenting with novel approaches to international policing, these challenges are neither surprising nor insurmountable. While it is still too early to say whether the IDG represents the future of international policing, other countries are looking to the IDG as a model for how they might manage their contributions. China, for instance, has established a dedicated training college for police officers slated for overseas employment, and the Royal Canadian Mounted Police is creating its own version of the IDG to give Canada a standing capacity to deploy police overseas. What is more, the original 2000 Brahimi Report's recommendation for a permanent stand-by pool of civilian police for rapid deployment became UN policy in September 2005 with the establishment of a standing police capacity within the UN. Altogether, these developments suggest the IDG will continue to be the one to watch when pondering the future of international policing.

CHAPTER TWO

MONITORING AND EVALUATION AND PERFORMANCE REPORTING

When placed against the backdrop of UNPOL, tracing the birth and evolution of the IDG provides some of the most useful learning opportunities to date in the space of international policing. From these collective experiences we can begin to induct any number of insights into how practices should be developed going forward. It is similarly helpful to look back at the historical evolution of M&E in police peace operations, which we do in this chapter, to sufficiently complete the background for conceptual discussions that begin in Chapter 3. In so doing this chapter recounts both domestic and international policing efforts in M&E, particularly UNPOL, highlighting inhibiting factors and current successes. It then delves more deeply into police capacity development operations and the concept of capacity and capacity building more generally.

Monitoring and Evaluation in Police Peace Operations: An Historical Overview

A recurrent challenge for those organisations deploying peace operations is to gauge whether or not these expeditions are successful and if so, to what extent. From a purely normative perspective, it is important for the international community to assess the efficacy of conflict management initiatives deployed in its name. In the simplest of terms, one of the key management challenges in peace operations is to monitor and evaluate (M&E) how the mission and components therein are contributing to achieving mandated objectives and how this is impacting upon society. For the peacekeeping organisation, M&E represent useful tools in managing, adjusting and learning from missions.

To date, attempts by the UN to evaluate its peace operations have been extremely limited and suffered from institutional inertia. This is typically due to a wide range of factors. Firstly, peace operations suffer from a shortage of the material and human resources required to conduct what can be expensive and time-consuming undertakings. In addition, the United Nations operates in some of the world's most insecure milieus, characterised by armed violence, instability and abject poverty. As a result, operational realities can dictate that areas of responsibility (AOR) are insufficiently secure, stable and predictable to meet the access needs of evaluators. These constraints are exacerbated further by a scarcity of data and the reality that obtainable information is of dubious or low fidelity. To compound this, the high-pressure operational environments and associated unwillingness to admit or demonstrate failure have acted to dis-incentivise buy-in to M&E processes.

Ultimately, despite a range of institutions and experts increasingly engaged in developing methodologies and applying M&E techniques to peacekeeping and peacebuilding,[117] there has been little momentum behind overcoming this reality due to the enduring paucity of context-specific methods and suitable tools to conduct such M&E. However, this deficit belies the utility of evaluation in the conduct of effective peace operations.

As Lewis describes,

> *The conflict-resolution community is ultimately presented with a 'Humpty Dumpty Problem'; it is extremely difficult, expensive, and risky to put back together societies that have been shattered by conflict. It is crucial that those working in the field improve upon their performance and better deploy their finite resources. As a tool for determining the value of conflict-resolution interventions, evaluation is an important means to achieving this end.*[118]

Furthermore, in 2007, the report of the Secretary-General on strengthening the capacity of the UN to manage and sustain peace operations recognised that: "The absence of a formal mechanism, structure and capacity to periodically evaluate... peace operations grossly limits the ability of the Department of Peacekeeping Operations to take informed decisions and provide guidance to mission leadership."[119]

In order to be effective, peace operations must function efficiently at and between these strategic, operational and tactical levels.[120] Meaningful M&E is

---

117 *Inter alia*: NUPI, CMI, ACCORD, PPC, and RPP.

118 Helen Lewis, "Evaluation and Assessment of Interventions," in *Beyond Intractability*, ed. Guy Burgess and Heidi Burgess (Boulder,Colorado: Conflict Information Consortium, University of Colorado, 2004).

119 Ban Ki-Moon, *Comprehensive Report on Strengthening the Capacity of the United Nations to Manage and Sustain Peace Operations*, Report of the Secretary-General (New York: United Nations, 2007), 21–22.

120 It is useful to observe and analyse peace operations at three functionally distinct but inter-related levels. Those being: Strategic (i.e. organisational HQ—policy); Operational (i.e. mission management—doctrine); and Tactical (i.e. conduct in field—Standard Operating Procedures).

critical in each of these dimensions. Strategically, M&E is important for three main reasons. First and foremost, in a context of scarce financial resources, donors and member states need a better understanding of the cost-effectiveness of these extremely expensive interventions. Detailed analyses provide a means of linking commitments and contributions to achievements.[121] Secondly, assessments provide a way of demonstrating success, substantiating intended outcomes and conferring legitimacy to policy decisions.[122] Third, and by extension, this information constitutes a solid foundation from which to garner and sustain political will amongst decision-makers and donors as well as respond to critics. Ultimately, it is this political support and material resource that remains the fundamental enabler of, and the umbilical cord to, peace operations.

M&E is similarly useful at the operational level. The *ad hoc* and evolutionary nature of peace operations demands, that, lessons are efficiently identified and best practice is committed to institutional memory.[123] The results of systematic and periodic M&E can provide the material necessary for informing future mission design, undergirding doctrinal development for field-mission planning and management structures and can also act as a training needs assessment.

Finally, but perhaps most importantly, the ability of a mission to function effectively is enhanced when its agents are provided with significant information on performance and progress. M&E of day-to-day activities can empower mission managers to identify implementation gaps and make real-time tactical adjustments in what is often a rapidly changeable environment.[124] These assessments can further inform the development of tactical directives or Standard Operating Procedures (SOPs).

In addition to these fundamental advantages, there are numerous cross-cutting benefits associated with an M&E regimen. Two noteworthy examples relate to: 1) identifying, and developing strategies to mitigate, the negative impacts and unintended consequences of peace operations on host populations; and 2) presenting illuminating information on the level of integration vertically (i.e. between these functional strata), as well as horizontally (i.e. across different mission components). Such examination can produce detailed analysis of interdependent programming in these increasingly integrated and multidimensional

121 This is particularly true in the context of limited involvement and/or consultation of troop and personnel contributors in opaque Security Council processes.

122 Agnes Hurwitz and Kaysie Studdard, *Rule of Law Programs in Peace Operations*, The Security-Development Nexus Program Policy Paper (New York: International Peace Academy, 2005), 13.

123 Joshua G. Smith, Victoria K. Holt, and William J. Durch, *Enhancing United Nations Capacity for Post-Conflict Policing and Rule of Law*, Report from The Project on Rule of Law in Post-Conflict Settings (Washington DC: The Henry L. Stimson Center, 2007), 43–44.

124 David H. Bayley, *Community Policing: Evaluation Programs* (New York: Civilian Police Division, DPKO, United Nations, 2005), 3.

endeavours, further improving the chance that operations will be efficacious. Put simply, meaningful M&E is critical to effective peace operations. In Mohan Nair's words, "Measurement is the driver of the next direction, not just the documenter of today's position."[125]

Monitoring & Evaluation of United Nations Police

In addition to the strategic, operational and tactical justification previously outlined, the complexity of contemporary peace operations requires that M&E can isolate the impact of a mission in a specific geographical area or on a particular policy area. Similarly, there is great value in an M&E system which can accurately analyse particular mission components and contingents therein. For these purposes, the most useful tools incorporate an ability to disaggregate. In doing so, they possess the potential to offer vital information for gauging how the police component is performing as a discrete mission component, but they can also point to how it may be contributing to overarching macro-level mission objectives of sustainable peace and security.

This argument gains further credence when one recalls the centrality of international police in re-establishing public security and the intrusive nature of domestic RoL and security sector reform processes conducted by, or at least occurring under the auspices of, the UN. In a 2007 report on enhancing UN capacity to support its post-conflict policing operations, the Stimson Centre identified the lack of evaluation and performance measurement as one of the four most pressing challenges facing the UN police division and its missions.[126] A view backed up by many scholars and practitioners writing about international policing and UN peacekeeping.[127]

There are a number of policing-specific reasons for such targeted M&E. The importance of the United Nations Police during the earliest stages of a mission cannot be overstated. In difficult circumstances, practitioners at all levels require meaningful information about the impact of their actions if they are to lay sound foundations for the future success of the mission. Equally, in this context, both

---

125 Mohan Nair, *Essentials of the Balanced Scorecard* (Hoboken, New Jersey: John Wiley and Sons, 2004), 2.

126 Joshua G. Smith, Victoria K. Holt, and William J. Durch, *Enhancing United Nations Capacity for Post-Conflict Policing and Rule of Law*, Report from The Project on Rule of Law in Post-Conflict Settings (Washington DC: The Henry L. Stimson Center, 2007), 44.

127 Annika S. Hansen, "From Congo to Kosovo: Civilian Police in Peace Operations," *Adelphi Papers* 41, no. 343 (2002): 31; William G. O'Neill, *Police Reform in Post-Conflict Societies: What We Know and What We Still Need to Know*, The Security-Development Nexus Program Policy Paper (New York: International Peace Academy, 2005), 11; Gordon Peake and Kaysie Studdard-Brown, "Policebuilding: The International Deployment Group in the Solomon Islands, "*International Peacekeeping* 12, no. 4 (2005): 528–29.

the domestic and international police are the visible arm of the public security apparatus. As such, they constitute the primary interface between the state's monopoly on the legitimate use of force and the citizenry. Policebuilding and supporting the provision of safety and justice is more than a formal institutional restructuring process and is perhaps better understood as a socio-cultural narrative. Such processes of social change require genuine local ownership and participation, which has not been the strength of UNPOL missions to date. Therefore, ascertaining a clear picture of how providers are performing in a range of areas as well as how their actions are received in this complex environment lies at the heart of enhancing efficacy and producing sustainable outcomes. Meaningful evaluations which are indicative of outcomes and impacts in the realm of policing and the RoL provide an insight into what effect policing activities are having, as opposed to simply recording and documenting what they have done and basing assumptions on that.

However, in the realm of policing—as in general—DPKO has been unable to develop meaningful ways to monitor and evaluate its success in restoring public order and longer-term police reform objectives.[128] The rare and limited attempts to assess UNPOL missions have been blighted by unrealistic goals, reflected in erroneous evaluation criteria. This inaccurate goal-setting can lead to inadequate M&E results as documentary realities fail to reflect the situation on the ground. As Hansen states: "After all, we are not looking to transform war-torn societies into crime-free ones, but to identify and arrive at tolerable levels of crime and instability . . . The key is to reach for an outcome that lies between the likely and the desirable."[129]

The major inhibiting factors to measuring short-term stabilisation outcomes are three-fold. First, as mentioned above, police missions are notoriously slow at deploying and often insufficient in number to perform even core activities at the outset and for significant periods.[130] Second, this limited capacity is thrown into a relatively chaotic 'post-conflict' environment characterised by uncertainty and limited access. Finally, the distinct lack of accurate and trustworthy data to analyse has inhibited extant systems predominantly reliant on synthesising crime statistics. Combined, these factors have acted to reduce the opportunity and severely limit the ability of police to conduct their own self-evaluation in a rigorous and timely fashion. More protracted police and RoL reform missions have

---

[128] Joshua G. Smith, Victoria K. Holt, and William J. Durch, *Enhancing United Nations Capacity for Post-Conflict Policing and Rule of Law*, Report from The Project on Rule of Law in Post-Conflict Settings (Washington DC: The Henry L. Stimson Center, 2007), 43.

[129] Annika S. Hansen, "From Congo to Kosovo: Civilian Police in Peace Operations," *Adelphi Papers* 41, no. 343 (2002): 107–8.

[130] Joshua G. Smith, Victoria K. Holt, and William J. Durch, *Enhancing United Nations Capacity for Post-Conflict Policing and Rule of Law*, Report from The Project on Rule of Law in Post-Conflict Settings (Washington DC: The Henry L. Stimson Center, 2007), 44.

faced similar constraints but numerous supplementary hurdles to accurately capturing progress of domestic police service transformation and public perceptions of them. In practice, these programmes are even more *ad hoc* and inconsistent in terms of the mission environment, context and *modus operandi*.[131] Furthermore, conventional approaches to monitoring and evaluating these efforts suffer from distorting and misleading trends in the data.[132] These circumstances have been reflected in the (lack of) M&E of these UNPOL efforts.

Despite—and indeed because of—these constraints, there is much value in evaluating the efficacy of police components. The idiosyncrasies of international police missions, the way they are constructed, and the work they perform, mean that additional benefits accrue when M&E can be disaggregated and tailored to the policing context. Given the expansion in both magnitude and functionality of UNPOL deployments in recent times, it is perhaps more salient than ever to develop ways to monitor and evaluate their impact. As Mobekk attests: "While crucial lessons have been learned, there is still significant progress to be made in ensuring high-quality efficient international policing and subsequently successful local police reform."[133]

As peace operations have evolved to face the changing nature of conflict the number of police deployed has burgeoned as their mandates have become increasingly ambitious. From plugging the 'post-conflict' public security gap to instigating and managing protracted police reform programmes, international police are now a mission-critical and indelible component of contemporary peace operations and attempts to address the root causes of conflict, laying the foundations for sustainable peace.[134]

Attempts to assess their impact are currently unsatisfactory. In general, the UN has been slow to recognise the importance of M&E in managing and improving its peacekeeping architecture. However, in his 2007 report on strengthening the capacity of the UN to manage and sustain peace operations, the Secretary-General described 'self-evaluation' of mission performance as:

---

131 Joshua G. Smith, Victoria K. Holt, and William J. Durch, *Enhancing United Nations Capacity for Post-Conflict Policing and Rule of Law*, Report from The Project on Rule of Law in Post-Conflict Settings (Washington DC: The Henry L. Stimson Center, 2007), 44.

132 For example, reduction in the number of crimes reported is a traditional indicator of success for police organisations. However, it is often the case that as police services become more trustworthy, the rate of reporting of increases. This is particularly true in 'post-conflict' environments.

133 Eirin Mobekk, "Identifying Lessons in United Nations International Policing Missions," *Policy Paper* 9 (Geneva: Geneva Centre for the Democratic Control of Armed Forces (DCAF), 2005), 3.

134 Gordon Peake and Kaysie Studdard-Brown, "Policebuilding: The International Deployment Group in the Solomon Islands," *International Peacekeeping* 12, no. 4 (2005): 530.

> ... *key to identifying areas in which managerial oversight, operational implementation or performance must be improved... identify policy shortcomings, training inadequacies or business process and structural disharmonies, therefore improving management, strengthening performance and enhancing accountability.*[135]

This acknowledgement has created the space for M&E to claim its necessary place as a central tenet in the management and evolution of UN peace operations and the various components therein. Given similar recognition within the UN's policing apparatus, but the enduring limitations of the Police Division in this area, it seems clear that a tool for assessing UNPOL missions is much-needed. As Hansen asserts, "There is much work to be done in evaluating the performance of international civilian police."[136] In light of the potential benefits accruing and the conspicuous absence of suitable tools at present, developing a meaningful way of monitoring and evaluating if, and how, operations are producing successful outcomes and intended impacts would be an invaluable tool for political decision-makers, headquarters staff, police-specific mission managers and recipient communities alike.

Whilst there is a wealth of literature on measuring the performance of policing in a domestic context,[137] this is of limited use in international policing. Even in societies where the RoL has strong roots, the eclectic nature of policing functions and responsibilities means that the most appropriate way to measure performance of police organisations remains an area of debate.[138]

---

135 Ban Ki-Moon, *Comprehensive Report on Strengthening the Capacity of the United Nations to Manage and Sustain Peace Operations*, Report of the Secretary-General (New York: United Nations, 2007), 21–22.

136 Annika S. Hansen, "From Congo to Kosovo: Civilian Police in Peace Operations," *Adelphi Papers* 41, no. 343 (2002): 31.

137 William J. Bratton and Sean W. Malinowski, "Police Performance Management in Practice: Taking Compstat to the Next Level," *Policing* 2, no. 3 (2008); Peter Neyroud, "Past, Present and Future Performance: Lessons and Prospects for the Measurement of Police Performance," *Policing* 2, no. 3 (2008); Police Executive Research Forum, *Quantifying Quality in Policing*, ed. Bill Blackwood Law Enforcement Management Institute of Texas (Washington DC: Police Executive Research Forum (PERF) 1996); Nigel Fielding and Martin Innes, "Reassurance Policing, Community Policing and Measuring Police Performance," *Policing and Society: An International Journal of Research and Policy* 16, no. 2 (2006); David I Ashby, "Policing Neighbourhoods: Exploring the Geographies of Crime, Policing and Performance Assessment," *Policing and Society* 15, no. 4 (2005); Isabelle Lelandais and Julie Bodson, "Measuring Police Performance," (Montreal: International Centre for the Prevention of Crime, 2007); Robert Langworthy, "Measuring What Matters: A Police Research Institute," in *Measuring What Matters: Proceedings from the Police Research Institute Meetings*, ed. Robert Langworthy (Washington DC: National Institute of Justice, 1999).

138 Rick Sarre, "Community Policing—Success or Failure? Exploring Different Models of Evaluation," in *The Police and the Community*, ed. Julia Vernon and Sandra McKillop (Canberra: Australian Institute of Criminology, 1992).

Domestic and International Policing

In the West, assessments of policing performance utilise extensive crime statistics and sophisticated computer programmes. One such example is the *Compstat* program which has been heralded for its impact upon the performance of the New York and Los Angeles Police Departments.[139] This is a sophisticated model using a range of data sources to assess performance of police managers against prioritised policing objectives in specific precincts. The model conceptualises cause-and-effect relationships by mapping policing activities through to outcomes.[140] Smith has argued that this programme, or similar, could be used to enhance the performance of police in UN peace operations when viewed as an international public service.[141]

However, the context for international policing renders such methods inappropriate. As argued in the previous chapter, (post-) conflict environments are tumultuous, dynamic and typically absent the rich data sets and abundant resources required to employ and maintain such technologies. Furthermore, the extent to which such systems measure complex social phenomena akin to the intended impact of peace operations is debatable given their managerial focus and dependence upon crime statistics. Monitoring and evaluating the effectiveness of police in peace missions requires a tailored approach, due to the unique operating environment, but also the nature of international policing work.

With regard to police in peace operations the scarcity of literature and attention to suitable M&E approaches is significant and manifest in the absence of widely used tools. The rare attempts to evaluate policing in this setting tend to centre on the longer-term goals of reforming and restructuring of police services.[142]

---

139 Dennis Smith, "Managing Civpol: The Potential Performance Management in International Public Services," in *Rethinking International Organizations: Pathology and Promise*, ed. D. Dijkzeul and Y. Beigbeder (New York: Berghahn, 2003), 276–79; William J. Bratton and Sean W. Malinowski, "Police Performance Management in Practice: Taking Compstat to the Next Level," *Policing* 2, no. 3 (2008); William J. Bratton and D. C. Smith, "Performance Management in New York City: Compstat and the Revolution in Police Management," in *Quicker Better Cheaper? Managing Performance in American Government*, ed. D. Forsythe (State University of New York Press 2001); Mark H. Moore and Anthony A. Braga, "Measuring and Improving Police Performance: The Lessons of Compstat and Its Progeny," *Policing* 26, no. 3 (2003).

140 Mark H. Moore and Anthony A. Braga, "Measuring and Improving Police Performance: The Lessons of Compstat and Its Progeny," *Policing* 26, no. 3 (2003).

141 Dennis Smith, "Managing Civpol: The Potential Performance Management in International Public Services," in *Rethinking International Organizations: Pathology and Promise*, ed. D. Dijkzeul and Y. Beigbeder (New York: Berghahn, 2003), 282.

142 William G. O'Neill, *Police Reform in Post-Conflict Societies: What We Know and What We Still Need to Know*, The Security-Development Nexus Program Policy Paper (New York: International Peace Academy, 2005); Charles T. Call, "Challenges in Police Reform: Promoting Effectiveness and Accountability," in *From Promise to Practice:*

The most sophisticated of such attempts is probably the 'Police Reform Indicators and Measurement Evaluation' (PRIME) System developed at Princeton University.[143] The project assessed police reform in post-conflict environments and was developed and field-tested in three UN peace operations—UNMIK in Kosovo, UNAMSIL in Sierra Leone and (as was) UNOTIL in Timor-Leste. Given this focus, the system conceptualised the prerequisites for an effective reformed police service and developed indicators to "measure the extent to which a police service has made overall progress on key outcomes"[144] for the recipient community. Although it is a complex framework, PRIME claims to provide a 'real world' solution whereby practical data sources are relied upon.[145] It comprises sixteen core predominantly qualitative indicators, which are divided into four main pillars of 'outcomes'. These cover: (1) performance effectiveness; (2) management and oversight; (3) community relations; and (4) sustainability.

The paucity of comprehensive frameworks addressing the impacts of policing in peace operations means that PRIME's use of a policing-specific lens in the design process provides the opportunity to capture the organisational and operational idiosyncrasies associated with UNPOL missions. For example, the results point to some of the enabling competencies within the police component, which may facilitate more efficacious missions.[146] However, despite the benefits derived from more qualitative methods,[147] the system's bias towards such measures disregards the value quantitative methods can provide. That is, it misses detailed task-oriented performance measures, which are more tightly linked to the day-to-day conduct of international police which are easily and already captured within missions. This, in turn, can be inhibitive to demonstrating contributions from basic activities and their outputs to overarching mission outcomes. Perhaps the major failing of the PRIME system is its inability to internalise exogenous factors and unintended consequences.[148] That is, the approach struggles to account for

---

Strengthening UN Capacities for the Prevention of Violent Conflict ed. Chandra Lekha Sriram and Karin Wermester (New York: International Peace Academy, 2003).

143 Ylber Bajraktari, Arthur Boutellis, Fatema Gunja, Daniel Harris, James Kapsis, Eva Kaye and Jane Rhee, *The PRIME System: Measuring the Success of Post-Conflict Police Reform*, (Princeton: Princeton University, 2006).

144 Ylber Bajraktari, Arthur Boutellis, Fatema Gunja, Daniel Harris, James Kapsis, Eva Kaye and Jane Rhee, *The PRIME System: Measuring the Success of Post-Conflict Police Reform*, (Princeton: Princeton University, 2006), 15.

145 Ylber Bajraktari, Arthur Boutellis, Fatema Gunja, Daniel Harris, James Kapsis, Eva Kaye and Jane Rhee, *The PRIME System: Measuring the Success of Post-Conflict Police Reform*, (Princeton: Princeton University, 2006), 13.

146 Ylber Bajraktari, Arthur Boutellis, Fatema Gunja, Daniel Harris, James Kapsis, Eva Kaye and Jane Rhee, *The PRIME System: Measuring the Success of Post-Conflict Police Reform*, (Princeton: Princeton University, 2006), 105–6.

147 See below.

148 For further discussion of unintended consequences of peacekeeping, also known as 'displacement effects' when they have negative connotations, see: Aoi Chiyuki,

negative impact of external influences, such as significant countervailing levels of organised criminality. Ultimately, the focus on reform, and corollary decision to locate the domestic police service as the unit of analysis, inhibits the ability of PRIME to draw conclusions about the impact of the peace operation mandated to support the reform process under scrutiny. Assessments about the impact of UNPOL itself are consequently reduced to assumptions by proxy.

Another rare example of evaluating international policing can be found amongst the UN DPKO-commissioned guidance on Community Policing in peace operations. The compendium includes a manual on how to evaluate UN programs promoting community policing in peacekeeping contexts.[149] The handbook lays out the benefits and principles of evaluation in this context and suggests ways of addressing the following questions: Firstly, how well has UNCIVPOL implemented its community policing programs? How successful have local police been in incorporating UN-sponsored community policing into their operational programs? And finally, how successful has UN-sponsored community policing been locally in improving crime control and prevention and in improving relations between police and the public?

These tiered questions can be understood to fit a logical framework whereby the first level addresses UNPOL outputs, the second the associated outcomes and the third the ensuing impact. Although conventional in this sense, the second and third do provide useful insight into more inclusive and participatory approaches to evaluating impact, targeting public perceptions etc. Although this constitutes a guide rather than a ready-to-use tool, it does propose a method, potential performance indicators and sources of validation which range from statistical data and bureaucratic documentation to survey results and first hand observations.[150] The stated intention is to simplify and economise the process in order to overcome bureaucratic inertia and inhibitive costs. Although this presents rare specificity in the realm of M&E for police peacekeepers, the focus on community policing neglects the rest of UNPOL's mandated goals in these settings, particularly in the short-term. The approaches described therein reflect that concentration at the expense of other important components of UNPOL work.

Despite the ubiquitous recognition of the importance of police functions in modern peace operations, there is a paucity of literature dedicated to understanding and assessing their impact. Furthermore, there has been no attempt to

---

Cedric de Coning, and Ramesh Thakur, eds., *Unintended Consequences of Peacekeeping Operations* (Tokyo: United Nations University Press, 2007).

149 David H. Bayley, *Community Policing: Evaluation Programs* (New York: Civilian Police Division, DPKO, United Nations, 2005).

150 David H. Bayley, *Community Policing: Evaluation Programs* (New York: Civilian Police Division, DPKO, United Nations, 2005), 9–10.

develop or conduct M&E of the early stages of UNPOL missions. This in itself is a significant gap in the literature, especially given widespread acknowledgement of the importance of policing in the critical early stages of a mission.[151]

Current Practices in Police Capacity Development M&E

Police capacity building is one crucial aspect of SSR. Whilst it is by no means always carried out in the context of a broader SSR process, it is desirable for the M&E of capacity building to be compatible with SSR[152] frameworks in the interests of working with international 'providers' in such environments. There is currently no consensus on how SSR should be monitored and evaluated. However, it worth noting for the purpose of this book, that the Balanced Scorecard approach to M&E in SSR appears to be a dominant recommendation.[153] Other Logical Framework models and metrics systems are also generally supported.

Much has, and is, being done in the area of police capacity building and reform specifically, and whilst the international community is far from achieving a universally accepted and consistently implemented model for M&E the subject has been gaining increasing attention. Work in this area has produced a range of guides, predominantly presented in the form of 'check lists'. Long lists of indicators are available from various sources[154] which, to varying degrees of comprehensiveness, list the indicators of a successful police force.[155] This 'ideal type' provides a reference point to measure 'unsuccessful' police organizations against with the intention of 'filling the gaps' and measuring the action taken. Despite the increasing interest in this field the measurement of success is done largely on an ad hoc basis. Even in cases where evaluations are conducted thoroughly

---

151 United Nations High-Level Panel on United Nations Peace Operations, *Report of the Panel on United Nations Peace Operations* (New York: United Nations, 2000), 15; Joshua G. Smith, Victoria K. Holt, and William J. Durch, *Enhancing United Nations Capacity for Post-Conflict Policing and Rule of Law*, Report from The Project on Rule of Law in Post-Conflict Settings (Washington DC: The Henry L. Stimson Center, 2007), 39–40, 50; United Nations Department of Peacekeeping Operations, *Capstone Doctrine: United Nations Peacekeeping Operations: Principles and Guidelines*, (New York: UN DPKO, 2008), 62–63.

152 As well as other internationally coordinated multifaceted reform projects.

153 Ann Fitz-Gerald and Sylvie Jackson, "Developing a Performance Measurement System for Security Sector Interventions," *Journal of Security Sector Management* 6, no. 1 (2008).

154 Sources include academic institutions, government bodies and multilateral agencies and NGOs.

155 For example see excerpt from I. Clegg, R. Hunt, and J. Whetton, *Policy Guidance on Support to Policing in Developing Countries*, (Swansea: University of Wales, Centre for Development Studies, 2000).

they tend not to be ongoing or introduce different approaches each time making comparisons difficult, if not impossible.[156]

Examples of more comprehensive approaches to M&E in police reform do exist. In 2005 the Organization [sic] for Security and Cooperation in Europe (OSCE) Mission in Kosovo (OMiK) published a guide to police capacity building in transition and post-conflict states.[157] Included in this guide was a comprehensive section on M&E recommending the Kirkpatrick evaluation model as one possible tool for M&E. This model requires the collation of data at four defined operational levels set against overall objectives. The four levels include: the results level; performance level; training level; and reaction level. The M&E is set out according to the following figure:[158]

Advanced level of evaluation	Results level	Impact of capacity building on the police organisation and its objectives
	Performance level	Impact of the capacity building on workplace performance/ behaviour
Basic level of evaluation	Training level	Impact of the capacity building in terms of what the trainee officers learned
	Reaction level	Impact of the capacity building in terms of the trainee officers' satisfaction

Figure 2: Kirkpatrick's evaluation model.[159]

156 Ylber Bajraktari, Arthur Boutellis, Fatema Gunja, Daniel Harris, James Kapsis, Eva Kaye and Jane Rhee, *The PRIME System: Measuring the Success of Post-Conflict Police Reform*, (Princeton: Princeton University, 2006).

157 Frank Harris, *The Role of Capacity-Building in Police Reform.* (Pristina: Department of Police Education and Development / Organisation for Security and Cooperation in Europe—Mission in Kosovo, 2005).

158 Note this book is informed by the experiences in Kosovo. Such experience was based on the mission mandate—see *237th Plenary Meeting—PC Journal No 237, Agenda item 2—Decision No 305*, Organisation for Security and Cooperation in Europe Permanent Council, 1 July 1999.

159 Frank Harris, *The Role of Capacity-Building in Police Reform.* (Pristina: Department of Police Education and Development / Organisation for Security and Cooperation in Europe—Mission in Kosovo, 2005), 160.

It should be noted from the outset that the precondition for this approach is an existing local desire for reform. That is, it requires a commitment from Government officials and Ministers, the Police Commissioner, Executive and Senior Police Officers to be willing and motivated to achieve a democratic community-centric police force.[160] The strategy is based on Results Based Management (RBM). It is a technical, mechanistic, gap-filling approach, adopting rational systematic style capacity building,[161] to which we dedicate significant space in Chapter 6's critique of mainstream approaches.

Another recently published approach to M&E in Police Reform comes from Princeton University. The PRIME (Police Reform Indicators and Measurement Evaluation) System is an 'evidence-based' qualitative measurement tool designed around '16 core indicators' making up the four central pillars: Performance Effectiveness; Management Oversight; Community Relations; and Sustainability.[162] Ultimately this is a guide to identifying information (organised data collation) in a systematic and consistent way in line with the key priorities of Police Reform. There are many benefits inherent in this approach. The move to qualitative measures is not only welcome (providing flexibility and the opportunity for meaningful data) but necessary, according to the authors, as base line quantitative data is unreliable (if available at all) in a post-conflict environment.

Whilst the above approaches to M&E suffer from some obvious weaknesses that we critique in Chapter 6, much of these could be ameliorated with improvements to the operationalisation of their processes. Rather the real problem lies in the relationship between high-level macro performance management and what is happening on the ground. The following explores the 'top-down' tendencies of such M&E practices. We argue if these operations are to be successful, the information channel will need to be reversed. Furthermore, the process of problem diagnosis, planning, defining success and the practice of meaningful data collation requires the utilisation of inclusive and innovative methods. To understand the importance of this we first need to address the concept of 'capacity building'.

---

160 Frank Harris, *The Role of Capacity-Building in Police Reform.* (Pristina: Department of Police Education and Development / Organisation for Security and Cooperation in Europe—Mission in Kosovo, 2005), 23.

161 Frank Harris, *The Role of Capacity-Building in Police Reform.* (Pristina: Department of Police Education and Development / Organisation for Security and Cooperation in Europe—Mission in Kosovo, 2005), 50–4.

162 Ylber Bajraktari, Arthur Boutellis, Fatema Gunja, Daniel Harris, James Kapsis, Eva Kaye and Jane Rhee, *The PRIME System: Measuring the Success of Post-Conflict Police Reform,* (Princeton: Princeton University, 2006), 5.

The Monitoring and Evaluation of Capacity Building

Expanding on the explanations in Chapter 1, the following exploration delves more deeply into capacity development addressing evolving concepts in the discussion on capacity development. Primarily, these are sustainable organisational capacity development and results based M&E.

The Concept of Capacity

Capacity as a concept has recently attracted a great deal of attention. The mixed results of capacity development programs has led the international development community to question just what is capacity, and what are the conditions which allow an organisation to evolve into a self sustaining system? In March 2006 the European Centre for Development Policy Management facilitated a workshop as part of the larger 'Study on Capacity, Change and Performance'. This workshop considered the work and views of a wide range of agencies and development practitioners (scholars and so on) regarding the nature of capacity development and experiences in monitoring and evaluating such capacity.[163] The workshop report lists five dimensions of capacity relating to the five core capabilities:[164]

- The capability to act and survive;
- The capability to generate results;
- The capability to relate;
- The capability to adapt and self-renew; and,
- The capability to achieve coherence;

The ECDPM goes on to provide the following definition:

> *Capacity is that emergent combination of attributes, assets, capabilities and relationships that enables human systems to perform, survive and self-renew.*[165]

More recently the ECDPM has produced a report on *Capacity, Change and Performance*[166] which reflects the findings of this workshop together with the

163 AusAID is one of the international supporters of this study: 'Study on Capacity, Change & Performance'. For more information see ECDPM's website at http://www.ecdpm.org.

164 Julia Zinke, *Monitoring & Evaluation of Capacity and Capacity Development: Workshop Report*, (Maastricht, The Netherlands: European Centre for Development Policy Management, 2006), 2–5.

165 Julia Zinke, *Monitoring & Evaluation of Capacity and Capacity Development: Workshop Report*, (Maastricht, The Netherlands: European Centre for Development Policy Management, 2006), 5.

166 H. Baser & Peter Morgan, *Capacity Change & Performance: Study Report*, Discussion Paper No 59b, (Maastricht, the Netherlands: European Centre for Development Policy Management, 2008), 22–35.

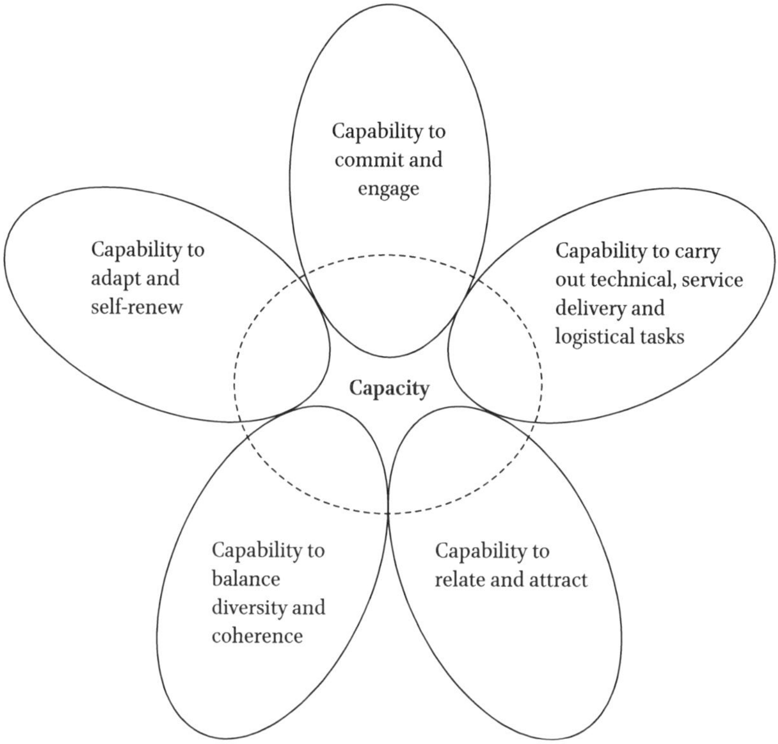

Figure 3: Capacity and Capabilities.[167]

findings of a broad ranging study on the subject of capacity. As a result of widespread consultation and much debate the report settled on the below figure of overlapping core capabilities.

What is evident here is that the concept of capacity has moved a long way from its technocratic origins and is now being defined as something far less tangible, something that reflects concern for sustainability, fluidity, flexibility, agency and relatedness. Simply put an organisation has to be able to access what it needs and respond to circumstances—and crucially it has to want to.

Capacity Development

The process of capacity development therefore, is certainly concerned with building and developing technical capabilities and competencies but it must do so in a way that nurtures the development of the above more abstract conditions.

[167] H. Baser & Peter Morgan, *Capacity Change & Performance: Study Report*, Discussion Paper No 59b, (Maastricht, the Netherlands: European Centre for Development Policy Management, 2008), 22–35.

Sustainable Organisational Capacity Development

In light of the decades of problematic capacity development programs the international aid community, along with development scholars, have been working to understand the aspects of capacity development that result in lasting and sustainable change and improvements. The literature shows that the technical transfer of skills and equipment to local personnel who are treated as passive recipients of external expertise has had limited success.[168] Whilst this approach has some success in teaching partner personnel how to do the job (according to technical experts) and why they should do the job (imported logic) often there is no commitment to the change, so in practice the new procedures are not followed.

The contemporary understanding of capacity development still values the development of technical skills as a core component but suggests a need to deliver capacity development programs in a manner which harnesses local energy and develops sustainable *organisational capacity.* Organisational capacity refers to the practical aspects of those more abstract concepts highlighted in the previous section on the concept of capacity. Organisational capacity (as it is referred to here) does not just refer to the hierarchy's capacity to organise and co-ordinate (although this is certainly part of it). Rather, it refers to the organisations' capacity to relate, establish internal and external coherence, survive and self-renew.

Rather than deliver technical assistance to components of the organisation (units) with little regard to their broader function—sustainable organisational capacity development considers how the unit fits into a broader system. This is because the unit does not operate in isolation.[169] The unit's capacity to function is dependent on external factors and its capacity to engage and relate with those outside its immediate unit. This obviously includes those within the broader organisation—but it can also, and often does, include other agencies[170] as well as the broader system in which it needs to survive—that being the broader political and social system. An organisation and its respective components (units) rely on its capacity to relate and be relevant to the broader system for its legitimacy.

Other crucial aspects of *sustainable* capacity development relate to the manner in which capacity is developed. Externally imposed solutions that make little sense in the context in which they are being introduced are at best met with resistance. Instead sustainable capacity development means engaging in processes which generate local ownership and commitment. This means finding out

---

168 Such an approach is only appropriate in cases where organisational capacity already exists and technical training is responding to demand.

169 Organization for Economic Co-operation and Development, *The OECD DAC Handbook on Security Sector Reform: Supporting Security and Justice*, (Paris: OECD, 2007), 191.

170 Organization for Economic Co-operation and Development, *The OECD DAC Handbook on Security Sector Reform: Supporting Security and Justice*, (Paris: OECD, 2007), 199.

what is relevant for those local people undertaking the change process and ensuring systems are appropriate for the context and in line with social expectations.

Contemporary approaches are concerned with the *process* of capacity development. It is now seen to be important to approach capacity development in a manner which explicitly facilitates the emergence of sustainable conditions and organisational capacity.

In summary the evolution of the capacity building field, and the growing international consensus on the subject, demonstrates a definite move towards the holistic understanding of capacity as outlined by the ECDPM key points and defined by Peter Morgan above. Such an understanding of capacity requires a complex approach to capacity building, particularly in cases such as the IDG's offshore organisational capacity building projects.

"All models are wrong, some models are useful"[171]

It is impossible to discuss the potential approaches to measuring the effectiveness of capacity building initiatives in isolation. How capacity building is conceptualised, consequent approaches to it, and the following M&E processes are inseparable, as they inherently impact upon each other. This is evident in the following summary of *some* key criticisms of RBM which have emerged through the experience of the development community. Our intention is to learn from these lessons, to avoid repeating M&E mistakes in police capacity building operations.

Results Based Management Approaches to M&E

The UN Development Program (UNDP) has been using RBM approaches in SSR[172] and as previously mentioned RBM is already utilised in police capacity building operations. However, as the OMiK example highlights, its utility is limited as the approach is arguably only appropriate in cases of existing capacity and genuinely established internal motivation for reform.

RBM is a corporate based method of strategic performance management. It is focused on streamlining every tangible aspect of capacity development and has a heavy emphasis on accountability. In this approach all aspects of resource allocation and funding, process and action, reporting and accountability should directly relate to the desired 'outcomes' as defined by the donor.[173] In reality,

---

171 Box as cited in Peter Morgan, *The Concept of Capacity* (Maastricht, the Netherlands: European Centre for Development Policy Management, 2006).

172 Ann Fitz-Gerald and Sylvie Jackson, "Developing a Performance Measurement System for Security Sector Interventions," *Journal of Security Sector Management* 6, no. 1 (2008), 5.

173 United Nations Development Programme. *Results Based Management: Concepts & Methodology.* (New York: UNDP: 2000), 2–3.

however, the process is only accountable to the 'output' stage.[174] The important points to recognise here are that problem diagnosis and subsequent performance indicators are generally developed by the donor staff. Whilst outcomes are monitored, the actual performance measure for the donor staff is generally the delivery of the stipulated outputs and not the broader social impact of the overall organisational capacity of the host country institution. This is largely because the units of analysis are the technical components of the institution (treated as a closed system).

The 'typology of results' encourages standardisation in the interest of generating data and performance information comparable across locations and time.[175] 'Soft' assistance or 'soft' issue intervention such as attempting to influence the external environment the organisation engages with or creating enabling conditions is recognised as being important, however, very difficult to measure. The importance of 'securing the trust and cooperation' of partners[176] is acknowledged, although it is not central to the approach. There is a notion that if the donors prove themselves as being valuable contributors to and instigators of, change the local participants will learn to trust them.[177]

The benefits of standardisation in M&E, is that it allows comparative analysis and can provide 'snap shots'. Trends can be identified and abnormalities detected, potentially prompting action. RBM and similar approaches are concerned particularly with accountability.[178] Therefore, a crucial benefit, or at least goal, of the framework is the establishment of clear expectations. With clearly defined expectations managers and practitioners (and to varying degrees staff and 'in country' partners) are explicitly aware of the priorities, their roles in meeting these expectations and what aspects they will be assessed and measured against.[179] The manner in which outcomes are broken down into manageable outputs provides transparent start and end points, as does the reporting period applicable.

---

174 For a more detailed discussion of the strengths and weakness see forthcoming papers (Jodie Curth-Bibb—details of which to be published at http://www.uq.edu.au/idg-international-policing/.

175 United Nations Development Programme. *Results Based Management: Concepts & Methodology.* (New York: UNDP: 2000), 12.

176 United Nations Development Programme. *Results Based Management: Concepts & Methodology.* (New York: UNDP: 2000), 4.

177 United Nations Development Programme. *Results Based Management: Concepts & Methodology.* (New York: UNDP: 2000), 4–10.

178 David Watson, *Monitoring and Evaluation of Capacity and Capacity Development* (Maastricht, the Netherlands: European Centre for Development Policy Management, 2006), 17.

179 United Nations Development Programme. *Results Based Management: Concepts & Methodology.* (New York: UNDP: 2000), 10.

Performance measurements utilising a framework such as RBM enjoy the perceived legitimacy of *objectivity*[180] and resource flows are easily identifiable.

It is useful to briefly summarise some potential criticisms as alternative approaches are largely informed by the perceived failures associated with RBM and other 'Logical Frameworks'. It should be noted development agencies (donors) are typically aware of the following outlined problems and the model of RBM is being constantly reviewed to address many inherent weaknesses.[181]

Arguably the strongest and most frequent criticism relates to notions of ownership. The interventionist model of external diagnosis, 'gap filling' and accountability reduces the sense of ownership for local participants—due to a lack of comprehensive local input from the outset. This stems from the misguided notion that problem identification and solving is an objective, logical process and resultant measurements of reform (i.e. indicators of success) are knowable through rational linear prediction and objective observation. This is a problem in the building of capacity itself, as local participants are not central to the planning stages or the prescription and utilisation of measurements, consequently opportunity for participatory learning is reduced.[182] As change is prescribed from the outside there is often a lack of mutual understanding and limited agreement on what 'success' might look like. Another considerable criticism of RBM and similar approaches is the heavy reliance on specific problem diagnosis in an environment notoriously difficult to accurately assess.[183] The multitude of complex contributing disabling factors in a capacity building environment makes simple problem-solution strategies extremely difficult and to attempt to address capacity issues in this manner is to achieve only partial solutions which may in fact undermine capacity on the whole.[184]

In the interests of demonstrating success there is a tendency in this model to divert resources toward areas of quick realisation with quantifiable outcomes.

---

180 A. Binnendijk, *Results Based Management in the Development Cooperation Agencies: A Review of Experience—Executive Summary (Draft)* (Paris: Development Assistance Committee of Organisation for Economic Cooperation and Development, 2000), 3.

181 A. Binnendijk, *Results Based Management in the Development Cooperation Agencies: A Review of Experience—Executive Summary (Draft)* (Paris: Development Assistance Committee of Organisation for Economic Cooperation and Development, 2000), 3.

182 The degree of consultation varies between donors and projects—what is important is the trend.

183 David Watson, *Monitoring and Evaluation of Capacity and Capacity Development* (Maastricht, the Netherlands: European Centre for Development Policy Management, 2006), 16.

184 Peter Senge, *The Fifth Discipline: The Art and Practice of the Learning Organization* (Sydney: Random House, 1992), 7; Peter Morgan, *The Idea and Practice of Systems Thinking and their Relevance for Capacity Development.* (Maastricht, the Netherlands: European Centre for Development Policy Management, 2005), 4–7.

This is particularly problematic when the result is a reduced focus on 'soft' less tangible aspects of capacity building. The artificial construct of time-blocks and reporting periods can also motivate short-term goal orientation. 'In country' partner personnel may be sidelined, undermining sustainability, as intervening practitioners attempt to meet predetermined goals on a timeline. RBM is often criticised for a preoccupation with 'hard' indicators and micro aspects of the organisation. This relates to criticisms of compartmentalising the organisation rather than treating it as a whole. This can be problematic as it stems from the assumption that the organisation can be broken down into discrete units and 'treated' in isolation, potentially undermining the 'whole'.

A key element of any police peace operation should be evaluating the success and sustainability of the deployment, recognising that these operations do not exist in isolation. They represent myriad historical influences and theoretical and practical evolutions both in terms of policing deployments, M&E and capacity development but also within the host nations and the nations deploying these policing forces. By establishing these contexts, these first two chapters have set the stage for an examination of the ontological and epistemological aspects that influence the evolution of these ideas and the way this book envisages their contribution to this discussion.

PART TWO

RECASTING KEY ONTOLOGICAL AND EPISTEMOLOGICAL ASPECTS

CHAPTER THREE

RESHAPING THE SUBSTANCE OF INTERNATIONAL CONTRIBUTIONS—BEYOND RETHINKING THE 'STATE OF THE STATE'

Chapters 1–2 provided a useful and necessary grounding for a comprehensive interrogation of international policing. They have set up an historical and contextual backdrop from which to make a meaningfully critical contribution to rebuilding how we think about international policing. The ensuing three chapters delve deeply into the key conceptual debates that *should* be acknowledged as comprising the points from which the conventional wisdom needs to shift from its current, unfounded moorings. Beginning with this chapter, we endeavour to redress the numerous misconstrued assumptions that have contributed to the current widespread fallacies. All together, we argue for a move beyond the problematic state-centric prism in order to begin to appreciate the myriad forces that do indeed warrant the attention of the international community as it strives to contribute in appropriate and fruitful ways.

To that end, the blind spot most damaging to successful peace support interventions may be that the broad church of international assistance continues to misunderstand the nature of recipient societies.[185] That is, interveners persist in viewing conflict-affected societies through a self-image lens which wrongly presumes the Weberian state ideal, with its centralised and hierarchical structures and formalised distinctions between public and private. Crucially, orthodox Western notions of the security sector and therefore of security sector reform (SSR) are informed by this mistaken view of the mission environment. The reality

---

185 This viewpoint builds upon what Bruce Baker and Eric Scheye, "Access to Justice in a Post-conflict State: Donor-supported Multidimensional Peacekeeping in Southern Sudan", *International Peacekeeping* 16 no. 2, (2009): 171–185, 172, express as: 'A key challenge of donor-supported multidimensional peacekeeping operations, which typically occur in post colonial environments, is to understand the structure and limitations of the state where assistance is being provided'.

in most cases however is far from this idealised Western conception. Rather, as an increasingly irrefutable case now attests, the 'majority world'[186] in which interventions take place is marked by often complex layers of political orders combining practices and actors from formal and informal, traditional and new origins.[187] To be clear, this is not the same environmental complexity talked about in donor circles, which refers to the relationships among the array of intervening actors on the one hand and the host-government and its often monolithically-portrayed 'local population' on the other.

Failing to accept the true nature[188] of the majority world means that security and development programs risk missing the mark. The consequences can be grave indeed; atrocities committed by incorrigible state militaries constitute only some of the tragic outcomes of a misplaced reliance on state actors. The longer-term ramifications for sustainable peace can of course be devastating; with some arguing that such conventionally conceived interventions can do more harm than good.[189] Near term problems thrown up can be equally thorny since multi-layered realities often come with conflicting, or at least inconsistent, notions of law and order.[190] Eric Scheye opines: 'For effective donor support to take place,

---

186 We borrow from the *New Internationalist* magazine for this apt—and substantively less patronising—term. Herein it is meant to encompass basically everything outside the OCED countries that drive the global assistance realm.

187 See, *inter alia*, Sinclair Dinnen and John Braithwaite, "Reinventing Policing Through the Prism of the Colonial Kiap", *Policing and Society* 19 no. 2, (2009): 161–173; Bruce Baker and Eric Scheye, "Access to Justice in a Post-conflict State: Donor-supported Multi-dimensional Peacekeeping in Southern Sudan", *International Peacekeeping* 16 no. 2 (2009): 171–185.; Bruce Baker and Eric Scheye, "Multi-Layered Justice and Security Delivery in Post Conflict and Fragile States", *Conflict, Security & Development* 7 no. 4 (2007): 503–528; Volker Boege, Anne Brown, Kevin Clements and Anna Nolan, *On Hybrid Political Orders and Emerging States: What is Failing—States in the Global South or Research and Politics in the West?* (Berlin: Berghof Research Centre for Constructive Conflict Management, 2009); M. Anne Brown, "Security, Development and the Nation-Building Agenda—East Timor", *Conflict, Security & Development* 9 no. 2 (2009): 141–164.

188 Importantly, the use of the terms 'true' and 'nature' are not to be confused with essentialising environments. To the contrary, our arguments consistently maintain that we consider the environment to be contested, fluid, and multi-perspective.

189 Carolyn Bull, "Building the Rule of Law Under UN Transitional Administration", *Policy Brief No. 7* (United Nations University Press, 2007), 2–3; Nat J. Colletta and Robert Muggah, "Rethinking Post-War Insecurity: From Interim Stabilization to Second Generation Security Promotion", *Journal of Humanitarian Assistance* (February 2009): 1–20, 1.

190 For instance, in contrast to some state legal codes, moral codes based on the Koran often criminalise homosexuality; similarly, in Sierra Leone, taxi associations enforce the prohibition of carrying pregnant women on motorbikes, an act which is permitted by state codes, Bruce Baker, *Grasping the Nettle of Nonstate Policing*, Paper presented at Making Sense of Peace and Capacity building: Rethinking Policing and Beyond Workshop, (Brisbane, July 2009), 4. Both examples raise troublesome practical ques-

what is required is an accurate analysis of the nature and structure of the post-colonial fragile state as it is, rather than as one may wish it to be'.[191]

The underlying argument of this chapter is that the international community (or more accurately, the OECD states and their donor appendages that generally speak for the international community) needs to accept forthwith that the nature of recipient societies is one of hybrid systems and therefore very different 'solutions' to what have been on the menu heretofore may be required. The state itself may not even be the most appropriate referent with which to begin our analyses.[192] The crux of the problem is not, as the conventional wisdom maintains, the rather straightforward case of needing more resources for largely the same approaches. To be clear, well-intending donor states and organisations have no less a role to play; a need for intervention is the common denominator. The roles themselves however must change. As such, the debate must turn to explore how and where exogenous actors can assist societies characterised by non-state and hybrid institutions, practices and actors. This entails creating the space in which *internal* processes of transformation can occur,[193] rather than continuing to attempt transplantation of foreign ideas and institutions.

An important corollary is that we must sincerely interrogate what these societies *should* look like in the longer term—beyond the short-term peacekeeping and medium-term peacebuilding goals. What kinds of societal norms and institutions will emerge out of nearer term rebuilding activities?[194] Contrary to the widely-held view that the actions of interveners can somehow be value and thus impact free, this means acknowledging that the forms of assistance inescapably affect how a society's norms and institutions evolve. Conducting training courses on democratic policing modus operandi, for instance, is about instilling a particular set of values, some of which are not espoused in many parts of the world. The same applies to the myriad programs to institutionalise ideals ranging from

---

tions as to which order is to be upheld, particularly since non-state codes often enjoy greater traction among the majority of the populace.

191 Eric Scheye, *The Structure of the Post-Colonial State: The Role and Function of NonState/Local Justice and Security Networks* (OECD, forthcoming), 2; See also Bryn Hughes and Charles Hunt, "The Rule of Law in Peace and Capacity Building Operations: Moving Beyond a Conventional State Centred Imagination", *Journal of International Peacekeeping* 13 no. 3–4 (2009): 267–293

192 Saskia Sassen, 'Cities and New Wars: After Mumbai', (2008) http://www.opendemocracy.net/article/the-new-wars-and-cities-after-mumbai-0.

193 Carolyn Bull, "Building the Rule of Law Under UN Transitional Administration", *Policy Brief No. 7* (United Nations University Press, 2007), 5.

194 See the work of Michael W. Doyle and Nicholas Sambanis, *Making War and Building Peace: United Nations Peace Operations* (Princeton: Princeton University Press, 2006); and Virginia Fortuna, *Does Peacekeeping Work? Shaping Belligerents' Choices After Civil War* (Princeton: Princeton University Press, 2008) for examples of critical perspectives and alternate paradigms.

the extant human rights agenda to liberal economic structures. If we consider frankly the endemic problems of many OECD countries, such as the United States with its high crime and incarceration rates, wide gaps between rich and poor, extreme carbon footprint and current economic malaise, it becomes questionable that longer term 'state-building' goals should be permitted to tend toward the 'free-market', ecologically-irresponsible, individualistic orders that have so far gone largely unquestioned as the end game of international interventions.[195] Indeed, these same globalising forces have tended to create significant problems in the majority world.[196]

A serious re-think of both the mission environment and the future form of societies thus prompts us to ask what Western mindsets can learn from traditional societies (e.g. parts of Papua New Guinea). In other words, what valuable 'post-Weberian' characteristics—meaning forward-looking hybrid systems of governance in which both state and informal actors comprise plausible sources of law and order, justice, and other public goods[197]—might be held out as 'better practice' models than what has been assumed to date?[198] Restorative approaches to justice stand tall as one of many such potential facets.[199] 'Relative universalism' frameworks[200] offer invaluable guidance about how to avoid outcomes

195 See: M. Anne Brown, "Security, Development and the Nation-Building Agenda—East Timor", *Conflict, Security & Development* 9 no. 2 (2009): 141–164.

196 Volker Boege, M. Anne Brown, Kevin P. Clements, and Anna Nolan, "States Emerging from Hybrid Political Orders—Pacific Experiences", *Occasional Paper Series Number 11* (Australian Centre for Peace and Conflict Studies, September 2008).

197 These evolving hybrid orders contrast the Weberian ideal which presupposes that formal state mechanisms alone deliver public goods. See: Joel S. Migdal and Klaus Schlitche, "Rethinking the State", in *The Dynamics of States: The Formation and Crises of State Domination*, ed. K. Schiltche. (Surrey, UK.: Ashgate Publisher, 2005); and Bryn Hughes and Charles Hunt, "The Rule of Law in Peace and Capacity Building Operations: Moving Beyond a Conventional State Centred Imagination", *Journal of International Peacekeeping* 13 no. 3–4 (2009): 267–293.

198 See: Michael Barnett, "Building a Republican Peace: Stabilizing States after War", *International Security* 30 no. 4 (2006): 87–112 for a useful discussion covering these kinds of issues.

199 The following are some of the arguably preferred characteristics non-Western approaches have to offer: 'often restorative (not punitive) justice; non-adversarial; a focus on reconciliation and social harmony; consultative and consensual decisions; a collective and not individual view of problems; holistic rather than a strict division of criminal and civil matters; incorporating public participation (victim and accused); addressing root issues of the dispute and not just behavioural symptoms; and not being dominated by legal professionals... (and) well suited to low levels of literacy'; Bruce Baker, *Grasping the Nettle of Nonstate Policing*, Paper presented at Making Sense of Peace and Capacity building: Rethinking Policing and Beyond Workshop (Brisbane, July 2009), 14.

200 Jack Donnelly, "The Relative Universality of Human Rights", *Human Rights Quarterly* 29 no. 2 (2007): 281–306; and Bryn Hughes and Charles Hunt, "The Rule of Law in

plagued by either Western liberal impositions or, on the other hand, oppressive traditional practices. Similarly, better practice approaches must rely on the often tough and always politically-charged contestation between the myriad intervening and indigenous perspectives.

Related is the question of the *sustainability* of the (typically foreign) systems and institutions being developed. A closer look underscores the structural challenge that recipient governments are typically forced to rely upon a fraction of the tax revenue donor nations enjoy domestically,[201] while straining to meet Western expectations of state pervasiveness and service provision. It should come as little surprise that, even with massive yet temporary influxes of donor monies, police and other state provider institutions suffer from chronic under-funding. The problems that accompany an insufficiently paid public security sector in the post-war phase are well known. Whereas in sharp contrast, most customary practices require comparatively few resources and at the same time often serve significantly more of the population.[202] The upshot is a perspective which grasps the actual nature of the mission environment, while also appreciating how near term activities link to long term success. Today's endeavours are thereby more likely to bear the type of fruit which not only addresses immediate needs but also promises to supply sustenance for generations to come.

These inter-related arguments—aimed at reshaping international assistance to fit with a re-considered conception of recipient societies—are developed in three main sections. The first section examines flaws in mainstream views of the mission environment which have so far resisted the mounting evidence that a reliance on Western state-centric solutions is a pernicious model to follow. While the reticence to acknowledge and ultimately adapt may have much to do with the

---

Peace and Capacity Building Operations: Moving Beyond a Conventional State Centred Imagination", *Journal of International Peacekeeping* 13 no. 3–4 (2009): 267–293 provide examples by which universal markers can nevertheless allow for meaningful local content in the areas of human rights and rule of law, respectively.

201 A glance at global gross national income per capita comparisons shows an enormous gap between recipient countries such as Timor Leste and Sierra Leone (at $400 and $901 per annum respectively) and those such as the USA, Norway and Australia ($41,557, $41,941, and $31,020 respectively) from which these state provider ratios derive; *Nations Online*. See also: Bruce Baker and Eric Scheye, "Access to Justice in a Post-conflict State: Donor-supported Multidimensional Peacekeeping in Southern Sudan", *International Peacekeeping* 16 no. 2 (2009): 171–185, 176–177, who offer a more detailed analysis of the situation in southern Sudan to demonstrate how utterly improbable the establishment and running of OECD-like state systems can be in the majority world.

202 See: Bruce Baker and Eric Scheye, "Access to Justice in a Post-conflict State: Donor-supported Multidimensional Peacekeeping in Southern Sudan", *International Peacekeeping* 16 no. 2 (2009): 171–185; and Volker Boege, M. Anne Brown, Kevin P. Clements, and Anna Nolan, "States Emerging from Hybrid Political Orders—Pacific Experiences", *Occasional Paper Series Number 11* (Australian Centre for Peace and Conflict Studies, September 2008).

conservative forces of the bureaucratic structures which constitute those predominantly in charge of assistance programs (e.g. the UN and the EU), and therefore the success of state-building programs may depend largely on fundamental reforms of the organisations themselves,[203] the underlying conceptual impediments must be made visible in order to be overcome. The next part of the article follows on to explore the true nature of recipient societies, in stark contrast to mainstream visions. These sections provide the context for the key challenge facing the international community: namely, developing what *should* be done with this new awareness. The final section therefore takes up the challenge of rethinking the international assistance paradigm in a fashion which is based on the realities of the majority—rather than the minority—world. In doing so, it concentrates on areas in which international policing components may be able to foster a sustainable war-to-peace transition in the critical periods following ceasefire agreements. More specifically, it describes potential innovations in terms of how policing components might contribute to 'interim stabilization' and 'second generation security promotion' programs. The important point is that future programs be targeted to assist the multiple layers of existing networks and mechanisms.

Recognition of the 'State of the State'

OCED/DAC importantly recognises the need to understand the 'state of the state'. In a report on state-building, they note that 'state-building policy in any given fragile state must be grounded first and foremost in a specific, historically informed assessment of the state of the state.'[204] This rhetorical willingness to accept whatever may comprise recipient societies constitutes a paradoxical part of the mainstream narrative on issues pertaining to peace and capacity building operations. That is, despite the fact that practitioners and scholars alike have increasingly emphasised the importance of appreciating local context and capacity in the realm of justice and security, the foundations upon which they base reform programs remain steadfastly the state—whereby the Western, Weberian ideal of a state is what they really mean. This ideal envisages a society in which the formal state, with its centralised and hierarchical structures and formalised separation between the public and private realms, pervades social life. Important to present purposes, it presupposes that state mechanisms are capable of

---

203 Carolyn Bull, "Building the Rule of Law Under UN Transitional Administration", *Policy Brief No. 7* (United Nations University Press, 2007), 7.

204 Organization for Economic Co-operation and Development, *The OECD DAC Handbook on Security Sector Reform: Supporting Security and Justice*, (Paris: OECD, 2007), 23, emphasis in original.

delivering law and justice to the populace as a whole.[205] Such assertions are often matter-of-fact, as exemplified by the following OECD statement: 'States retain central responsibility for assuring the safety and security of their citizens, protecting property rights and providing public goods to enable a functioning market'.[206]

The assumption of the state pre-eminence is made plainer by the labels that comprise the interrogations themselves. The terms 'fragile' or 'failed' *state* and *state*-building reveal this inbuilt bias which presumes that what exists is state-like. For decades mainstream voices have talked about conflict-affected areas as though the modern, Weberian, notion of the state was the only game in town. The SSR debate provides a clear example in that its main focus is about how to get the *state* military under the control of *state* parliaments. The possibility that the security sector could be—let alone *should be*—populated by either non-state or quasi-state actors and/or institutions, is basically out of the question.

The false dichotomy of the state versus 'those in direct opposition to the state', which underpins this lens, can have grave consequences. For instance, although non-state elements, such as militia, are a major consideration in most Disarmament, Demobilisation and Reintegration (DDR) programs, large sections of traditional actors which may not have been involved in violence against the state, or even during the political conflict can be overlooked.[207] These sections may nevertheless command loyalty of many and therefore possess a clear potential *either* to hinder or to help a war to peace transition. Gangs are one such example. They can be a source of significant armed violence, and yet they are typically overlooked altogether by the state-centric lens which views 'non-state armed groups' narrowly as those which directly oppose the state's security sector. This conceptual oversight can impede success in many ways, but expressed in general terms, if interventions are targeted at state-blinkered realities, then the multitude of actors and processes out of sight constitutes a potentially enormous sector that is destined, at best, to go without assistance in their endeavours to improve the prospects for peace and, at worst, to turn in to precisely the kinds of spoilers meant to be overcome by interventions in the first place.[208] As such, only when

---

205 See: Joel S. Migdal and Klaus Schlitche, "Rethinking the State", in *The Dynamics of States: The Formation and Crises of State Domination*, ed. K. Schiltche. (Surrey, UK.: Ashgate Publisher, 2005), 36–40.

206 Organization for Economic Co-operation and Development, *The OECD DAC Handbook on Security Sector Reform: Supporting Security and Justice*, (Paris: OECD, 2007), 11.

207 See: Robert Muggah and Keith Krause, "Closing the Gap Between Peace Operations and Post Conflict Insecurity: Towards a Violence Reduction Agenda", *International Peacekeeping* 16 no. 1 (2009): 136–150, 140; and, Dennis Rodgers and Robert Muggah, "Gangs as Non-State Armed Groups: The Central American Case", *Contemporary Security Policy* 30 no. 2 (2009): 301–317.

208 See: Dennis Rodgers and Robert Muggah, "Gangs as Non-State Armed Groups: The Central American Case", *Contemporary Security Policy* 30 no. 2 (2009): 301–317, for this

the full spectrum of local entities is recognised can genuinely comprehensive solutions be developed.

The overlapping RoL sector is another crucial realm in which this narrow, state-centric imagination can undermine success.[209] To be sure, pre-eminent peace organisations such as the UN, the EU and the World Bank promote particular Western notions rather than effectively embracing the wealth of diversity which is likely to exist in the mission environment. Bull, for instance, observes that "the RoL agenda in UN state-building has sought to support a particular normative order based on a cluster of values characteristic of liberal democratic states".[210] Reform programs have been overwhelmingly about transplanting extraneous models, presumed as the sole bastion of best practice.[211]

Indicative of mainstream conceptions, the World Justice Project,[212] highlights the need for 'human rights, commercial law, and corruption' while tacitly relying upon state-based actors to deliver these outcomes. Likewise, in spite of stressing the need for 'local community solutions', David Bayley's summary of UN community policing evaluations within peace operations puts forward recommendations that are limited to state-based actors delivering policing, rather than recognising the potential for non-state sources which may provide or complement UN community policing efforts.[213] In these ways, the orthodox imagination is narrowed implicitly by a top-down, state-centric premise.[214]

Making Space beyond the State

Improving the RoL should not, however, be equated with establishing state-based mechanisms such as state law, judicial and police systems.[215] A main reason is that in most conflict-affected areas access to effective state systems is largely non-

oversight as it relates to gangs and the problematic conceptions of 'non-state armed groups'.

209 Laura Grenfell, "Promoting the Rule of Law in Timor-Leste", *Conflict, Security & Development* 9 no. 2, (2009): 213–238.

210 Carolyn Bull, "Building the Rule of Law Under UN Transitional Administration", *Policy Brief No. 7* (United Nations University Press, 2007), 2.

211 Gordon Peake and Kaysie Studdard-Brown, "Policebuilding: The International Deployment Group in the Solomon Islands," *International Peacekeeping* 12, no. 4 (2005): 520–532, 525–526.

212 World Justice Project, Website (2009), http://www.worldjusticeproject.org/.

213 David H. Bayley, *Community Policing: Evaluation Programs* (New York: Civilian Police Division, DPKO, United Nations, 2005).

214 Stephen Golub, "A House Without a Foundation", in *Promoting the Rule of Law Abroad: In Search of Knowledge*, ed. Thomas Carothers (Washington, D.C.: Carnegie Endowment for International Peace, 2006), 105.

215 Bryn Hughes and Charles Hunt, "The Rule of Law in Peace and Capacity Building Operations: Moving Beyond a Conventional State Centred Imagination", *Journal of International Peacekeeping* 13 no. 3–4 (2009): 267–293.

existent.[216] But as Baker and Scheye point out: it is a flawed assumption to suggest that lack of access to *state* justice means an absence of justice.[217] The reality is that not only do the majority of the population settle their disputes and RoL-related activities through informal channels, but that they actually prefer these systems to the state.[218]

In spite of the mainstream insistences across the entire spectrum of multinational interventions, labelled variously DDR, SSR, peacekeeping, peacebuilding, and so on, the majority world scarcely resembles a Western state self-image. For example, in a critique of SSR in West Africa, Adedeji Ebo points out that at hardly any point in time have states had a monopoly on force as the Western notion of the state presumes; rather a vast array of security providers hold sway.[219] Thomas Carothers moreover notes that civil society, as is understood in the West, does not exist in the many fragile, post-colonial states which cover the globe.[220] And in Melanesia, the state, as depicted above, is largely irrelevant to over 85% of the population.[221]

The problem to date has been that international initiatives have been characterised by cursory understanding of traditional forms of order and justice and existing informal mechanisms.[222] Understanding will only improve when it has been possible to push past Euro-American images of security, judicial, and corrections

---

216 Bruce Baker and Eric Scheye, "Access to Justice in a Post-conflict State: Donor-supported Multidimensional Peacekeeping in Southern Sudan", *International Peacekeeping* 16 no. 2 (2009): 171–185. See also: Denis M. Tull, "Peacekeeping in the Democratic Republic of Congo: Waging Peace and Fighting War", *International Peacekeeping* 16 no. 2 (2009): 215–230, 220, who argues that in the case of the DRC and MONUC peace operations, the transitional state government was 'dysfunctional'.

217 Bruce Baker and Eric Scheye, "Access to Justice in a Post-conflict State: Donor-supported Multidimensional Peacekeeping in Southern Sudan", *International Peacekeeping* 16 no. 2 (2009): 171–185, 171.

218 Bruce Baker and Eric Scheye, "Access to Justice in a Post-conflict State: Donor-supported Multidimensional Peacekeeping in Southern Sudan", *International Peacekeeping* 16 no. 2 (2009): 171–185; and Agnes Hurwitz and Kaysie Studdard, *Rule of Law Programs in Peace Operations*, The Security-Development Nexus Program Policy Paper (New York: International Peace Academy, 2005), 5.

219 Adedeji Ebo, "Non-State Actors, Peacebuilding and Security Governance in West Africa: Beyond Commercialisation", *Journal of Peacebuilding and Development* 3 no. 2 (2007): 53–69, 61–62.

220 Thomas Carothers, "The End of the Transition Paradigm", *Journal of Democracy* 13 no. 1 (2002): 5–21.

221 Australian Federal Police (AFP), *Inquiry into the Main Economic and Security Challenges Facing Papua New Guinea and the Island States of the Southwest Pacific*, Report to the Parliament of Australia Senate Standing Committee on Foreign Affairs, Defence and Trade, (Canberra: Australian Federal Police, 2008).

222 Writing for The World Bank, Samuels acknowledges that the preference for formal over informal or traditional mechanisms is among the major lessons *not* yet learned; Kirsti Samuels, "Rule of Law Reform in Post-Conflict Countries: Operational Initiatives

as silos inhabited by state-based providers. Channell argues against assuming that the government is the key to the kinds of reform which comprise multi-national interventions.[223] The underlying point is that we cannot overlook the existing institutions, norms and practices by assuming that either broken down Weberian state machinations or no institutions to speak of exist in these places.

To be sure, this dearth of knowledge is an indication of the vexing nature of the challenge to fully understand 'other' complex forms of being. To begin with, there is the matter of language impediments. Brand points out that an often overlooked problem is that the literal translations of the term RoL can mean any number of different things to those not from the Anglo-American tradition.[224] Similarly, others highlight the fact that the institutions of the state are regularly conveyed in languages not spoken by most of the populace.[225] This 'lost in translation' problem cuts both ways, with interveners commonly unable to apprehend local languages and the beliefs transmitted through them. It is not hard to imagine that many practical problems may flow from this cultural disconnect.[226] Altogether, these and other impediments have meant that the extent to which customary and non-state or traditional justice mechanisms constitute part of a substantively different indigenous conception of the RoL has been extremely limited.[227] Crucially, the practice of attempting to transplant a common template of institutions into the majority world can in fact harm pre-existing mechanisms that deal with

and Lessons Learnt," *Social Development Papers: Conflict Prevention and Reconstruction* 37 (2006), 16–23.

223 Wade Channell, "Lessons Not Learned about Legal Reform," in *Promoting the Rule of Law Abroad: In Search of Knowledge*, ed. Thomas Carothers, (Washington, D.C.: Carnegie Endowment for International Peace, 2006).

224 Marcus Brand, *Promoting the Rule of Law, Transparency and Fighting Against Corruption*, Paper presented at Building Capacity for Democracy, Peace and Social Progress (Doha: The 6th International Conference of New or Restored Democracies (ICNRD-6), October–November, 2006), 2.

225 Bruce Baker, *Grasping the Nettle of Nonstate Policing*, Paper presented at Making Sense of Peace and Capacity building: Rethinking Policing and Beyond Workshop (Brisbane, July 2009), 14.; Volker Boege, M. Anne Brown, Kevin P. Clements, and Anna Nolan, "States Emerging from Hybrid Political Orders—Pacific Experiences", *Occasional Paper Series Number 11* (Australian Centre for Peace and Conflict Studies, September 2008): 9–11.

226 Marcus Brand, *Promoting the Rule of Law, Transparency and Fighting Against Corruption*, Paper presented at Building Capacity for Democracy, Peace and Social Progress (Doha: The 6th International Conference of New or Restored Democracies (ICNRD-6), October–November, 2006), 6.

227 Eirin Mobekk, "Identifying Lessons in United Nations International Policing Missions," *Policy Paper* 9 (Geneva: Geneva Centre for the Democratic Control of Armed Forces (DCAF), 2005), 11.

critical issues such as property ownership or conflict resolution.[228] The underlying approach should instead be about how to incorporate extant local mechanisms with an eye to facilitating the right balance between state and non-state providers.[229]

Having pointed out the mainstream's current addiction to a flawed notion of recipient societies, the interrogation now examines the true nature of the majority world. Both discussions help to unsettle the tacit acceptance of extant policies and practices as well as open space to explore what the international community should in fact be doing with its assistance resources.

Realities beyond the State

The realities of the mission environment are not of course limited to state organs. To the contrary, the state is often the least relevant entity in most peoples' lives, most of the time. Furthermore, formal institutions will have little positive influence without the support of the embedded networks of the people comprising and affected by them.[230] What, then, do these realities look like? Before we delve into that question, however, we must first recognise what a society looked like prior to the onset of armed conflict; with that backdrop, we can strive to understand what it may have mutated into during the violence.

The majority world, as indicated previously, is best understood as consisting of hybrid systems, orders characterised by multiple layers which stem from an often wide array of legacies from various periods and cultures. Boege *et al.*, provide a useful schema by which to locate the majority world vis-à-vis the Western state ideal for which it is otherwise mistaken.[231] Their three ideal types present political order and governance along a spectrum, each of which, according to Boege *et al.*, can provide effective and legitimate governance, capable of delivering social peace. At one pole is the Weberian state ideal—best approximated by OECD Westernised states, with the characteristics outlined at the outset of the article. On the opposing pole are customary orders (which they note are scarcely

---

228 Frank Upham, "Mythmaking in the Rule-of-Law Orthodoxy", in *Promoting the Rule of Law Abroad: In Search of Knowledge*, ed. Thomas Carothers (Washington, D.C.: Carnegie Endowment for International Peace, 2006), 1.

229 Sinclair Dinnen, Abby McLeod and Gordon Peake, "Police-Building in Weak States: Australian Approaches in Papua New Guinea and Solomon Islands", *Civil Wars* 8 no. 2 (2006): 87–108; and Adedeji Ebo, "Non-State Actors, Peacebuilding and Security Governance in West Africa: Beyond Commercialisation", *Journal of Peacebuilding and Development* 3 no. 2 (2007): 53– 69, 61–62.

230 M. Anne Brown, "Security, Development and the Nation-Building Agenda—East Timor", *Conflict, Security & Development* 9 no. 2 (2009): 141–164, 144.

231 Volker Boege, M. Anne Brown, Kevin P. Clements, and Anna Nolan, "States Emerging from Hybrid Political Orders—Pacific Experiences," *Occasional Paper Series Number 11* (Australian Centre for Peace and Conflict Studies, September 2008): 9–11.

practiced today). Mobekk describes customary justice structures as the 'mechanisms for solving disputes, conflicts and crime at community level in which a village or tribal council, community meeting or council of elders deals with crimes committed against the community or individuals, or focuses on resolving conflicts such as marital disputes';[232] such mechanisms can be restorative as well as retributive.[233] It is important to dispel the myth that customary practices remain fixed, whereas in fact they are entirely capable of evolving,[234] and in directions readily acceptable to most universal norms.

In the middle are hybrid systems, which exhibit a complex mix of liberal institutional and customary mechanisms, and, they maintain, comprise the majority of the Global South states, including the Pacific region.[235] This category is also known as the 'post-colonial' state, but the defining quality is the existence of 'parallel authorities and regimes'.[236] In other words, there are a number of actors and mechanisms delivering the full gamut of public goods and services—not just those on the formal state's payroll. This realisation is crucial since it means that interventions must firstly be aware of the panoply of authorities and regimes in order to be able to engage with and possibly assist them in such endeavours that could bear fruit towards peace and security.

Scheye uses the term 'second state' to describe those which are beyond the formal state, yet still typically responsible for the preponderance of delivery of all public goods.[237] Figures indicate that from as much as 70 to 90 percent of justice and security matters are handled by these providers across the globe.[238] A key

---

232 Eirin Mobekk, "Identifying Lessons in United Nations International Policing Missions," *Policy Paper* 9 (Geneva: Geneva Centre for the Democratic Control of Armed Forces (DCAF), 2005), 11.

233 See: Sinclair Dinnen, Abby McLeod and Gordon Peake, "Police-Building in Weak States: Australian Approaches in Papua New Guinea and Solomon Islands," *Civil Wars* 8 no. 2 (2006): 87–108.

234 Volker Boege, M. Anne Brown, Kevin P. Clements, and Anna Nolan, "States Emerging from Hybrid Political Orders—Pacific Experiences," *Occasional Paper Series Number 11* (Australian Centre for Peace and Conflict Studies, September 2008): 10–12.

235 Volker Boege, M. Anne Brown, Kevin P. Clements, and Anna Nolan, "States Emerging from Hybrid Political Orders—Pacific Experiences," *Occasional Paper Series Number 11* (Australian Centre for Peace and Conflict Studies, September 2008): 9.

236 Bruce Baker and Eric Scheye, "Access to Justice in a Post-conflict State: Donor-supported Multidimensional Peacekeeping in Southern Sudan," *International Peacekeeping* 16 no. 2 (2009): 171–185, 173.

237 Eric Scheye, *The Structure of the Post-Colonial State: The Role and Function of NonState/Local Justice and Security Networks* (OECD, forthcoming). Note that even someone with a critical take of this space opts to use the word 'state', emblematic of its primacy in these discussions.

238 Bruce Baker and Eric Scheye, "Access to Justice in a Post-conflict State: Donor-supported Multidimensional Peacekeeping in Southern Sudan," *International Peacekeeping* 16 no. 2 (2009): 171–185,174; Sinclair Dinnen, Abby McLeod and Gordon Peake, "Police-Building in Weak States: Australian Approaches in Papua New Guinea and

attribute, for the purposes herein, is that the 'second state' and the formal state are found time and again to work together. Examples include the following: in Rwanda and Uganda, the state has authorised volunteers to conduct everyday policing; elsewhere in Africa the state 'allows' lesser criminal and civil cases to be heard by customary chiefs; and PNG has a state-customary hybrid court system throughout the villages. The symbiotic nature of the relationship—contrary to those who might surmise a competitive or antagonistic interaction—paves the way for this productive collaboration to continue when the society is challenged with the need to restore peace and development. Equally important, the authority as well as legitimacy of the state regularly hinges on how it relates to the second state providers.[239] This could be predicted given that the (colonial) legacy of the formal state is typically much shorter historically, less familiar, and nearly always more brutal than many of the customary authorities. The international community must therefore be willing to enable the broadest spectrum of resources when pursuing its broad intervention goals.

Baker's work on African policing identifies the myriad sources that would fit a post-Weberian awareness. He points out that each of the following sources are known to provide 'policing' services. From state sources, there are local councils; state police; and violent crime crack units; whereas non-state sources can include crime prevention panels; commercial security firms; traders associations; (illegal) mob justice;[240] ethnic or clan militias; customary structures; restorative justice community based organisations; religious police; civil defence forces; semi-commercial anti-crime groups; and informal local government security structures.[241] This move to extend dramatically the notion of those who 'do' policing requires a broadened conception of policing itself. Baker obliges with the type of all-encompassing definition of what constitutes policing that could be developed to work equally well for other sectors comprising peace and capacity building missions: 'any organised activity, whether by state or non-state groups, that seeks to ensure the maintenance of communal order, security and peace through elements of prevention, deterrence, investigation of breaches and punishment'.[242]

Solomon Islands," *Civil Wars* 8 no. 2 (2006): 87–108; Susanne Schmeidl and Masood Karokhail, "The Role of Non-State Actors in 'Community Based Policing'—An Exploration of the *Arbakai* (Tribal Police) in South-Eastern Afghanistan," *Contemporary Security Policy* 30 no. 2 (2009): 318–342.

239 Pierre Englebert, *State Legitimacy and Development in Africa* (Boulder, C.O.: Lynne Rienner Publishers, 2000).

240 Bruce Baker, "Multi-choice policing in Uganda," *Policing and Society* 15 no. 1 (2005): 19–41, 21.

241 Bruce Baker, *Grasping the Nettle of Nonstate Policing*, Paper presented at Making Sense of Peace and Capacity building: Rethinking Policing and Beyond Workshop (Brisbane, July 2009), 2.

242 Bruce Baker, *Multi-Choice Policing in Africa* (Uppsala: Nordiska Afrikainstituter, 2008), 9.

It may be surprising to those previously unfamiliar with this viewpoint that not only many times are the same policing activities shared by state and non-state sources alike, but that interactions between the two 'sides' are routine, open, and even formalised.[243] Baker's analysis also highlights the various working links between these state and non-state actors, underscoring the potential for systems and solutions which welcome both functioning in concert. To this view, concern over the nature of the provider is overshadowed by issues to do with efficacy and accessibility; at the same time, these providers ironically can often be more liberal than the state.[244] Local mechanisms have a number of benefits beyond being already in place. They tend to focus on restoration and harmony rather than contestation, offer quick settlement rather than protracted processes, and generally require significantly fewer resources for upkeep.[245] The following gives an indication of how these layers of order and 'jurisdiction' may look on the ground:

> *In the village the headman or maybe the imam is there to bring a settlement regarding 'men-women' problems. To settle the land dispute there is the paramount chief or there may be a restorative justice organisation. On the visit to the town a neighbourhood committee will be on the watch for armed robbers; a commercial security guard will protect the entrance to the bank; and a taxi-drivers association (or a mob) will deal with any pickpocket at the bus station. Finally, if there is a serious crime and a 'shedding of blood', there is the state police.*[246]

Among the numerous realisations to be gleaned from making visible what mainstream conceptions overlook is that a focus on the formal state is tantamount to a neglect of the majority of day to day maintenance of communal order. To be sure, it is all too common for interventions to be planned as if there is basically nothing at all already in place. The main point is to recognise that either hybrid or customary systems pervade the majority world, and this has clear implications for how interveners contribute.

---

243 Bruce Baker, *Multi-Choice Policing in Africa* (Uppsala: Nordiska Afrikainstituter, 2008).

244 Bruce Baker, *Grasping the Nettle of Nonstate Policing*, Paper presented at Making Sense of Peace and Capacity building: Rethinking Policing and Beyond Workshop (Brisbane, July 2009), 4, 8.

245 Stephen Arthur Lamony, *Approaching National Reconciliation in Uganda: Perspectives on Applicable Justice Systems* (Kampala: Ugandan Coalition for the International Criminal Court, 2007).

246 Bruce Baker, *Grasping the Nettle of Nonstate Policing*, Paper presented at Making Sense of Peace and Capacity building: Rethinking Policing and Beyond Workshop (Brisbane, July 2009), 8.

Dealing With a Post-Weberian Reality

The first two sections have been dedicated to demonstrating that the mainstream view continues to work off a flawed notion of recipient societies, as well as, enquiring about the true nature of the majority world. Those explorations set the foundation for this final section, which focuses on ways in which the international community should be helping.

There are two key points, however, which warrant re-emphasis before we proceed. First, rather than rejecting everything that does not fit with idealised Western notions of how conflict-affected areas *should* look, it is incumbent upon intervening actors to accept the true nature of the environment at the outset, in order to get on with the job of improving these realities as quickly as possible and with the limited resources at hand. Given the reconsidered realities outlined above, if state and peace-building missions are truly concerned with improving the lives of as many as possible as quickly as possible, it seems, in Baker's words, 'misguided to focus all reform efforts and all resources on the state security agencies'.[247] After all, in many cases state police are neither more capable nor more willing to act effectively and appropriately.

Second, before intervention designs are completed we should pause to ask what a society may look like in the longer term in areas related to justice and security, remembering that what is done today inescapably affects what tomorrow brings. Thorny as they may be, these questions—and thus the answers—about what lies beyond the horizon must come predominately from endogenous voices. This is not to suggest exogenous actors should be excluded from the processes. To the contrary, outsiders are undoubtedly needed if we take as fact that interventions have come about because local actors have failed to resolve conflict by non-violent means. Some go further, suggesting that reform processes will inevitably draw on foreign models and/or experiences, since the context of justice and security sector reform connotes that what exists is 'inadequate and requires modification'.[248] Notwithstanding the degree to which foreign ideas ultimately embed, it is ill-advised simply to include local voices in what can essentially be foreign solutions.

---

247 Bruce Baker, *Grasping the Nettle of Nonstate Policing*, Paper presented at Making Sense of Peace and Capacity building: Rethinking Policing and Beyond Workshop (Brisbane, July 2009), 14.

248 Charles T. Call, "Challenges in Police Reform: Promoting Effectiveness and Accountability," in *From Promise to Practice: Strengthening UN Capacities for the Prevention of Violent Conflict* ed. Chandra Lekha Sriram and Karin Wermester (New York: International Peace Academy, 2003), 4.

Accordingly, a comprehensively participatory approach must be employed in order to maximise local ownership and capacity.[249] Who the local owner is, vis-à-vis questions of local ownership, however is not as simple as is often assumed. Rather than skimming over this critical issue—too often being satisfied with an expedient 'tick in the box' from a small minority of typically expatriate national elites—Scheye offers a useful typology of how to begin to unpack, and therefore include in meaningful ways, local voices: (1) national government and elite; (2) local government and elite; (3) justice and security service providers and; (4) customers of the public good delivered.[250] Only after these complex layers have been allowed to become centrally involved will there be a reasonable understanding of what local actors want for the longer term.

Upham maintains that 'societies must develop a mix of formal and informal mechanisms that can produce optimal results given their respective social, political, economic, and cultural contexts'.[251] Baker and Scheye advocate for a hybrid system in which a key role of the state is basically to act as an arbiter of the various informal layers.[252] While others have emphasised that there are tenable concepts of justice and implementing mechanisms which can and should be utilised.[253] But beyond the general aim of assisting the appropriate development of both state and non-state providers, what should the international community shift towards vis-à-vis peace support operations?

---

249 See: Jessica Howard and Bruce Oswald, eds., *The Rule of Law on Peace Operations: A 'Challenges of Peace Operations' Project Conference* (Melbourne: Asia-Pacific Centre for Military Law, 2002), 279, where they argue that: 'From the earliest moment, international civil actors must seek to incorporate local participation and create consultative mechanisms'.

250 Eric Scheye, "Unknotting Local Ownership Redux: Bringing Non-State/Local Justice Networks Back In," in *Local Ownership and Security Sector Reform*, ed. Timothy Donais (Geneva: Geneva Centre for the Democratic Control of Armed Forces (DCAF), 2008), 63–4.

251 Frank Upham, "Mythmaking in the Rule-of-Law Orthodoxy," in *Promoting the Rule of Law Abroad: In Search of Knowledge*, ed. Thomas Carothers (Washington, D.C.: Carnegie Endowment for International Peace, 2006), 1.

252 Bruce Baker and Eric Scheye, "Access to Justice in a Post-conflict State: Donor-supported Multidimensional Peacekeeping in Southern Sudan," *International Peacekeeping* 16 no. 2 (2009): 171–185.

253 Jessica Howard and Bruce Oswald, eds., *The Rule of Law on Peace Operations: A 'Challenges of Peace Operations' Project Conference* (Melbourne: Asia-Pacific Centre for Military Law, 2002), 267–277 noted that 'Many of the communities that we have worked with have interesting and viable concepts of communal justice that can be utilised and drawn upon in this respect'. See also: Otwin Marenin, "Restoring Policing Systems in Conflict Torn Nations: Process, Problems, Prospects," *Occasional Paper No. 7* (Geneva: Geneva Centre for the Democratic Control of Armed Forces (DCAF), 2005), 48–55, who notes the need to identify and build the capacity of locals.

What Should Interveners Do in the Early Post-War Period?

Having previously pressed for the need to engage the longer term vision prior to making decisions on assistance activities, the interrogation shifts to what the international community *should* do in the near to medium term timeframes.[254] The responses predictably centre on ways to assist the myriad local networks and providers already in place. In this commonly mislabelled 'post-conflict' realm,[255] the discussions range from peacekeeping to peacebuilding activities, including DDR and SSR. The composition and priorities of this space unsurprisingly vary according to organisation and scholar. For instance, the military component sometimes gets left out, whereas in other cases, such as the traditional SSR debates, policing might be omitted.

Of the vast array of peace and capacity building operation facets, the following exploration continues the emphasis on policing, but in the particular periods following the signing of ceasefire and peace agreements. These agreements are typically the beginning—rather than the end—of the peace process.[256] What follows are suggestions for novel developments in which international policing resources can enable existing policing providers of all kinds to achieve the unconventional measures comprising both 'interim stabilization' and 'second generation security promotion'. We need, more generally, to engage with the emerging body of research surrounding these concepts, a literature which has not been a significant part of the conventional peace operations debate. After all, traditional state police reform tends to be superficial and temporary in both its nature and effect.[257] As such, these areas represent, in Colletta and Muggah's words, 'a new horizon for stabilization missions and offer a challenging forward-looking agenda for the

254 See also Robert Muggah and Keith Krause, "Closing the Gap Between Peace Operations and Post Conflict Insecurity: Towards a Violence Reduction Agenda", *International Peacekeeping* 16 no. 1 (2009): 136–150, 147–148 who explore similar issues with the same broad aim.

255 'Post-conflict' is a term based on a false dichotomy, mainly because the level of armed violence and excess morbidity and mortality often remains near to that during hot wars; Robert Muggah, "No Magic Bullet: A Critical Perspective on Disarmament, Demobilization and Reintegration (DDR) and Weapons Reduction in Post-conflict Contexts," *The Round Table* 94 no. 379 (2005): 239–252. Moreover, as conflict is an endemic part of all societies, there cannot be a post-conflict society; Nat J. Colletta and Robert Muggah, "Rethinking Post-War Insecurity: From Interim Stabilization to Second Generation Security Promotion," *Journal of Humanitarian Assistance* (February 2009): 1–20, 1–2. Adapting Saskia Sassen's terms might result in these areas being known as 'fragile spaces' to give it a term least encumbered by fallacious connotations; Saskia Sassen, "Cities and New Wars: After Mumbai," (2008), http://www.opendemocracy.net/article/the-newwars-and-cities-after-mumbai-0.

256 Christine Bell, "Peace Agreements: Their Nature and Legal Status," *American Journal of International Law* 100 no. 373, (2006): 373–412.

257 Alice Hills, "The Dialectic of Police Reform in Nigeria," *Journal of Modern African Studies* 46 no. 2 (2008): 215–234, 217.

humanitarian, development and security sectors alike'.[258] We must look beyond the traditional tasks of patrols, arrests, and investigations in order to develop creative means that further enhance the prospect for a lasting peace.

The reasons for this focus are twofold. First, the period immediately following ceasefires holds significant promise for innovative contributions from international police contingents because it is then that armed conflict usually shifts from politically to criminally motivated violence; yet traditional DDR and SSR programs—in addition to being relatively slow to come into effect—have yet to adapt accordingly.[259] Policing expertise should be at a premium to help redress this gap. Even more so than an intervening military, policing resources could benefit greatly from enlisting the assets and sympathies of local providers.[260] Second, interim stabilization and second generation measures rely on local ownership, as explained below. This reliance complements a post-Weberian lens with its embrace of the realm of actors and practices outside of the formal state. The context in which these emerging areas should be examined is, after all, a prism which recognises the true 'state of the state'; namely, one which foregrounds the myriad of informal providers and institutions that are likely to comprise the mission environment alongside strictly state agents.

Notwithstanding which particular intervention component or organisation undertakes this reformulation exercise, two core assertions remain: firstly, the nature of conflict areas necessitates working with non-state actors and mechanisms; secondly, the forms of assistance should be adapted accordingly—and not just to reflect engagement with non-state sources but also the need to rethink what kind of assistance should occur, in general, according to the discussion at the outset about how the long term form of a society is shaped by near term assistance.

Given a now realistic representation of the mission environment, with its multiple layers of formal and informal policing orders and providers, we can turn our attention to the areas with significant potential for the development of new forms of international policing assistance. The first step is to identify new ways current policing organisations can help. The ensuing step is to identify what skills policing contingents *should* have in years to come. Changing and evolving roles may

---

258 Nat J. Colletta and Robert Muggah, "Rethinking Post-War Insecurity: From Interim Stabilization to Second Generation Security Promotion," *Journal of Humanitarian Assistance* (February 2009): 1–20, 2.

259 Robert Muggah and Keith Krause, "Closing the Gap Between Peace Operations and Post Conflict Insecurity: Towards a Violence Reduction Agenda," *International Peacekeeping* 16 no. 1 (2009): 136–150, 137.

260 The 2006 Australian-led Operation Serene in Timor Leste is a prime example of the need to enlist local providers and mechanisms to assist their own policing efforts to mitigate the law and order problems. See: Andrew Goldsmith, "It Wasn't Like Normal Policing: Voices of Australian Police Peacekeepers in Operation Serene, Timor-Leste 2006," *Policing and Society* 19 no. 2 (2009): 119–133.

not be easy. Innovative strategies are certain to be accompanied by tensions, such as the prospect that police might feel they have now been asked to become social workers as well.[261] Retaining the status quo of striving diligently to implement misconceived strategies, however, is a far worse fate.

The next section therefore briefly elaborates upon particular interim stabilization and second generation security promotion initiatives with the capacity for exogenous policing organisations to offer assistance, while crucially sketching out specific ways in which that assistance could occur. These emergent areas comprising alternative forms of violence reduction and prevention represent the synthesis of an ever-widening array of scholars and practitioners acquainted with public health, criminology, and sociology.[262]

Developing Post-Weberian Interim Stabilization Measures

Pressured by the need to show progress, parties to peace negotiations often skim over the detailed planning required to ensure the conditions for peace have the best chance to take root while the planning for conventional security promotion measures is being done.[263] However, the risk of a slide back into armed conflict is significant in these early post-war days. Interim stabilization measures are therefore about buying time in the immediate post-war periods. It does, after all, take time to constitute the bureaucratic structures, policies and legal content which typically go into the conventional security promotion programs of DDR and SSR. Putting aside for the moment a critique of DDR/SSR themselves, these initiatives can accompany conventional programs as part of a broader transitional approach. The point is to ensure that the types of sinister elements and processes that commonly become impediments to sustainable peace are not allowed a foothold during this precarious period. By setting immediate and limited objectives, apart from buying time for the roll out of conventional programs, they aim to: significantly diminish armed violence; improve real and perceived security; and help build confidence and trust.[264] It may now seem obvious that to achieve these aims requires enlisting the support and resources of the *de facto* existing mechanisms and providers. Furthermore, without these stop-gap measures designed to

---

261 Caroline Moser, "Urban Violence and Insecurity: An Introductory Roadmap," *Environment and Urbanisation* 16 no. 2 (2004): 3–16, 13.

262 Robert Muggah and Keith Krause, "Closing the Gap Between Peace Operations and Post Conflict Insecurity: Towards a Violence Reduction Agenda," *International Peacekeeping* 16 no. 1 (2009): 136–150, 147–148.

263 Robert Muggah, "Securing the Peace: Post-Conflict Armed Violence and Security," in *Small Arms Survey 2009: Shadows of War*, ed. Small Arms Survey Geneva (Cambridge: Cambridge University Press, 2009), 22.

264 Robert Muggah, "Securing the Peace: Post-Conflict Armed Violence and Security," in *Small Arms Survey 2009: Shadows of War*, ed. Small Arms Survey Geneva (Cambridge: Cambridge University Press, 2009), 23.

convert potential spoilers into stakeholders it is less likely that DDR and SSR programs will ever have a chance to be launched in the first place.[265]

While this article's focus is not conventional measures, questions about their efficacy cannot go unmentioned; highlighting their deficiencies adds to the case to re-think the ways in which the international community engages the conflict environment. For instance, due to their narrow conception of arms availability and violent actors, they are typically ill-equipped to deal with the complexity of issues commonly at hand across conflict-affected areas. The case of the 2006 Australian-led Operation Serene in Timor Leste, for example, showed how difficult establishing law and order was due largely to youth gangs often armed with little more than rocks and darts.[266] Moreover, conventional approaches remain evidence-agnostic rather than evidence (of context specific factors that either facilitate or exacerbate armed violence) led.[267] Perhaps the most troubling aspect is their detachment from local inputs, based on a one-size-fits-all approach. Whereas, in fact, the success of security promotion initiatives necessitates that they be tailored to the specific macro and micro-level characteristics of the conflict itself.[268] The upshot is that this cursory list of deficiencies augments the case for the expanded emphasis on alternative measures herein.

That noted, many interim stabilization initiatives are not particularly well-suited to the present day capacities of external policing organisations such as UNPOL (e.g. patrols, crowd control, and investigations); some, however, are. Consider what potential the following interim stabilization areas may possess towards reshaping the way in which international policing contingents contribute to peace and capacity building missions. One such area is that police may be able to offer at least some assistance in helping to transition former military groups into either a) single yet decentralised transitional security forces, or b) civilian service corps capable of conducting a number of civilian activities,[269]

265 Robert Muggah, "Securing the Peace: Post-Conflict Armed Violence and Security," in *Small Arms Survey 2009: Shadows of War*, ed. Small Arms Survey Geneva (Cambridge: Cambridge University Press, 2009).

266 See: Andrew Goldsmith, "It Wasn't Like Normal Policing: Voices of Australian Police Peacekeepers in Operation Serene, Timor-Leste 2006," *Policing and Society* 19 no. 2 (2009): 119–133.

267 Robert Muggah and Keith Krause, "Closing the Gap Between Peace Operations and Post Conflict Insecurity: Towards a Violence Reduction Agenda," *International Peacekeeping* 16 no. 1 (2009): 136–150, 147.

268 Nat J. Colletta and Robert Muggah, "Rethinking Post-War Insecurity: From Interim Stabilization to Second Generation Security Promotion," *Journal of Humanitarian Assistance* (February 2009): 1–20.

269 Nat J. Colletta and Robert Muggah, "Rethinking Post-War Insecurity: From Interim Stabilization to Second Generation Security Promotion," *Journal of Humanitarian Assistance* (February 2009): 1–25, 9–13.

as it is increasingly common for police to deploy alongside the military. Engaging with local security networks in order to gain their assistance promises to make these initiatives much more productive. So too could police become robustly and formally involved in sensitisation programs and halfway house arrangements, whereby the former is concerned with conducting dialogue sessions designed to work through the conflict issues, and the latter uses urban cooperatives or agricultural farms to provide a period of adjustment to re-socialise problematic mindsets.[270] Meanwhile, civilian police could offer *substantial* assistance toward 'security sector integration' measures; namely by helping bring together warring parties in order to 'right-size' policing (as well as military) structures. Most of these immediate measures pertain to ensuring combatants are positively occupied while the more elaborate DDR and SSR programs are planned. Knowing which groups exist across the entirety of this space reduces the likelihood that some will turn against you. That many peace missions now involve policing components from the earliest days means that police are ideally situated to assist with many interim stabilization initiatives—all the while building their own capacity in these areas for future deployments.

Developing Post-Weberian Second Generation Security Promotion

Second generation security measures, though often times overlapping or even following DDR/SSR programs, are distinct nevertheless in their focus on criminal and quasi-political violence.[271] That is, while DDR/SSR strive to address violence based on political motivations, according to the SSR principle that combatants of political conflicts must be demobilised and ultimately held accountable to politicians, second generation initiatives recognise that often times the most damaging forms of violence in the aftermath of war may lack political aims. A key feature of these measures is that their approach to engendering local ownership consciously engages with existing institutions rather than attempting to build new bureaucratic structures.[272]

This is in keeping with the post-Weberian vision concerning peace and capacity building operations which emphasises that improvements to RoL are not only quicker to materialise but also typically more sustainable when they come

270 Nat J. Colletta and Robert Muggah, "Rethinking Post-War Insecurity: From Interim Stabilization to Second Generation Security Promotion," *Journal of Humanitarian Assistance* (February 2009): 1–25, 9–13.

271 Robert Muggah, "Securing the Peace: Post-Conflict Armed Violence and Security," in *Small Arms Survey 2009: Shadows of War*, ed. Small Arms Survey Geneva (Cambridge: Cambridge University Press, 2009), 8.

272 Nat J. Colletta and Robert Muggah, "Rethinking Post-War Insecurity: From Interim Stabilization to Second Generation Security Promotion," *Journal of Humanitarian Assistance* (February 2009): 1–25, 10.

from endogenous institutions rather than foreign implants.[273] Moreover, second generation programs are marked by a scaled-back and facilitative role by the international community,[274] further reinforcing that the primary roles should be occupied by local providers. Similarly, these initiatives highlight a re-shaping of the ways in which donor organisations and states should assist, particularly once the need to embrace informal providers towards these ends is internalised. This thinking also shares the same philosophical ground of community policing, pushing further to the fore the role of the local populace while simultaneously fostering social capital and efficacy.[275]

What, in brief, are some second generation security promotion measures and in what ways could international policing help? 'Community security mechanisms' is one such vehicle which strives to reduce violence from the ground-up by eliciting the 'routine involvement of formal and informal security agents and affected communities'. This reliance on the 'influence of indigenous powerbrokers and agents of change'[276] makes it a quintessential example whereby post-Weberian policing could occur since the majority of actors involved in these processes are bound to exist outside the traditional state-centric lens. The emphasis is on a bottom-up, locally-driven identification and development of security issues, distinct from the typical top-down UN mandated processes which tend to be divorced from local contexts.[277] 'Rather than being entrenched in formal national institutions, programs are embedded in both formal and informal municipal authority structures, including elected officials, university faculties, faith-based centres, councils of elders and customary authorities, so as to promote a degree of local legitimacy'.[278] These are the same kinds of sources of local policing provision, underscoring again the complementary nature of these initiatives with a post-Weberian vision. International policing organisations should therefore first identify those relevant to these processes (employing the above RoL provider

273 Bryn Hughes and Charles Hunt, "The Rule of Law in Peace and Capacity Building Operations: Moving Beyond a Conventional State Centred Imagination," *Journal of International Peacekeeping* 13 no. 3–4 (2009): 267–293.

274 Nat J. Colletta and Robert Muggah, "Rethinking Post-War Insecurity: From Interim Stabilization to Second Generation Security Promotion," *Journal of Humanitarian Assistance* (February 2009): 1–25, 14.

275 See: Mark Ungar and Desmond Arias "Community Policing and Latin America's Citizen Security Crisis," *Comparative Politics* 41 no. 4 (2009): 409–429.

276 Robert Muggah, "Securing the Peace: Post-Conflict Armed Violence and Security," in *Small Arms Survey 2009: Shadows of War*, ed. Small Arms Survey Geneva (Cambridge: Cambridge University Press, 2009), 26.

277 Robert Muggah and Keith Krause, "Closing the Gap between Peace Operations and Post Conflict Insecurity: Towards a Violence Reduction Agenda," *International Peacekeeping* 16 no. 1 (2009): 136–150, 144–45.

278 Robert Muggah and Keith Krause, "Closing the Gap Between Peace Operations and Post Conflict Insecurity: Towards a Violence Reduction Agenda," *International Peacekeeping* 16 no. 1 (2009): 145.

framework) and then either help to establish or buttress existing community security mechanisms—all of which should be based on local evidence and voices of the areas and facets most in need. On the question of which skill sets might become part of the international policing arsenal, 'urban anthropologists'—along with architects, builders and transportation planners—could be valuable assets indeed.[279]

The emphasis on local voices brings us back to an aspect which frequently troubles international interventions: namely, the discussion in a previous section about when it comes to the question of 'local ownership', what constitutes 'local'? Without delving deeply, suffice it to say that we must unpack that term well beyond looking for a few expatriate national elites as a proxy. Scheye's helpful (post-Weberian) typology of local actors is a good starting point. As Scheye points out, discussions heretofore have largely overlooked the *predominant* category of service provider: the non-state or *local* justice networks.[280] These oversights can cause irreparable damage to the success of interventions. Hence a participatory approach must be employed in order to maximise local ownership and capacity.[281] It is the job of external actors to *create* the space for security and development solutions, not fill the space. The context-specific results will no doubt be innovative, locally-driven strategies in which both state and non-state providers receive external resources in the quest to improve the levels of security within precarious communities.

'At-risk youth and gang violence reduction' is another area under the second generation banner with clear potential for 'plugged-in' international policing involvement. The obstacles to peace caused by youth gangs in Timor Leste provide a stark example of the need for initiatives in this space. Programs aim to strengthen the mechanisms by which youth avoid lives of crime. This entails, for example, providing at-risk youth with mentoring, risk education, and alternative livelihoods for would-be perpetrators. The skill sets of international police already approximate many that would be required, and therefore they should contemplate taking on these tasks in a more formalised manner. By engaging directly with existing justice and security provider networks, the reach and resonance of these initiatives can be increased many fold. Equally within present

279 Caroline Moser, "Urban Violence and Insecurity: An Introductory Roadmap," *Environment and Urbanisation* 16 no. 2 (2004): 3–16, 3.

280 Eric Scheye, "Unknotting Local Ownership Redux: Bringing Non-State/Local Justice Networks Back In," in *Local Ownership and Security Sector Reform*, ed. Timothy Donais (Geneva: Geneva Centre for the Democratic Control of Armed Forces (DCAF), 2008), 60.

281 See: Jessica Howard and Bruce Oswald, eds., *The Rule of Law on Peace Operations: A 'Challenges of Peace Operations' Project Conference* (Melbourne: Asia-Pacific Centre for Military Law, 2002), 279, where they argue that: 'From the earliest moment, international civil actors must seek to incorporate local participation and create consultative mechanisms'.

day international policing capacity are the opportunities to add value to both 'weapons for development' and 'safer community/city' initiatives. 'Weapons for development' entails preventative strategies with an eye to the demand side of gun violence (rather than simply the supply-side approach of traditional arms collection programs within DDR).[282] Police could be integrally involved in these initiatives—alongside local security providers—in aspects such as community outreach and capacity building training aspects.

'Safer community/city' programs concentrate on innovative design of the urban and built environment with the aim to reduce the opportunity for predatory violence. Police should often be well situated to advise the myriad existing providers on these matters. That noted this is yet another area where new skill sets may be welcomed.[283] Particular interventions, which could benefit clearly from the application of—albeit perhaps evolved in many cases—international policing resources, include the following:

> *'surveillance' through the identification of 'hot spots'; 'hierarchy of space' through the encouragement of use and ownership of public space; 'target hardening' through the strategic use of physical barriers and security devices; 'environment harmonizing' by reducing space for conflicting groups; 'image maintenance' through creating well-maintained spaces; targeted activities to integrate youth; and supporting 'territoriality' by fostering neighbourhood interaction and vigilance.*[284]

---

282 Nat J. Colletta and Robert Muggah, "Rethinking Post-War Insecurity: From Interim Stabilization to Second Generation Security Promotion," *Journal of Humanitarian Assistance* (February 2009): 1–25, 14.

283 Caroline Moser, "Urban Violence and Insecurity: An Introductory Roadmap," *Environment and Urbanisation* 16 no. 2 (2004): 3–16, 13.

284 Nat J. Colletta and Robert Muggah, "Rethinking Post-War Insecurity: From Interim Stabilization to Second Generation Security Promotion," *Journal of Humanitarian Assistance* (February 2009): 1–20, 15. For more detailed explanations of these and other interim stabilization and second generation security promotion activities see: Henry G. Cisneros, *Defensible Space: Deterring Crime and Building Community* (Washington, D.C.: U.S. Department of Housing and Urban Development, 1995); Candace J. Cross-Drew, *Target Hardening: A Literature Review* (Washington D.C.: Office of the Attorney General, 1989); Adam Sutton, Adrian Cherney and Rob White, *Crime Prevention* (Cambridge: Cambridge University Press, 2008). Elaborations follow: Territoriality—fostering residents' interaction, vigilance, and control over their neighbourhood; Surveillance—maximising the ability to spot suspicious people and activities; Activity support—encouraging the intended use of public space by residents; Hierarchy of space—identifying ownership by delineating private space from public space through real or symbolic boundaries; Access control/target hardening—using physical barriers, security devices and tamper-resistant materials to restrict entrance; Environment (harmonising)—a design or location decision that takes into account the surrounding environment and minimises the use of space by conflicting groups; Image/Maintenance—ensuring that a building or area is clean, well-maintained, and graffiti free (RCMP, 'Crime Prevention').

These approaches to crime prevention also complement community policing.[285] Moreover, it is not difficult to see how a robust engagement with the gamut of post-Weberian policing providers would lead to quicker, more effective, and more sustainable solutions. In other words, looking at ways to reshape policing contributions along the lines sketched out above promises to better leverage their own comparatively meagre resources with the more abundant local resources that are destined to remain under-utilised if intervening actors either ignore or alienate them.

Summary

Although at only an exploratory stage of conceptualisation, the purpose of this chapter has been to identify concrete ways in which the resources and talents of international police may be better employed, given a realistic conception of conflict-affected spaces. The crux of the matter is that an acceptance of the post-Weberian conception of the conflict environment means that the future direction of policing contributions becomes clear: upon identification of the many layers of policing, determine how best to develop the capacities of the many state, quasi-state, and non-state organisations that act to ensure the maintenance of communal order. It is both impractical and undesirable to strive to do the heavy lifting of putting on the ground the numbers of intervening agents otherwise needed to make a widespread difference; the human resources and materiel required are simply too grand, whereas an added detriment could be the creation of a culture of dependency.

International assistance must instead begin to 'plug-in' to the existing provider networks in an advisory capacity rather than straining in vain to have the limited reach of state providers achieve the needed improvements. Bull makes the important point that since informal systems are often widely accepted, unlike state mechanisms, they can rely on voluntary consent rather than coercion.[286] Another benefit is that capacity building then occurs where it should: namely, with the local population so as to ensure sustainability of the myriad developments. Limiting assistance to state actors alone must no longer be the default option, despite the need for ongoing diligence to ensure the various providers and mechanisms ultimately sanctioned by the international community keep from generating 'perverse practices'.[287] The central conventional goal of restoring

285 Royal Canadian Mounted Police (RCMP), *Crime Prevention Through Environmental Design Report* (1998) http://www.rcmp-grc.gc.ca/pubs/ccaps-spcca/safecomm-seccollecteng.htm.

286 Carolyn Bull, "Building the Rule of Law Under UN Transitional Administration," *Policy Brief No. 7* (United Nations University Press, 2007), 4.

287 Caroline Moser, "Urban Violence and Insecurity: An Introductory Roadmap," *Environment and Urbanisation* 16 no. 2 (2004): 3–16, 13, 11.

the state's monopoly on force has been based on an ill-founded assumption, since that condition never usually existed in the first place. This is not to say there is no room for state actors. They too have roles to play, particularly in areas such as transnational crime whereby local systems may be at extreme disadvantages to cope with international players.

In a similar manner as policing, other international assistance providers should revisit what they do—with the view to shifting beyond the traditionally narrow state-centric view and its attendant toolkits. Strategic re-tooling and re-directing of donor capacities is the next logical phase, but there is much to be gained in the near term by simply accepting and beginning to respond to the true nature of the mission environment. At the same time, a number of activities may remain unchanged. Assistance related to developing how societies interact with external entities, such as in the areas of international law and contracts in fishing or mining rights whereby powerful foreign interests may come to bear, may not benefit as greatly from thinking anew about the domestic environment.

For the most part, however, the time has come for the international community to accept many of the heretofore invisible entities and informal mechanisms recounted in this article. The pervasive thinking must change from bemoaning a lack of resources—and the political will ultimately responsible for this deficit—to the realisation that the diversity of the globe typically means recipient societies are not in need of Western solutions, regardless of how well resourced the currently misinformed approach to interventions could become. An increasing number of scholars and practitioners have been exhorting us to this realisation, knowing the vast ramifications to the way peace and capacity building missions are currently conducted.[288] Of the many challenges that accompany this realisation two deserve reiteration: firstly, having shed off the Western illusion that recipient societies are made in a Weberian state image, we must search for more appropriate and more effective ways in which the international community can help these societies to stand on their own two feet; and secondly, that we need to ask serious questions about what kinds of societies should be built from the dysfunctional elements of today's conflict, because the insights to come out of this debate will undeniably affect the substance of near term assistance. Going forward we should be under no illusions concerning the task at hand: engaging with 'other' forms of living and employing inclusive processes across diverse perspectives in order to determine the 'right' courses of action will be fraught with difficulty and laden with political contestation. Crucially, however, this contestation should be embraced not shied away from. Improvements on these various grounds can help the international community move beyond rethinking the 'state of the state' towards reshaping peace and capacity building operations to address the real problems of the majority world.

---

[288] M. Anne Brown, "Security, Development and the Nation-Building Agenda—East Timor," *Conflict, Security & Development* 9 no. 2 (2009): 141–164.

CHAPTER FOUR

THE RULE OF LAW IN PEACE AND CAPACITY BUILDING OPERATIONS: APPRECIATING MORE THAN THE STATE

This chapter extends Chapter 3's critique of the mainstream's 'state of the state' to investigate a little recognised, yet highly consequential, challenge facing the field of peace and capacity building operations,[289] which pertains to the RoL. On the one hand, there is now broad consensus that the RoL is critical to success.[290] The way to redress wide spread violence, all manner of social ills, and corruption is to resurrect—or erect—RoL.[291] Its prominence has risen to the point that it has been depicted as the "preeminent legitimating political ideal in the world today",[292] surpassing democracy and liberal economics as the dominant paradigm in the

289 Peace and capacity building operations are defined herein as: non-coercive as well as coercive multi-functional international interventions, short of war, conducted with the principle of impartiality and with the goal to establish and maintain sustainable peace. See: Marten Zwanenburg, *Accountability of Peace Support Operations* (Leiden: Martinus Nijhoff Publishers, 2005), 30, 49.

290 According to Jessica Howard and Bruce Oswald, eds., *The Rule of Law on Peace Operations: A 'Challenges of Peace Operations' Project Conference* (Melbourne: Asia-Pacific Centre for Military Law, 2002), ix, it is seen as "a cornerstone of effective peace operations". See also: Jane Stromseth, David Wippman, and Rosa Brooks, eds., *Can Might Make Rights: Building the Rule of Law after Military Interventions* (Cambridge: Cambridge University Press, 2006), 56–60.

291 Otwin Marenin, "Restoring Policing Systems in Conflict Torn Nations: Process, Problems, Prospects," *Occasional Paper No. 7* (Geneva: Geneva Centre for the Democratic Control of Armed Forces (DCAF), 2005), 4; Office for the High Commissioner for Human Rights, *Rule-of-Law Tools for Post-Conflict States: Mapping the Justice Sector* (New York and Geneva: United Nations OHCHR, 2006), foreword; Bruce Oswald, *Addressing the Institutional Law and Order Vacuum: Key Issues and Dilemmas for Peacekeeping Operations* (New York: UN DPKO, 2005), 4.

292 Brian Z. Tamanaha, *On the Rule of Law: History, Politics, Theory* (Cambridge: Cambridge University Press, 2004), 4.

post-Cold War era.[293] Those interested in promoting such varied aims as human rights, development, national security, and free markets can all agree.[294] Illustrations which bear out this lofty status include the 2005 World Summit's commitment to an international order based on the RoL[295] and the announcement of newly inaugurated US President Barak Obama that it will comprise the touchstone of his presidency.[296]

On the other hand, what is RoL? And how can it be realised? These questions frame a problem which troubles all of its many applications. The problem exists for three main reasons. Firstly, RoL's delineation remains vague and uninstructive among those most involved with its implementation.[297] A survey of the major organisations charged with restoring and maintaining peace around the globe, for instance, indicates wide-spread satisfaction with only cursory definitions. In fact, RoL is typically bundled together with democracy, good governance and human rights as a collective panacea to peaceful and stable societies, and thus it is used as a political ideal.[298] Expressing platitudes about the need for RoL appears to suffice in lieu of a precise definition. The result is that those charged with delivering this critical area lack sophisticated views about its meaning and therefore what may be required both to achieve and to measure it.[299]

Secondly, though there is a significant amount of agreement and overlap, to-date the numerous efforts to unpack this encompassing concept have failed to develop the necessary antidote: a widely-accepted understanding which is clear

---

293 Marcus Brand, *Promoting the Rule of Law, Transparency and Fighting Against Corruption*, Paper presented at Building Capacity for Democracy, Peace and Social Progress (Doha: The 6th International Conference of New or Restored Democracies (ICNRD-6), October–November, 2006), 5.

294 Jane Stromseth, David Wippman, and Rosa Brooks, eds., *Can Might Make Rights: Building the Rule of Law after Military Interventions* (Cambridge: Cambridge University Press, 2006), 58–62.

295 United Nations General Assembly Resolution 60/1, '2005 World Summit Outcome' (2005). 134 (a), 29.

296 Sheryl Gay Stolberg, 'On First Day, Obama Quickly Sets a New Tone', *The New York Times*, 21 January 2009.

297 Thomas Carothers, "The Problem of Knowledge," in ed. Thomas Carothers, *Promoting the Rule of Law Abroad: In Search of Knowledge* (Washington DC: Carnegie Endowment for International Peace, 2006), 16.

298 Marcus Brand, *Promoting the Rule of Law, Transparency and Fighting Against Corruption*, Paper presented at Building Capacity for Democracy, Peace and Social Progress (Doha: The 6th International Conference of New or Restored Democracies (ICNRD-6), October–November, 2006), 5; Thomas Carothers, "Promoting the Rule of Law Abroad: The Problem of Knowledge," *Carnegie Paper* no. 34 (Washington DC: Carnegie Endowment for International Peace, 2003), 5–7.

299 Rachael Kleinfeld-Belton, "Competing Definitions of the Rule of Law: Implications for Practitioners," *Rule of Law Series, Democracy and Rule of Law Project, Carnegie Papers* no. 55 (Washington D.C.: Carnegie Endowment for International Peace, 2005).

while at the same time flexible and comprehensive.[300] In fact, the assumptions concerning its apparent simplicity and moral clarity belie the challenges of defining its substance.[301] A review of these investigations reveals how difficult this task has been. Vastly different factors as well as perspectives are identified. Is RoL about the existence of formalised legal institutions, state governance across many other areas, the absence of street violence, or something else altogether? Rachel Kleinfeld-Belton likens the current state of affairs to the proverbial blind man's elephant, whereby what is a trunk to one person is a tail to another.[302]

Finally, largely unrecognised state-centric assumptions continue to restrain the debate from moving toward a more incisive and universally applicable understanding.[303] That is, Western-dominated conceptions and thus programs tend to view conflict-affected areas through a self-image prism which may bear scant resemblance to the realities of the societies targeted by the interventions. It is not enough to express the need to promote local ownership but then offer nothing more than state-specific solutions.[304]

The blind spots which emanate from these three characteristics have consequences far beyond conceptual debates. They present significant obstacles to the success of peace and capacity building operations in at least two inter-related ways: first, it means that scarce resources are too often wasted (or worse, end

---

300 "Academics, policy makers, and reformers have struggled to define the term "rule of law" and to date no universal definition has been widely accepted." Jim Parsons, Monica Thornton, Hyo Eun Bang, Ben Estep, Kaya Williams and Neil Weiner, *Developing Indicators to Measure the Rule of Law: A Global Approach*, A Report to the World Justice Project (Vera Institute of Justice, 2008), 3. See also: Rachael Kleinfeld-Belton, "Competing Definitions of the Rule of Law: Implications for Practitioners," *Rule of Law Series, Democracy and Rule of Law Project, Carnegie Papers* no. 55 (Washington D.C.: Carnegie Endowment for International Peace, 2005); Thomas Carothers, "The Problem of Knowledge," in ed. Thomas Carothers, *Promoting the Rule of Law Abroad: In Search of Knowledge* (Washington DC: Carnegie Endowment for International Peace, 2006), 19.

301 Marcus Brand, *Promoting the Rule of Law, Transparency and Fighting Against Corruption*, Paper presented at Building Capacity for Democracy, Peace and Social Progress (Doha: The 6th International Conference of New or Restored Democracies (ICNRD-6), October November, 2006), 2; Scott N. Carlson, *Legal and Judicial Rule of Law Work in Multi-Dimensional Peacekeeping Operations: Lessons-Learned Study* (New York: UN DPKO, 2006), 2.

302 Rachael Kleinfeld-Belton, "Competing Definitions of the Rule of Law: Implications for Practitioners," *Rule of Law Series, Democracy and Rule of Law Project, Carnegie Papers* no. 55 (Washington D.C.: Carnegie Endowment for International Peace, 2005): 32.

303 For a critique that is broadly consistent with ours herein, see Bruce Baker and Eric Scheye, "Access to Justice in a Post-conflict State: Donor-supported Multidimensional Peacekeeping in Southern Sudan," in *International Peacekeeping* 16, no. 2 (2009): 171–185.

304 See: Till Blume, "Security, Justice and the Rule of Law in Peace Operations," *International Peacekeeping*, 15, no. 5 (2008): 716–17. For examples of how local ownership is recognised but *not* critically enough and to the extent we suggest herein.

up having a counter-productive effect) because they go to the wrong places;[305] second, a consequence of this misplacement of resources is that the political will of well-intending donor states and organisations—who understandably look for results yet become frustrated if progress does not materialise—is put in jeopardy.

The purpose of this chapter is to help redress these definitional deficiencies, since their persistence has grave real-world ramifications. 'Sustainable peace' remains but a wishful expression in too many parts of the globe where genuine improvements in RoL could make an enormous difference to the lives of the world's most vulnerable. We do not expect that the universal adoption of any delineation will occur in the near term, due in part to the panoply of underpinning issues but also that current discussions remain dominated by state-based actors. We do however hope that, at the very least, this investigation helps to usher the debate toward a more incisive, post-Weberian notion[306] capable of informing wiser practices, whereby the term post-Weberian is meant to contrast the Weberian ideal which presupposes that formal state mechanisms alone can deliver credible law and justice practices.[307] By accepting that state and non-state actors alike can constitute plausible sources of law and justice, the focus of peace operations can then turn to identifying where and how the myriad RoL sources—if appropriate—can operate and potentially interact in a complementary fashion.

The pathway we advocate marries the wealth of mainstream knowledge and experience on the one hand with the emerging insights on how to incorporate extant local mechanisms in order to facilitate the right balance between state and non-state providers.[308] It is a hybrid form which pushes beyond the contemporary marriage of international and national to include the widest array of providers.[309]

---

305 Rachael Kleinfeld-Belton, "Competing Definitions of the Rule of Law: Implications for Practitioners," *Rule of Law Series, Democracy and Rule of Law Project, Carnegie Papers* no. 55 (Washington D.C.: Carnegie Endowment for International Peace, 2005): 64.

306 See: Joel S. Migdal and Klaus Schlitche, "Rethinking the State", in *The Dynamics of States: The Formation and Crises of State Domination*, ed. K. Schiltche. (Surrey, UK.: Ashgate Publisher, 2005), 1–40, 36–40.

307 Others before us have suggested the need to marry formal state with informal non-state mechanisms. See, for example, W. Clifford, L. Morauta, and B. Stuart, *Law and Order in Papua New Guinea* (Port Moresby: Institute of National Affairs and Institute of Applied Social and Economic Research, 1984), who made the argument that because Papua New Guinea's formal justice system was often entirely irrelevant to much of the population, it should be viewed within the broader context of the many informal social control mechanisms in order to enhance its performance.

308 Sinclair Dinnen, Abby McLeod and Gordon Peake, "Police-Building in Weak States: Australian Approaches in Papua New Guinea and Solomon Islands", *Civil Wars* 8 no. 2 (2006): 87–108.

309 We intend to embed robustly what many such as Stromseth *et al.* acknowledge (yet fail to explore in depth) in statements such as the following: "community-based

The framework we set out hinges on the following ideas. RoL conceptions must move beyond the magnanimous aim of accommodating local sensitivities to a non-state-centric awareness which is capable of recognising all manner of 'RoL providers' that may already exist locally. It is not enough simply to include local voices in *non*-indigenous processes or institutions, the approach which marks the overwhelming majority of reform activities. Limiting resource allocation to state-based actors can cause legitimate and effective indigenous institutions to be overlooked in lieu of more expensive, less sustainable and often less legitimate options. Global best practice conceptions[310] must be equally relevant to the many circumstances in which the Weberian ideal of the modern nation-state has never really applied (*e.g.* Melanesia).

We augment this insistence to use the most inclusive lens possible with specific principles that, together, promise the *experience* of RoL.[311] The intent is that managers of peace and capacity building operations begin to ask: 'Who or what has delivered (or may be capable of delivering) RoL?' As such, donors must come to accept that state providers can not only co-exist with non-state providers, but that they can complement each other. The framework we outline is therefore conceived specifically to enable the most efficient and sustainable use of scarce resources. It not only reduces the chance that resources will be poured into the building of 'foreign' institutions that may be wholly incompatible with local RoL providers when synergistic solutions are needed,[312] but at the

---

accountability proceedings that both enjoy local legitimacy and respect human rights can have an important immediate impact and also contribute to the longer-term goal of strengthening the rule of law." Jane Stromseth, David Wippman, and Rosa Brooks, eds., *Can Might Make Rights: Building the Rule of Law after Military Interventions* (Cambridge: Cambridge University Press, 2006), 308.

310 Randy Peerenboom, "The Future of Rule of Law: Challenges and Prospects for the Field," *Hague Journal on the Rule of Law* 1, no. 1 (2009), 6, makes an important point that we should guard against striving for a consensus definition, preferring instead to accept multiple perspectives. While agreeing with the essence of his point, we would argue that the absence of explicit understandings contains its own problems, including the risk of making RoL meaningless, and that we should therefore move toward a consensus which allows for multiple perspectives to be housed under the same roof. We see no reason to presume that a consensus definition would necessarily strangle the capacity for diverse perspectives.

311 We are also mindful that some contest whether the causal relationship between RoL and development may actually be the converse from what RoL advocates maintain. See: Stephen Golub, "A House Without a Foundation", in *Promoting the Rule of Law Abroad: In Search of Knowledge*, ed. Thomas Carothers (Washington, D.C.: Carnegie Endowment for International Peace, 2006), 105–36, 110.

312 See Michael Kelly in Jessica Howard and Bruce Oswald, eds., *The Rule of Law on Peace Operations: A 'Challenges of Peace Operations' Project Conference* (Melbourne: Asia-Pacific Centre for Military Law, 2002) 279, who argues that 'We have to avoid the paradigm paralysis of attempting to impose what we are familiar with, and what has worked elsewhere.'

same time it can take advantage of the otherwise problematic short-term results donor culture by enabling quicker 'wins'. In doing so a post-Weberian understanding, which interrogates the Euro-American assumption that modern state mechanisms permeate all facets of daily life, promises the most effectual path to sustainable RoL.

The chapter is divided into three main sections. The first section reviews the current state of affairs in order to establish how RoL is generally understood. Though brief, the review is wide-reaching, encompassing the views of researchers as well as a global cross-section of the organisations that fund and implement RoL programs. We delimit the debate according to four features, which include its state-centric lens. The second section takes up the issue of state-centrism in order to outline a way to move beyond its confines. The first two sections provide the platform for the final section in which we put forward an approach intended to redress the issues highlighted.

Delineating Rule of Law

Aristotle described the RoL succinctly as: "government of laws, not men."[313] The evolution of the concept of RoL can be characterised by a dichotomy between *Formalist* and *Substantive* conceptions.[314] The *Formalist* perspective relies on a government which conducts its affairs in a legally mandated and predictable fashion. *Substantivists* believe laws must be just, driven by moral vision and guarantee the common good.[315] These sentiments resonate with similar distinctions between 'positive' and 'natural' law, 'minimalist' versus 'maximalist' conceptions,[316] 'thin' versus 'thick', and 'rule *by* law' as opposed to 'rule *of* law'. Yet, the two perspectives can be seen as complementary, since the formalist understanding of

---

313 Jane Stromseth, David Wippman, and Rosa Brooks, eds., *Can Might Make Rights: Building the Rule of Law after Military Interventions* (Cambridge: Cambridge University Press, 2006), 56.

314 See: Paul Craig, "Formal and Substantive Conceptions of the Rule of Law: An Analytical Framework," *Public Law*, Autumn (1997): 467–87; Brian Z. Tamanaha, *On the Rule of Law: History, Politics, Theory* (Cambridge: Cambridge University Press, 2004), 91–113.

315 See: Paul Craig, "Formal and Substantive Conceptions of the Rule of Law: An Analytical Framework," *Public Law*, Autumn (1997): 467–87; Matthew Stephenson, *Rule of Law as a Goal of Development Policy*, (The World Bank)http://web.worldbank.org/WBSITE/EXTERNAL/TOPICS/EXTLAWJUSTINST/0,,contentMDK:20763583~menuPK:1989584~pagePK:210058~piPK:210062~theSitePK:1974062~isCURL:Y~DIR_PATH:WBSITE/EXTERNAL/TOPICS/EXTLAWJUSTINST/,00.html; Thomas Carothers, "The Rule of Law Revival," *Foreign Affairs* 77 no. 2 (1998): 96–97; Brian Z. Tamanaha, *On the Rule of Law: History, Politics, Theory* (Cambridge: Cambridge University Press, 2004), 91–113.

316 Rama Mani, "Contextualizing Police Reform: Security, the Rule of Law and Post-Conflict Peacebuilding," *International Peacekeeping* 6 no. 4 (1999): 17–18.

RoL is often a necessary component of substantive, morally justifiable RoL.[317] We, however, go further by explicitly including non-state providers; whereas the previous viewpoints operate from a largely unacknowledged state-centric prism.

While the above descriptions provide a useful starting point for advancing a best practice framework, let us not equivocate about the thorniness of the challenge ahead. To be sure, many have endeavoured to redress the existing definitional gremlins. Their efforts to unpack RoL have been much needed.

In spite of the recent attention, the debate remains hampered by four main features. First, RoL spans a dizzying breadth of elements and issues. Its domain can be understood to contain a network of interdependent systems, incorporating multiple institutions and actors, which hold disparate interpretations of associated legal-political concepts across the world.[318] This sphere constitutes an international phenomenon whereby numerous and diverse agencies and actors conduct programs across the globe.[319] As such, RoL is a product of its constituent parts, often a catch-all term for a wide range of functions and foci.[320] RoL nomenclature is used in programming that targets nearly everything ranging from anti-corruption to human rights. Most commonly the referent will be the criminal justice apparatus (particularly the police, judicial and corrections sectors), where programming ranges from judicial training, police reform, support to customs and maritime security services; prosecutors, defence lawyers, street law clinics, and legal education[321] Kleinfeld-Bolton stresses that RoL is not a unified good, but rather, in her view, composed of the following five discrete social goods: (1) a government bound by law (2) equality before the law (3) law and

---

317 Matthew Stephenson, *Rule of Law as a Goal of Development Policy*, (The World Bank) http://web.worldbank.org/WBSITE/EXTERNAL/TOPICS/EXTLAWJUSTINST/0,,contentMDK:20763583~menuPK:1989584~pagePK:210058~piPK:210062~theSitePK:1974062~isCURL:Y~DIR_PATH:WBSITE/EXTERNAL/TOPICS/EXTLAWJUSTINST/,00.html.

318 See: Till Blume, "Security, Justice and the Rule of Law in Peace Operations," *International Peacekeeping*, 15, no. 5 (2008): 718, who suggests that "Rule of Law should be seen as a set of institutions, not as single instruments and indicators."

319 Kirsti Samuels, "Rule of Law Reform in Post-Conflict Countries: Operational Initiatives and Lessons Learnt," *Social Development Papers: Conflict Prevention and Reconstruction* 37 (2006), 1.

320 Kirsti Samuels, "Rule of Law Reform in Post-Conflict Countries: Operational Initiatives and Lessons Learnt," *Social Development Papers: Conflict Prevention and Reconstruction* 37 (2006), 2.

321 Marcus Brand, *Promoting the Rule of Law, Transparency and Fighting Against Corruption*, Paper presented at Building Capacity for Democracy, Peace and Social Progress (Doha: The 6th International Conference of New or Restored Democracies (ICNRD-6), October November, 2006), 6; Kirsti Samuels, "Rule of Law Reform in Post-Conflict Countries: Operational Initiatives and Lessons Learnt," *Social Development Papers: Conflict Prevention and Reconstruction* 37 (2006), 2.

order (4) predictable and efficient rulings, and (5) human rights.[322] Simultaneously, RoL has become a central tenet in governing the conduct of peace operations, guiding the behaviours and ensuring the accountability of peacekeepers in the field.[323]

Second, its meaning is contested—in spite of a considerable amount of agreement and overlap. As illustrated above, it is used to describe a vast array of activities, principles, programs, and outcomes. It refers not only to the behaviour of the panoply of actors and institutions charged with its implementation but also the behaviour of the public at large, when considering that the level of criminal activity is a core facet of its understanding. Grote surmised that the RoL "belongs to the category of open-ended concepts which are subject to permanent debate"[324] Indeed, there is no universal understanding of what it encompasses or excludes.[325] Samuels points out how "... the terminology has no internationally accepted definition, and in practice is used in a fluid and uncertain fashion."[326] The underlying point is that its definition is highly contested, and thus in need of developments that could diminish this problematic status.[327]

Third, the viewpoint of those in charge of its implementation remains encumbered by a vague notion, comprised largely of platitudes. Yet there should be

---

322 Rachael Kleinfeld-Belton, "Competing Definitions of the Rule of Law: Implications for Practitioners," *Rule of Law Series, Democracy and Rule of Law Project, Carnegie Papers* no. 55 (Washington D.C.: Carnegie Endowment for International Peace, 2005): 27. Also see Kirsti Samuels, "Rule of Law Reform in Post-Conflict Countries: Operational Initiatives and Lessons Learnt," *Social Development Papers: Conflict Prevention and Reconstruction* 37 (2006), 7.

323 Jessica Howard and Bruce Oswald, eds., *The Rule of Law on Peace Operations: A 'Challenges of Peace Operations' Project Conference* (Melbourne: Asia-Pacific Centre for Military Law, 2002).

324 Rainer Grote, "Rule of Law, Rechtsstaat and Etat De Droit," in ed. Christian Starck, *Constitutionalism, Universalism and Democracy—a Comparative Analysis* (Baden-Baden: Nomos Verlagsgesellschaft, 1999), 271.

325 Joshua G. Smith, Victoria K. Holt, and William J. Durch, *Enhancing United Nations Capacity for Post-Conflict Policing and Rule of Law*, Report from The Project on Rule of Law in Post-Conflict Settings (Washington DC: The Henry L. Stimson Center, 2007), ix; Sean Mcfate, *Securing the Future: A Primer on Security Sector Reform in Conflict Countries*, Special Report 209 (Washington DC: United States Institute of Peace, 2008), 3; Marcus Brand, *Promoting the Rule of Law, Transparency and Fighting Against Corruption*, Paper presented at Building Capacity for Democracy, Peace and Social Progress (Doha: The 6th International Conference of New or Restored Democracies (ICNRD-6), October November, 2006), 18.

326 Kirsti Samuels, "Rule of Law Reform in Post-Conflict Countries: Operational Initiatives and Lessons Learnt," *Social Development Papers: Conflict Prevention and Reconstruction* 37 (2006), 2.

327 Rachael Kleinfeld-Belton, "Competing Definitions of the Rule of Law: Implications for Practitioners," *Rule of Law Series, Democracy and Rule of Law Project, Carnegie Papers* no. 55 (Washington D.C.: Carnegie Endowment for International Peace, 2005).

little doubt that how these actors conceptualise the term matters. Stephenson observes that "[p]olicymakers need to be clear about they mean by the RoL because answers to many of the questions they are interested in... depend crucially on what definition of the RoL is being used."[328] The multitude of RoL concepts breeds confusion between donors and recipients. The risk to political support follows inevitably.

A brief yet wide-reaching scan across the America's, Africa, Europe and Asia, illustrates the abstract nature with which RoL is understood. As the pre-eminent international organisation for peace and security, the view held by the United Nations is undoubtedly vital. Importantly, RoL programming is conspicuous throughout the UN system.[329] Reflecting a heightened emphasis, the Department of Peacekeeping Operations (DPKO) created the Office for Rule of Law and Security Institutions (OROLSI) in 2007. Perhaps the most renowned definition was proffered in a 2004 Report of the Secretary-General.

> *The rule of law... refers to a principle of governance in which all persons, institutions and entities, public and private, including the State itself, are accountable to laws that are publicly promulgated, equally enforced and independently adjudicated, and which are consistent with international human rights norms and standards. It requires, as well, measures to ensure adherence to the principles of supremacy of law, equality before the law, accountability to the law, fairness in the application of the law, separation of powers, participation in decision-making, legal certainty, avoidance of arbitrariness and procedural and legal transparency.*[330]

This articulation represents perhaps the most holistic and authoritative definition among the organisations charged with RoL operations. According to the Vera Institute, "[t]his definition of the RoL thoughtfully presents the concept as a collection of principles that can be used to inform the structure, operation, reform, and evaluation of law-related institutions across societies. It emphasizes equity, accountability, and avoidance of arbitrariness and is rooted in fundamental principles of human rights as well as the more traditional concept of the supremacy of the law."[331] The upshot however is that while the UN stresses the importance of RoL, their delineations remain at a high level of abstraction, meaning that its conception remains uninstructive, particularly for such a complex term.

---

328 Matthew Stephenson, *Rule of Law as a Goal of Development Policy*, (The World Bank) http://web.worldbank.org/WBSITE/EXTERNAL/TOPICS/EXTLAWJUSTINST/0,,contentMDK:20763583~menuPK:1989584~pagePK:210058~piPK:210062~theSitePK:1974062~isCURL:Y~DIR_PATH:WBSITE/EXTERNAL/TOPICS/EXTLAWJUSTINST/,00.html.

329 See for example UNDP, UN OHCHR, OCHA, etc.

330 Kofi Annan, *The Rule of Law and Transitional Justice in Conflict and Post-Conflict Societies*, Report of the Secretary-General (New York: United Nations, 2004), 4.

331 Jim Parsons, Monica Thornton, Hyo Eun Bang, Ben Estep, Kaya Williams and Neil Weiner, *Developing Indicators to Measure the Rule of Law: A Global Approach*, A Report to the World Justice Project (Vera Institute of Justice, 2008), 3.

Another key player in the RoL programming is the European Union. And while the emphasis on RoL is similarly high to the UN, the EU has not yet developed a clear definition.[332] Indeed, it uses the term to connote a number of different things depending on the structure and mandates of its missions.[333] Such inconsistencies are indicative of the wider discourse whereby RoL terminology is used to refer to any support offered in the criminal justice and security sectors.

The Organisation for Security and Cooperation in Europe (OSCE) conducts numerous field operations whereby RoL objectives are made explicit.[334] As with the UN and the EU, there is continual emphasis on the central importance of RoL to peace and security.[335] Under this banner, the OSCE approach identifies its support for "anti-corruption actions" and "launching strategies for law enforcement" as its core-business.[336] Moreover, the OSCE is clear in its commitment to a 'free market' economy as part of its RoL conception.[337] Yet again, however, we come to find the lack of a clear definition is evident in any number of documents.[338] This vagueness unsurprisingly transfers across to its actions.[339]

The African Union (AU) represents another globally significant regional organisation both engaged in and the recipient of peace operations with RoL

---

332 See: Differing conceptions for EUJUST LEX Iraq, EULEX Kosovo: http://www.consilium.europa.eu/showPage.asp?id=268&lang=en&mode=g, accessed 31 March 2009.

333 For example, current SSR processes in DRC and Guinea-Bissau are discussed as activities in the realm of RoL no different to the police, judiciary and customs focus in their Kosovo programs, despite the significant distinctions between what each entails.

334 See: Organisation for Security and Cooperation in Europe, Website, Rule of Law activities—http://www.osce.org/activities/13049.html; Organisation for Security and Cooperation in Europe, Website, Policing activities—http://www.osce.org/activities/13046.html, accessed 31 March 2009.

335 Organisation for Security Cooperation in Europe, Website, Strategic Police Matters Unit: Background, (December 2006) http://www.osce.org/publications/spmu/2004/11/13565_64_en.pdf, accessed 31 March 2009.

336 Organisation for Security and Cooperation in Europe, Website, Rule of Law activities http://www.osce.org/activities/13049.html, accessed 31 March 2009.

337 The OSCE, as with the World Bank and multinational corporations, stress the free market aspect of the sanctity of private property and enforcement of contracts. See: Jane Stromseth, David Wippman, and Rosa Brooks, eds., *Can Might Make Rights: Building the Rule of Law after Military Interventions* (Cambridge: Cambridge University Press, 2006), 58.

338 Organisation for Security and Cooperation in Europe, *Document of the Copenhagen Meeting of the Conference on the Human Dimension of the CSCE*, (Copenhagen: OSCE, 1990), 1, http://www.osce.org/documents/odihr/2006/06/19392_en.pdf, accessed 31 March 2009. (NB: The OSCE was then called the CSCE.)

339 For example, describing its on-going RoL activities, the OSCE proclaims that: "The concept of rule of law forms a cornerstone of the OSCE's human rights activities. It not only describes formal legal frameworks, but also aims at justice based on the full acceptance of human dignity." Organisation for Security and Cooperation in Europe, Website, Rule of Law activities, http://www.osce.org/activities/13049.html, accessed 31 March 2009.

components. Here too, RoL is also seen as integral to the achievement of peace. For example, its Political Affairs Department states how: "...The rule of Law, if managed well and successfully implemented at the level of Member States, will prevent conflicts and promote sustainable peace and development on the continent."[340] However, no different to the others above, there is little by way of detailed explanation of its meaning.[341]

Moving westward, the Organization of American States (OAS) is a key regional organisation, comprised of all 35 independent countries of America, including the USA. As with the organisations mentioned above, RoL is explicit in its foundational documents.[342] Not unusually, human rights, democratic governance and RoL are mentioned as inextricably tied. Unlike OSCE and others however, OAS avoids conflating democracy with the liberal commitment to free markets; they instead maintain that economic growth should be "based on justice and equity".[343] Yet despite these contrasting economic principles, RoL terminology is used—like the others above—with equally high levels of ambiguity and importance.

The Commonwealth of Independent States (CIS), a heavily Russian influenced regional organisation comprising 12 states from the former Soviet Union, provides an interesting contrast in that it serves as an example of an important actor which resists, for somewhat obvious reasons that the internal political make up of its main members are able only to satisfy 'rule *by* law', the otherwise global uptake of RoL. That is, while CIS is a significant player to be sure, having conducted a number of peace support operations in its sphere of influence, it has had very little to say about the RoL. With a few exceptions, CIS highlights a tension that accompanies those states or inter-state organisations which lack robust political commitments of their own to democratic governance and human rights (*e.g.* China).

One might ponder where the Association of South-East Asian Nations (ASEAN) might fit concerning this tension over espousing RoL versus internal political ideologies and practices. The reality is that it straddles the divide. While it does not explicitly define RoL, reference has been made to it in numerous organisational documentations and speeches of the Secretary-General.[344] Hence, ASEAN

---

340 AU Political Affairs Department, Website http://www.africaunion.org/Structure_of_the_Commission/depPOLITICAL%20AFFAIRS%20DIRECTORATE.htm, accessed 31 March 2009.

341 See, for example, African Union, *AU Constitutive Act: the Preamble*, http://www.africaunion.org/root/au/AboutAu/Constitutive_Act_en.htm, accessed 31 March 2009.

342 See Articles 3 &4 for example: Organisation of American States (OAS), *Inter-American Democratic Charter*, http://www.oas.org/charter/docs/resolution1_en_p4.htm, accessed 31 March 2009.

343 Organisation of American States (OAS), *Inter-American Democratic Charter*, http://www.oas.org/charter/docs/resolution1_en_p4.htm, accessed 31 March 2009.

344 Rodolfo C. Severino, Secretary-General of ASEAN, *The ASEAN Way and the Rule of Law*, Address at International Law Conference on ASEAN Legal Systems and Regional

provides another instance whereby the significance of RoL is clear, even though the detail of its definition is found wanting.

This brief but broad survey of major peace operation organisations therefore indicates that, with few exceptions, RoL occupies a core place in the vision of peace and security, while at the same time the term itself continues to be bandied about at an unhelpfully high level of abstraction. The delineations used have come to constitute 'definitions of convenience'; that is, they reflect the practicalities from which they materialized more than any conceptual or strategic clarity.[345]

Not yet addressed however is the assumption that the state is basically *the* vehicle for its delivery. While the first three characteristics of the RoL debate are problematic in their own right, this latter feature is particularly pernicious since it can cripple implementation efficiency and effectiveness though unbeknownst to interveners who may be striving diligently to do the wrong things well. Indicative of mainstream conceptions, the World Justice Project,[346] highlights the RoL elements of "human rights, commercial law, and corruption" while tacitly relying upon state-based actors—whether from external or internal sources—to deliver these outcomes. Likewise, despite stressing the need for 'local community solutions', David Bayley's summary of UN community policing evaluations within peace operations puts forward recommendations that are limited to state-based actors delivering policing, rather than recognising the potential for non-state sources which may provide or complement UN community policing efforts.[347] In these ways, the orthodox imagination is narrowed implicitly by a top-down, state-centric premise.[348]

Others make the state explicit, but in such a way that leaves the assumption nearly invisible. Stromseth *et al.*, for instance, put it this way:

> *The rule of law describes a state of affairs in which the state successfully monopolises the means of violence, and in which most people, most of the time, choose to resolve disputes in a manner consistent with procedurally fair, neutral, and universally applicable rules, and in a manner that respects fundamental human rights norms... this requires modern*

Integration, (Asia-Europe Institute/Faculty of Law, University of Malaya, Kuala Lumpur, 3 September 2001), http://www.aseansec.org/2849.htm, accessed 31 March 2009. See also: ASEAN, *ASEAN Vision 2020* (1997) http://www.aseansec.org/1814.htm, accessed 31 March 2009.

345 Marcus Brand, *Promoting the Rule of Law, Transparency and Fighting Against Corruption*, Paper presented at Building Capacity for Democracy, Peace and Social Progress (Doha: The 6th International Conference of New or Restored Democracies (ICNRD-6), October November, 2006), 6.

346 WJP, Website, http://www.abanet.org/wjp/rolindex.html, accessed 31 March 2009.

347 See: David H. Bayley, *Community Policing: Evaluation Programs* (New York: Civilian Police Division, DPKO, United Nations, 2005).

348 Stephen Golub, "A House Without a Foundation", in *Promoting the Rule of Law Abroad: In Search of Knowledge*, ed. Thomas Carothers (Washington, D.C.: Carnegie Endowment for International Peace, 2006), 105.

> *and effective legal institutions and codes, and it also requires a widely shared cultural and political commitment to the values underlying these institutions and codes.*[349]

According to this representation, RoL is achieved only through 'modern' (read, state) institutions and codes. Creative attempts to harness domestic capacity alongside international oversight, such as the development of 'hybrid courts' are often no better because they too rely on state mechanisms. We push back from this Weberian mindset.

A Critical Delineation: The Need for a Post-Weberian Evolution

Though many of the above viewpoints contain considerable merit, they remain hamstrung by these far-reaching commitments to the state. This is unsurprising given that the debate continues to be dominated by either state-based organisations or the researchers largely beholden to state-based organisations. Yet in much of the world, the Weberian state ideal is simply not relevant—neither today nor at any time in the past. In Melanesia, for example, the state is largely irrelevant to over 85% of the population.[350] We begin to see how this condition may pose significant problems when we recognise that international support to RoL reform programs has been overwhelmingly about transplanting extraneous models, presumed as the sole bastion of best practice.[351] Upham warns about the consequences:

> *... attempting to transplant a common template of institutions and legal rules into developing countries without attention to indigenous contexts harms pre-existing mechanisms for dealing with issues such as property ownership and conflict resolution.*[352]

Morgan and McLeod add, paradoxically, that the entire *state*-building mission will be undermined if the importance of local (often non-state) circumstances is ignored.[353] Simplistic approaches to RoL reform are reliant on the idea

349 Jane Stromseth, David Wippman, and Rosa Brooks, eds., *Can Might Make Rights: Building the Rule of Law after Military Interventions* (Cambridge: Cambridge University Press, 2006), 78.

350 Australian Federal Police (AFP), *Australian Federal Police Submission to the Senate Standing Committee on Foreign Affairs, Defence and Trade: Inquiry into the Main Economic and Security Challenges Facing Papua New Guinea and the Island States of the Southwest Pacific* (Canberra: Commonwealth of Australia, 2008).

351 Gordon Peake and Kaysie Studdard-Brown, "Policebuilding: The International Deployment Group in the Solomon Islands," *International Peacekeeping* 12, no. 4 (2005): 520–32, 525–26.

352 Frank Upham, "Mythmaking in the Rule-of-Law Orthodoxy", in *Promoting the Rule of Law Abroad: In Search of Knowledge*, ed. Thomas Carothers (Washington, D.C.: Carnegie Endowment for International Peace, 2006), 1.

353 Michael G. Morgan and Abby McLeod, "Have We Failed Our Neighbour?", *Australian Journal of International Affairs* 60 no. 3 (2006): 426.

that institutional change will engender social change.[354] In fact, effective and self-sustaining RoL is inherently dependent upon the consent and support of the people who constitute society.[355] Furthermore, it is not uncommon for the same state-based actors (which the dominant viewpoint presumes will provide the remedies) to be considered at the heart of the problem.[356]

Despite the fact that scholars and practitioners alike—including many of the organisations mentioned above—have increasingly emphasised the importance of appreciating local context and capacity in the realm of justice and security,[357] this acknowledgement has yet to be reflected in the field.[358] Rather, international initiatives have been characterised by cursory understanding of traditional forms

---

354 Kirsti Samuels, "Rule of Law Reform in Post-Conflict Countries: Operational Initiatives and Lessons Learnt," *Social Development Papers: Conflict Prevention and Reconstruction* 37 (2006), 1.

355 Marcus Brand, *Promoting the Rule of Law, Transparency and Fighting Against Corruption*, Paper presented at Building Capacity for Democracy, Peace and Social Progress (Doha: The 6th International Conference of New or Restored Democracies (ICNRD-6), October November, 2006), 22.

356 In a 2008 survey in eastern DRC, for example, the Government military was widely seen as dangerous, with only a third seeing them as 'protectors'. On the other hand, when asked how justice should be achieved, 15% mentioned traditional/customary means with a further 34% mentioning other non-state mechanisms; Patrick Vinck, Phuong Pham, Suliman Baldo and Rachel Shigekane, *A Population-Based Survey on Attitudes about Peace, Justice, and Social Reconstruction in Eastern Democratic Republic of Congo* (Washington DC: International Centre for Transitional Justice, August 2008). 26, 45. Findings from northern Uganda show a similar need to take seriously non-state sources. Specifically, when asked who they thought could "bring justice," 40% replied the government, whereas 44% cited various non-state sources as being best suited for the task; International Centre for Transitional Justice, *Forgotten Voices: A Population-Based Survey on Attitudes about Peace and Justice in Northern Uganda* (Washington DC: International Centre for Transitional Justice, July 2005), 31, http://www.ictj.org/images/content/1/2/127.pdf, accessed 31 March 2009. Yet these beliefs, and plausibly the existing institutions and capacities that underpin them, tend to be invisible to dominant models.

357 Jessica Howard and Bruce Oswald, eds., *The Rule of Law on Peace Operations: A 'Challenges of Peace Operations' Project Conference* (Melbourne: Asia-Pacific Centre for Military Law, 2002), 279; Organization for Economic Co-operation and Development, *The OECD DAC Handbook on Security Sector Reform: Supporting Security and Justice*, (Paris: OECD, 2007), 195.

358 In a 2004 report on RoL (Kofi Annan, *The Rule of Law and Transitional Justice in Conflict and Post-Conflict Societies*, Report of the Secretary-General (New York: United Nations, 2004.), the Secretary General stated that: "unfortunately, the international community has not always provided rule of law assistance that is appropriate to the country context. Too often, the emphasis has been on foreign experts, foreign models and foreign-conceived solutions to the detriment of durable improvements and sustainable capacity. Both national and international experts have a vital role to play, to be sure. But we have learned that effective and sustainable approaches begin with a thorough analysis of national needs and capacities, mobilizing to the extent possible expertise resident in the country." See also: Jessica Howard and Bruce Oswald, eds.,

of order and justice and existing informal mechanisms.[359] This 'lost in translation' problem cuts both ways. As Brand points out, an often overlooked problem is that the literal translations of the term RoL itself can mean any number of different things to those not from the Anglo-American tradition; it is not hard to imagine that many practical problems may flow from this cultural disconnect.[360] Altogether, these and other impediments have meant that the extent to which customary and non-state or traditional justice mechanisms constitute part of a substantively different indigenous conception of the RoL has been extremely limited.[361]

Upon reflection, however, this neglect appears counter-intuitive given that *state* RoL capacities are often entirely dysfunctional when programs are being planned and rolled out. The reality is more likely that in "... conflict-ridden countries, the majority of the population, and especially those outside of capital cities, may settle disputes and handle RoL related activities through non-formal, or customary, channels."[362] The reliance on state-based solutions is similarly counter-intuitive when one considers that customary practices are, by definition, already widely-known and in-place; whereas the importation of institutions or models unavoidably requires a greater amount of time and resources to become equally known and practiced. The delay in uptake not only equates to a greater drain on already limited resources and continued suffering, but it increases the likelihood of sinister elements filling the vacuum, thereby further exacerbating progress toward sustainable peace.

Non-state Providers

The suggestion to broaden our imagination regarding viable RoL providers requires that we ask about the capacities as well as the appropriateness of non-state sources. To this point, Peake and Studdard-Brown emphasise the credibility,

---

The Rule of Law on Peace Operations: A 'Challenges of Peace Operations' Project Conference (Melbourne: Asia-Pacific Centre for Military Law, 2002), 276–77.

359 Writing for The World Bank, Samuels acknowledges that the preference for formal over informal or traditional mechanisms is among the major lessons *not* yet learned. Kirsti Samuels, "Rule of Law Reform in Post-Conflict Countries: Operational Initiatives and Lessons Learnt," *Social Development Papers: Conflict Prevention and Reconstruction* 37 (2006), 16–23.

360 Marcus Brand, *Promoting the Rule of Law, Transparency and Fighting Against Corruption*, Paper presented at Building Capacity for Democracy, Peace and Social Progress (Doha: The 6th International Conference of New or Restored Democracies (ICNRD-6), October November, 2006), 6.

361 Eirin Mobekk, "Identifying Lessons in United Nations International Policing Missions," *Policy Paper* 9 (Geneva: Geneva Centre for the Democratic Control of Armed Forces (DCAF), 2005), 11.

362 Agnes Hurwitz and Kaysie Studdard, *Rule of Law Programs in Peace Operations*, The Security-Development Nexus Program Policy Paper (New York: International Peace Academy, 2005), 5.

legitimacy and salience of non-state spheres;[363] and they are not alone. Others have emphasised that there are tenable concepts of justice and implementing mechanisms which can and should be utilised.[364]

What, however, do we mean when we discuss non-state (*i.e.* customary, traditional, and so forth) RoL 'deliverers'? And what might they look like on the ground? Mobekk suggests that traditional justice structures are the "mechanisms for solving disputes, conflicts and crime at community level in which a village or tribal council, community meeting or council of elders deals with crimes committed against the community or individuals, or focuses on resolving conflicts such as marital disputes; such mechanisms can be restorative as well as retributive."[365] This idea is consistent with the view which recognises that "The RoL is as much a culture as a set of institutions, as much a matter of the habits, commitments, and beliefs of the ordinary people as of legal codes."[366]

One example is the local justice system (called 'Ailuc') among the Iteso peoples of Uganda. It is applied to a wide variety of justice issues ranging from murder and incest to disrespecting parents. Its purpose is both to punish and deter wrongs. Its many facets include investigations, the opportunity for all parties to be heard, formal apologies, compensation, and importantly, safeguards to ensure fairness for all the parties involved as well as that the compensation mechanism must be clearly spelt out and applied equally to protect the weak.[367] The striking overlaps with the conception of RoL held by the Western orthodoxy are apparent.

---

363 Gordon Peake and Kaysie Studdard-Brown, "Policebuilding: The International Deployment Group in the Solomon Islands," *International Peacekeeping* 12, no. 4 (2005): 527.

364 Jessica Howard and Bruce Oswald, eds., *The Rule of Law on Peace Operations: A 'Challenges of Peace Operations' Project Conference* (Melbourne: Asia-Pacific Centre for Military Law, 2002), 276–77, said: "Many of the communities that we have worked with have interesting and viable concepts of communal justice that can be utilised and drawn upon in this respect." See also: Otwin Marenin, "Restoring Policing Systems in Conflict Torn Nations: Process, Problems, Prospects," *Occasional Paper No. 7* (Geneva: Geneva Centre for the Democratic Control of Armed Forces (DCAF), 2005), 48–55, who notes the need to identify and build the capacity of locals. Further, Frank Upham, "Mythmaking in the Rule-of-Law Orthodoxy", in *Promoting the Rule of Law Abroad: In Search of Knowledge*, ed. Thomas Carothers (Washington, D.C.: Carnegie Endowment for International Peace, 2006), 75–104, points out how Hernando de Soto's investigations of Peru should be interpreted to highlight how well informal systems can function—in specific contrast to Peru's formal RoL providers.

365 See: Eirin Mobekk, "Identifying Lessons in United Nations International Policing Missions," *Policy Paper* 9 (Geneva: Geneva Centre for the Democratic Control of Armed Forces (DCAF), 2005), 11.

366 Jane Stromseth, David Wippman, and Rosa Brooks, eds., *Can Might Make Rights: Building the Rule of Law after Military Interventions* (Cambridge: Cambridge University Press, 2006), 310.

367 Stephen Arthur Lamony, *Approaching National Reconciliation in Uganda: Perspectives on Applicable Justice Systems* (Kampala: Ugandan Coalition for the International Criminal Court, 2007), 15–18.

On the other hand, the emphasis on harmony rather than blame, and getting past offences in order to restore peace are redeeming qualities not often associated with Western solutions.

Similarly, Bruce Baker's work on African policing identifies myriad sources that would fit a post-Weberian awareness. He points out that each of the following sources are known to provide 'policing' services: local councils (state actors); Uganda police (state); the Violent Crime Crack Unit (state); crime prevention panels (citizens); commercial security (private) traders associations (citizens); and (illegal) mob justice (citizens).[368] His analysis also highlights the various working links between these state and non-state actors, which underscores the potential for systems and solutions which welcome both in concert. In addition, Baker, provides the type of all-encompassing definition of what constitutes policing that we suggest could be developed to work equally well for the broader realm of RoL: "any organised activity, whether by state or non-state groups, that seeks to ensure the maintenance of communal order, security and peace through elements of prevention, deterrence, investigation of breaches and punishment".[369] Expanded to RoL, this might become something along these lines: any organised activity, whether by state or non-state group, that seeks to ensure law and order or dispense justice according to internationally-accepted standards.

The final clause about acceptable standards highlights a crucial, and often vexing, point for the direction we embrace. Customary systems related to justice can be deeply flawed—no different to their state-based alternatives. Hence, they must be scrutinised to ensure they adhere to fundamental human rights standards and do not discriminate against vulnerable sections of society, since many contain practices that are entirely unacceptable in terms of inhumane punishments or marginalisation of various segments of society such as women and youth.[370] Informal systems can also impede international efforts to carry out justice in numerous ways.[371] Further, they too are not immune to the eroding or corrupting afflictions of conflict; and the need for support and resources in order to rebuild their capacity and legitimacy is also likely to exist.[372] The key point,

---

368 Bruce Baker, "Multi-Choice Policing in Uganda", *Policing and Society* 15, no. 1 (2005): 19–41, 21.

369 Bruce Baker, *Multi-Choice Policing in Africa* (Uppsala: Nordiska Afrikainstituter, 2008).

370 Australian Federal Police (AFP), *Inquiry into the Main Economic and Security Challenges Facing Papua New Guinea and the Island States of the Southwest Pacific*, Report to the Parliament of Australia Senate Standing Committee on Foreign Affairs, Defence and Trade, (Canberra: Australian Federal Police, 2008).

371 Australian Federal Police (AFP), *Inquiry into the Main Economic and Security Challenges Facing Papua New Guinea and the Island States of the Southwest Pacific*, Report to the Parliament of Australia Senate Standing Committee on Foreign Affairs, Defence and Trade, (Canberra: Australian Federal Police, 2008), 5.

372 Organization for Economic Co-operation and Development, *The OECD DAC Handbook on Security Sector Reform: Supporting Security and Justice*, (Paris: OECD, 2007), 195.

however, is that rather than rejecting everything that does not meet our quixotic notions of how RoL *should* look, and thus risking little if any near term progress, it is better to consider how to improve as quickly as possible and with our limited resources what does exist. While this is not to say that mainstream, state-building initiatives should be repudiated; it is to say that significant and unnecessary suffering may occur in the typically long periods required for them to bear fruit.

When considering RoL providers in the most inclusive sense, Joerg Friedrichs refers to a triad of potential providers of force: "the state monopoly of force, the commodification of force, and community self-help."[373] The model offers a useful way to think of the three potential categories of RoL providers: state-based actors; privately contracted (often but not necessarily by the state) providers; and the myriad of community-based or informal providers. When combined with Black's general theory of law,[374] which maintains that the strength of a society's formal legal institutions will vary inversely with the strength of its informal ones, the model can be extended to RoL to offer this specific insight: that if a society's *formal* RoL institutions are weak, then its *informal* institutions are likely to be comparatively strong. Of course, in many cases both may be badly weakened; but this insight can nevertheless instruct program managers to consider when, where, and how best to harness local institutions. Specifically, it causes managers to consider appropriate private and community sectors when state-based options are problematic due either to their absence or their unacceptability.

As with all human practices, the above justice and policing systems are ultimately fluid, not fixed, which opens up the possibility of evolving or hybrid institutions (but not limited to state-based actors such as 'hybrid courts' cited above). Upham maintains that "societies must develop a mix of formal and informal mechanisms that can produce optimal results given their respective social, political, economic, and cultural contexts."[375] We accept that the context of RoL reform connotes that what exists is "inadequate and requires modification" and

---

373 Joerg Friedrichs, *Transformative Consequences of Private Force: The Provision of Security from State to Market and Society*, ISA's 50th Annual Convention—"Exploring the Past, Anticipating the Future" (New York Marriott Marquis, New York, USA, 2009), 3. It is important to note that Friedrich's main argument—that the state should in effect maintain exclusive control over the delivery of force—is basically the opposite of ours. Concerning the community 'self-help' sources, Friedrichs uses the example of the deputisation of local sheikhs after the recent US-led invasion of in Iraq as a warning of the unintended consequences which, to him, predictably occur when the state does not maintain a monopoly on the use of force. However his selective examples are limited to objectionable sources (*e.g.* Sharia law or merciless gangs). We repudiate his over-generalisation that community providers will predictably result in negative outcomes, in recognition of the many that might assist in positive outcomes.

374 Donald Black, *The Behaviour of Law* (New York: Academic Press, 1976).

375 Frank Upham, "Mythmaking in the Rule-of-Law Orthodoxy", in *Promoting the Rule of Law Abroad: In Search of Knowledge*, ed. Thomas Carothers (Washington, D.C.: Carnegie Endowment for International Peace, 2006), 1.

that—whether driven locally or externally—reform processes will invariably draw on foreign models and/or experiences.[376] At the same time, a comprehensively participatory approach must be employed in order to maximise local ownership and capacity.[377] The overall point for the present purposes is that we cannot overlook the existing institutions, norms and practices by assuming that they cannot contribute to RoL solutions. Local mechanisms have a number of benefits beyond being already in place. They tend to focus on restoration and harmony rather than contestation, offer quick settlement rather than protracted processes, and generally require significantly fewer resources for upkeep.[378] The need to appreciate non-state RoL providers is further underscored by the fact that of the four types in Otwin Marenin's typology of contexts for RoL programs—namely, "(1) Following period of state repression (*e.g.* South Africa); (2) After destructive/divisive inter-communal violence (*e.g.* Rwanda); (3) State failure (*e.g.* Liberia/East Timor/Afghanistan); and (4) Transitional/developing societies",[379] the latter three are arguably circumstances in which traditional/customary systems would likely predominate. For its part, the Australian Federal Police recognises that a 'sound understanding of traditional law and justice systems can inform the appropriateness and scope of service provision' in such contexts.[380] Even so, as with other intervening actors, their policebuilding approach continues to rely on narrow Western notions of RoL providers.[381]

The above alternative contentions supply invaluable insights. They go a long way toward illuminating what may actually exist in mission areas rather than what some might wish existed. By doing so they have the potential to explain why

376 Charles T. Call, "Challenges in Police Reform: Promoting Effectiveness and Accountability," in *From Promise to Practice: Strengthening UN Capacities for the Prevention of Violent Conflict* ed. Chandra Lekha Sriram and Karin Wermester (New York: International Peace Academy, 2003), 4.

377 See: Jessica Howard and Bruce Oswald, eds., *The Rule of Law on Peace Operations: A 'Challenges of Peace Operations' Project Conference* (Melbourne: Asia-Pacific Centre for Military Law, 2002), 279. They argue that: "From the earliest moment, international civil actors must seek to incorporate local participation and create consultative mechanisms."

378 Stephen Arthur Lamony, *Approaching National Reconciliation in Uganda: Perspectives on Applicable Justice Systems* (Kampala: Ugandan Coalition for the International Criminal Court, 2007).

379 Otwin Marenin, "Restoring Policing Systems in Conflict Torn Nations: Process, Problems, Prospects," *Occasional Paper No. 7* (Geneva: Geneva Centre for the Democratic Control of Armed Forces (DCAF), 2005), 4.

380 Australian Federal Police (AFP), *Inquiry into the Main Economic and Security Challenges Facing Papua New Guinea and the Island States of the Southwest Pacific*, Report to the Parliament of Australia Senate Standing Committee on Foreign Affairs, Defence and Trade, (Canberra: Australian Federal Police, 2008): 5.

381 Australian Federal Police (AFP), *Inquiry into the Main Economic and Security Challenges Facing Papua New Guinea and the Island States of the Southwest Pacific*, Report to the Parliament of Australia Senate Standing Committee on Foreign Affairs, Defence and Trade, (Canberra: Australian Federal Police, 2008), 5.

peace and capacity building operations heretofore have enjoyed limited success. Unfortunately they reside on the margins of mainstream awareness and practice. The realities they reveal have to date flown largely under the mainstream radar. The framework proposed below aims to incorporate these perspectives into an emerging best practice RoL conception.

A Post-Weberian Best Practice Framework

The point of discussions concerning best practice developments, like that generated herein, is to articulate compelling gains in efficiency and effectiveness. In RoL terms this means not only finding better ways to (re)establish this crucial ingredient, but ensuring its sustainability. A main goal must be eliminating the need for perpetual intervention activities and funding as witnessed in many places such as Timor Leste and the DRC. The framework we sketch out in this penultimate section aims to overcome the deficiencies highlighted above. In particular, those elements which overlook complex local realities because they view RoL through their own narrow (state-centric) image. It is often neither practical nor desirable to ignore the many non-state sources for RoL. Importantly, rather than promoting an 'artificial consensus' by culling alternative perspectives,[382] our approach aims to embrace the diversity which exists across the globe, but in a way that allows for both precise and comparative evaluations.

We draw from extant views in particular ways to arrive at the initial iteration of a framework which contains three main facets. The first part maintains that RoL should be delimited to cover security, judicial, and correctional *functions*.[383] For the purposes herein, security extends both to personal safety and those who provide it; judicial denotes the systems of rules and practices used to settle matters of justice; and corrections refers to mechanisms of internment and rehabilitation. Often referred to as either the 'justice' or 'security triad', these are the key organs which *work together* to enable RoL. In other words, similar to human organs, the health of one affects the others, and thus if the corrections functions are significantly flawed or non-existent, for instance, this will undoubtedly have a negative impact on both the security and judicial areas. In policy and praxis, this means we cannot treat any in isolation without the risk of backlash from the others.

---

[382] Randy Peerenboom, "The Future of Rule of Law: Challenges and Prospects for the Field," *Hague Journal on the Rule of Law* 1, no. 1 (2009), 6.

[383] In a 2005 think-piece for the Department of Peacekeeping Operations (DPKO) Best Practices Section, Oswald refers to local criminal justice structures of police, judiciary and corrections as the contextually important "law and order authorities." See: Bruce Oswald, *Addressing the Institutional Law and Order Vacuum: Key Issues and Dilemmas for Peacekeeping Operations* (New York: UN DPKO, 2005), 4.

Furthermore, these categories, understood in the most inclusive manner possible, cover the breadth of activities that comprise the mainstream's programs.[384] As such, it is not only an accurate way to order the rest of the framework but a productive one since it can be readily adopted by the major actors discussed throughout. Equally important, however, is its capacity to recognise and subsequently encompass the non-Euro-American institutions and processes which may approximate RoL.[385]

Second, and following from the last point, we maintain that the *experience* of RoL can be known by the fulfilment of a set of principles.[386] The crucial aspects of the RoL that must be present in any best practice approach are the principles, such as transparency and equal access to justice,[387] while at the same time the focus must be on their *de facto* delivery rather than *de jure* principles of law.[388] The approach of this second facet is consistent with many viewpoints, including Marenin's opinion that it is crucial to "stress principles and goals, not models"[389] and the Substantitivist viewpoint which maintains that we must go well beyond the presence of formal institutions in order to realise what RoL is about. Furthermore, the realisation of these principles should be understood across each of the three aforementioned functional categories.

---

384 Though we concur with Jane Stromseth, David Wippman, and Rosa Brooks, eds., *Can Might Make Rights: Building the Rule of Law after Military Interventions* (Cambridge: Cambridge University Press, 2006), 184–5, for the need to reframe this triad as encompassing those institutions and processes which contribute 'upstream', the attempt to do so vis-à-vis our framework unnecessarily complicates the aim for precision. For that reason, we advocate the more narrow delimitation of the justice triad, without losing an appreciation of its wider linkages.

385 See: Randy Peerenboom, "The Future of Rule of Law: Challenges and Prospects for the Field," *Hague Journal on the Rule of Law* 1, no. 1 (2009), 6–7, for the need for a 'process' oriented understanding.

386 In this vein, see how Vera-Altus has adapted the World Justice Project's useful but state-centric RoL Index. (World Justice Project, Website, http://www.abanet.org/wjp/rolindex.html, accessed 31 March 2009)

387 Jim Parsons, Monica Thornton, Hyo Eun Bang, Ben Estep, Kaya Williams and Neil Weiner, *Developing Indicators to Measure the Rule of Law: A Global Approach*, A Report to the World Justice Project (Vera Institute of Justice, 2008), ii.

388 Jim Parsons, Monica Thornton, Hyo Eun Bang, Ben Estep, Kaya Williams and Neil Weiner, *Developing Indicators to Measure the Rule of Law: A Global Approach*, A Report to the World Justice Project (Vera Institute of Justice, 2008), 8. See also: David Mednicoff, "Middle East Dilemmas", in ed. Thomas Carothers, *Promoting the Rule of Law Abroad: In Search of Knowledge* (Washington DC: Carnegie Endowment for International Peace, 2006), 254, whereby he uses Arab nation examples to argue that "the most promising approaches ... tie ideals to practices."

389 Otwin Marenin, "Restoring Policing Systems in Conflict Torn Nations: Process, Problems, Prospects," *Occasional Paper No. 7* (Geneva: Geneva Centre for the Democratic Control of Armed Forces (DCAF), 2005), 53.

With that foundation in place, the third and final facet addresses the sources that may be capable of *providing* RoL functions—in accordance with the RoL principles. Unlike dominant views (*e.g.* World Justice Project and the UN) we do not place our reliance in state based providers. An example of this underlying state dependency is presented by how Vera juxtaposes '*Non-state justice mechanisms*', with the functional capacities of (state-based) police, prisons and the judiciary, under the principles of 'accountability, unbiased and efficient' delivery of justice. This approach means that though non-state sources are mentioned, it is done in a way that places them on the periphery. The clear implication is that they are always less tenable, less desirable, and therefore only to be tolerated in the absence of state systems. While concurring with the need to ensure these non-state mechanisms are "adequately resourced, accountable to high standards, fair and transparent,"[390] and denying the type of cultural relativist viewpoint which may be inclined to accept customary practices at odds with RoL principles, we go the next step by arguing that informal sources must be *fully* considered *within* the functional categories of police/security, judicial and corrections, rather than as a separate element.

None of this is to suggest that RoL deliverers exist in a vacuum. On the contrary, our approach conceptualises RoL as a complex system comprising a multiplicity of interacting entities which exist in an even broader system of beliefs and practices. Indeed, it is the mainstream prism which problematically compartmentalises specific areas for particular activities. At the same time our framework of three functional areas examined according to the *five* principles described next, constitutes a less convoluted design to many who dwell in this area (*e.g.* Vera-Altus).

We maintain that the following selection of principles (drawn from the broader debate) can be used to comprehensively assess the way in which RoL providers *behave*. For example, the principle listed fourth below, transparency may be used to query whether the judicial processes have been developed so that judges conduct their matters in a public rather than secretive environment. The only exception, as we clarify below, is the principle of 'equal access' when it is combined with 'security' functions. The upshot is that our conception of RoL is an ideal in which absolute adherence to each principle transpires across all three functional areas. As an ideal, its realisation is highly improbable, but nevertheless it provides a clear—yet flexible and comprehensive—benchmark by which to gauge any given particular circumstance, regardless of whether or not *de facto* providers are state actors.

---

390 Jim Parsons, Monica Thornton, Hyo Eun Bang, Ben Estep, Kaya Williams and Neil Weiner, *Developing Indicators to Measure the Rule of Law: A Global Approach*, A Report to the World Justice Project (Vera Institute of Justice, 2008), 11.

The first principle (not in order of importance) is '*equal access*'.[391] This means that each inhabitant (*i.e.* not just those with formal citizenship status) should be able to receive a similar level of RoL services as all others. Certain individuals or groups cannot have access to demonstrably more effective RoL functions due to, for instance, geographic location, ethnicity, or financial wherewithal. This principle offers perhaps the best opportunity to point out the advantage of a post-Weberian conception, since *access* to RoL is most likely to be the first casualty of donor efforts which focus principally on state actors for delivery. That is, in the many circumstances whereby the state is not (and perhaps never has been) a particularly relevant entity, access to RoL is bound to grow increasingly unequal if intervening parties ignore traditional RoL providers. Accordingly, both formal and informal sources must be taken seriously. Simply put, do inhabitants have equal access to appropriate security, judicial, and corrections services, no matter what forms they may take?[392]

'*Accountability*' is our second principle. That is, each of the functional areas of police, judiciary, and prisons (including non-state mechanisms) must be accountable for their actions. The point is to ensure that those delivering RoL do not operate with impunity. They must be accountable to those whom their activities affect, in that they must be capable of being scrutinised then, if appropriate, reformed, disciplined or stopped altogether.[393] The mechanisms to hold providers to account can of course take many forms, but the idea must be upheld regardless of delivery mode. '*Lack of Bias*' is the third. RoL requires an absence of discrimination, which may be based on any criteria such as ethnicity or gender. Equal treatment is essential. Applied across the three functional areas, questions should be raised as to whether and how the experiences of security, judicial, and correctional functions are being provided without bias to a person or group's multiple markers. Fourth is '*transparency*'. This refers to the public having a

---

391 See: Jim Parsons, Monica Thornton, Hyo Eun Bang, Ben Estep, Kaya Williams and Neil Weiner, *Developing Indicators to Measure the Rule of Law: A Global Approach*, A Report to the World Justice Project (Vera Institute of Justice, 2008), 12, as they apply it to access to justice.

392 As mentioned above, equal access concerning the 'security' function is the one exception wherein our principles do not refer solely to the behaviour of RoL providers since security conceptions should also refer to the behaviour of the public at large in terms of crime rates. We can, however, continue to enquire as to whether security providers deploy relatively equally so that access to security can be experienced equally as opposed to neglecting certain areas. The experience of law and order, in other words, can be uncoupled from the provision of security. The lesson to take from this distinction is that one eye should be on the levels of crime committed by the public while the other should consider the behaviour, resources and coverage of security providers.

393 For a useful discussion on the accountability of intervening parties in a peace support operation context, see: Marten Zwanenburg, *Accountability of Peace Support Operations* (Leiden: Martinus Nijhoff Publishers, 2005), 287–314.

sound understanding of RoL functions, and the way in which they are enacted and developed. As with 'access', customary mechanisms are likely to have a distinct edge on imported Western notions in many societies concerning transparency, in that they are generally widely known already. Finally, it is not enough that inhabitants have equal access to an accountable, transparent and unbiased RoL system. In keeping with Vera, we maintain that the principle of '*Participation*' must be present for the full experience of RoL to exist. Participation can be understood in conventional terms as a public which can influence state legislation in ways such as town meetings.[394] We go beyond the implication that participation is limited to state-based systems in order to conceive participation as the general public's ability to influence norms, conventions and practices—regardless of whether they are formalised and codified. As such, if members of a society have the capacity to participate in deciding how their RoL affairs are conducted, then we would argue that is an appropriate experience, even if none of the systems pertain to formal state processes or providers.

Hence, analyses begin by posing the question of how each of the functions of security, judicial, and corrections are going vis-à-vis the principles. First level questions ask, for instance, 'how transparent, accountable, and unbiased are security providers?' Second level questions might look like this: regards the security element, how transparent is policing behaviour? Or how transparent are the military type-services' behaviour? Third level questions would then unpack the investigation further by establishing what (formal or informal) sources are or could be providing policing, and then applying each principle to each source so that the outcome is a precise analysis For example, when the 'unbiased' principle is applied to the security sector, one could look at a) the state police; b) the state military; or c) a potentially vast array of non-state security providers, asking of each how 'unbiased' is RoL under that provider? For instance, are certain ethnic groups treated differently? The same is done for the other principles. For the security category, we can ask questions from the three perspectives about (1) the conduct of providers; (2) access to providers; and (3) the level of crime.

Within the limits of this chapter, we do not have room to discuss the crucial matter of how to evaluate the various aspects which comprise this framework. For the purposes herein, suffice it to say that we subscribe to a modified version of Vera-Altus' approach designed to evaluate each aspect (and by extension, each provider) against our five RoL principles with a *basket* of indicators developed specifically for each context, The key is that there are a variety of indicators in each basket that utilise different methods such as data from expert opinion and public surveys, hard data from governments or non-governmental organisations, and so on. As such, analysts can arrive at straightforward yet comprehensive and

[394] Jim Parsons, Monica Thornton, Hyo Eun Bang, Ben Estep, Kaya Williams and Neil Weiner, *Developing Indicators to Measure the Rule of Law: A Global Approach*, A Report to the World Justice Project (Vera Institute of Justice, 2008), 10.

realistic evaluations of each functional area of RoL—the kind which is currently lacking. Regarding the security function, for example, the various sources that 'provided' security could be assessed according to a basket of indicators aimed at understanding how each stacked up against the five principles. There would be further indicators to evaluate the relationships between each functional area to ensure a holistic view, which recognises each facet as a part of an overall system, is not lost.

These types of in-depth and inclusive assessments can only be achieved by synthesising the core functional components of RoL with a comprehensive list of principles and the widest imagination of providers. Underpinned by our conception of RoL, the framework renders a precise yet flexible approach, which draws attention to the indigenous systems and practices that are normally missed by importing a culturally alien conception. Hence, it redresses the current deficiencies outlined at the beginning of the chapter by striking the balance between flexible and thus universally applicable on the one hand, while clear and thus instructive on the other. Moreover, it is compatible with the views and practices of the major organisations tasked with implementing RoL, which also recognise that RoL consists of interrelationships between many institutions. As aforementioned, this latter quality smooths the way for its adoption.

Concluding Thoughts

When the context for international engagement is one of supporting fragile states on the road towards self-sustaining peace, good governance, and stable economic livelihoods, we concur with Smith *et al.* that "the common foundation on which such institutions and outcomes must be built is respect for and deference to the rule of law."[395] The enormous significance of these efforts means we must get its conception right. The underlying purpose of this chapter has been to expand the conception of the RoL to fit in the many places on earth which do not resemble a modern Western state. This post-Weberian notion challenges the practice whereby those implementing RoL stop at asking local actors for their opinion on Western processes and institutions. It intends to correct the practice whereby the scarce resources applied to reconstituting RoL are misapplied towards building an alien 'part', which may be rejected in the same manner that the human body rejects an incompatible organ.

Moving global best practice understandings[396] forward requires a hybrid delineation to inform systems that go beyond the current understanding of

---

395 Joshua G. Smith, Victoria K. Holt, and William J. Durch, *Enhancing United Nations Capacity for Post-Conflict Policing and Rule of Law*, Report from The Project on Rule of Law in Post-Conflict Settings (Washington DC: The Henry L. Stimson Center, 2007), xi.

396 It might be better termed: 'relevant or successful' practices to underscore the need to leverage fully local realities as opposed to a one-size fits all supposition.

international and national actors combining to pursue a Weberian ideal of RoL. It needs to push past Euro-American images of security, judicial, and corrections as silos inhabited by state-based providers. Channell points out that a lack of implementation is the litmus test for failed RoL programs, and that it is a mistake to assume that the government is the key to reform;[397] whereas we would take that point one step further to maintain that implementation commonly fails because the environment is not the Weberian ideal that interveners presume.

The vision we have put forward in this chapter exhorts us to look for the right balance of traditional/customary, state or international RoL providers. The extent to which non-state providers exist, are relevant and acceptable to universally held standards will of course vary depending on context. What is not context specific however is that "attempting to create all at once the full panoply of legal institutions found in developed countries is generally not the best use of limited resources."[398] Further research is needed to discover more the potential—or successes and failures—of this notion of hybrid systems. To be clear, this is not to suggest that the non-state sector is more important; it is to say that we cannot go forward in conceptualising RoL without taking seriously the multitude of 'informal' providers.

In the context of peace and capacity-building operations, the RoL domain is best located at the confluence of multiple interdependent formal and informal institutions, mechanisms and networks. It is vital that international actors not only recognise, but expeditiously harness the utility of locally-driven processes and traditional mechanisms if RoL is to prevail in the fabric of society and the mindset of its people. The recipe can be developed to ensure the most appropriate mixture. Despite the inevitable contextual differences, this promises to achieve the most immediate yet sustainable amalgam.

In conflict-ridden Uganda, someone recently said: "In my opinion peace is sleeping with one's door open, on a full stomach, and walking on the road during day or night without fear of attack."[399] This notion of peace is consistent with the vision of RoL developed herein. The key point is that, like countless others made vulnerable by conflicts around the planet, it matters little *which* RoL providers contribute to the realisation of peace and security. What they care about is that improvements come sooner rather than later and that they last.

---

397 Wade Channell, "Lessons Not Learned about Legal Reform", in *Promoting the Rule of Law Abroad: In Search of Knowledge*, ed. Thomas Carothers, (Washington, D.C.: Carnegie Endowment for International Peace, 2006), 137–60.

398 Randy Peerenboom, "The Future of Rule of Law: Challenges and Prospects for the Field," *Hague Journal on the Rule of Law* 1, no. 1 (2009), 10.

399 Stephen Arthur Lamony, *Approaching National Reconciliation in Uganda: Perspectives on Applicable Justice Systems* (Kampala: Ugandan Coalition for the International Criminal Court, 2007), 21.

CHAPTER FIVE

THE CASE FOR PEACE OPERATIONS TO ENGAGE THE 'POLITICAL'

Having now demonstrated how main aspects of today's conventional wisdom misrepresent what indeed exists on the ground, as well as ways in which an alternative view can bring us closer to the kinds of peace and capacity building missions talked about as the international community's reason for involvement in foreign spaces, this chapter tackles head on the stumbling block that provides perhaps the most stubborn blind spot: that of apprehending and negotiating with ways of living and thinking alien to our own.

The reason this exploration is so vital is because in order for us to enjoy a future filled with effective and sustainable peace support operations,[400] the international community should stop maintaining that such a future will come basically from imparting the 'right' institutions, mustering an 'appropriate' level of resources, or honing the technical and managerial skills of interveners and recipients alike. On the contrary, successful missions will become possible only when external actors engage with the 'political' as core practice. Political herein does not mean the formal workings of government or the power struggles within and between organizations; rather, it refers to 'the socio-cultural value systems that determine which behaviour, arguments, and actions are (deemed) legitimate'.[401] It is these phenomena that constitute the heartbeat of human existence and therefore deserve utmost attention because of the ways they inexorably shape behaviour through constraining and enabling agency.

---

400 For present purposes, the term 'peace support operations' is used synonymously to encompass the broad spectrum of peace and capacity development endeavours, to include peacekeeping, stabilization, humanitarian aid, and peacebuilding missions, with the view that the arguments herein are relevant across this wide range of international involvement.

401 Andrew Harrington and Tanja Chopra, *Arguing Traditions: Denying Kenya's Women Access to Land Rights*, Research Report No. 2 (World Bank Justice for the Poor, 2010), v.

Equipped with a 'political consciousness',[402] the international community would then recognise that truly fruitful engagements entail working *with* existing sources of power and legitimacy and the social orders they enable rather than dismissing them, with the underlying aim being to achieve 'socially generative' change.[403] To this point, Oliver Richmond cautions that problems arise when local belief systems fail to match those of external actors.[404] Realizing this admittedly daunting paradigm shift means a commitment to navigating the precarious shoals among the political exigencies and aspirations of recipient societies on the one hand, and the myriad political imaginations and imperatives of the international actor's constituent parts on the other.

The overwhelming tendency of external actors to date has instead been to contemplate local societies through a reductionist conception bereft of the rich, multilayered, dynamic interaction that makes up any social context.[405] With the general exception of the peacebuilding field,[406] interveners commonly enter the fray with purportedly objective approaches, maintaining they can somehow divorce their own life's socialization and worldview from the 'facts on the ground' they seek to uncover and repair through technical solutions.[407] Seemingly without

---

402 Rory Keane, "Peace Operations and Crisis Management: Not Benign Tasks but Political Acts" in *Measuring What Matters in Peace Operations and Crisis Management*, ed. Sarah Meharg (Montreal: McGill-Queen's University Press, 2009), 153–58.

403 See Sinclair Dinnen, Doug Porter and Caroline Sage, *Conflict in Melanesia: Themes and Lessons*, World Development Report 2011, Background Paper (World Bank: 2010).

404 Oliver Richmond, "Emancipatory Forms of Human Security and Liberal Peacebuilding," *International Journal* 62 no. 3 (2007) 460.

405 Bryn Hughes, "Moving Beyond Rethinking the State of the State: to the Challenge of Reshaping International Contributions to Peace operations," *Conflict Security & Development* 10 no. 3 (2010): 329–352; Marion Jacka, "Security and Development: Conflict and Resilience in the Pacific Islands Region" in *Security and Development in the Pacific Islands: Social Resilience in Emerging States,* ed. M. Anne Brown (Boulder, CO: Lynne Rienner, 2007).

406 While much of the peacebuilding literature and practice has been *de facto* liberal statebuilding, a significant and burgeoning portion nevertheless strives to engage with the political in the kinds of culturally appropriate and effective manner we advocate herein. For examples which bear this claim out, see: John Paul Lederach, *The Moral Imagination: The Art and Soul of Building Peace* (New York: Oxford University Press, 2005); Timothy Donais, "Empowerment or Imposition? Dilemmas of Local Ownership in Post-Conflict Peacebuilding Processes," *Peace & Change* 34 no. 1 (2009). Oliver Richmond ed., *Palgrave Advances in Peacebuilding: Critical Developments and Approaches* (Hampshire: Palgrave Macmillan, 2010).

407 Oliver Richmond maintains the widespread lack of understanding of local politics to date by the international community. As he puts it: they believe their approaches are 'unbiased by cultural or historical proclivities', being 'naively ill-equipped to reform the politics of post-conflict states'. See Oliver Richmond ed., *Palgrave Advances in Peacebuilding: Critical Developments and Approaches* (Hampshire: Palgrave Macmillan, 2010), 1–2.

having realised it, the international community now finds itself embarking on staggeringly ambitious efforts to rebuild entire societies—from the ground up, yet ironically with largely top-down approaches that in effect ignore the political.[408]

While diverse motivations circulate beneath this veneer of neutrality and political atheism, the intentions of many interveners have not been pure.[409] The UN Security Council, for example, routinely devises the parameters for peace operations with little concern for local contexts.[410] Attitudes on the ground are scarcely better, with peacekeeping forces, for example, having commonly approached local orders with disdain.[411] Hence, even though our conversations with practitioners from the UN, OECD, the EU and the Australian Federal Police (AFP) have detected a genuine concern for the wellbeing of local systems, including an appreciation that the political should be left unmolested wherever it does not affront international norms, many conspire to impose their own value systems. This presents an overall picture of current circumstances wherein local political considerations are deliberately shunned by innumerable external actors.

Intentions aside, this peculiar combination of practitioner and policymaker mindsets creates a toxic brew. Such an apolitical, self-image fails to account for the fact that most indigenous orders have never approximated the Westphalian state; their socio-cultural notions of how to live together, more generally, are usually far from OECD country experiences.[412] The realities of the lives of ordinary

408 The *kiap* epitomized the perfunctory and minimalist colonial approach. The kiap served as the colonial agent in an all-in-one executive, judicial and enforcer role intended to pacify the local population—but only to the degree that the European states could extract what they wanted (See Abby McLeod, "Police Reform in Papua New Guinea" in *Security and Development in the Pacific Islands: Social Resilience in Emerging States,* ed. M. Anne Brown (Boulder, CO: Lynne Rienner, 2007), 76–79). This model however never came close to the intense level of resources and wide-ranging expectations contemplated in today's peace operation imagination. See also Sinclair Dinnen and John Braithwaite, "Reinventing Policing Through the Prism of the Colonial Kiap", *Policing and Society* 19 no. 2, (2009).

409 Jarat Chopra, "The UN's Kingdom of East Timor," *Survival* 42 no. 3 (2000): 27–40; Roger MacGinty, "Indigenous Peace-Making Versus the Liberal Peace," *Cooperation and Conflict* 43 no. 2 (2008).

410 Beatrice Pouligny, *Peace Operations Seen from Below: UN Missions and Local People* (Bloomfield, CT: Kumarian Press, 2006), 1.

411 Beatrice Pouligny, *Peace Operations Seen from Below: UN Missions and Local People* (Bloomfield, CT: Kumarian Press, 2006), 1.

412 Volker Boege, M. Anne Brown, Kevin P. Clements, and Anna Nolan, "States Emerging from Hybrid Political Orders—Pacific Experiences", *Occasional Paper Series Number 11* (Australian Centre for Peace and Conflict Studies, September 2008); Sinclair Dinnen and John Braithwaite, "Reinventing Policing Through the Prism of the Colonial Kiap", *Policing and Society* 19 no. 2, (2009); Bryn Hughes, "Moving Beyond Rethinking the State of the State: to the Challenge of Reshaping International Contributions to Peace operations," *Conflict Security & Development* 10 no. 3 (2010): 329–352.

people are often overlooked.[413] Time and again this leads to the type of debilitating, yet scarcely recognized, tension whereby local actors are made to enforce politico-legal orders 'that conflict openly with their internal beliefs and external... social obligations'.[414]

Indeed, the relationship between insiders and outsiders is integral to effective missions,[415] and peacekeeping is inherently political.[416] Yet resistance from indigenous elements is often because programmes have ignored the cultural, ethical and social (the political, in other words).[417] The effect is to severely undermine the dual goals of effective and sustainable operations. The broader point is that ill-conceived adventures can ensue when local political considerations are discounted, with the imposition of the liberal peace providing the most prominent example to date.[418] In its particular case, the political has been circumvented by those who have maintained that there is only one set of universal values (liberal, Western), whereas an emphasis on the political would undoubtedly trouble attempts to impose foreign notions of order.

Hence, while the shortcomings of peace support operations have been amply chronicled,[419] it is the under-acknowledged failure to navigate the political that does more work explaining the dubious outcomes of peace support operations

---

413 As Beatrice Pouligny, *Peace Operations Seen from Below: UN Missions and Local People* (Bloomfield, CT: Kumarian Press, 2006), 276, puts it: we should adopt an image of peace operations according to 'the image conveyed by the people themselves'. 'See also Paul Higate and Marsha Henry, *Insecure Spaces: Peacekeeping, Power, and Performance in Haiti, Kosovo, and Liberia* (London: Zed Books, 2009), 155, who argue for a need to 'reorient peacekeeping' to fit with what local actors might want.

414 Abby McLeod, "Police Reform in Papua New Guinea" in *Security and Development in the Pacific Islands: Social Resilience in Emerging States*, ed. M. Anne Brown (Boulder, CO: Lynne Rienner, 2007), 80.

415 Timothy Donais, "Empowerment or Imposition? Dilemmas of Local Ownership in Post-Conflict Peacebuilding Processes," *Peace & Change* 34 no. 1 (2009).

416 Paul Higate and Marsha Henry, *Insecure Spaces: Peacekeeping, Power, and Performance in Haiti, Kosovo, and Liberia* (London: Zed Books, 2009), 155.

417 Marion Jacka, "Security and Development: Conflict and Resilience in the Pacific Islands Region" in *Security and Development in the Pacific Islands: Social Resilience in Emerging States,* ed. M. Anne Brown (Boulder, CO: Lynne Rienner, 2007), 34.

418 Timothy Donais, "Empowerment or Imposition? Dilemmas of Local Ownership in Post-Conflict Peacebuilding Processes," *Peace & Change* 34 no. 1 (2009): 5–6; Paul Higate and Marsha Henry, *Insecure Spaces: Peacekeeping, Power, and Performance in Haiti, Kosovo, and Liberia* (London: Zed Books, 2009), 156; Roland Paris, "International Peacebuilding and the Mission Civilsatrice," *Review of International Studies* 28 (2002).

419 See Paul Higate and Marsha Henry, *Insecure Spaces: Peacekeeping, Power, and Performance in Haiti, Kosovo, and Liberia* (London: Zed Books, 2009), 156 and Beatrice Pouligny, *Peace Operations Seen from Below: UN Missions and Local People* (Bloomfield, CT: Kumarian Press, 2006), who set out widespread practices of sexual predation by UN peacekeepers and other gender-related maladies, as well as the unintended consequences caused by a lack of organisational accountability or short-term contract arrangements.

thus far. That is, even in a best-case hypothetical scenario whereby donor practitioner incompetency, maleficence, and organisational politics were to vanish altogether, international operations would still falter if they continued to take decisions at odds with local value systems and the corresponding institutions. Many renowned problems, such as corruption that funds insurgency, would in fact be downstream manifestations of choices that botched the political.

The purpose of this chapter is to make a foray into this consequential space. As would be clear by this point, the underlying argument hinges on the need to concentrate on the political rather than the technical, with the expectation that the political views of *intervening* actors be aired and added to the mix of indigenous voices instead of pretending they neither exist nor enter into decision making considerations. The admittedly difficult yet central challenge is to negotiate arrangements amenable to all. We have chosen two main components to develop this argument. The initial section highlights a few of the many—and largely unappreciated—fissures between how Western and recipient societies conceive security and justice. This aspect is vital because the recognition of difference regarding beliefs and corresponding practices is a prerequisite for effective mission programming. The political, as with other key forces, should not however be viewed as though it exists in a mechanistic, closed system. Hence the second section explores the notion of 'complex social systems' in order that we may begin to conceptualise peace operations through a lens which emphasizes the fluid and interactive nature of what emerges during programming. Importantly, the discussion continues with how the political forms the space for agency, employing the notion 'regimes of truth' to appreciate the power-knowledge nexus that underpins the political.

Recognising Political Diversity

Part of the reason the political is not upfront and centre in mainstream peace operations thinking is a lack of awareness of 'other' forms. That is, it might astonish many of the conscientious members of interceding forces from Western countries to learn the depth to which their own values and notions of the social world can differ from those to which they aim to transfer skills and institutions. The cultural sensitivity training undertaken by many peacekeeping forces, for instance, seldom has time to do more than skim the surface. This section puts forward a small sampling of some major areas of disconnect while illustrating how stark the differences often are. The challenge for orthodox mindsets is how to conceive societies whose notions of political community seldom resemble whatsoever the modern, Weberian notion of a state.[420] Yet such awareness is vital because what

420 Sinclair Dinnen and John Braithwaite, "Reinventing Policing Through the Prism of the Colonial Kiap", *Policing and Society* 19 no. 2, (2009): 161–173; Bryn Hughes, "Moving Beyond Rethinking the State of the State: to the Challenge of Reshaping International

is palatable for each constituency can vary dramatically and in the worst cases begin from incompatible or even mutually exclusive stances. Identifying and acknowledging difference—rather than glossing over what may be integral pillars of recipient societies—is a crucial step toward negotiating mutually acceptable directions.

Violence is a germane area beset with often dramatically divergent viewpoints. Whereas Western conceptions of society hinge on a homeostatic view in which violence is considered a dysfunctional aberration to order, many traditional societies have considered violence as 'normal' part of life.[421] More specifically, violence in certain circumstances is viewed as legitimate, a conflict resolution tool in response to a problem, not the problem itself; while to the Western idealized notion it is only deemed legitimate by formal state actors.[422] This difference could prove disastrous to unaware program managers.

Related is a more nuanced but nevertheless equally significant divergence which pertains to the Western idea of 'impartial' justice. On the one hand, Westerners have been taught the primacy of the abstract concept of the state; allegiances and legitimacies are meant to flow from this abstract. Crime, for example, is understood as a transgression against the abstract subject of the state. One's position in society, ethnicity, gender, and so on is propagated as irrelevant to this notion of impartial justice (despite the discrimination that commonly occurs in practice). Many traditional societies however see wrongs as committed against *particular* people, property or the supernatural order.[423] The many layers of identity that the 'impartial' perspective seeks to ignore, in other words, are at the very heart of how traditional justice is designed and carried out. In some customary imaginations, the referent object of crime is not solely the individual, with the kin *group* being held equally responsible.[424]

Similarly, traditional societies have lacked the specialized systems of courts, police, and prisons. Since the times of the colonial *kiaps*, and before, these functions have commonly been performed by single entities. Social, economic,

Contributions to Peace Operations," *Conflict Security & Development* 10 no. 3 (2010): 329–352.

421 Abby McLeod, "Police Reform in Papua New Guinea" in *Security and Development in the Pacific Islands: Social Resilience in Emerging States,* ed. M. Anne Brown (Boulder, CO: Lynne Rienner, 2007), 77.

422 Sinclair Dinnen, *State Society and Governance in Melanesia: Law, Order and State in Papua New Guinea*, Discussion Paper 97/1, The Australian National University, 1997, 6, http://rspas.anu.edu.au/papers/melanesia/discussion_papers/ssgmdinnen.pdf.

423 Abby McLeod, "Police Reform in Papua New Guinea" in *Security and Development in the Pacific Islands: Social Resilience in Emerging States,* ed. M. Anne Brown (Boulder, CO: Lynne Rienner, 2007).

424 Tanja Chopra, "When Peacebuilding Contradicts Statebuilding: Notes from the Arid Lands of Kenya", *International Peacekeeping* 16, no. 4 (2009): 534.

religious, political, and justice aspects historically have not been understood as the ostensibly independent silos of the OECD states of the Twenty-First Century. Rather these areas regularly intermingle, overlap, or function seamlessly.[425] How can these be reconciled, or conversely, upon which model should programming rely?

On the matter of justice processes, Western approaches insist on a 'winner', 'loser' approach which, *inter alia*, permits only a narrow discussion of the conflict, insofar as evidence not directly related to the case at hand is generally impermissible.[426] By contrast, Melanesian traditional approaches focus on restoring social relations, and interestingly include a practice known as 'airing the talk' which vitally allows for all parties to make public their grievances—thus affording a significantly greater chance of fleshing out and repairing root causes.[427] Emblematic of this divide, the practice of incarceration was introduced and largely imposed on peoples for whom the Western concept of a jail was previously unfamiliar. In Kenya today, for example, local concepts of justice dictate that punishment of a perpetrator is handled through payment of compensation—leaving Western practices of incarceration impotent to restore peace in a justice imagination whereby the 'lost' values of the victim's group are meant to be reinstalled.[428]

Albeit brief, the above exploration makes clear that there can be wide gaps between the political imaginations of many recipient societies and those offering to craft the 'solutions'. The recognition of diverse worldviews opens space to consider how to engage unfamiliar forms when striving to facilitate socially generative change. This is not to suggest that the values and institutions of (Western) donor sources are necessarily invalid. It is to make the point that attempts to transfer-in Western practices wholesale are likely to run up against the values and beliefs that have been instilled in local populations since birth. It is a lot to ask to have someone's lifelong teachings suddenly supplanted by several months of training that, for instance, the Western separation of law and order functions is *the* correct model.

425 Sinclair Dinnen and John Braithwaite, "Reinventing Policing Through the Prism of the Colonial Kiap", *Policing and Society* 19 no. 2 (2009).

426 Abby McLeod, "Police Reform in Papua New Guinea" in *Security and Development in the Pacific Islands: Social Resilience in Emerging States*, ed. M. Anne Brown (Boulder, CO: Lynne Rienner, 2007), 78.

427 Abby McLeod, "Police Reform in Papua New Guinea" in *Security and Development in the Pacific Islands: Social Resilience in Emerging States*, ed. M. Anne Brown (Boulder, CO: Lynne Rienner, 2007), 78.

428 Tanja Chopra, "When Peacebuilding Contradicts Statebuilding: Notes from the Arid Lands of Kenya", *International Peacekeeping* 16, no. 4 (2009): 534.

The Ocean in which the Political Lives

The investigation to this point has explored numerous facets of the political, ranging from its central importance to highlighting how starkly different Western and indigenous societies can conceive the political itself. Insights generated from these interrogations could not however yield sufficient guidance without an understanding of the overarching milieu in which it is (re)produced, including the interrelated matter of how it affects and is affected by agency. Coming to grips with these elements builds the bridge between sincere intentions to engage and having the conceptual tools to do so. An analogy might be that attempting to understand fish necessitates knowledge of the ocean. The broad milieu's conceptualisation is based on, for reasons set out below, the notion of 'complex social systems'. Following that discussion is an articulation of how the political forms an integral part of the space in which agency plays out, thereby enabling and constraining human behaviour. Together these explorations sketch out a pragmatic perspective by which the political can feature in mission programming.

Complex Social Systems

On one hand, mainstream views have unwittingly treated peace operation environments as though problems, such as corrupt practices or lack of law and order, can be identified and then isolated on their way to being 'solved'. Time and again we witness program planning and implementation according to this static conceptualization. Indeed it is difficult to find any major EU or UN mission articulation that does not take that approach. Training indigenous police forces, for instance, is a common tactic thought to 'solve the problem' that law and order is precarious due to a dearth of competent state police, with UNPOL in Liberia and EUJUST-LEX Iraq offering two examples. Once enough police have been trained to a sufficient degree, the problem of law and order is meant to be remedied—so the reductionist thinking goes. The social world is viewed implicitly as if focusing resources on police training could have no unforeseen or negative spill over effects.

However, not only is this approach about technical solutions—which pay little attention to political issues such as who may be perceived as winners or losers, or even what forms of policing might be preferred by particular stakeholders—but it supposes that elements of the environment can be treated in isolation. This is basically the peace operations' version of *ceteris paribus*—the economic term meaning 'all else remaining the same'.

In stark contrast to this conventional wisdom lens, an increasing number of thinkers reject that underlying assumption, opting instead to view programming through a lens informed by 'complex social systems'. This alternative perspective, which places *relationships* as the central organizing concept, informs fields as diverse as nuclear physics, biology and organisational development.[429] As Margret Wheatley puts it, 'nothing in the universe exists as an isolated or independent entity. Everything takes the form of relationships, be it subatomic particles sharing energy or ecosystems sharing food. In the web of life, nothing living lives alone.'[430] While we undertake a detailed examination of complex social systems in Chapter 7, this next section serves as an entrée with the crucial advantage of illustrating how the political and complexity intertwine—and in so doing, help prepare the reader for what we mean by 'complex, political realities' represented in this book's title.

As such, to a complexity lens, the centrality of relationships accrues special meaning when contemplating peace and capacity development operations. Contrary to how traditional Western social science has informed our views of conflict-affected environments, complexity thinking introduces heterogeneity of actors, interaction, dynamism, and the notion that behaviour *will adapt*.[431] Individuals and communities live within 'a web of relationships' with their enemies.[432] Peter Coleman identifies five paradigms that have been used to understand and address intractable conflicts. 'Systems Theory' is one of these. Its main contribution, to our thinking, is that it shifts our understanding away from static, simplified views of conflict into an appreciation of what Coleman describes as 'the complex, multilevel, dynamic, and cyclical nature of these phenomena'.[433] Whereas Coleman treats each paradigm as rough equivalents—credible in their own ways, we maintain that conflict-affected societies should be understood as *existing within complex social systems*; the other paradigms can serve a support role by providing guidance in the many areas by which they can enrich our acumen.

Similarly instructive, Kenneth Menkhaus argues that we should think of the circumstances of so-called state fragility, into which peace support operations deploy, as 'wicked' rather than 'tame' problems.[434] Of note, these delineations

---

429 John Paul Lederach, *The Moral Imagination: The Art and Soul of Building Peace* (New York: Oxford University Press, 2005), 29.

430 Margaret Wheatley, *Turning to One Another*, (San Francisco: Barrett-Koehler, 2002), 89.

431 Morgan Brigg, *The New Politics of Conflict Resolution: Responding to Difference* (New York: Palgrave MacMillan, 2008), 143–8.

432 John Paul Lederach, *The Moral Imagination: The Art and Soul of Building Peace* (New York: Oxford University Press, 2005), 31.

433 Peter Coleman, "Paradigmatic Framing of Protracted, Intractable Conflict: Toward the Development of a Meta-framework—II" *Peace and Conflict: Journal of Peace Psychology* 10 no. 3 (2004): 226.

434 Kenneth Menkhaus, "Arrangements sécuritaires locaux dans les régions somalies de la Corne de l'Afrique", [Local security arrangements in the Somali regions of the Horn of Africa] *Politique Africaine* no. 11 (2008). For a further explanation of tame versus wicked problems, see Horst Rittel and Melvin Webber, "Dilemmas in General Theory of Planning," *Policy Sciences* 4 (1973): 155–169.

parallel the distinction of 'complex' versus 'complicated', respectively: unlike 'complicated' systems (e.g. wiring in an aircraft) which are ultimately knowable, the interaction between many agents in complex systems, by contrast, results in unpredictable and surprising outcomes.[435] Chief among the characteristics that distinguish wicked from tame problems are that they not only morph continually due to societal interactions, but their solutions are neither true nor false 'because they are judged in a social context in which different stakeholders have different values and goals'.[436] This latter attribute reinforces that social conditions, and the programming activities that strive to improve them, resist singular interpretations. Indeed, the 'god-eye from nowhere' is fallacy.[437] To the contrary, this realm is about the perennially contested, fluid and inter-subjective concepts that flow from the processes of social interactions,[438] as elaborated upon below through an exploration of power, knowledge and legitimacy.

When the above characteristics are amalgamated into an accessible form, the context in which the ongoing production of the political occurs can be understood as follows. First, interactions are the key to what exists. What ultimately emerges is a product of the interdependent exchange between each of myriad levels. A vital dynamic of this interaction is that agents 'adapt to the behaviour of other agents, who in turn adapt'.[439] As a result particular relationships or patterns of behaviour cannot be reduced and quarantined as if they occur in a vacuum or closed system. Second, multiple perspectives will continue to make up those engaged in these relationships. *Inter alia*, this denies the possibility of a single (i.e. Western) viewpoint whilst at once lending itself to a 'de-centred universalism' approach wherein difference is always welcome.[440] 'Success for whom and how so?', in other words, are questions that do not lend themselves to one-dimensional responses. This underscores a critical pragmatic issue: if external actors grant resources to one actor or group but not another, the potential for negative unintended consequences looms large since those left out might consider

---

[435] Diane Hendrick, "Complexity Theory and Conflict Transformation: An Exploration of Potential and Implications," Working Paper 17 (Bradford: Centre for Conflict Resolution, Department of Peace Studies, University of Bradford, 2009), 5.

[436] Kenneth Menkhaus, "Arrangements sécuritaires locaux dans les régions somalies de la Corne de l'Afrique", [Local security arrangements in the Somali regions of the Horn of Africa] *Politique Africaine* no. 11 (2008): 86.

[437] Morgan Brigg, *The New Politics of Conflict Resolution: Responding to Difference* (New York: Palgrave MacMillan, 2008), 147.

[438] See Nicholas Onuf, *World of our Making: Rules and Rule in Social Theory and International Relations* (Columbia: University of South Carolina Press, 1989).

[439] Diane Hendrick, "Complexity Theory and Conflict Transformation: An Exploration of Potential and Implications," Working Paper 17 (Bradford: Centre for Conflict Resolution, Department of Peace Studies, University of Bradford, 2009), 7.

[440] Morgan Brigg, *The New Politics of Conflict Resolution: Responding to Difference* (New York: Palgrave MacMillan, 2008), 163.

international intervention as a threat to the continuance of their identity and livelihood. Third, 'the whole' is what matters; yet it is not simply the sum of the parts but rather exhibits qualities unique to an ever-emerging *synthesis* in the space between chaos and order. The fourth characteristic follows directly from this: unforeseeable consequences are virtually assured in this constantly emerging world. Rigid programming, locked in at long timeframes is thus highly problematic because of its incapacity to adapt to changing circumstances along the way. And while the notion of complex systems will be unpacked in significantly greater depth in chapter 10, the above synopsis helps bring its characteristics and importance into focus.

The international community however continues to plan, implement and evaluate peace operations as though they were about tame problems—somehow afforded with well-defined stopping points, solutions that could be 'objectively' arrived at and evaluated, and existing in stable and thus predictable environments.[441]

Agency and Change within the Political Space

Similarly lost on the mainstream vision is how the political affects the interactions which are at the heart of our complex social systems and, as such, agency and change. To our way of thinking, however, these are the reasons the political deserves our full attention because they correspond to the key ingredients underpinning conflict transformations. That is, if we take as plausible the above claims that the social world is constantly adapting as the result of interactions among myriad agents under the influence of innumerable factors, then questions concerning *how* certain adaptations take root when others do not should be posed in order to become better equipped to facilitate socially generative transformations. Such 'facilitation' may indeed turn out to mean staying out of a space altogether rather than giving in to the tendency to bulldoze ahead in what may invite highly inefficient and even harmful misuses of donor resources. Continuing the aim for uncomplicated guidance that is therefore well suited for program managers in the field, the following examines how the political affects the contours of what may be possible (and advisable) in terms of agency and change.

Throughout human history value systems have enabled the production and maintenance of social orders, evolving in lock step. An examination of power is thus a useful point of departure for understanding the political since, in general terms, power is about how outcomes are produced and how actors are either

441 Kenneth Menkhaus, "Arrangements sécuritaires locaux dans les régions somalies de la Corne de l'Afrique", [Local security arrangements in the Somali regions of the Horn of Africa] *Politique Africaine* no. 11 (2008): 86.

constrained or enabled.[442] Although power assumes many forms, two have special import to the present discussion: how power regulates and controls social life; and how it affects actors' capacity to control their fates.[443]

Michel Foucault's notion 'regimes of truth' helps us to appreciate how the political is produced and maintained.[444] It aids our understanding in at least three ways. First, it highlights the power-knowledge nexus wherein each is reliant on the other for its existence. This means, *inter alia*, peace operations managers should pay attention to the sources of power (e.g. material or institutional) in addition to prevailing forms of legitimacy[445] in order to become a positive force in the war-to-peace-to-development transformations. Second, the political can be likened to regimes of truth since the socio-cultural value systems that comprise the political constitute bodies of knowledge that have come about from a mutually-constitutive relationship with power. How each group interprets mission activities, as well as other developments more generally, will therefore come through their own political lens in the manner conceptualised for regimes of truth. At minimum, this claim underscores the central influence that political forces have on peace and development transformations. Following from this second point, agency can be seen as enabled or constrained by the elements which constitute each 'political regime of truth'.

Problems arise in the field when exogenous actors fail to appreciate first, the existence of different regimes of truth, and second, how integral such regimes are to the capacity and substance of change processes. To be sure, peace and capacity development endeavours unavoidably operate in the spaces between various regimes of truth. Yet, historically this has been a site of enormous tension because a liberal state self-image has instead been substituted. The prospect of

---

442 Michael Barnett and Raymond Duvall, "Power in Global Governance" in *Power in Global Governance* ed. Michael Barnett and Raymond Duvall (Cambridge: Cambridge University Press, 2005), 3.

443 See Michael Barnett and Raymond Duvall, "Power in Global Governance" in *Power in Global Governance* ed. Michael Barnett and Raymond Duvall (Cambridge: Cambridge University Press, 2005), 2–3.

444 Conveyed in general terms, "'Truth' is linked in a circular relation with systems of power which produce and sustain it, and to effects of power which it induces and which extend it." Michel Foucault, *Power/Knowledge: Selected Writing and Other Writings 1972–1977*, ed. Colin Gordon (New York: Pantheon Books, 1980), 133.

445 Although a popular way to conceptualise legitimacy is in terms of its logics (i.e. 'legal-rational', 'traditional', 'charismatic', 'democratic' and 'international'); Louise Anten, *Strengthening Governance in Post-Conflict Fragile States*, Issues Paper (The Hague: Netherlands Institute of International Relations, 2009), 48–49. This view is insufficient in two respects. First, because it represents legitimacy as a static end form, it fails to consider the power-knowledge processes of *how* something has come to be considered legitimate in the first place. Second, it similarly neglects the role of agency in how legitimacy is produced; whereas what actors do and say is pivotal to what ultimately becomes perceived as legitimate.

engendering resistance therefore continues to looms large from such mismatches unless a change in our thinking emerges. As Eric Scheye observes: 'If a significant percentage of the citizenry perceives that their formal state provided justice and security system is foreign, incomprehensible, and contrary to their beliefs, cultural values, and expectations, there is little likelihood that that system can be deemed legitimate, accessible or effective.'[446] Bruce Baker and Eric Scheye's work on the justice and security sector in post-colonial environments not only reinforces the necessity of the complex system's interactions focus by drawing attention to the 'parallel authorities and regimes' that pervade the vast majority of places where peace operations tread,[447] but it also underscores the existence of multiple regimes of truth. Coming out of this section's discussions, we can therefore see the etchings of a framework in which the space for peace operations is constantly adapting based on a complex interdependence of interactions, all of which are influenced by the ideas bound up in the political.

Concluding Thoughts

The underlying argument of this chapter has been that the international community must shift from its overwhelming tendency of concentrating on technical solutions and instead begin any engagement with a political consciousness. As such, external attempts to promote peace and development will only succeed when local notions of order are at least taken seriously and accommodated, if not accepted.[448] Importantly, the discussion also developed a view of the milieu in which the political exists. The hope is that the current reductionist thinking eventually gives way to a complex social systems thinking, which reflects reality and thereby leads to conceptual tools with the capacity to work in practice instead of merely on paper. The discussion also pointed out how the political forms the space from which the capacity to get things done (agency) derives.

Admittedly, appreciating other socio-cultural value systems takes time. Understanding will come in stages similar to how an onion is peeled back in layers. An explicit, reflexive awareness of the incompleteness of our understanding is therefore vital so that decisions are taken with a large degree of caution (and humility) while at the same time demanding that we think through the possible ramifications. A big part of the challenge for the international community is to

---

446 Eric Scheye, "The Statebuilding Misconception in the Fragile and Post-conflict State," *Journal of International Peacekeeping* 14 no. 3 (2010): 270.

447 Bruce Baker and Eric Scheye, "Access to Justice in a Post-conflict State: Donor-supported Multidimensional Peacekeeping in Southern Sudan," *International Peacekeeping* 16, no. 2 (2009): 173.

448 Abby McLeod, "Police Reform in Papua New Guinea" in *Security and Development in the Pacific Islands: Social Resilience in Emerging States*, ed. M. Anne Brown (Boulder, CO: Lynne Rienner, 2007), 73.

accept that what eventuates may not approximate the Western liberal democratic model.[449]

Our plea for this approach however stands in stark contrast to those who would argue that the international community should steer clear of these admittedly murky waters for risk of exacerbating circumstances. To this view, 'outsiders' could never get close to properly apprehending the politics of local ordering, and therefore incomplete understandings would invariably result in more harm than good. To be sure, assistance done badly can be far worse than none at all,[450] with the example of Somaliland suggesting societies can in fact be better off without (current modalities of) international 'assistance'.[451] More to the point, countless examples illustrate how a limited knowledge of local politics can lead to invidious outcomes. Some would maintain the most valuable contribution may be simply to initiate conversations under a peacekeepers' security umbrella between local enemies who have previously been unable or unwilling to work together.[452]

We would counter these thoughtful positions, which are the reflections on extensive experience in the field, by pointing out that it is a false dichotomy to suggest that we can *either* ignore politics altogether *or* flounder while grappling with them. While concurring with a cautious mentality and preference for 'creating the space' for local solutions to evolve, we would point out that interventions to date have nearly always eschewed the political rather than having botched what could be considered erudite approaches. As such, efforts to engage the political with a high degree of acumen, such as we are only now beginning to accumulate in other areas has not been given a chance. The case of the Luo communities in Kenya, whereby external actors successfully navigated the local political on the way to improving the lot of some of the most disadvantaged women in that society proves heartening in this regard.[453] Progress in Bougainville offers another ray of hope.[454] And the case of the Marshall Islands, which we dedicate significant

---

[449] Oliver Richmond, "Emancipatory Forms of Human Security and Liberal Peacebuilding," *International Journal* 62 no. 3 (2007) 460.

[450] M. Anne Brown, "Security and Development: Conflict and Resilience in the Pacific Islands Region" in *Security and Development in the Pacific Islands: Social Resilience in Emerging States*, ed. M. Anne Brown (Boulder, CO: Lynne Rienner, 2007).

[451] Louise Wiuff-Moe, *Negotiating Political Legitimacy: the Case of State Formation in Post-conflict Somaliland*, Issues Paper (Canberra: Centre for International Governance and Justice, ANU, 2009).

[452] John Braithwaite, Hilary Charlesworth, Peter Reddy and Leah Dunn, *Reconciliation and Architectures of Commitment Sequencing Peace in Bougainville* (Canberra: ANU Press, 2010), 1.

[453] Tanja Chopra, "Promoting Women's Rights by Indigenous Means: An Innovative Project in Kenya," *The World Bank Briefing Note* 1 no. 2 (2007).

[454] Volker Boege, "Bougainville and the Discovery of Slowness: an Unhurried Approach to State-Building in the Pacific," *The Australian Centre for Peace and Conflict Studies Occasional Papers Series* 3 (2006).

space to in the final part of the book, will illuminate how eliciting views from the broadest spectrum of stakeholders practicable can be useful in helping to redress this awareness gap.

Finding the heartbeat means learning about the role of the state, cultural information related to taboo, power structures, and sources of legitimacy—all of which are integral to appreciating the political realities that constitute a society. As pointed out above, regimes of truth and the corresponding notions of the political are fluid and thus will change over time, so we should aim to play a positive role in the direction the socio-cultural ideas and values evolve. Importantly, this is not the same as suggesting that heavy footprints are desirable. On the contrary, we share with a growing number of practitioners and academics the belief that the international community's underlying role should be about creating the space in which the political can evolve in productive ways. What should be beyond doubt is that 'business as usual' promises more of the same failings to date. Therefore, to deliberately refuse to deal with what is arguably the most important variable seems a path fraught with far more peril than the alternatives.

PART THREE

PUSHING BACK ON CONVENTIONAL MONITORING AND EVALUATION

CHAPTER SIX

AN UNCONVENTIONAL APPROACH TO MONITORING AND EVALUATION

Together, chapters 3–5 conducted an in-depth critical analysis of the major conceptual assumptions underpinning international policing. The thinking constitutes the philosophical heartland of our critique. The under-acknowledged state centrism, failure to engage the 'political', and existence of complex rather than static systems are core facets of the conventional wisdom that were unpacked and then re-packed in alternative notions and directions. The examinations made the case that the very foundations of the conventional wisdom are in need of being recast.

In a similar break with mainstream imaginations, the ensuing three chapters are dedicated to challenging the conventional M&E that feeds in and out of conventional mission design, programming and implementation. Reiterating a key point made in the **Introduction**: the nexus between M&E and conventional wisdom is integral because of how underlying views about the field itself inform M&E (its design and interpretation) and vice versa, with the conclusions of M&E informing mission programming and the interpretation of the mission environment itself. In order to break this mutually reinforcing cycle of misinterpretation, M&E must begin to convey environments and dynamics as they are—rather than as the contemporary international policing mindsets would have them construed. Each with their own foci, the subsequent chapters direct their investigations toward issues concerning M&E in order to come out the other side equipped to effect learning and programming based on alternative assumptions.

The purpose of this chapter is to provide an entrée into the areas whereby our notions about the nature of peace operations depart from how conventional mindsets approach M&E. It deliberately retraces ground made familiar in previous chapters due to the need to have these elements fresh in our minds for the ensuing interrogations. More specifically, it provides a synopsis contrasting the main points of how conventional M&E views peace and development operations versus how we would argue these same facets can and should be understood and approached. Conventional M&E (CM&E), despite providing some obvious benefits to peace and development operations—at the very least by drawing attention to the need to examine and learn from our environments—has been the subject of many and varied criticisms concerning both its practice and theory. This chapter summarises these critiques thus setting a platform from which innovative approaches can spring, in addition to introducing the framework methodology that comprises the authors' contribution to collaborative policing M&E. This conceptual backdrop also paves the way for a detailed interrogation of complex systems theory in Chapter 8, knowledge which is indispensable when grappling with the inherent societal complexities in which peace and development programs operate.

Critiquing Conventional M&E

To the conventional mindset, contemporary evaluations of official development assistance are intended principally for diagnostic and accountability purposes. The underlying belief is that aid effectiveness will improve when the particular agents and technical processes comprising its delivery are scrutinised periodically by external experts.[455] For our purposes, it is important to note that today's mainstream approaches to M&E comprise particular commitments that have developed over decades. Unsurprisingly then these beliefs about 'legitimate' M&E have become deeply entrenched in the evaluation industry, making it necessary to explain fundamentally different approaches from the outset.

Chief among these commitments are the beliefs that M&E should be conducted by specialists in order to generate and articulate the most insightful assessments; that M&E specialists should be independent of the processes and persons being evaluated to preclude the corruption of data and thus findings; that legitimate data stems from state-based and quantitative sources rather than informal or qualitative forms; and that the purpose of M&E is foremost accountability, with learning being another stated use.[456] In so doing, this approach looks back in time nearly always in an attempt to isolate cause and effect pertaining to one or a few programs.

Notwithstanding the obvious benefits, Conventional M&E (CM&E) approaches toward capacity building environments and methods of data collation have been

---

455 Joshua G. Smith, Victoria K. Holt, and William J. Durch, *Enhancing United Nations Capacity for Post-Conflict Policing and Rule of Law*, Report from The Project on Rule of Law in Post-Conflict Settings (Washington DC: The Henry L. Stimson Center, 2007), 43–44.

456 David Watson, *Monitoring and Evaluation of Capacity and Capacity Development* (Maastricht, the Netherlands: European Centre for Development Policy Management, 2006), 17.

heavily criticised in recent years. The following critique is based on the Results Based Management (RBM) model because its features are indicative of most conventional models based on 'objective' or 'logical frameworks' and therefore any criticisms apply to varying degrees. Indeed, donors are typically aware of these criticisms and many are working to address the accompanying problems. It is important, however, to outline them at this juncture because they inform the alternative methodology framework that we have devised.

Specific problem diagnosis:[457] A harsh criticism of RBM and similar approaches is the heavy reliance on specific problem diagnosis in an environment notoriously difficult to accurately assess. The multitude of complex contributing disabling factors in a capacity building environment make simple problem-solution strategies extremely difficult and to attempt to address capacity issues in this manner is to achieve only partial solutions which may in fact undermine capacity on the whole. Given the narrow focus of RBM and the tunnel vision it can create, the model is largely incapable of detecting such unintended consequences.

Short-term goal orientation: CM&E has a tendency to create a detrimental focus on short-term goals.[458] In the interests of demonstrating success resources are diverted toward areas of quick realisation with quantifiable outcomes. This can be problematic for long-term sustainability if it results in a reduced focus on 'soft' less tangible aspects of capacity building as these tend to be the enabling factors. Artificial timeframes constructed according to reporting periods can also motivate short-term goal orientation. The consequence is too often the sidelining of 'in country' partner personnel in the interests of meeting a predetermined timeline—again inherently undermining opportunities to build capacity.

Utilising hard indicators: The focus on hard indicators, through quantitative measures encourages prioritising things that can be counted such as equipment delivery, number of people trained, technical skills and alike. Apart from distorting program delivery and inefficient allocation of resources, this can create problems in demonstrating change in a data poor environment (as is the case for the majority of post-conflict or unstable and 'fragile' states) as baseline indicators are difficult to ascertain and notoriously unreliable.

A preoccupation with 'hard' indicators and micro aspects of local partner organisations (rather than the whole) are related to the need for demonstrable short-term success. Breaking the organisation into discrete units or programs artificially isolates the funded activities from the wider organisation and society. This focus leads to the consequent failure to detect and absorb disabling aspects and

---

457 David Watson, *Monitoring and Evaluation of Capacity and Capacity Development* (Maastricht, the Netherlands: European Centre for Development Policy Management, 2006), 16.

458 Ylber Bajraktari, Arthur Boutellis, Fatema Gunja, Daniel Harris, James Kapsis, Eva Kaye and Jane Rhee, *The PRIME System: Measuring the Success of Post-Conflict Police Reform* (Princeton: Princeton University, 2006).

actors from outside the activities subject to M&E. Simply put, this model will only see what it is looking for. There is particularly strong evidence of this in relation to gender sensitive reforms where there has been a detrimental effect created by the model's inability to capture broader social dynamics and impacts.

Disconnect with Practice: Another common problem with CM&E generally is the creation of what Atkinson and Coffey term 'documentary realities', whereby planning and reporting procedures connect the dots in the paper trail rather than with their corresponding context.[459] Similarly, when reporting procedures and performance information collation is centred on jargon, links are created with current bureaucratic orthodoxies rather than practical efforts. This compromises opportunities to evaluate activities and can create a 'cultural' barrier between donors and locals with potentially divisive consequences. Externally imposed performance measurements can be perceived as threatening—and thereby become an impetus for defensive or passive behaviour. Faith in the M&E system is undermined if the value of reporting and measuring information is not understood. When this is the case there is considerable scope for inaccuracies and failure to report.

Accountability stops at outputs: Related to the disconnect with practice, there is a disconnect with consequences of actions on the ground. In a model preoccupied with accountability the emphasis of reporting tends to focus on inputs and outputs (or 'activities level'), with only rhetorical connection with the broader impact. This is only true in some instances however; it is not uncommon for the accountability aspects of M&E to explicitly stop at outputs. This problem stems from the difficulties of proving attribution. It is considered unreasonable to hold donor personnel accountable to the impact or even outcome level as there are too many variables in an open system to prove causation. Whilst this is a perfectly understandable concern, the emphasis on outputs tends to distort behaviour and create a limited view of the donor's responsibilities to account for the broader impacts of an operation's intervention.

Local institutional knowledge: There is a problem with CM&E approaches in their reliance on external evaluation experts. The availability of external assessors can cause considerable problems in the interpretation of M&E, creating a disjointed and ad hoc evaluation process.[460] External evaluation can also have a detrimental impact on institutional knowledge because M&E capacity and the associated knowledge is not transferred to local people.

Reduced local ownership: One of the strongest and most frequent criticisms of RBM and conventional approaches is that they are a product of the intervention-

---

459 Atkinson, P. and Coffey, A., 'Analysing documentary realities', in D. Silverman (Ed.), *Qualitative research* (London: Sage: 45–62).

460 David Watson, *Monitoring and Evaluation of Capacity and Capacity Development* (Maastricht, the Netherlands: European Centre for Development Policy Management, 2006), 17.

ist model which relies on external problem diagnosis.[461] In this process the partner organisation is compared with an 'ideal' institutional model and the gaps and shortfalls of the partner organisation are identified. The M&E process is derived from this analysis as steps towards improving such shortfalls are prescribed and translated into indicators and measurement of success. The undermining of local ownership is therefore inherent in the M&E planning stages—as local people lack comprehensive input from the outset.[462] This compromises relevance of the M&E framework, local motivations, and opportunities for mutual learning. In a worst case scenario it can be perceived and used as a punitive measure linked to future funding. Such conditions make it difficult to harness local energy. So important is this feature that the matter of its handling is taken up again below in an area which extends well beyond RBM.

Perverse Consequences: A corollary of the above characteristics relates to one of the lurking problems associated with these models, which can be summed up by the adage that "*what gets measured, gets done*". Instead of these models being utilised as a reporting mechanism (which they were arguably only ever intended to do) they too often serve a prescriptive function. The common upshot is the perverse consequences that come when behaviour is altered—in often unhelpful ways—to accommodate the pressures of successfully achieving RBM objectives.

To wrap up this section focusing on RBM, it is important to reiterate that the above criticisms are presented here to inform the proposed methodology for M&E, not necessarily to agitate for the abandonment of RBM and similar models altogether. In fact, the framework we put forward works in the current international context *because* it has the capacity to hook into these traditional models, and in so doing can function compatibly with the currently ubiquitous RBM frameworks. Expressed differently, RBM or CM&E frameworks should be used for what they are good at: namely, to be treated as a convenient and efficient way of presenting and managing data for reporting purposes to illustrate the actions and impacts on the ground—not to dictate them.

Change Theories and Realising Local Ownership

A critique of the mainstream M&E approaches is not sufficiently complete however until the interrogation is broadened from a focus on the characteristics and consequences of RBM. Sitting beneath the thinking that goes into the design and prosecution of RBM reporting is the more rudimentary thinking about what needs to be accomplished from an intervention. This is the realm of 'change

---

461 David Watson, *Monitoring and Evaluation of Capacity and Capacity Development* (Maastricht, the Netherlands: European Centre for Development Policy Management, 2006), 16.

462 Aoi Chiyuki, Cedric de Coning, and Ramesh Thakur, eds., *Unintended Consequences of Peacekeeping Operations* (Tokyo: United Nations University Press, 2007).

theories', and as aforementioned, this realm poses grave implications for local ownership.

In general terms, a 'theory of change is a set of beliefs about how change happens'.[463] From the beginning of the international community's foray into other state territories, theories about how the situation should change (read, improve) have underpinned peace support operations. Such 'theories', also referred to as 'programme logic' or 'intervention logic',[464] do not have to be formal in a codified sense of the term, nor do they need to adhere to a particular ideological project (for example, part of the liberal statebuilding project). They can instead be general, succinct, and commonsensical notions of how to transform circumstances. They can be combined and used in concert,[465] or broken down further into the various categories of change, including changes in: knowledge, behaviour, outlook (e.g. optimistic mindset from suspicious to united), relationships, status (e.g. rebel leader to parliamentarian), and circumstance (e.g. politically marginalised to able to vote).[466]

The below example comprises articulations of 'Theories of change for the Community Peace Councils':[467]

> **Theory #1**: By establishing a new community-level mechanism for handling a range of dispute types, we will contribute to keeping the peace and avoiding incidents that have the potential for escalating into serious violence.
>
> **Theory #2**: By creating inclusive structures for community problem solving, we can improve communication, respect, and productive interactions among subgroups in the community, and improve the access of disenfranchised groups to decision making.
>
> **Theory #3**: By creating a new leadership group infused with democratic concepts and provided with critical skills, we can foster more effective and responsive leadership.

---

463 Cheyanne Church and Mark M. Rogers, 'Understanding Change', in *Designing for Results*, (Washington D.C.: Search for Common Ground, 2006), http://www.sfcg.org/Documents/dmechapter2.pdf, 11.

464 Organisation for Economic Cooperation and Development (a), *INCAF Task Team on Peacebuilding, Statebuilding, Security—Room Document 5: Draft Justice and Security Monitoring and Evaluation Toolkit*, (Paris, France: OECD, 2009), 8.

465 Cheyanne Church and Mark M. Rogers, 'Understanding Change', in *Designing for Results*, (Washington D.C.: Search for Common Ground, 2006), http://www.sfcg.org/Documents/dmechapter2.pdf, 17.

466 Cheyanne Church and Mark M. Rogers, 'Understanding Change', in *Designing for Results*, (Washington D.C.: Search for Common Ground, 2006), http://www.sfcg.org/Documents/dmechapter2.pdf, 19.

467 Organisation for Economic Cooperation and Development (b), *Guidance on Evaluating Conflict Prevention and Peacebuilding Activities*, (Paris: France: OECD, 2008) http://www.oecd.org/secure/pdfDocument/0,2834,en_21571361_34047972_39774574_1_1_1_1,00.pdf, 79.

There are myriad theories in use today—whether or not their presence has been made explicit—providing the logic and direction for all that the international community undertake. We have included a substantial survey of these theories in Appendix 1 due to its instructional value in appreciating why particular interventions have taken the foci they have to date. At the very least, this compendium—which reflects a variety of sub-fields, particularly the peacebuilding and security sector reform realms—will make clear many of the areas in which peace and capacity development operations can focus their energies.

The presence of some form of change theory is however as unavoidable as it is powerful. That is, a view about what may be needed to improve (change) a situation is inescapably a part of the planning of what goes into such endeavours, whether such theories are explicitly and consciously recognised or not. The risk for overall failure is clear should the underlying change theory with its accompanying programme design fail to provide a suitable means for change.[468] In terms of extant practices, the initial problem is that many times activities may be disjointed and lack an explicit theory about how such activities are meant to bring about change. As OECD[469] put it: 'Theories of change are seldom made explicit during the planning or implementation stages of a project, and it often falls to evaluators to identify and express these by interrogating programme documents and staff and then testing the programme logic against the realities of the local context.'

Yet by examining and understanding the assumptions behind selected change theories means that not only can detailed plans be developed but also that indicators to measure progress become more obvious[470] and the program design itself can be assessed.[471] Hence, the link to M&E—and therefore a critique of the CM&E which flows out of its underlying change theory—is powerful: because change theories inform what is to be undertaken and ultimately achieved, they therefore inform what should be measured in order to determine if progress towards the stated goals has been met. In other words, the program planning that is the focus of M&E derives directly from whatever theory of change underpins it.

---

468 Organisation for Economic Cooperation and Development (a), *INCAF Task Team on Peacebuilding, Statebuilding, Security—Room Document 5: Draft Justice and Security Monitoring and Evaluation Toolkit*, (Paris, France: OECD, 2009), 8.

469 Organisation for Economic Cooperation and Development (a), *INCAF Task Team on Peacebuilding, Statebuilding, Security—Room Document 5: Draft Justice and Security Monitoring and Evaluation Toolkit*, (Paris, France: OECD, 2009), 8.

470 Cheyanne Church and Mark M. Rogers, 'Understanding Change', in *Designing for Results*, (Washington D.C.: Search for Common Ground, 2006), http://www.sfcg.org/Documents/dmechapter2.pdf, 13.

471 Simon Rynn and Dustin Hiscock, *Evaluating for Security and Justice*, (London, UK: Saferworld, 2009) http://www.saferworld.org.uk/downloads/pubdocs/Evaluating%20for%20security%20and%20justice.pdf, 28.

The greater risk, foregrounded previously, is that the determination of change theory(s) is undertaken with little or no input from local stakeholders.[472] The main problem is that, to date, the overwhelming tendency has been to have that process dominated by external actors and experts with only occasional input coming from the breadth of local stakeholders. This practice is ill-advised by how it undermines local ownership and demand-driven solutions, as discussed above in our conceptual investigations. The ramifications of this mistake cannot be overstated since the impact touches on virtually every aspect of a mission's progress. The conventional approach not only sanctions a de facto external problem analysis but in turn hollows out local input regarding the downstream decisions about solutions and, similarly important, their prioritisation. In order to deliver on the rhetorical promise of meaningful local ownership, the upshot is the need for the content to be developed principally by local actors.

'Home Grown' Change

Given the variety of underlying logic for peace and capacity development operations (set out in the Appendix), one might be forgiven for being inclined to continue the mainstream approach of focusing our energies and intellect on which change theory is best suited to each circumstance. We would agree that many of them have considerable merit and may be generally suited to particular contexts across the globe. That is not what matters, however. What matters is that while none of these predetermined theories is wrong, per se, insofar as they reflect considered logic about how to make societal improvements, the process of implanting a model developed elsewhere is the wrong *approach*. To the contrary, whatever change theory is to underpin a peace operation should be determined by negotiations between local and (to be realistic) external stakeholders if it is to have any lasting and positive impact on a society's efforts to change its circumstances for the better. It is, in other words, to be 'home-grown' as opposed to the common approach of being pre-determined by external experts with little input from the ground. No matter how clever and experienced they may be, outsiders cannot proxy on these vital decisions. Not only is local ownership best realised by enabling local actors to identify and pursue those areas which are most important to them, but this approach guarantees context-relevance devoid of the oftentimes irrelevant and excessive elements that mark pre-packaged theories.

In practical terms, the process entailed involves having the mission staff first put forward their *initial* assumptions concerning change when needing to

---

472 See Cheyanne Church and Mark M. Rogers, 'Understanding Change', in *Designing for Results*, (Washington D.C.: Search for Common Ground, 2006), http://www.sfcg.org/Documents/dmechapter2.pdf, 13, whereby they conclude that 'Ultimately, the definition '*Who defines what success is?*' of success is the responsibility of the people in conflict'.

estimate resources required before the intervention commences. Importantly, making change theories explicit at the outset allows all of the stakeholders to discuss and agree upon the advantages of one over others.[473] This means considered thought about why certain theories will be more effective than others should be prompted.[474] However, the point is that these early outlines are understood to be rough guides that are meant to be developed when in theatre rather than kept off the discussion table as if somehow an external appraisal would know better.[475] The real work begins when the myriad of local stakeholders can begin to be accessed for their viewpoints. By asking 'what is happening currently?' and accordingly 'what should change?' practitioners will begin to learn what change processes are felt necessary and appropriate by those whom matter most to sustainable peace. After having identified and prioritised what is wanted, the aim is to describe the path forward for change. What activities might help achieve identified areas of change? This planning and mission design phase involves determining what needs to change in the environment in a broad sense and how such change can be achieved in more specific terms. The upshot, for our purposes, is that whatever specific change theory emerges from this locally-owned, locally-driven process, it has the best opportunity to resonate where it matters most—among those responsible to support and sustain its activities and direction. Change theories will almost certainly end up being entirely specific, *sui generis*, and in so doing create the most effective approach to program activities and priorities—the exact qualities we should want.

Contrasting M&E: Conventional versus Democratising

Spurred by the above critique of mainstream M&E approaches, the need to develop and operationalise an alternative framework becomes clear. Fortunately, the germane emerging research not only highlights how these conventional monitoring and evaluation (M&E) methodologies have faltered, but more usefully suggests that alternative methodologies can achieve greatly expanded

473 See Cheyanne Church and Mark M. Rogers, 'Understanding Change', in *Designing for Results*, (Washington D.C.: Search for Common Ground, 2006), http://www.sfcg.org/Documents/dmechapter2.pdf, 16, whereby they talk about an assumption of theory selection being the strategic advantage of the chosen theory over other theories for the context.

474 Cheyanne Church and Mark M. Rogers, 'Understanding Change', in *Designing for Results*, (Washington D.C.: Search for Common Ground, 2006), http://www.sfcg.org/Documents/dmechapter2.pdf, 17.

475 Serge Loode aptly refers to this mindset as the "privilege of universal knowledge over local knowledge" ("Peacebuilding in Complex Social Systems", *Journal of Peace, Conflict & Development*, 18, 2011), 69.

purposes not previously envisaged by traditional notions of M&E.[476] Specifically, in addition to genuinely delivering on the crucial diagnostic and accountability aims, approaches such as those outlined in this document can be powerful tools through which to: help resolve the conflicts themselves; deliver on the promise of local ownership; and build local capacity—all of which feature in the international community's more recent commitments to enhance aid effectiveness. What is more, the social dynamics set in motion by implementing a 'Democratising M&E' framework—go beyond cultivating the conditions needed for sustainable peace and development towards instilling democratic beliefs and behaviours because of how the methods encourage direct participation across the spectrum of society.

In keeping with a democratising ethos intended to disperse power across society, the role of the evaluator is delimited to facilitating data collation rather than extending to the determination of findings. In the context of M&E, *democratisation* entails expanding the circles of those able to participate meaningfully, thus helping to instil a core pillar of democracy which applies across time and culture. As such, the 'experts' comprise the intended aid beneficiaries as well as the practitioners involved in its implementation, while traditional M&E experts act as facilitators for the key processes such as indicator selection, data capture, and report development. This broadening of participation necessarily brings with it 'grounded' accountability and transparency, and engenders local ownership and capacity building—thereby delivering on many of the international community's stated aims for security and development cooperation. Not only does the approach retain the rich diversity of perspective which does indeed exist in any society, the processes entailing wide collaboration are used to feed into program adaptation and resource identification—thereby serving the dual purpose of contributing to a snapshot evaluation while more importantly helping a society towards sustainable peace and development. The upshot is that the ideas that populate an evaluation now come from those for whom the aid was intended. This shift in the role of external actors from 'determiner' to facilitator mirrors the trend in the delivery of assistance itself.

The Democratising M&E mindset is concerned with the following questions:

- Did M&E processes help bring people together by sharing their challenges and mobilising their resources rather than treating them as objects to assess or sources of data?

---

476 Eirin Mobekk, "Identifying Lessons in United Nations International Policing Missions," *Policy Paper* 9 (Geneva: Geneva Centre for the Democratic Control of Armed Forces (DCAF), 2005), 3; Annika S. Hansen, "From Congo to Kosovo: Civilian Police in Peace Operations," *Adelphi Papers* 41, no. 343 (2002): 31.

- Did it help build the capacity of local actors in order to give them the tools and relationships to craft sustainable peace and development pathways?
- Did it give voice to previously marginalised/powerless segments of society (*e.g.* women)?
- Did it reflect the diversity of viewpoints on the ground rather than presenting a falsely narrow, state-centric view of the situation?
- Did it focus on what matters—the beliefs and behaviours that result from the myriad forces combining in the complex social system—instead of recounting the completion of isolated outputs?
- Did it produce a rich picture of the cause and effect dynamics from triangulated perceptions rather than superficial accounts or statistics of trends?
- Were evaluation findings accessible to the widest possible audience or conversely were they produced in complicated formats to be reviewed (read) by only a few?

The debate comprising the distinctions between conventional and democratising M&E can be summarised in the format below (Figure 4). Its intent is to assist the change in mindset required for those accustomed to conducting M&E based on conventional assumptions.

Issue/area	Conventional M&E	Democratising M&E
Diagnosis of development environment and program effect	Largely outputs focus that tells little about crucial beliefs/behaviour trends with quantitative preference from frequently unreliable data sources	An outcomes focus which reflects the all-important synthesis of forces that make up each situation. Qualitative stakeholder input is recognised as paramount both to an accurate picture and democratisation processes
Accountability	Punitive—an 'us versus them' approach is deemed to offer effective accountability, when in fact hidden resistances are often built, creating new forms of conflict	Collaborative/restorative ethos removes antagonisms while broad awareness means actors become de facto accountable to a degree previously unknown when findings were disseminated narrowly among offending parties & donors

Transparency	Limited mainly to donor and partner country elites, thereby failing to provide wide spread transparency	Strives to develop transparency among an ever-expanding set of stakeholders, on the ground, so that each can hold the others to account; recognises that straightforward and uncomplicated reporting formats are the best way to ensure widest consumption
Conflict resolution	Not a consideration	Explicit aim, with methodologies designed specifically to establish stakeholder forum for ongoing dialogue and development of solutions
Local ownership	Embraced in rhetoric, yet in actuality external experts choose not only processes but determine focus, priorities, indicators, and interpret data, thereby precluding local input and the ownership that would accrue and in turn creating resentment and resistance	Focus is on local voices, with them populating the content, with external experts to facilitate the capture and collation of local voices resulting in the most local ownership possible short of no outside involvement
Local capacity building	External experts run evaluation and, accordingly, little local capacity is built	The thinking and doing of monitoring and evaluations comes from local actors and program practitioners, guaranteeing local capacity is built in these vital areas
Contribution to program planning and adaptation	Requires separate step to marry diagnostic findings to program design, insisting a hand over stage from one set of staff to another, thus opening likelihood of knowledge and intent being lost in the process	Unlike the bolt-on traditional model, M&E is part and parcel of program (embedded) planning, thereby ensuring M&E contributes directly and robustly to planning and adaptation

View of reality	Linear development progress assumed, intervention logic nearly always Western centric, cause and effect dynamics conceived in isolation, state-centric both in terms of who provides and should provide public services	Embraces ongoing variances of multiple perspectives and interpretations while also accepting that war-to-peace & development transitions are seldom linear; also, appreciates non-state and hybrid sources often provide services
Perceived legitimacy of data sources	Primarily state-based and quantitative, often traditional state statistics (e.g. crime reporting) or broad surveys which direct feedback while avoiding in-depth understanding of cause and effect	Qualitative elicitation of stakeholder viewpoints is the key. Interviews, focus groups and workshops understood as most practical ways to glean accurate picture of environment. Quantitative acceptable but only if adjudged accurate. State sources are vital part but broad elements of society are essential.

Figure 4: Contrast Table

Developing an Alternative Framework Methodology

Equipped with the above perspective, one is now in a position to develop and pursue a different kind of M&E. Below is an outline of a concrete and readily implemented framework that we have developed to fill the gap left by the comprehensive critiques of mainstream. While the framework's detail is described in Appendix 2, requiring more space than a mere outline to explain the nuance that indeed sets it apart, two main aspects are of particular importance to highlight broadly: it is process focused, allowing stakeholders to make context specific and truly-owned decisions, and the nature of the processes themselves enshrine the vast array of stakeholder viewpoints in a way that means it is their ideas that drive the missions, rather than as is today's practice of having decisions made by external actors, with only lip service paid to those on whom sustainable success actually depends.

An Alternative Framework Methodology—Stages Summary

Mission Context

Involves identifying and understanding the context into which missions deploy, including its own capacity and mandate.

Stakeholders

Involves the identification of key stakeholders across the broadest possible spectrum of society, coupled with the determination of how these stakeholders can best interact.

Situation Analysis

Involves determining benchmarks—what is happening *now*, and why? This may also include gleaning stakeholders' aims through their 'Visions of Success".

Planning

Change-processes are planned so as to move from benchmarks generated in the Situation Analysis down the agreed upon paths.

Monitoring Loops

An ongoing monitoring process is designed for collating data on the deliverance of work plans set out in the Planning stage, and monitoring change.

Community Communications

Strategies are devised to keep the broadest circle of stakeholders informed. This includes those stakeholders not already involved (such as the broader community).

Unintended Consequences

This stage looks specifically for information not previously targeted, or unplanned/ unintended effects.

Evaluation Reporting

Information is adapted to feed into various donor and performance management reporting systems.

After Action Review

Lessons learned and ways to adapt going forward are explored through joint reviews and/or feedback.

The above framework outline merely hints at an approach that has significant capacity to overcome the main points of critique of extant mainstream practices enumerated in this chapter. Its complete form, which provides sufficient explanation for practitioners in the field to employ new and contrasting techniques, is contained in the Appendix. As indicated at the outset, this book extends beyond critique to include offering viable alternatives based upon an awareness of the deficits and pitfalls of CM&E. The subsequent chapter moves from an overall critique to an in-depth analysis of one of the core areas which fuels the need to make dramatic changes to conventional wisdom: complex social systems. It thoroughly unpacks the notion of complexity that constitutes the environments in which missions operate, and thus proves crucial to learning how better to design and implement missions.

CHAPTER SEVEN

APPLYING SYSTEMS THINKING TO M&E: LEARNING IN SPITE OF 'UNCERTAINTY'

Having made plain many points of departure distinguishing conventional M&E from our preferences for collaborative, democratising approaches, the critical examination turns to an emerging area of thought that is as integral to learning about the impact of peace and capacity development operations as it may be a challenge to apprehend: how the notions of systems thinking and complexity theory should inform M&E. To elaborate: M&E provides the most obvious vehicle for learning both about an environment and the effect particular courses of action may be having upon the various segments of societies within that environment; therefore, when accepting that environments are complex social systems—as we contend—the aim becomes how to use the characteristics of complex systems (broached in Chapter 5) to learn what is indeed happening. Hence, in spite of the warning about the difficulty many may have in coming to grips with the content of this chapter, the basis for its inclusion is quite simple: the international community must begin to view mission environments through a lens that reflects their true complexity; otherwise we resign ourselves to repeating the mistakes that come from believing we can isolate then 'fix' aspects of inter-connected social systems.

Fortunately, this endeavour already enjoys a substantive and growing body of knowledge. As a matter of fact, systems thinking approaches (to capacity development in particular) have been advocated as an alternative to the static, reductionist mainstream lens for over a decade. The European Centre for Development Policy Management (ECDPM) have been notably influential in their exploration of systems thinking as it relates to the concept of capacity itself—as well as what this means for the practice of capacity development, program management and M&E. With the shift away from reductionist approaches and a growing focus on the 'whole', systems and emergence proponents have moved towards complexity theory in recent times. For their part, the Overseas Development Institute (ODI)[477] have comprehensively considered the relevance of complexity theory to development practice, while the ECDPM[478] have also begun to draw on complexity concepts in their thinking about organisational change and capacity development.

We access such existing literature as the foundation for our own, specific, exploration. The review of the literature on the use of systems thinking and complexity theory in social sciences includes a particular focus on their relevance to capacity development and M&E. The concepts are explored with an emphasis on their utility toward informing improvements in practice. Many of the foregoing criticisms of conventional approaches stem from critiques of the ontological and epistemological assumptions inherent in the managerial methodologies. Systems thinking and complexity theory offer an alternative lens, which in many ways informs the critique of conventional practice.

The chapter proceeds by first laying out the relevant concepts of systems thinking as they have been adopted in the capacity development field. It then moves on to unpack the component concepts which make up complexity theory, exploring the relevance of these concepts for capacity development and M&E. Whilst this review draws extensively on a range of literature including complexity in social science generally, complexity and systems thinking in the organisational and management fields, development and evaluation more broadly—it will be centred on the work of ODI and ECDPM due to their leading roles. Given the practical emphasis of this book, the consideration of practice orientated scholarship is given priority here.

Systems Thinking

The renewed interest in systems thinking approaches to capacity building and M&E, addresses many of the criticisms made of conventional approaches to M&E.[479] In Peter Morgan's earlier work on capacity building and performance

---

477 Ben Ramalingam and Harry Jones, *Exploring the Science of Complexity: Ideas and Implications for Development and Humanitarian Efforts*, Working Paper 285 (Overseas Development Institute, 2008); Harry Jones, *Tackling Complex Problems: Linking Knowledge and Decision-making*, Presentation for Governance Ecosystems Livelihoods (GEL) World Vision CAS Conference, (Tanzania, 2010).

478 Tony Land, Volker Hauck and Heather Baser, *Capacity Change and Performance: Capacity Development: between Planned Interventions and Emergent Processes—Implications for Development Cooperation*, Policy. Management Brief No. 22 (Maastricht: European Centre for Development Policy Management, 2009).

479 Volker Hauck, *Applying systems thinking to capacity development: Systems thinking is back on the agenda*, (ECDPM/UNDP, 2005).

measurements he recommends thinking in terms of 'systems'.[480] There is broad scope for interpretation in relation to systems thinking and the actual application of Soft Systems Management (SSM—a branch of management techniques stemming from systems thinking, related to 'Interpretive Systems Perspectives (ISP)'[481] is not necessarily utilised, but rather the systems thinking behind it informs alternative approaches to M&E.[482]

To reiterate the idea introduced in Chapter 6: systems thinking is based on the understanding that no individual, organisation, institution or other human or social structure can be understood in isolation, as it is all 'bound by invisible fabrics of interrelated actions'[483] and to attempt to do so is at best futile and at worst detrimental. Therefore, 'you can only understand a system by contemplating the whole, not any individual part of the pattern'[484] SSM was developed to deal with the complexities of the above 'reality' and in particular to deal with 'problem situations'—that is when optimum circumstances are not present and specific problem diagnosis is complex. SSM is particularly suited to problem solving which attempts to accommodate 'multiple interpretations of complex interrelated issues'.[485] It is concerned with the 'whole'[486] and aspects of the whole that cannot be broken down into parts or components—that being the emergent properties.[487]

SSM assumes a number of things from the outset. That is that human beings attach meaning to everything,[488] and we therefore cannot understand, manage, monitor, influence or change human action effectively without considering

480 NOTE: the term 'systems thinking' is controversial and used in different ways—we use it here in reference to its use in the capacity development literature.

481 Peter Morgan, *The Idea and Practice of Systems Thinking and their Relevance for Capacity Development.* (Maastricht, the Netherlands: European Centre for Development Policy Management, 2005), 5; H. Tsoukasl, "Panoptic Reason and the Search for Totality: A Critical Assessment of the Critical Systems Perspective," *Human Relations* 45, no. 7 (1992): 637–657.

482 David Watson, *Monitoring and Evaluation of Capacity and Capacity Development* (Maastricht, the Netherlands: European Centre for Development Policy Management, 2006), 20.

483 Peter Senge, *The Fifth Discipline: The Art and Practice of the Learning Organization* (Sydney: Random House, 1992), 7.

484 Peter Senge, *The Fifth Discipline: The Art and Practice of the Learning Organization* (Sydney: Random House, 1992), 6.

485 K. K. J. Ho and D. Sculli, "Organisational Theory and Soft Systems Methodologies," *The Journal of Management Development* 13 no. 7 (1994): 47–58, 49.

486 Peter Checkland and Jim Scholes, *Soft Systems Methodology in Action* (West Sussex: John Wiley & Sons, 1990), 18.

487 Peter Checkland and Jim Scholes, *Soft Systems Methodology in Action* (West Sussex: John Wiley & Sons, 1990), 19.

488 Peter Checkland and Jim Scholes, *Soft Systems Methodology in Action* (West Sussex: John Wiley & Sons, 1990), 2.

context and meaning. Any interpretation of the 'reality' of a situation or problem will be incomplete.[489] Such interpretations are what inform our 'purposeful action' as a human being—that is that people act to improve a *perceived* problem situation. Purposeful action then impacts upon the *perceived* world and brings about change, which again human beings will perceive and learn from... and so the cycle continues.[490] Knowledge acquisition is therefore part of a cycle: experience creates knowledge > informs purposeful action > leads to change (transformation) > leads to new experience >generating new knowledge > and so on. It is possible to be part of a problematic cycle and this may be cause for intervention. Such intervention should utilise this knowledge acquisition and action cycle.[491]

In this world of complex interpretation and meaning a definitive problem-solution scenario will often be elusive. The best we can do is develop a 'rich picture' of the problem situation through the active involvement and participation of interested parties.[492] Whilst situations will differ, generally stages will continue from identifying the 'messy' problem situation to identifying the problem 'expressed'. According to systems thinking it is not only important to identify avenues for improvement but to consider 'through whose eyes improvement is to be judged'.[493] The process is 'intrinsically collaborative'.[494] The learning generated by the process of enquiry is deliberate and valuable.[495]

The emphasis is heavily in favour of substantial stakeholder and problem 'owner' input and even driving of the process.[496] The assumption causal determinants in the social sciences always include human intentions[497] means the possibilities are infinite in a study of 'open systems'. Therefore, it aims to maximise discussion and debate in the interests of moving forward with a common under-

---

489 K. K. J. Ho and D. Sculli, "Organisational Theory and Soft Systems Methodologies", *The Journal of Management Development* 13 no. 7, (1994): 47–58, 48.

490 Peter Checkland and Jim Scholes, *Soft Systems Methodology in Action* (West Sussex: John Wiley & Sons, 1990), 8.

491 Peter Checkland and Jim Scholes, *Soft Systems Methodology in Action* (West Sussex: John Wiley & Sons, 1990), 2.

492 K. K. J. Ho and D. Sculli, "Organisational Theory and Soft Systems Methodologies", *The Journal of Management Development* 13 no. 7 (1994): 47–58, 48.

493 Peter Checkland and Jim Scholes, *Soft Systems Methodology in Action* (West Sussex: John Wiley & Sons, 1990), 28.

494 Peter Checkland and Jim Scholes, *Soft Systems Methodology in Action* (West Sussex: John Wiley & Sons, 1990), 28.

495 Volker Hauck, *Applying systems thinking to capacity development: Systems thinking is back on the agenda*, (ECDPM/UNDP, 2005).

496 K. K. J. Ho and D. Sculli, "Organisational Theory and Soft Systems Methodologies", *The Journal of Management Development* 13 no. 7 (1994): 47–58, 49.

497 Peter Checkland and Jim Scholes, *Soft Systems Methodology in Action* (West Sussex: John Wiley & Sons, 1990), 2.

standing amongst interested parties[498] to achieve a picture of perceived realities regarding causality to identify avenues for 'improvement' which are meaningful for those concerned and 'deemed to be improvements by those carrying out the process'.[499]

This approach takes a definite step away from conventional approaches to program management in that it is less concerned with measuring tangible outputs and more concerned with the *process* and how this may bring about the 'emergent property'. In this case the emergent property is the *impact* of capacity building itself—in other words, capacity. Stakeholders play a central role, and accordingly this characteristic improves problem diagnosis, the understanding of external and influencing factors and nurtures ownership in solution development, action and accountability. As the complete process is inherently inclusive genuine participation is established from the outset.[500] The comprehensive understanding of the inter-subjective relationships relevant to that specific operating environment increases the likelihood of the organisation surviving as it is well placed to absorb external shocks. Contributing to survival is the knowledge, and inclusion, of those with disabling capabilities in the consultation process.

In the systems thinking approach addressing 'soft issues' (that which informs human intention), is the key to meaningful, sustainable change. 'Soft issues' will include things like meaning, fear, motivation, identity, values, legitimacy, hope and confidence.[501] A concern with 'soft issues' and full participation facilitates the harnessing of social energy. Furthermore, it provides a basis for 'demand side' capacity building[502] through addressing the demands of those directly involved and benefiting from such. It increases awareness of reasonable expectations of the organisation and therefore fuels realistic external 'in country' demand and increases local accountability.[503]

The potential problems and limitations of systems thinking will depend largely on the situation. It is heavily dependent on highly variable factors. For example, participants may be reluctant to contribute for a range of reasons, including: the sensitivity of the subject, cultural differences or barriers, intimidation and power

498 K. K. J. Ho and D. Sculli, "Organisational Theory and Soft Systems Methodologies", *The Journal of Management Development* 13 no. 7 (1994): 47–58, 48.

499 Peter Checkland and Jim Scholes, *Soft Systems Methodology in Action* (West Sussex: John Wiley & Sons, 1990), 4.

500 Peter Morgan, *The Design and Use of Capacity Development Indicators*, Paper prepared for the Policy Branch of the Canadian International Development Agency (1997), 13.

501 Peter Morgan, *The Design and Use of Capacity Development Indicators*, Paper prepared for the Policy Branch of the Canadian International Development Agency (1997), 5.

502 Callisto Madavo, *Building Effective States: Forging Engaged Societies*, Report of the World Bank Task Force on Capacity Development in Africa, (Washington D.C.: World Bank, 2005), 48.

503 Heather Baser, "What is Capacity? Going beyond the Conventional Wisdom" *News from the Nordic Africa Institute* no. 2 (2004): 14.

relations and imbalances.[504] Ideas and concepts produced by the process may prove to be irreconcilable or mutually exclusive. The potential for bias is difficult to eliminate in such a subjective approach. The possibility for bias to affect the process is present at every point.[505]

Critical systems thinking (CST) considers the potential for power relations to undermine the above approach to be so great as to render the approach useless unless explicitly deal with.[506] Critical systems thinkers draw on Habermas[507] in that they assert that systems participants will suffer from *false consciousness.*[508] According to CST it is therefore inadequate to draw only on their held perspectives within the existing power/knowledge paradigm. This school of thought argues that it's 'only when an 'ideal speech situation' has been created will system participants be able to freely participate in negotiating fairer outcomes from all.'[509]

As will become apparent in the subsequent exploration of complexity theory concepts, there are some close parallels between systems thinking and complexity. Complexity emerges within systems, concepts such as emergence, feedback, non-linearity and the focus on multidimensional/directional relationships are common to both. The step away from reductionist approaches and the compartmentalisation of the whole is in the same direction. In fact the above description of systems thinking highlights aspects of it which appear to be very much compatible with *complexity science.* The discussion turns now to examine how complexity relates to systems.

---

504 Critical systems thinking is an attempt to address many of the limitations outlined regarding bias, cultural sensitivities, trust and power imbalances (see K. K. J. Ho and D. Sculli, "Organisational Theory and Soft Systems Methodologies", *The Journal of Management Development* 13 no. 7 (1994): 47–58, 58.)

505 K. K. J. Ho and D. Sculli, "Organisational Theory and Soft Systems Methodologies", *The Journal of Management Development* 13 no. 7 (1994): 47–58, 53.

506 It is important to note that CST has been heavily criticised for its 'inadequate' conceptualisation and operationalisation of power. (For a detailed critique of CST see H. Tsoukasl, "Panoptic Reason and the Search for Totality: A Critical Assessment of the Critical Systems Perspective", *Human Relations* 45 no. 7 (1992): 637 657.)

507 R. L. Flood, "Liberating Systems Theory: Towards Critical Systems Thinking," *Human Relations* 43 no. 1 (1990): 49–75; John Brocklesby and Stephen Cummings, "Foucault Plays Habermas: An Alternative Philosophical Underpinning for Critical Systems Thinking" *The Journal of the Operational Research Society* 47 no. 6 (1996): 741–754.

508 Foucauldian approaches to understanding power and emancipation through making visible the 'unwritten categories and rules of the system' has also been used in CST theory (Brocklesby and Cummings above).

509 Steven Phelan, "A Note on the Correspondence Between Complexity and Systems Theory", *Systemic Practice and Action Research* 12 no. 3 (1998): 238–246.

Despite the obvious relationship between these concepts the complexity literature tends not to acknowledge it.[510] When these theories are compared they are often treated as fixed things, making permanent inflexible statements of fact regarding the nature of the world and how we can know about it. In reality both are a collection of ideas which have changed and evolved over time and manifest in different ways depending on how they are being interpreted for the purposes of social science. Some have critiqued old systems notions (in the realm of hard systems) and compared them unfavourably with recent complexity thinking.[511] Other arguments are inconsistent, offering comparisons between complexity and systems—providing contradictory explanations without reference to the changed position of systems thinking over time.

Steven Phelan[512] gives a useful account of the status quo in the late 90's and, whilst there are some problems, he provides a platform to move forward from. He argues that systems and complexity theory share a vocabulary but not an ontology or epistemology. He claims that complexity theory 'remains firmly in the positivist camp' and that this is at odds with the newly found interpretivist or at least critical feeling of the new systems approaches (soft systems and critical systems). Other differences stand including the tendency of systems theory to aim to predict and control[513] as well as its 'problem-solving' emphasis. According to Phelan complexity theory is exploratory, looking to explain a system's aggregate behaviour, whilst systems theory is trying to change it. This is again an excellent example of the problems with analysing these schools of thought as if they were a static set of concepts. As Phelan himself, acknowledges complexity theorists move on to prediction and control as the knowledge and methodologies in this area evolve to allow this.

The positivist stance of complexity theory seems too to be more flexible than is often argued. As Phelan points out there has long been the potential for the incorporation of 'constructionist' ideas in the use of agent-based modelling:[514]

> *One of the strengths of agent-based modelling is its ability to model heterogeneous behaviour among agents. It is conceivable that a model could be developed to allow agents to have different perceptions of an underlying ontological reality. These differences in*

---

510 Steven Phelan, "A Note on the Correspondence Between Complexity and Systems Theory", *Systemic Practice and Action Research* 12 no. 3 (1998): 238–246.

511 Walby as cited in Malcolm Alexander, "We do complexity too! Sociology, chaos theory and complexity science", *The Future of Sociology*, (The Australian Sociological Association, 2009).

512 Steven Phelan, "A Note on the Correspondence Between Complexity and Systems Theory", *Systemic Practice and Action Research* 12 no. 3 (1998): 238–246.

513 There is not the space here to explore this in detail, but we would suggest that these claims are less true of soft and critical systems—depending on the way it is interpreted and used.

514 Steven Phelan, "A Note on the Correspondence Between Complexity and Systems Theory", *Systemic Practice and Action Research* 12 no. 3 (1998): 238–246.

> *perception would lead to divergent learning experiences and an inevitable variation in preference and actions among agents.*

The following exploration of complexity reveals a great deal of overlap between these schools of thought. Importantly, the final section of this chapter argues that whilst the ontological compatibility between the two can be disputed to no end the actual utility of these concepts for the purposes of program management and M&E can be interpreted in similar ways and both schools of thought can be drawn upon to improve practice in complementary ways.

At this juncture it is useful to take a step back and look at the origins of the theory. Complexity sciences originated in the natural sciences and there are still many who argue that the relevance of complexity science does not go beyond the physical world. Others, including Urry, have argued that complexity sciences actually overcome the physical/social science divide.[515] Complexity concepts have been developed in the fields of physics, biology, mathematics, ecology, chemistry' and more recently they have become what Urry terms of the new 'turn' in social sciences. Complexity sciences derive from a number of related concepts including one of the earliest and most famous manifestations known as 'chaos theory'.[516] Like other aspects it derives from observations made in the physical sciences, with popular understanding of this stemming from Edward Lorenz's 'butterfly effect'. This early work highlighted the nonlinear dynamics which can lead to unpredictable change. It is this thinking that challenges the reductionist model and clearly demonstrates the problems with the compartmentalisation of complex systems.

Newton's reductionist model for investigation was premised on the assumption that complex phenomena can be divided into scientifically knowable component parts—these parts could be analysed and their behaviours explained, these component explanations then fit together to describe the behaviour of the whole. This way of thinking informs conventional approaches to program management and M&E. The 'butterfly effect' challenged these assumptions by instead analysing patterns in a system's behaviour.[517] Complexity sciences reject the notion that a complex system is knowable through the analysis of its individual parts as the relationship between parts and the impact on the system is not proportional, and importantly the emergent property of such interaction is in any case 'more than the sum of its parts'.

It is not however practical to arrive at definitions. This is because the complexity *sciences* or *theory* is not a coherent and definitive formula of ontology, epistemology and corresponding methodology and method but rather it has been

---

515 John Urry, "The Complexity Turn", *Theory, Culture & Society* 22 no. 5 (2005): 1–14, 5.
516 Which importantly includes notions of deterministic chaos.
517 John Urry, "The Complexity Turn", *Theory, Culture & Society* 22 no. 5 (2005): 1–14, 5.

described as a 'collection of ideas and principles'[518] drawing on a range of influences from both the natural and the social sciences. In reviewing the literature it is clear that users of the *theory* are often drawing on very different understandings.[519] Included in this difference is the centrality of the concepts themselves. In some cases a concept will be considered critical and in other descriptions and applications the same concept will be largely ignored. As is noted by Hendrick,[520] scholars also differ in their picking and choosing of concepts, with some advocating that the list of concepts can be drawn on as is convenient. For this reason it is impossible to provide a definition which captures all these elements and perspectives. Ramalingam and Jones[521] do however, offer a helpful description:

> *Complexity sciences look at the phenomena that arise in systems of interconnected and interdependent elements and multiple dimensions... Both positive and negative feedback processes take place... acting to dampen or amplify change; emergent properties result from the interactions of the elements, but these are not properties of the individual elements themselves.*

Complexity theories and methodologies are more advanced in some disciplines than in others and some phenomena lend themselves to *scientific* investigation more than others. Consequently not all inquiries that are underpinned by complexity understandings could be classified as 'complexity science'. In line with Hendrick's[522] observation regarding the different accounts of the field and the flexibility of its concepts I will borrow a term from David Byrne[523] and refer

518 Diane Henderick, "Complexity Theory and Conflict Transformation: An Exploration of Potential and Implications", *Working Paper 17*, (Bradford: University of Bradford, Centre for Conflict Resolution, Department of Peace Studies, 2009); Ben Ramalingam and Harry Jones, *Exploring the Science of Complexity: Ideas and Implications for Development and Humanitarian Efforts*, Working Paper 285 (Overseas Development Institute, 2008).

519 Paul Cilliers, "Complexity, Deconstruction and Relativism", *Theory, Culture & Society* 22 no. 5 (2005): 255–267.

520 Diane Henderick, "Complexity Theory and Conflict Transformation: An Exploration of Potential and Implications", *Working Paper 17*, (Bradford: University of Bradford, Centre for Conflict Resolution, Department of Peace Studies, 2009).

521 Ben Ramalingam and Harry Jones, *Exploring the Science of Complexity: Ideas and Implications for Development and Humanitarian Efforts*, Working Paper 285 (Overseas Development Institute, 2008).

522 Diane Henderick, "Complexity Theory and Conflict Transformation: An Exploration of Potential and Implications", *Working Paper 17*, (Bradford: University of Bradford, Centre for Conflict Resolution, Department of Peace Studies, 2009).

523 David Byrne, *Working within a complexity frame of reference—the potential of 'integrated methods' for understanding transformation in complex social systems* (Communication For Social Change Consortium, 2009). (This paper is a contribution towards the Communication For Social Change Consortium's paper for UNAIDS on expanding the monitoring and evaluation of Social Change Communication for HIV/AIDS prevention).

(unless otherwise appropriate) to the concepts more broadly as the 'complexity frame of reference'.

Before moving on to unpack the concepts comprising the CFoR it is important to acknowledge the real and credible objections to the use of complexity theory. There are scholars who argue that complexity is only applicable to the physical or natural sciences. Others who acknowledge its resonance with social science have suggested that its descriptive similarities mean it is a useful metaphor, while others still suggest it is a useless coincidence. Less dismissive are those that suggest it may be valuable but so far its theoretical and methodological development in the social sciences is still too crude to be sure of its value.[524]

This chapter will engage with some of these criticisms. However, we would state from the outset that we are inclined to agree with the latter of the criticisms. It is clear that conventional approaches to social science, as it relates to social change, capacity development and its M&E, is of limited use when it comes to the analysis and evaluation of complex social systems and it is highly probable in our view that the solution lies in a complexity understanding of the world. How we operationalise these concepts remains a challenge as is the extent to which these claims can be adequately *proven.*

The 'collection of ideas' which make up the CFoR will be addressed below as this chapter unpacks and briefly describes the various concepts. This section summarises the key concepts as identified in the literature including those highlighted by Ramalingam and Jones[525] in their review of the applicability of complexity sciences to development practice. The list of concepts include: interconnectedness and interdependence (interrelatedness); coupling; emergence; localised interactions producing the global; complex adaptive agents; self-organisation; coevolution; feedback processes; sensitivity to initial conditions; non-linearity; strange attractors; chaos and the edge of chaos; and phase space.

Interconnectedness

All systems display varying degrees of interconnectedness. A system is complex when it is made of multiple elements and processes which are constituted and influenced by other elements and processes within the system—as well as being shaped and influenced by the system (or the environment) itself. 'Complexity arises when dependencies among the elements become important'.[526] This is

524 Another objection to the *fad* of complexity stems from its shallow application by management and organisational '*gurus*'. This is a valid criticism and damages of the reputation of serious scholars.

525 Ben Ramalingam and Harry Jones, *Exploring the Science of Complexity: Ideas and Implications for Development and Humanitarian Efforts*, Working Paper 285 (Overseas Development Institute, 2008).

526 John Miller and Scott Page, "Complexity is Social Worlds" in *Complex Adaptive Systems: An Introduction to Computational Models of Social Life* (Princeton: Princeton University Press, 2007), 9.

what Ramalingam and Jones[527] describe as 'interdependence' as well as aspects of 'interconnectedness'. In a social system this refers to the interconnectedness and interdependence of social and political actors (people), their relationships with each other, the physical and political/social environment and the processes of social construction and exchange, historical conditions and the shared and competing meanings of the actors in the system.

The manner in which these (and many other) elements or aspects of the system *relate* is dependent on the interrelatedness of the elements and process in the system. In other words the relationship between one element and another cannot be understood through isolating and analysing the two elements. Rather the relationship between the two elements is informed, shaped and influenced by the relationships with other aspects of the system. The elements and processes of the system are therefore, mutually constituting—that is not to say all elements would cease to exist without reference to all other elements, only that each element which is connected to the same system is in some way dependent on the others for its composition/manifestation.

> *As the elements react, the aggregate changes; as the aggregate changes, elements react anew.*[528]

Interconnectedness refers not only to the connections between elements of a system, but also interconnectedness occurs between systems, as wells as levels of systems and subsystems. This interconnectedness 'leads to interdependence' and 'gives rise to complex behaviour'.[529] Interconnectivity results in the emergence of complexity and non-linear relationships.[530]

The degree of interconnectedness can vary and therefore so too does the depth of interrelatedness—this will have an effect on how influential a change within the system might be. The extent to which elements and agents are interdependent is referred to as coupling.[531] Loosely coupled systems are not as responsive or susceptible to changes in a wide spread or dramatic way. Therefore, there is a greater likelihood of maintaining a localised equilibrium despite changes in the system. Whilst this makes it more difficult to effect change throughout the

---

527 Ben Ramalingam and Harry Jones, *Exploring the Science of Complexity: Ideas and Implications for Development and Humanitarian Efforts*, Working Paper 285 (Overseas Development Institute, 2008).

528 W. B. Arthur, "Complexity and the Economy", *Science* 284 (April 2, 1999): 107–109.

529 Ben Ramalingam and Harry Jones, *Exploring the Science of Complexity: Ideas and Implications for Development and Humanitarian Efforts*, Working Paper 285 (Overseas Development Institute, 2008).

530 John Miller and Scott Page, "Complexity is Social Worlds" in *Complex Adaptive Systems: An Introduction to Computational Models of Social Life* (Princeton: Princeton University Press, 2007).

531 John Miller and Scott Page, "Complexity is Social Worlds" in *Complex Adaptive Systems: An Introduction to Computational Models of Social Life* (Princeton: Princeton University Press, 2007).

system, loosely coupled systems are generally more resilient and independent.[532] There is a sense that this may refer to systems that are highly de-centralised. For example, in a social context decentralised government and localised decision-making mechanisms and social ordering may benefit from its loose coupling with the system, as local level changes are not dependent on the 'whole system to respond.'

Emergence

Emergence 'describes how the behaviour of systems emerges—often unpredictably—from the interaction of the parts'.[533] The commonly used phrase 'the whole is more than the sum of its parts' goes some way to illuminating the concept of emergence, although as Urry[534] argues... 'It is not that the sum is greater than the size of its parts—but that there are systems effects that are different from their parts'.[535] Simply put emergence describes the process of producing that emergent property, through the interaction of component parts (elements). 'These are non-linear consequences that are non-reducible to the very many individual components that comprise such activities. Such emergent characteristics emerge from, but are not reducible to, the micro-dynamics of the phenomenon in question'.[536] Or as explained by DeWolf and Holvoet...

> *In short, the uses of the concept of emergence refer to two important characteristics: a global behaviour that arises from the interactions of the local parts; and that global behaviour cannot be traced back to the individual parts.*[537]

It is fundamental to the critique of Newtonian understandings. It is this emergent property which differentiates a complex system from a complicated system. It is also a crucial factor in the unpredictability of a system. The interaction of elements within the system produce any number of emergent proprieties, such properties influence elements and produce emergent properties in an ongoing process of dynamic interaction. It is these unknowns, influencing the emergence of other unknowns, which make prediction with certainty extremely unlikely, if not impossible. That said, depending on the complexity of the system and the

---

532 Ben Ramalingam and Harry Jones, *Exploring the Science of Complexity: Ideas and Implications for Development and Humanitarian Efforts*, Working Paper 285 (Overseas Development Institute, 2008).

533 Ben Ramalingam and Harry Jones, *Exploring the Science of Complexity: Ideas and Implications for Development and Humanitarian Efforts*, Working Paper 285 (Overseas Development Institute, 2008).

534 John Urry, "The Complexity Turn", *Theory, Culture & Society* 22 no. 5 (2005): 1–14.

535 John Urry, "The Complexity Turn", *Theory, Culture & Society* 22 no. 5 (2005): 5.

536 John Urry, "The Complexity Turn", *Theory, Culture & Society* 22 no. 5 (2005).

537 Tom DeWolf and Tom Holvoet, "Emergence Versus Self-organisation: Different concepts but Promising When Combined" *Lecture Notes in Artificial Intelligence: Subseries of Lecture Notes in Computer Science* 3464, (2005): 1–15.

context, we would argue that a well informed intervention (that being one gathering data from multiple sources) can still make useful approximations, but it must expect to be inaccurate in varying degrees.

The concept of emergence challenges the fundamental assumptions of state-building, as it clearly argues that social and political ordering is not the result of careful planning and management from the top, but rather the generation of an emergent order through multi-directional interaction of elements and process. As Marion argues the direction may indeed be the other way...

> *a [complex] system emerges from the interactions of individual units... The units... are driven by local rules... and are not globally coordinated*[538]

By this rationale *global order*, whilst no doubt heavily influence by top down pressures, is essentially the emergent property of local interactions. As Urry[539] explains in drawing on the work of Resnick ant colonies, highway traffic, market economies, immune systems etcetera...'in all these systems, patterns are determined... by local interactions among decentralised components.' That being the case, we need to find new tools to explore things from the 'ground up'.[540]

Adaptive Agents

'Certain kinds of systems are made up of individual agents acting for their own purposes, and with their own view of the situation. A special class of complex systems is made up of adaptive agents [complex adaptive systems], which react to the system and to each other, and which may make decisions and develop strategies to influence other agents or the overall system'.[541]

'All living things are adaptive agents'[542] and in some way they all sense the environment and broader system and they respond. In the case of complex social systems these agents include people (actors), intelligent agents that are capable of receiving and analysing information about the system and acting accordingly. Actors in the system are also a product of the system and their inherent knowledge in which they draw on to analyse and respond to the system is the emergent

---

538 Marion cited in Ben Ramalingam and Harry Jones, *Exploring the Science of Complexity: Ideas and Implications for Development and Humanitarian Efforts*, Working Paper 285 (Overseas Development Institute, 2008).

539 John Urry, "The Complexity Turn", *Theory, Culture & Society* 22 no. 5 (2005): 1–14.

540 John Miller and Scott Page, "Complexity is Social Worlds" in *Complex Adaptive Systems: An Introduction to Computational Models of Social Life* (Princeton: Princeton University Press, 2007).

541 Ben Ramalingam and Harry Jones, *Exploring the Science of Complexity: Ideas and Implications for Development and Humanitarian Efforts*, Working Paper 285 (Overseas Development Institute, 2008), 44.

542 Ben Ramalingam and Harry Jones, *Exploring the Science of Complexity: Ideas and Implications for Development and Humanitarian Efforts*, Working Paper 285 (Overseas Development Institute, 2008), 44.

property of their historical experience and learning of the system. Whilst thought processes and ways of knowing will differ between agents generally speaking they will have their own 'internal information processing and decision-making capacities'[543] enabling them to engage in ongoing situational analysis, assessing the state of the system, considering how they will affect the system in their actions and comparing this with their desired state. Or as Miller and Page[544] put it…

> *Social agents are also capable of change via thoughtful, but not necessarily brilliant deliberations about the worlds they inhabit. Social agents must continually make choices, either by direct cognition or a reliance on stored (but not immutable) heuristics, about their actions.*

As Arthur[545] points out 'this adds a layer of complication… not experienced in the natural sciences'. Social agents also predict and react to the behaviours of other agents,[546] they also anticipate future states 'based on internationalised models of change' (which may be incomplete and/or incorrect').[547] This self awareness together with an awareness of surroundings and possibilities is the reflexive agency that Byrne[548] refers to in considering the possible influences in a system that need to be taken account of.

This notion of intelligent adaptive actors with the ability to 'perceive the system around them and act on these perceptions'[549] and how this 'view of the world dynamically influences, and is influenced by, events and changes within

---

543 Ben Ramalingam and Harry Jones, *Exploring the Science of Complexity: Ideas and Implications for Development and Humanitarian Efforts*, Working Paper 285 (Overseas Development Institute, 2008), 44.

544 John Miller and Scott Page, "Complexity is Social Worlds" in *Complex Adaptive Systems: An Introduction to Computational Models of Social Life* (Princeton: Princeton University Press, 2007).

545 WB. Arthur, "Complexity and the Economy", *Science* 284 (April 2, 1999): 107–109.

546 John Miller and Scott Page, "Complexity is Social Worlds" in *Complex Adaptive Systems: An Introduction to Computational Models of Social Life* (Princeton: Princeton University Press, 2007); WB. Arthur, "Complexity and the Economy", *Science* 284 (April 2, 1999): 107–109.

547 Ben Ramalingam and Harry Jones, *Exploring the Science of Complexity: Ideas and Implications for Development and Humanitarian Efforts*, Working Paper 285 (Overseas Development Institute, 2008).

548 David Byrne, *Working within a complexity frame of reference—the potential of 'integrated methods' for understanding transformation in complex social systems*, (Communication For Social Change Consortium, 2009) (This paper is a contribution towards the Communication For Social Change Consortium's paper for UNAIDS on expanding the monitoring and evaluation of Social Change Communication for HIV/AIDS prevention).

549 Ben Ramalingam and Harry Jones, *Exploring the Science of Complexity: Ideas and Implications for Development and Humanitarian Efforts*, Working Paper 285 (Overseas Development Institute, 2008), 44.

the system',[550] has strong resonance with the soft systems conceptions of knowledge and purposeful action cycles. The process of receiving information and analysing it will necessarily be impacted by the agent's framework. A framework includes beliefs as well as knowledge construction processes. These are a consequence of the agent's socialisation including the influence of societal culture, history, institutional culture, national culture, religion, gendered constructs and so on. The way an agent responds to the system and its other agents will invariably be biased by the agent's lens. Once tied to the notion of 'rational choice', economic modelling too now acknowledges that there are other influencing factors stemming from an agent's perception. Accordingly, market simulations have been accounting for 'irrationality[551] and adaptation' for well over a decade.[552]

Not all agents have the same capacities. Whilst these differences can be subtle and manifest in any number of ways, complexity theory generally uses the concept of weak and strong agents to explain these differences.[553] Weak agents[554] describe those agents who are generally reactive. They respond to the immediate forces, they are not able to recognise the forces in a manner which could potentially liberate them from these forces. Weak agents might also see simple cause-and-effect patterns which alter their behaviour directly without considering the broader system at work. This description of weak agents aligns with the observations of CST, in that agency as well as the actors' position to negotiate is compromised by an inability to make visible crucial aspects of the system (often related to power). 'Weak agents' are also less inclined to set ambitious goals followed by plans to negotiate a path to achieving them. Strong agents will identify and negotiate such paths to achieving goals. They will attempt to influence other agents in the system and they have an increased capacity to identify the forces at work (albeit still far from complete) within a system. I would argue that weak and strong agents can be seen as having varying degrees of agency as their autonomy is bounded in different ways and their activity and behaviour is informed by a

550 Ben Ramalingam and Harry Jones, *Exploring the Science of Complexity: Ideas and Implications for Development and Humanitarian Efforts*, Working Paper 285 (Overseas Development Institute, 2008), 44.

551 The use of the term irrationality is in opposition to economic conceptions of rationality. The extent to which such a concept is indeed rational is debated for good reason.

552 T. Grimm, J. Mitlöhner, and W. Schönfeldinger, *Bounded rationality and adaptive agents in economic modelling* Conference paper. (New York: Association for Computer Machinery, Array Programming Languages, Special Interest Group on Programming Languages, 1995).

553 Ben Ramalingam and Harry Jones, *Exploring the Science of Complexity: Ideas and Implications for Development and Humanitarian Efforts*, Working Paper 285 (Overseas Development Institute, 2008), 44–45.

554 This is a simplified explanation of a concept which is already an oversimplified representation of reality.

type of 'bounded rationality'.[555] In short, 'the common knowledge assumption' of rational approaches is flawed[556]—agents have differing levels of agency depending on their ability to uncover the layers of reality.

The manner in which agents relate to one another and the system creating an emergent order is incredibly complex. Agents that do not share the same physical space, who have never met and may not even be explicitly aware of the other's existence, collaborate, compete and are in conflict through indirect but interconnected relationships. It is not only individual human beings who are adaptive agents in complex social systems, so too are the organisations and institutions.[557] This notion of organisations as complex adaptive agents illustrates again the hierarchy of systems. Human beings are complex physical beings in their biology. They are also complex social beings. It is these multifaceted adaptive agents that make up the complex adaptive agent which is an organisation.

Agent-Based-Modelling (ABM)

Methodologies such as agent-based-modelling (ABM) are designed to capture and analyse such relationships and process between agents—shedding light on how emergent systems behaviours evolve. ABM is literally a model based on agents. It is the agent and their activity and interaction which the artificial system is comprised of—'bottom up'.[558] ABM model dynamic interaction between agents in a social context through the use of computer generated communities informed by empirical research. Generally speaking these models are made up of three key components: agents; social space/context/environment; and rules. Examples of this type of thinking being used in the development context include the use of 'actor-orientated analysis'.[559] What is also known as computer simulation of Multi-agent systems can be used to understand the manifestation of Intelligent Complex Adaptive Systems (CAS made up of intelligent actors). As with other agent based approaches it relies on rules to dictate behaviour such

555 T. Grimm, J. Mitlöhner, & W. Schönfeldinger, *Bounded rationality and adaptive agents in economic modelling* Conference paper. (New York: Association for Computer Machinery, Array Programming Languages, Special Interest Group on Programming Languages, 1995).

556 WB. Arthur, "Complexity and the Economy", *Science* 284 (April 2, 1999): 107–109.

557 Ben Ramalingam and Harry Jones, *Exploring the Science of Complexity: Ideas and Implications for Development and Humanitarian Efforts*, Working Paper 285 (Overseas Development Institute, 2008).

558 Ben Ramalingam and Harry Jones, *Exploring the Science of Complexity: Ideas and Implications for Development and Humanitarian Efforts*, Working Paper 285 (Overseas Development Institute, 2008).

559 Long 2002 cited in Ben Ramalingam and Harry Jones, *Exploring the Science of Complexity: Ideas and Implications for Development and Humanitarian Efforts*, Working Paper 285 (Overseas Development Institute, 2008).

as 'a belief-desire-intention model'.[560] Once such rules are applied the methodology starts to reveal some contradictions as external control is counterintuitive with the observations of a CFoR, as the concept of self-organisation helps to illuminate.

Miller and Page[561] discuss the exciting potential of computational models to 'give us a way to grow worlds from the ground up'. In their example using the phenomena of standing ovations they demonstrate how crude measurement and abstracted predictions of average behaviour as conventional modelling provides tell us very little about process or the multiple effects of interconnectedness and social agent adaptation that really generate social phenomena. By moving from a simple model to one based on the logic of complex systems they change the equation from one of identical individuals (audience members) responding to a single stimuli (the performance) to a complex social system with adaptive agents informed by social interaction, norms, context and circumstances. Whilst this example is useful it also serves to demonstrate the range of other factors which may have influenced the outcome that the model fails to account for. The endless arrays of social and historical factors which may have influenced the behaviour of the agents on the night were not and cannot be accounted for. Miller and Page[562] suggest that for ABM to be useful it should avoid be bogged down with the extraordinarily complex realities of the idiosyncrasies of individual agents. Rather it needs to create a realistic set of prototypical agents.

While ABM and computer simulation is very useful in helping us conceptualise the interaction between agents and how this creates emergent phenomena as well as possible methodologies for partially reflecting such reality, it is not (as will be explored later) particularly useful for the ongoing practical management and M&E of social change programs. Importantly, ABM does not at this stage promise to make the unknowable future predictable.[563] It is rather at best a tool for explaining what has happened or modelling what could happen with knowable elements but not what WILL happen.

Self-organisation

An important concept which helps to make sense of the behaviour of adaptive agents and their impact on the system is the concept of self-organisation.

---

560 Y. Shan & A. Yang, *Applications of Complex Adaptive Systems*, (Hershey, Philadelphia: IGI Publishing, 2008).

561 John Miller & Scott Page, "Complexity is Social Worlds" in *Complex Adaptive Systems: An Introduction to Computational Models of Social Life* (Princeton: Princeton University Press, 2007).

562 John Miller & Scott Page, "Complexity is Social Worlds" in *Complex Adaptive Systems: An Introduction to Computational Models of Social Life* (Princeton: Princeton University Press, 2007).

563 Chris Mowels, "Successful or not? Evidence, emergence, and development management", *Development in Practice* 20 no. 7, (2010): 757–770.

'Self-organisation describes how the adaptive strategies of individual agents in particular settings give rise to a whole range of emergent phenomena'.[564] The process of self-organisation results in the emergence of patterns of behaviour, collectively comprising the system and sub-systems, through the interconnectedness and interactions between adaptive agents. Most work on self-organisation and emergence combine these concepts or sees them as working together. This point of view treats self-organisation as causing emergence.[565] This is very important from the point of view of an intervener as this suggests that top-down reforms and impositions of change will not succeed as planned. Rather it will be just one of many factors feeding into the system which adaptive agents will account for, as they experience it (only partially), and respond to in their self-organisation. This too, becomes a significant problem for modelling and agent orientated software engineering (AOSE).[566]

Studies on how self-organisation works in complex social systems have revealed that direct orders from the top, calls for mobilisation by respected or influential leaders, dramatic system changing events and alike do not produce straight forward cause-and-effect behavioural changes in adaptive agents as the structures are not derived from external control.[567] Rather these strongly influencing factors feed into a complex social system resulting in adaptive agents interpreting this information and absorbing it into self-organising processes (see for example Bhavnani's[568] work on the Rwandan genocide).

Co-evolution

Throughout this exploration of complexity theory there is reference to the mutually constituting nature of elements within a system. This notion is also known as mutualism and is partly understood as co-evolution. 'When adaptable autonomous agents or organisms interact intimately in an environment, such

564 Ben Ramalingam and Harry Jones, *Exploring the Science of Complexity: Ideas and Implications for Development and Humanitarian Efforts*, Working Paper 285 (Overseas Development Institute, 2008).

565 Tom DeWolf and Tom Holvoet, "Emergence Versus Self-organisation: Different concepts but Promising When Combined" *Lecture Notes in Artificial Intelligence: Subseries of Lecture Notes in Computer Science* 3464, (2005): 1–15.

566 Jan Sudeikat & Wolfgang Renz, "Building Complex Adaptive Systems: On Engineering Self-Organizing Multi-Agent Systems", in *Applications of Complex Adaptive Systems*, ed. Y. Shan & A. Yang, (Hershey, Philadelphia: IGI Publishing, 2008).

567 Jan Sudeikat & Wolfgang Renz, "Building Complex Adaptive Systems: On Engineering Self-Organizing Multi-Agent Systems", in *Applications of Complex Adaptive Systems*, ed. Y. Shan & A. Yang, (Hershey, Philadelphia: IGI Publishing, 2008).

568 Bhavnani as cited in Ben Ramalingam and Harry Jones, *Exploring the Science of Complexity: Ideas and Implications for Development and Humanitarian Efforts*, Working Paper 285 (Overseas Development Institute, 2008).

as in predator-prey and parasite-host relationships, they influence each other's evolution—this effect is called co-evolution'.[569]

In simple terms this means that the manifestation of agents and their behaviour within the system will be influenced by, and at least partially dependent on, the evolution of other agents and elements within the system—the relationship, for example, between co-adaptors (frog and fly).[570] In this way 'adaptive agents are seen to have porous boundaries'.[571] By this it is meant that they are not separate from the system, but rather they are of the system and they evolve in relation to other elements of the system. In cases when the adaptive agents are exactly the same the co-evolution is a basic cause-and-effect relationship. In social systems this is not the case. The agent still evolves in relation to other agents or properties—however, there is no standard effect as the manifestation of the agent (and its properties) is unique and multifaceted and therefore so too will be the response/co-evolution.

Co-evolution in social systems relates to power and adaptation. Those in a position of less power co-evolve with their more powerful counterparts. This may be for survival or it may be to gain something. In a donor/recipient relationship co-evolution can manifest in many different ways, some of which can be positive. However, too often co-evolution in this relationship creates dependency. Another problematic example of co-evolution in this type of relationship is when those who wish to benefit from aid adapt to mimic the interveners.

Feedback and Path Dependency

The impact of agent activity is generally very difficult to isolate as agent activity (as with other activity in the system) results in feedback. Feedback can be positive or negative. It is basically the influence that moves through the system as a consequence of activity. Such activity may produce positive feedback which essentially sets in motion a change process that continues in the trajectory of the initial activity, it may amplify the change process through the emergence of

569 Ben Ramalingam and Harry Jones, *Exploring the Science of Complexity: Ideas and Implications for Development and Humanitarian Efforts*, Working Paper 285 (Overseas Development Institute, 2008).

570 M. B. Holbrook, "Adventures in Complexity: An Essay on Dynamic Open Complex Adaptive Systems, Butterfly Effects, Self-Organizing Order, Coevolutions, the Ecological Perspective, Fitness Landscapes, Market Spaces, Emergent Beauty at the Edge of Chaos, and All That Jazz", *Academy of Marketing Science Review*, (2003), http://www.amsreview.org/articles/holbrook06-2003.pdf.

571 Ben Ramalingam and Harry Jones, *Exploring the Science of Complexity: Ideas and Implications for Development and Humanitarian Efforts*, Working Paper 285 (Overseas Development Institute, 2008).

'reinforcing pressures'.[572] In the case of negative feedback the activity may result in a response in the system which is counteracting. Negative feedback may only balance the system back or close to its initial state, it can however push the system in another direction. A simple example of this in a complex social system may be a message for change in a particular direction, for example gender equality in the public service that then triggers negative feedback resulting in increased levels of gender-based violence in the home. Feedback can be *masked* or *disregarded*—if feedback signals are not detected or do not obviously correlate with the activity this can be referred to as *masked feedback*. In the case of the above example the M&E of gender equality inventions often miss the negative feedback which takes place outside the official spheres of intervention (i.e. at home, rather than at work).

There is obviously a complex interaction of feedback in a complex system—with any change in the elements or dimensions of a system resulting in feedback. This means that feedback in the system is multidirectional as it comes from a myriad of sources simultaneously. Feedback is therefore a process of continuous dynamic interaction. As implied above wholly positive feedback is not necessarily optimal. If legitimate problems exist with following a particular path but negative feedback is weak or non-existent there is the possibility of 'runaway' positive feedback, whereby the system gains momentum in one direction 'leading to accelerated changes and potentially a radically different configuration of the system'.[573]

Similarly if positive feedback processes create a magnifying effect it can lock the system into a self-perpetuating pattern. This pattern is referred to by economists as path dependence.[574] 'Positive feedback loops exacerbate initial stresses in the system, so rendering it unable to absorb shocks and re-establish the original equilibrium.'[575] This positive feedback is evident in cases of increasing returns, generating path dependency. 'Such irreversible path dependency occurs when *contingent* events set into motion institutional patterns or event chains over time that have deterministic properties through what Arthur terms are lock-ins'.[576]

---

572 Ben Ramalingam and Harry Jones, *Exploring the Science of Complexity: Ideas and Implications for Development and Humanitarian Efforts*, Working Paper 285 (Overseas Development Institute, 2008).

573 Ben Ramalingam and Harry Jones, *Exploring the Science of Complexity: Ideas and Implications for Development and Humanitarian Efforts*, Working Paper 285 (Overseas Development Institute, 2008), 18.

574 W. B. Arthur, "Complexity and the Economy", *Science* 284 (April 2, 1999): 107–109.

575 John Urry, "The Complexity Turn", *Theory, Culture & Society* 22 no. 5, (2005): 1–14.

576 Arthur as quoted in John Urry, "The Complexity Turn", *Theory, Culture & Society* 22 no. 5, (2005): 1–14.

Initial Conditions

The manner in which feedback plays out will depend on the elements within the system, the state of the system and the agents at the moment of activity. The initial conditions refer to the state of the system at any given time in its evolution. It will generally coincide with a purposeful assessment of the system. It is invariably an arbitrary point in time which may be considered the starting point in the interests of utility.[577] The notion of *sensitivity to the initial conditions* is crucial as it emphasises the critical importance of paying attention to the idiosyncratic composition of every complex system at any moment. It is an explicit acknowledgment of the potentially significant impact seemingly trivial and often invisible aspects of system can have on the behaviour of the system.[578] As such any input will be absorbed into the system and outcomes will manifest according to the unique state of the system or the *initial condition.* Importantly the *initial condition* is the product of all that has gone before—its specific manifestation is therefore highly contingent on its historical context. In line with Lorenz's observations regarding the massive impact of the most minor irregularities, the subtlest of difference between one system and another at the point of intervention (the initial condition) can have widespread effects throughout the system and result in very different outcomes. The initial conditions 'refers to situations where small changes in the initial system configuration may lead to large, non-linear effects'.[579] Accordingly, initial misdiagnosis which informs future predictions will magnify in their inaccuracies over space and time.[580]

The importance of the initial condition is emphasised in particularly exaggerated (although not necessarily uncommon) examples whereby the system sets up a self perpetuating cycle or becomes locked in, as discussed briefly above. This is most obvious in particularly harmful patterns of entrenched systems behaviour or path dependency such as fossil fuel consumption/reliance,[581] consumerism and alike. Whilst complexity scientists might challenge the absoluteness of the extent to which a system is locked into a particular course—citing the closed

577 However, it is recognised that complex systems are ongoing and do not have beginnings and ends perse.

578 M. B. Holbrook, "Adventures in Complexity: An Essay on Dynamic Open Complex Adaptive Systems, Butterfly Effects, Self-Organizing Order, Coevolutions, the Ecological Perspective, Fitness Landscapes, Market Spaces, Emergent Beauty at the Edge of Chaos, and All That Jazz", *Academy of Marketing Science Review*, (2003), http://www.amsreview.org/articles/holbrook06-2003.pdf.

579 Steven Manson, "Simplifying complexity: a review of complexity theory", *Geoforum* 32 no. 1 (2000): 405–414.

580 Edward Lorenz, *Predictability: Does a Flap of a Butterfly's wings in Brazil Set off a Tornado in Texas?* Conference paper presented at the American Association for the Advancement of Science (139th Meeting, Massachusetts Institute of Technology, 1972).

581 Gregory Unruh, "Understanding carbon lock-in" *Energy Policy* 28 no. 12 (2000): 817–830.

system thinking which informs such assumptions as well as the importance of 'attractors' and potential shocks to the system—there is certainly much to be learnt from understanding how these system become 'path dependent', even if it is not a permanent state.

Non-linearity

In contrast to the macro predictability of path dependent trajectories the non-linear nature of complex systems means that impacts within a system based on any particular input are disproportional and unpredictable. Complexity approaches to social science argue that social and human systems cannot be understood in terms of linear relationships. Given the multiple and mutual interdependence of any number of elements, dimensions and processes within a complex system causal relationships cannot be identified in a linear cause-and-effect pattern. The concept of non-linearity in complex systems shares its emphasis with systems thinking in that it refers to the need to study the system as a whole. Unlike linearity which 'describes the proportionality assumed in idealised situations where responses are proportional to forces and causes are proportional to effects', non-linear patterns of a whole cannot be neatly 'broken down into pieces, with each piece analysed separately'.[582] Importantly, inputs into a complex system are not proportional to system outputs or outcomes.[583]

Central to the understanding of nonlinear systems is the limited value of models utilising a select number of variables in attempting to prove causal relationships in a complex social system. One variable does not *cause* a change in another—but rather any number of variables interact producing feedback and altering the system and its elements. Indeed variables themselves are elements influenced by a myriad of other interacting variables. Accordingly isolating them for analysis produces a simplified distorted picture of a complex reality.

Phase Space

The recognition that the initial conditions will significantly affect the behaviour of the system as well as the importance of micro aspects of the system in the initial condition and on the manifestation of emergent properties has not resulted in complexity science conceding to the unknowability of a complex system. Instead

[582] Ben Ramalingam and Harry Jones, *Exploring the Science of Complexity: Ideas and Implications for Development and Humanitarian Efforts*, Working Paper 285 (Overseas Development Institute, 2008).

[583] M. B. Holbrook, "Adventures in Complexity: An Essay on Dynamic Open Complex Adaptive Systems, Butterfly Effects, Self-Organizing Order, Coevolutions, the Ecological Perspective, Fitness Landscapes, Market Spaces, Emergent Beauty at the Edge of Chaos, and All That Jazz", *Academy of Marketing Science Review*, (2003), http://www.amsreview.org/articles/holbrook06-2003.pdf.

it has shifted the emphasis of analysis away from the component parts onto the whole. In this analysis the concept of 'phase space' is employed. Phase space is the term given to the 'space of the possible' based on the mapping of the dimensions of the initial condition. 'The phase space is literally the set of all possible states—or phases—that a system can occupy.' It is essentially a mathematical tool which attempts to map and account for all the relevant aspects of the system and represent all the possible values these dimensions can have.

This appears to be a problematic contradiction in terms of social systems as it relies on identifying 'all the dimensions that are relevant to understanding the system' and knowing the range of possible values. Moreover, despite the emphasis on the whole, the identification of dimensions and their possible values can look a bit like reductionism in practice. We would argue that for the purposes of this inquiry *this* conceptualisation of phase space is not particularly useful as all the dimensions of the system are not knowable. Whilst we do not discount the merits of this approach in theory and the potentially promising possibilities of its application, we have serious reservations about the current capacities of social scientists to collate and analyse such a volume of data. We are severely hampered by our inability to know what is important or even where to look. As illustrated by Lorenz's[584] assessment of the data collation problems experienced in predicting the weather—social science too has not overcome these limitations:

> *Since we do not know exactly how many butterflies there are, nor where they are all located, let alone which ones are flapping their wings at any instant, we cannot, if the answer to our question is affirmative [Does the flap of a butterfly's wings in Brazil set off a tornado in Texas?], accurately predict the occurrence of tornados at a sufficiently distant future time.*

Strange Attractors; Chaos and the Edge of Chaos

Whilst it is acknowledged that complex systems are not predictable, it is argued that they are not entirely random either. Mapping[585] of the phase space over time is said to reveal a pattern of order despite the continual change and turbulence in the system. This pattern is what is known as a 'strange attractor'.[586] The pattern which emerges when mapped over time resembles butterfly wings.[587] It is

---

584 Edward Lorenz, *Predictability: Does a Flap of a Butterfly's wings in Brazil Set off a Tornado in Texas?* Conference paper presented at the American Association for the Advancement of Science (139th Meeting, Massachusetts Institute of Technology, 1972).

585 In a complex system, mapping generally requires the use of computers.

586 In simple systems the attractor such as the periodic attractor and the point attractor are predictable. These attractors are generally only relevant to physical systems which are made of limited components with knowable relationships these do not apply to complex social systems.

587 Ben Ramalingam and Harry Jones, *Exploring the Science of Complexity: Ideas and Implications for Development and Humanitarian Efforts*, Working Paper 285 (Overseas Development Institute, 2008).

important to note, however, that an illustration of this pattern is deceiving as the lines do not represent sequential movement, but rather the points in the system jump from line to line and wing to wing. When there is a dramatic jump, referred to as bifurcation, it is generally illustrative of a shift in the 'value' of a dimension in the system and the consequent feedback it produces.[588] Despite the 'ordered' pattern which emerges over time through mapping the system it remains unpredictable 'in its detail'. As Lorenz[589] explains after suggesting a tornado could be set off by the flap of a butterfly's wings...

> *...I am proposing that over the years minuscule disturbances neither increase nor decrease the frequency of occurrence of various weather evens such as tornados; the most that they may do is to modify the sequence in which these events occur.*

It is argued that complex systems will keep within a certain boundary (phase space) and feedback does provide a certain control of the chaos. Complex systems are said to be in a constant state of turbulence, often referred to as the 'edge of chaos'. This continually changing environment provides the room for innovative adaptation and perhaps sometimes romantically it is seen as the space where 'creativity flourishes'. The system can come under stress or can experience a dramatic change in an element which shifts the system and a new set of attractors emerges. It is possible to bring about change if the 'basic rules' which reinforce the existing attractor patterns were to be changed.[590]

> *Essentially, chaos refers to the phenomenon wherein systems composed of inter-related parts or interdependent agents—each of which follows very simple, highly regular rules of behaviour—generate outcomes that reflect these interactions and feedback effects in ways that are inherently nonlinear and intractably unpredictable.*[591]

---

588 Ben Ramalingam and Harry Jones, *Exploring the Science of Complexity: Ideas and Implications for Development and Humanitarian Efforts*, Working Paper 285 (Overseas Development Institute, 2008).

589 Edward Lorenz, *Predictability: Does a Flap of a Butterfly's wings in Brazil Set off a Tornado in Texas?* Conference paper presented at the American Association for the Advancement of Science (139th Meeting, Massachusetts Institute of Technology, 1972).

590 Ben Ramalingam and Harry Jones, *Exploring the Science of Complexity: Ideas and Implications for Development and Humanitarian Efforts*, Working Paper 285 (Overseas Development Institute, 2008).

591 This definition explains the logic of a large degree of ABM—such rules are not so easily identified, if they do indeed exist, in human behaviour—chaos in this sense is a useful concept but fails to account for agency. (M.B. Holbrook, "Adventures in Complexity: An Essay on Dynamic Open Complex Adaptive Systems, Butterfly Effects, Self-Organizing Order, Coevolutions, the Ecological Perspective, Fitness Landscapes, Market Spaces, Emergent Beauty at the Edge of Chaos, and All That Jazz", *Academy of Marketing Science Review*, (2003), http://www.amsreview.org/articles/holbrook06-2003.pdf.).

The idea of lever points in a system pushing the system to tipping point, bringing on bifurcation as the system tips from state into another—is one of the possibilities complexity theory presents for inducing change which have the potential to be very useful in program management.

> *To appreciate the power of epidemics, we have to abandon this expectation about proportionality. We need to prepare ourselves for the possibility that sometimes big changes follow from small events, and that sometimes these changes can happen very quickly.*[592]

Key Implications for Program Management and M&E

In a complex social system the multiple elements and processes which ultimately constitute each other, the environment and the system itself mean external diagnoses will always be too shallow to accurately account for the factors at play. Consequently local knowledge of the interrelatedness of the system is invaluable in situational analyses. The interconnectedness and interdependence of aspects of the system mean that, in line with soft systems analysis, no individual components of a complex social system can be understood (or changed) in isolation. In practical terms this means that interventions which rely on the compartmentalisation of the organisation and treatment of isolated units will fail. So too will interventions that treat the organisation as separate from society.

For example, a capacity development operation focussed on police reform has a heavy emphasis on the top-down elimination of corruption. The Professional Standards Unit (PSU) is responsible for reducing the consumption of fuel by 30% as this is the estimated rate of theft. The PSU's performance indicator reflects this goal. The capacity development advisers are successful in promoting a change in ethos within the unit and the PSU becomes committed to the enforcement of professional standards. The rest of the organisation however is not. All other officers continue to balance the expectations of professional ethical standards and social expectations of reciprocity and sharing access to resources (in line with social conventions which are critical in the provision of welfare). The Store adapts to these new pressures, the records start to add up—but fuel consumption does not go down. The PSU becomes isolated from the rest of the organisation. PSU officers are excluded from social events and they can no longer access fuel for their own personal use reducing their social capital. Capacity development benchmarks in the PSU are not met, performance indicators suggest capacity

592 Gladwell, quoted in M. B. Holbrook, "Adventures in Complexity: An Essay on Dynamic Open Complex Adaptive Systems, Butterfly Effects, Self-Organizing Order, Coevolutions, the Ecological Perspective, Fitness Landscapes, Market Spaces, Emergent Beauty at the Edge of Chaos, and All That Jazz", *Academy of Marketing Science Review*, (2003), http://www.amsreview.org/articles/holbrook06-2003.pdf.

development efforts in this area have failed. The Log Frame report does not capture the complex relations which led to this outcome.

There are many things to learn from the interconnected nature of complex systems for the program management and M&E of interventions. The importance of being aware of linkages means that situational analyses must be based on local knowledge regarding the interconnected factors at play in any reform effort. Capacity development must treat the organisation as a connected organism both internally and externally (rather than a machine that breaks into parts). Intervention activities need to account for and manage the impact on other aspects of the organisation as well as the social impacts (interconnectedness within the system, between systems and sub-systems).

The extent of interdependence or coupling offers some interesting challenges and opportunities. For example, the degree in which donor government policy changes actually influences practices on the ground (elements and processes) will depend on how tightly the government, its relevant agency, it's in country office and practitioners on the ground are coupled. In many cases the government is more likely to be tightly coupled with its agency, with looser coupling closer to the ground. In this case there is an increased opportunity to implement locally derived solutions, allowing greater autonomy at least in practice and greater local level resilience. There is however, also the increased possibility of masked feedback to occur as the relationship between elements throughout the levels of the system is less obvious. In loosely coupled systems it is difficult to implement system wide changes—but on the other hand the gap between top level bureaucracy and local out posts of an organisation offers the room to implement locally appropriate policy/practice.

Consequently any analysis, including situational analysis and M&E, needs to identify whether the system is loosely or tightly coupled as this will dramatically effect what is achievable in terms of system wide changes. Once coupling relationships are understood strategies should be devised accordingly. For example, it may be necessary to address loose links—can relationships be improved? Or should the strategy exploit the gap and work with semi-autonomous groups within the organisation to achieve localised solutions? Social Network Analysis techniques are very useful tools in addressing these questions. The analysis should be mindful that loosely coupled systems can have distorted impacts as weak links undermine communication and exchange between levels of the system. Others too may try to exploit the gap by taking advantage of misunderstandings due to weak communication links. M&E and program management needs to be aware of the increased risk of masked feedback in loosely coupled systems and to allow for this in data collection processes. If a decision is made to tighten coupling interventions should be careful not to ignore what is lost in attempting to implement this change.

Often what interventions are attempting to achieve is the product of emergence. For example, capacity itself is something that emerges and is not reducible to its very many individual and interconnected parts. This emergence is the product of localised activity including the self-organisation of agents within the system. This means that the manifestation of organisational capacity emerges from the ground-up. In the case of interventions in the RoL system it is typical that donors, often with varying degrees of host government input, design and implement a top-down change process by virtue of its focus on the state institutions. This does not mean that such interventions do not change the local; on the contrary, they are absorbed by the local as they feed into complex dynamic systems of interconnected and interdependent elements and feedback processes. They do not, however, change the local according to plan. Local systems take on the pressures from interventions and they adapt in unpredictable ways.

State-building as a concept therefore, needs rethinking—it is likely that the ordering and hierarchies assumed by intervening actors is the wrong way around. Capacity may need to be developed from the ground-up or at least from both directions, meaning top-down forces must adapt and respond to localised changes which produce global emergence. Only so much can be achieved by technical interventions as skill and technologies are only part of capacity. Importantly, the concept of emergence means that the outcome of interventions will be unpredictable. This does not mean program management cannot make plans or predictions it just means that programming should expect to be wrong or only partly right about the outcomes. This is why M&E is so important. An M&E system must capture unintended consequences and feed back into the planning cycle immediately. Program management needs to be iterative as each emergent property impacts upon the system in unexpected ways the intervention must adapt. More attention should be paid to localised interventions. Local level changes will produce high level changes.

> *Overall, the principles of emergence mean that over-controlling approaches will not work well within complex system—that in order to maximise system adaptiveness, there must be space for innovation and novelty to occur. While this may be obvious, this is often the reverse of what happens in the real world, because of a tendency to over-define and over-control rather than simply focus on the critical rules that need to be specified and followed.*[593]

As Arthur puts it governments should not attempt to predict and coerce—but push gently... 'Not a heavy hand, not an invisible hand, but a nudging hand'.[594]

In line with the knowledge acquisition and action cycle (described in SSM) the activities of adaptive agents in capacity development programs will be motivated by factors which are largely unknown to program managers and practitioners. The information which motivates program managers and practitioners will be

593 Peter Morgan, *The Concept of Capacity* (Maastricht, the Netherlands: European Centre for Development Policy Management, 2006).

594 W. B. Arthur, "Complexity and the Economy", *Science* 284 (April 2, 1999): 107–109.

unknown to the other adaptive agents in the system. All actors, both local and interveners, will be operating based on partial understandings (bounded rationality). Whilst ABM is not a practical tool for program management and M&E at this stage the ideas behind it can be useful for analysis. For example, program managers and practitioners along with their counterparts can ask the following questions: Who are the intelligent adaptive agents in this system? What motivates their behaviour? What information/inputs is this based on? Are there general rules that govern their responses? How do they view the situation? How will they respond to a particular intervention? How will this play out with the interaction of other agents? This analysis will be vastly improved by drawing on the knowledge of such agents (stakeholders).

The best way to gain an understanding of how the agents of a system will respond to intervention and what might be the best approach to change is to facilitate the broad inclusion of intelligent agents which make up that complex system. This inclusive analysis will need to include different ways of knowing and account for, or at least be aware of, the different knowledge verification processes different agents engage in (i.e. how does information become something that compels action?). The analysis will need to be power sensitive and politically aware. Not only do power and politics influence what agents will be willing to reveal it also impacts upon motivation and behaviour generally. Agents will all be operating based on differing information. It is therefore critical that the process of planning, change and M&E communicates widely to try to build a common understanding and gain a rich picture of messy problem situations. The recognition of agency and how actors work to improve their situation not only improves analysis but it reminds interveners of the crucial need to draw on and harness existing capacities and processes and perceptions in the interests of bringing about sustainable change.

Program management and practitioners need to be aware of the potentially powerful implications of co-evolution in interventions. Not only are agents co-evolving with each other and the system itself ensuring that things are in a state of flux, local systems and their agents are co-evolving with the intervention. There are many examples of problematic adaptation which occurs within host country institutions and communities. Some of these examples include increased donor dependency. This can happen when the intervener sets up systems that the host personnel adapt to and become dependent on, but then find they are not sustainable after donor withdrawal. A simple of example of this is the overuse of paper and computers which donor introduced systems encourage and local economies cannot support. Another common problem is the withdrawal of counterparts. This often happen when practitioners take over a job within a host organisation and change it so that local personnel no longer have ownership over their workplace, often local staff cope by withdrawing from the work.

The introduction of donor knowledge and the systems of interveners systematically devalues local knowledge, it is a prevalent response in host countries for counterparts to absorb this hierarchy of knowledge and come to devalue local knowledge—this is highly problematic when it results in a disconnection of the host organisation's personnel from broader society. Local actors are also known to mimic state actors and adopt bureaucratic approaches not because they work, but because they attract funding. Whilst donor practitioners are generally pleased when local organisations begin to mimic their language and structures (as this makes them easier to deal with within their own existing structure) it can be, and often is, a negative development. It is critical that program management and M&E does not reward such damaging co-evolutionary responses to their presence as it sets up perverse and unsustainable systems.

When attempting to influence change in a system it is crucial that change agents are at least aware of the positive and negative feedback processes at play. For planning and adaptation purposes it is critical to have current information about the impact of feedback in the interests of enhancing positive feedback and counterbalancing negative feedback. Of course this assessment in itself is quite simplistic. If negative feedback does occur, working against the planned change processes, it is extremely important to be informed and mindful as to why this is happening. It may be that an intervention is having unintended consequences and/or the system is correcting itself for good reason. Also imperative for situation diagnosis, responsive adaptation and monitoring is the identification of masked and ignored feedback.

It is also important to consider feedback between systems and subsystems. If interveners or change agents are focussed on one level of a system for example they can be blind to the impact of feedback from other levels of the system which may be pushing pressure back into the system. For example, a myopic focus on a subsystem in the RoL space may result in change agents limiting their attention to the local social ordering system at the sub-national level. The risks may be perceived differently at the national political level, this may fuel objections and countering activities which impact upon the donor government. In turn negative feedback may feed back into the local level subsystem. Local knowledge will be invaluable in the identification of feedback. Any program management/M&E system should take stock of unintended consequences and ensure the identification of such involves as broader group of stakeholders as possible. Including perspectives from outside of the immediate system will also help to identify path dependent or run away positive feedback and may provide insights into how vicious cycles can be broken. Ramalingam and Jones[595] point out, the use of Log Frames themselves might be seen as a case of damaging path dependency.

595 Ben Ramalingam and Harry Jones, *Exploring the Science of Complexity: Ideas and Implications for Development and Humanitarian Efforts*, Working Paper 285 (Overseas Development Institute, 2008).

The idea that the way in which a system will behave relies heavily on the initial conditions seems obvious. It is therefore surprising how often this is ignored or obscured in the process of interventions—as well as in social scientific analysis generally. The understanding that no two systems are the same is followed by the reasonable assumption then that no two interventions in a system will be the same. The initial conditions will always be different—so too will be the outcome of any activity or change. This has several implications for conventional approaches to planning, program management, M&E and the fundamental assumptions which underpin them: For one, context specific situational analysis is critical in setting successful interventions up. Such analyses are dependent on local knowledge and as many different sources of knowledge as possible. Given the importance of initial conditions there can be no such thing as 'Best Practice' in terms of prescribed universally appropriate intervention activities. As conventional approaches to program management and M&E rely methodologically on standardised results to activities and inputs and/or comparable environments, log frames, RBM, comparative analysis and RCT are methodologically flawed tools for the evaluation of interventions. Inaccuracies in the diagnosis of the initial conditions can start a chain of inaccuracies which will magnify over time—interventions must therefore work *with* uncertainty and the unpredictable nature of complex systems. All things are *never* equal and any methodology which uses this as its starting point is grossly inadequate.

The observations regarding the inadequacy of linear projections and analysis of complex nonlinear systems are critical in understanding the woeful track record of logical or rational program management tools. Tools such as the logical framework or log frame have been explicitly criticised by those forced to use them for exactly this reason. Activity completion, leading to said output, resulting in predetermined outcome and ultimately resulting in a particular impact on the system is nothing like the experienced realties of practitioners and their counterparts. The disproportionate way in which the system responds to particular inputs means that program management and M&E tools which rely on such linear projections need to be at least recognised for what they are—flawed change theories or partially informed guesses. The importance of non-linearity in complex systems reinforces the need to use program management and M&E tools which focus on the whole and explicitly recognise the likelihood that inputs may not be followed by proportional outputs and outcomes.

Concepts such as the strange attractor, chaos and the 'edge of chaos' are helpful in that they remind us that complex systems are both orderly and unpredictable—recurrent but changeable. The commonly found pattern of order despite the turbulence in the system tells us several important things for understanding capacity development. Feedback can often keep a system within a certain boundary. This goes some way towards explaining the common complaint of practitioners and aid professionals that despite the enormous inputs there is often very little noticeable long term change achieved. It is not that the system reverts back, as is often asserted, but rather it absorbs the inputs and responds in a way that often 'corrects' the disturbance. That said radical shifts, or tipping points, are possible as is the ability to influence the system when it sits on the 'edge of chaos'. Despite its apparent 'boundaries' the system is porous, social structures are always in a state of flux and capacity development programs should be looking for opportunities to take advantage of these points.

The practical methodological limitations of comprehensively mapping a phase space which are briefly outlined above are further exacerbated in a program management and M&E context as practitioners are not social scientists. It is fair to assume that capacity development personnel are not likely to use computer modelling in program management and ongoing M&E (at least not in the immediate term). That said, the concept of a phase space may still be useful in its emphasis on the whole—the focus on the 'overall shape of the system' and the patterns and relationships which comprise it. If we accept that it is at least not practical to map all of the dimensions of the system and know the possible 'values' in an objective and comprehensive way then what is important is that we identify the crucial elements and processes of the system. Through an inclusive approach of local participation and constant ongoing reflection this is both manageable and has its own productive value. In this way the concept of the phase space can be utilised in mapping the stakeholders within that phase space and mapping their contributions to illuminating the aspects of the system.

Summarising Complexity

The above exploration has covered a wide range of ethereal facets to provide an in-depth look at the concept of complex social systems. It would be disingenuous—and unnecessary—to suggest that these intricate notions were anything but challenging to grasp. It may be many years to come before someone has managed to articulate this dense space into a straightforward manner that is widely accessible—particularly to those working in the field where it is needed most. While such delineation would indeed enhance our capacity to navigate through these areas more adeptly, making day to day programming and design more palatable, its absence is not entirely cause for concern, given that the growing recognition and awareness of the underlying notion of complexity in and of itself provides sufficient ammunition to push back on the static, linear, reductionist notions in use for decades. Simple insights such as the need to focus on the fluid interconnectedness of the many key relationships comprising mission environments should go a long way towards shifting our attention onto the forces that matter, and altering our imaginations as to what actually constitutes the spaces in which peace and capacity development endeavours operate.

Complexity and Policing for Capacity Development

How might these heady conceptual discussions translate into a key area of contemporary policing? As mentioned in Chapter 1, the trend into building the capacity of indigenous police forces is perhaps the most significant change in practice regarding the overall space of international policing. Its ramifications are relevant not only to the allocation of resources but also to M&E by virtue of the fact that how one delineates capacity development affects how policing assessments should be made. This fact alone warrants the brief section that follows wherein key components, such as defining capacity building, are examined while underscoring the need to view this space holistically through a complex social systems lens.

Defining Capacity Building

"I can't define capacity but I know it when I see it".[596] The concept of capacity building both in theory and in practice is not well established. It has not attracted a lot of attention at a scholarly level and there are no blueprints.[597] Prior to the 1990s capacity building projects were tailored to address short-term, technical issues—focused on filling gaps in skills and competencies. There was a tendency to diagnose problems from the outside and respond to these shortfalls with training programs and equipment delivery.[598] The World Bank describes this as technical rather than institutional capacity.[599] Similarly, we use the terms 'technical capacity' and 'organisational capacity' when making the distinction.

The distinction between technical and organisational capacity is crucial in understanding appropriate approaches to capacity building assistance and corresponding performance M&E. Despite the criticisms of technical approaches, such assistance is still useful and highly appropriate in some contexts. For example, when organisational capacity already exists, targeted gap filling approaches may be exactly what are required. In the case of the AFP, technical approaches are common through the Law Enforcement Cooperation Program (LECP).[600] The

---

596 Peter Morgan, *The Concept of Capacity* (Maastricht, the Netherlands: European Centre for Development Policy Management, 2006), title page.

597 Peter Morgan, *The Concept of Capacity* (Maastricht, the Netherlands: European Centre for Development Policy Management, 2006), title page.

598 Callisto Madavo, *Building Effective States: Forging Engaged Societies*, Report of the World Bank Task Force on Capacity Development in Africa, (Washington D.C.: World Bank, 2005), 38.

599 Callisto Madavo, *Building Effective States: Forging Engaged Societies*, Report of the World Bank Task Force on Capacity Development in Africa, (Washington D.C.: World Bank, 2005), 38.

600 Australian Federal Police (AFP), *Australian Federal Police Submission to the Senate Standing Committee on Foreign Affairs, Defence and Trade: Inquiry into Australia's*

AFP acknowledges "a key requirement for LECP is the existence of a functioning police force that is ready to build on core police knowledge and skills".[601] As we argue throughout, it is the *process* of reaching this point which should be the key concern. That is, contemporary capacity building approaches should aim at a far broader idea of capacity than merely technical skills and capabilities. Capacity building has since been recognised as being both a means and an end of development.[602] By this, it is meant that the *process* of developing capacity is in fact itself capacity building. It is generally recognised this process is non-linear[603] and is the subject of open systems,[604] therefore highly susceptible to an enormous range of influencing and external factors.[605]

The concept of capacity building is not easily defined and the range of definitions is enormous. The following definitions have been selected to complement each other as they best encapsulate the enormity and complexity of the subject.

> *Capacity development is taken to mean the growth of formal organizational [sic] relationships and abilities; i.e. those changes in organizational behaviour, values, skills and relationships that lead to the improved abilities of groups and organizations to carry out functions and achieve desired outcomes over time . . . Capacity development can thus refer to either process or outcomes—i.e. those efforts to improve organizational performance and/or results of those efforts in terms of capacities developed.*[606]

> *Capacity is that emergent combination of attributes, assets, capabilities and relationships that enables human systems to perform, survive and self-renew.*—Peter Morgan[607]

Involvement in Peacekeeping Operations (Canberra: Commonwealth of Australia, 2007b).

601 Australian Federal Police (AFP), *Australian Federal Police Submission to the Senate Standing Committee on Foreign Affairs, Defence and Trade: Inquiry into Australia's Involvement in Peacekeeping Operations* (Canberra: Commonwealth of Australia, 2007b).

602 Julia Zinke, *Monitoring & Evaluation of Capacity and Capacity Development: Workshop Report*, (Maastricht, The Netherlands: European Centre for Development Policy Management, 2006), 2.

603 Julia Zinke, *Monitoring & Evaluation of Capacity and Capacity Development: Workshop Report*, (Maastricht, The Netherlands: European Centre for Development Policy Management, 2006), 14.

604 Simeon Yates, *Doing Social Science Research*, (London: Sage Publications, 2004), 10.

605 Nils Boesen, *Institutional Assessment and Capacity Development: Why, what and how?*, Concept Paper on Aid Delivery Methods (Luxembourg: EuropeAid, European Commission, 2006), 7.

606 Peter Morgan, *The Design and Use of Capacity Development Indicators*, Paper prepared for the Policy Branch of the Canadian International Development Agency (1997), iii.

607 Julia Zinke, *Monitoring & Evaluation of Capacity and Capacity Development: Workshop Report*, (Maastricht, The Netherlands: European Centre for Development Policy Management, 2006), 5.

Official Development Assistance (ODA)

When planning the M&E process it is crucial to note that policing organisations operating in an international capacity building environment are increasingly required to meet the challenges of the development agenda. The use of ODA for police operations is now common practice in the evolving security-development nexus. For participating OECD DAC countries this means there is enormous pressure on police to produce development outcomes. Policing organisations are not in the practice of looking for 'development outcomes' and meeting the reporting requirements will require a reorientation of focus.[608] This is a highly political arena and concern to use ODA funding for development priorities is crucial for the legitimacy of policing organisations delivering assistance. ODA criteria specify that for assistance to be classified as ODA it must be "administered with the promotion of the economic development and welfare of developing countries as its main objective". "The supply of donor police services to control civil disobedience is not reportable", nor is the interruption of violence or "enforcement aspects of peacekeeping".[609]

Not only are police confronted with the challenge of demonstrating development outcomes from policing initiatives, they are subject to the same accountability priorities applicable to development agencies. This means meeting the requirements specified by the international community (particularly DAC) regarding process, reporting and accountability in relation to aid effectiveness. The principle international agreements include: The Paris Declaration; Millennium Development Goals (MDGs); DAC Criteria for Evaluating Development Assistance; and other DAC guidelines.

There is not space within the scope of this book to discuss the contents of these agreements, however to appreciate the relevance of the proposed methodology it is important to note the heavy emphasis on partner country priorities present in these declarations. Of particular importance are the 'Paris' priorities of ownership, harmonisation, alignment, mutual accountability, and managing for results. The MDGs illustrate a focused concern with 'development partnerships' and the DAC Criteria emphasises the principles of relevance, effectiveness, efficiency, impact and sustainability. The DAC Evaluation Quality Standards too, recommend genuine stakeholder involvement in the process of evaluation.[610]

---

608 Various interviews with AFP police practitioners and program management. 2009–2010.

609 Organisation for Economic Cooperation and Development, *Is it ODA?*, OECD Fact Sheet (2008) http://www.oecd.org/dataoecd/21/21/34086975.pdf.

610 Organisation for Economic Cooperation and Development—Development Assistance Committee, *DAC Evaluation Quality Standards* (2006), http://www.oecd.org/dataoecd/34/21/38686856.pdf.

In summary, the capacity building field is evolving and international consensus regarding the subject is growing. This demonstrates a more holistic understanding of capacity and as such requires a complex approach to capacity building and development that encapsulates this understanding particularly in the kinds of international capacity development projects the IDG and similar organisations are involved in. Increasingly, these policing organisations are called upon to act outside the roles that are commonly used for and to adapt to structures and programmes they are unfamiliar with, such as ODA, which will require them to redefine their approaches to policing and capacity building with a development framework in mind.

CHAPTER EIGHT

BECOMING EMOTIONAL ABOUT ASSESSMENT

The previous chapter covering the notion of complexity was as important as it was challenging. As slippery as these concepts may appear, it is vital that we come to grips with what their advice means to the manner in which international interventions are designed, implemented, and ultimately evaluated. The ensuing chapter is no easier insofar as it too takes a radically unorthodox vantage point that requires a leap from conventional imaginations. Its details concern the relationship between human behaviour and emotion, which in itself is anything but straightforward. In plain terms, we posit that emotion is central to human behaviour, and thus an improved appreciation of how emotions affect and are affected by mission activities stands to significantly enhance our understanding of what is happening now and therefore how to go forward.

Underlying this practical exploration of emotion's utility to M&E however is a much larger debate. In short, the examination takes on conventional social science approaches in terms of what is considered legitimate versus illegitimate forms of knowledge, which includes a critique of the mythical construct of 'rational' behaviour. Insights from such explorations further destabilise conventional wisdom by problematising its core while serving us well with the endeavour of forging new approaches.

We begin an investigation of these broad topics by pointing out a rather specific problem: that while emotions are at the core of human behaviour, they have received little attention in conceptions of international policing where only 'rational' behaviour tends to be taken seriously. This blind spot is problematic, *inter alia* because it leads to an impoverished understanding of what contributes to the successes or failures of peace operations. This chapter makes a foray into this space, positing that a better understanding of the relationship between emotions (of local and intervening actors alike) and international policing performance could lead to improvements in mission design as well as implementation. The chapter identifies methods with the capacity to assess performance through the lens of emotion.

Although international policing missions deploy into conflict environments charged with emotions, the role of emotions remains starkly under-conceptualized. In particular, contemporary frameworks designed to assess performance fail to take account of emotion in any considered manner.[611] Emotions are seen as 'deviations from rationality'; incapable and undeserving of the kind of attention other more concrete factors demand.[612] However, not only are emotions at the core of human existence, situating us in relation to others and to the world around us, they take on even greater importance during times of conflict and in the aftermath.[613] Indeed, some place this factor at the heart of policing goals by arguing that the reduction of fear is tantamount to curtailing the injuries and economic losses suffered by victims.[614] Positive feelings too, such as hope and solidarity, must not be overlooked since they are equally likely to arise among both the local population and the intervening parties. Not only are processes of conflict and reconciliation underpinned and influenced by emotion,[615] there is a need to engage emotion actively in order to rebuild communities after the trauma of conflict.[616] It is within the emotional cauldrons that characterize peace and capacity building missions that civilian police are expected, indeed relied upon, to achieve their mandates to do with establishing sustainable law and justice.

Neta Crawford sums up the main problem of this lack of engagement: that peacebuilding efforts too often fail—leading to a renewal of violence.[617] Yet no different to other mission components, if policing activities evoke the 'wrong'

---

611 Ylber Bajraktari, Arthur Boutellis, Fatema Gunja, Daniel Harris, James Kapsis, Eva Kaye and Jane Rhee, *The PRIME System: Measuring the Success of Post-Conflict Police Reform*, (Princeton: Princeton University, 2006); Cheyanne Church and Julie Shouldice, *The Evaluation of Conflict Resolution: Framing the State of Play* (Derry: INCORE International Conflict Research, 2002); Todd Foglesong, Zainab Latif, Cybele Merrick, Janet Miller, James Parsons and Timothy Ross, *Measuring Progress toward Safety and Justice: A Global Guide to the Design of Performance Indicators in the Justice Sector* (New York: Vera Institute, 2003).

612 Jonathan Mercer, "Rationality and Psychology in International Politics", *International Organization* 59 (2005), 97.

613 Roland Bleiker and Emma Hutchinson, "Fear No More: Emotions and World Politics," *Review of International Studies* 34 (2008): 123. For the emotional bonds forged among Dutch peacekeepers, see Joanne Mouthan, Martin Euwema and Jos Weerts, "A Band of Brothers in U.N. Peacekeeping: Social Bonding Among Dutch Peacekeeping Veterans," *Military Psychology* 17 no. 2 (2005): 104.

614 Wesley Skogan and Kathleen Frydal, *Fairness and Effectiveness in Policing: The Evidence* (Washington DC: National Academies Press, 2004), 85.

615 Sara Ahmed, *The Cultural Politics of Emotion* (Edinburgh: Edinburgh University Press, 2004), 28–31.

616 Emma Hutchinson and Roland Bleiker, "Emotional Reconciliation: Reconstituting Identity and Community after Trauma," *European Journal of Social Theory* 11 no. 3 (2008), 385–403.

617 Neta Crawford, "The Passion of World Politics: Propositions on Emotion and Emotional Relationships," *International Society* 24 no. 4 (2000): 116.

emotional responses at the wrong times (including among the peacekeepers themselves), the prospect of a sustainable peace can be severely diminished. While coercion may of course be necessary, resentment and anger from the local population regarding the manner in which peacekeepers have conducted themselves is an all too recurrent theme, which contains clearly negative ramifications toward 'success' insofar as it is liable to instil resistance to future mission activities.[618] On the other hand are examples whereby winning the hearts and minds of the people has proved beneficial to efforts for sustainable peace.[619]

Given the key role that emotions undoubtedly play in mission outcomes it may seem surprising that the dominant discussions have resisted diving beneath the surface of this aspect.[620] Symptomatically, managers are expected to rise above such 'corrupting' forces which would apparently only weaken decision making. This oversight may be less startling when it is acknowledged that the same gap exists in the broader realm of international relations, but it is no less problematic.[621] What explains this? While there may be difficulties in accurately acquiring 'hard' data such as how many arrests have been made or how many weapons have been collected, admittedly it is another challenge altogether to comprehend the emotional relationships influencing the actions and reactions between the panoply of intervening and local actors. Following others,[622] I maintain that the social science traditions which dominate this field are ill-equipped to deal with a phenomenon that is as ephemeral, internal and seemingly 'irrational'. The challenges associated with capturing emotion do not however excuse

618 See, for example, Jonathan Wald, "Sex Abuse of Girls in Congo Continues", CNN, 8 Jan. 2005 (at: www.cnn.com/2005/WORLD/africa/01/08/congo.peacekeepers.sex/index.html).

619 E.g., see the Liberian experience outlined in 'New UN Military Advisor Takes up Post amid Surge in Peacekeeping', UN News Centre, 24 July 2008 (at: www.un.org/apps/news/story.asp?NewsID=27483&Cr=Peacekeeping&Cr1=html).

620 See periodic UN Secretary General reports on peacekeeping missions: UN Peace Operations 2002/Bosnia/Herzogovina; UN Peace Ops 2002/Sierra Leone; EUPM Report 2003.

621 See Roland Bleiker and Emma Hutchinson, "Fear No More: Emotions and World Politics," *Review of International Studies* 34 (2008): 115–35; Neta Crawford, "The Passion of World Politics: Propositions on Emotion and Emotional Relationships," *International Society* 24 no. 4 (2000): 116–56.

622 See Roland Bleiker and Emma Hutchinson, "Fear No More: Emotions and World Politics," *Review of International Studies* 34 (2008); Neta Crawford, "The Passion of World Politics: Propositions on Emotion and Emotional Relationships," *International Society* 24 no. 4 (2000); Richard Ned Lebow, "Reason, Emotion, and Cooperation", *International Politics* 42 no. 3 (2008): 283–313; George Marcus, "Emotions in Politics", *Annual Review of Political Science* 3 no. 1 (2000): 221–50; Christine Sylvester, "Bringing Art/Museums to Feminist International Relations", in *Feminist Methodologies for International Relations*, ed. Brooke Ackerly, Maria Stern and Jacqui True (Cambridge: Cambridge University Press, 2006): 201–2.

its neglect. After all, if those relinquishing their weapons continue to harbour malice, the knowledge of this 'indicator' seems more important to the prospect for peace than does the number of weapons removed from circulation.

The purpose of this chapter extends beyond generating an awareness of how emotion both affects and is affected by international policing in order to begin to outline ways in which these relationships may be assessed. Although the focus is policing, there is clear potential to apply insights generated across the gamut of peace operation components. This endeavour to take emotions seriously contains three facets. In the first instance, the vital role that emotions play in the outcomes of policing missions must be recognized. Accordingly, the chapter proceeds with a discussion about emotions in general and then in the context of policing more specifically. That discussion is followed by a brief review of the prevailing manner in which international policing (and peace operations more broadly) is conceived. The point is to highlight the absence of emotion in contemporary conceptions despite its presence being ubiquitous. The second line of argument advanced is that we need to go beyond the dominant social science methods to more fully understand the relationship between emotions and policing. This section of the book examines the reasons for the absence of emotion in mainstream conceptions, concluding that the social science approaches which inform the dominant conceptions of international policing lack the ability to account for emotion in a robust manner. In practice this reliance on rationality leads to blinkered solutions. The final facet of our exploration outlines methods that can be developed to assess policing activities—from an emotional vantage point.

Conceptualizing Emotion

A necessary starting point for this exploration is a delineation of emotion itself. What do we mean by the term? What are the relationships between emotion and both perception and cognition? What arouses particular emotions at particular times? And, perhaps most importantly, how can emotion affect behaviour? Responses to these core questions are set out in this section.

While there is no exhaustive list of what types of feelings comprise emotion, the following give an indication of the variations that such an investigation must consider—each of which may play a significant role in the effect and affect of international policing. Aristotle put forward ten emotions: anger, fear, shame, envy, jealousy, friendship, calm, favour, pity, indignation; whereas Darwin concentrated on anxiety, grief, dejection, despair, joy, love, devotion, ill temper, determination, hatred, anger, defiance, contempt, disgust, guilt, pride, shame, modesty and sulkiness. Hobbes' focus ranged from fear and contempt to honour and compassion. Although we should accept these labels as the linguistic artefacts handed down by the various cultures from which they were drawn, we can nevertheless enquire about an ontology that may apply across cultures. An in-depth examination of the many theories associated with emotion is beyond the scope of this chapter, yet a summary of main viewpoints is important in order to establish how might be understood relative to the questions posed above.

We therefore highlight the viewpoints of biological theorists, cognitive psychologists, and social constructivists to arrive at a position that serves as the basis for our understanding. As Crawford contends, each of these major vantage points offers something toward how emotion should be conceived.[623] Biological theorists, for their part, focus on the physical phenomena associated with emotion to point out how humans change physiologically depending on the types of emotions experienced.[624] The 'fight or flight' phenomenon marked by intense adrenaline is a credible example to come from this field of study.

However, a full understanding of the complexity of emotion cannot be reduced to a series of biological responses; there is much more to consider in the social world that makes up the environment for international policing missions. As Sara Ahmed observes,[625] there is immediacy to the biologist way of thinking about emotion that denies any cognitive or judgment link to informing the emotional reaction. The work of cognitive psychologists is thus crucial to such an expanded understanding. The tenets can be traced back to Aristotle as well as modern thinkers such as Martha Nussbaum or Jean-Paul Sartre. The key contribution is that emotions stem from (and therefore equate to) thoughts and beliefs.[626] *Inter alia*, emotions influence how we understand the past, and importantly, how we anticipate the future.[627] This viewpoint makes clear the value of accounting for emotions when one aims to understand the relationship between peacekeeping activities and the 'recipients' because it provides an avenue into what each is thinking.

---

623 Roland Bleiker and Emma Hutchinson, "Fear No More: Emotions and World Politics," *Review of International Studies* 34 (2008): 117, note that while psychologist and constructivist approaches can add useful insights, they should nevertheless be augmented by additional modes of enquiry including those from the humanities.

624 Paul Ekman, "An Argument for Basic Emotions", in *Emotion: Themes in the Philosophy of the Mind*, ed. Sean Crawford (Open University Worldwide, 2005), 230–46.

625 Sara Ahmed, *The Cultural Politics of Emotion* (Edinburgh: Edinburgh University Press, 2004), 5.

626 Gordon Bower, "Mood and Memory," *American Psychologist* 36 no. 2 (1981): 129–48; Neta Crawford, "The Passion of World Politics: Propositions on Emotion and Emotional Relationships," *International Society* 24 no. 4 (2000); Andrew Ortony, Gerald Clore and Allen Collins, *The Cognitive Structure of Emotion* (Cambridge: Cambridge University Press, 1988): 12–13.

627 Gordon Bower, "Mood and Memory," *American Psychologist* 36 no. 2 (1981): 129–48; George Marcus, "Emotions in Politics", *Annual Review of Political Science* 3 no. 1 (2000): 140; Andrew Ortony, Gerald Clore and Allen Collins, *The Cognitive Structure of Emotion* (Cambridge: Cambridge University Press, 1988): 12–13.

Social constructivists take this link between emotions and cognition further by arguing that our emotions are socially constructed and maintained.[628] According to this view, emotions are learned through social interactions.[629] Humans remember what happened and how it made them feel (as they interpreted it in a particular social context), and then use this 'learning' to inform how they feel and thus respond subsequently. The sight of a UN uniform, for example, could conjure up emotions ranging from relief to grief or even anger, depending upon the past experiences of the particular individual. Therefore, even though feelings may only be experienced *internally*, the meanings attached and the behaviours associated are cognitively and culturally constructed.[630] Socialization matters fundamentally. This means that we must recognise how a particular context and its historical forces may shape the emotion of the various actors. Crucial to post-conflict healing and reintegration processes is the corollary that if emotions can be learned so too they can be re-learned. Thus an awareness of these issues can be employed in order to more effectively institute the critical processes of change.

In sum, when emotion is understood not only as a phenomenon which affects us biologically but also as linked directly, through social interaction, to our thoughts, the utility of engaging emotions becomes apparent because it tells us about performance where it matters most: in the minds of relevant actors. More specifically, it can offer meaningful insights into whether particular activities have affected progress towards peace.

Emotion and Political Behaviour

Having outlined an understanding of emotion, the enquiry turns to the relationship between political behaviour (broadly construed) and emotion, before concentrating on the more specific relationship with international policing. What role might it occupy in politics? The view we subscribe to is that emotions are 'absolutely central' to politics.[631] Others agree, pointing out how emotion underpins everything from nationalism, leadership and decision making, and even the

---

628 Claire Armon-Jones, "The Thesis of Constructionism", in *Social Construction of Emotions*, ed. Rom Harre (Oxford: Blackwell, 1986), 33–4; James Averill, "A Constructionist View of Emotion," in *Emotion: Themes in the Philosophy of the Mind*, ed. Sean Crawford (Open University Worldwide, 2005), 250.

629 Sara Ahmed, *The Cultural Politics of Emotion* (Edinburgh: Edinburgh University Press, 2004), 6.

630 Neta Crawford, "The Passion of World Politics: Propositions on Emotion and Emotional Relationships," *International Society* 24 no. 4 (2000): 125.

631 Richard Ned Lebow, "Reason, Emotion, and Cooperation", *International Politics* 42 no. 3 (2008): 283.

creation of the polis itself.[632] Even the great philosophical and religious traditions have long recognised the connection between emotion and behaviour.

There is a crucial link to collective action. To understand cooperation we must understand how emotions and reason interact to create and sustain common identities.[633] If we consider the outpour of relief funds to the victims of the 2004 Tsunami or the global solidarity shown towards the United States immediately following the September 11, 2001 terrorist attacks, the linkages between emotional conditions and collective behaviour become clear. Of course, past emotional experiences must not be overlooked in the meantime since their legacy will influence future emotions, and thus behaviour. Judgements will depend on actors' pre-existing emotions and the emotional relationships among various actors.[634]

The 'politics of emotion' is a concept which highlights how emotion can be the driving ingredient binding collectives such as nations, kinship groups and religious communities through the shaping of memory and relationships.[635] This proposition is vital because cooperation underpins sustainable peace.

Appreciating Emotions in Peace and Policing Operations

Recognising that emotions play an omnipresent role in world politics, how does this translate to the narrower context of peace operations? This section explores how the lessons transfer into the narrower context. In short, emotions are no less important in the processes relating to peace operations than they are to politics generally.[636] Traumatic events not only generate powerful emotions, most notably fear, shock, anger and resentment, but they are more on display in crises.[637] This suggests that certain *clusters* of emotion may come into being during specific circumstances, an idea that holds significant promise for performance analyses. For instance, emotions such as fear and anger are likely to pervade periods high

632 Sara Ahmed, *The Cultural Politics of Emotion* (Edinburgh: Edinburgh University Press, 2004), 42–43; George Marcus, "Emotions in Politics", *Annual Review of Political Science* 3 no. 1 (2000): 222; Richard Ned Lebow, "Reason, Emotion, and Cooperation", *International Politics* 42 no. 3 (2008): 299.

633 Roland Bleiker and Emma Hutchinson, "Fear No More: Emotions and World Politics," *Review of International Studies* 34 (2008): 123; Richard Ned Lebow, "Reason, Emotion, and Cooperation", *International Politics* 42 no. 3 (2008): 283.

634 Neta Crawford, "The Passion of World Politics: Propositions on Emotion and Emotional Relationships," *International Society* 24 no. 4 (2000): 119.

635 Sara Ahmed, *The Cultural Politics of Emotion* (Edinburgh: Edinburgh University Press, 2004), 42–3.

636 Neta Crawford, "The Passion of World Politics: Propositions on Emotion and Emotional Relationships," *International Society* 24 no. 4 (2000): 119.

637 Jenny Edkins, *Trauma and the Memory of Politics* (Cambridge: Cambridge University Press, 2003), 4–5; Emma Hutchinson and Roland Bleiker, "Emotional Reconciliation: Reconstituting Identity and Community after Trauma," *European Journal of Social Theory* 11 no. 3 (2008), 385.

in violence, whereas feelings of calm and reconciliation should become apparent in post-conflict phases. This brief narrative—recounting a transformation of emotion within the UN peace operation in Timor Leste—offers a case in point.

> *"These are our forces!" chanted a group of children. They jumped and danced around, waving at a white UN helicopter that circled low over their neighbourhood... Slowly, Dili changed.... People started to feel safer. The suffocating atmosphere of fear began to dissipate, yielding to a joyous, but cautious, optimism.*[638]

Yet these kinds of observation, laden with emotional content, are not rare in accounts of peace operations. The problem is that such observations, which in this case reflect the unfolding success of mission activities, are taken for granted and not understood at deeper and more analytically rich levels. Recognising the need, for instance, to win hearts and minds is simply not enough. It is necessary to unpack and tap into the indicators which can tell us about international policing performance and the complex emotional relationships that exist between various actors. The key is to capture and interpret appropriately what emotions exist in a particular place and time among various groups. Performance analyses can be greatly enhanced accordingly.

More considered reporting on the sexual exploitation and abuse of local populations by international security forces is one such issue. It can be vital for the sustainable security of local populations as well as on future missions since abusive acts can breed cultures of resentment and mistrust. Speaking about the actions of peacekeeping forces in the Democratic Republic of Congo (DRC), the Under-Secretary for UN peacekeeping operations, Jean-Marie Guéhenno lamented, 'When I see people being tainted by the actions of those who've committed abuse, it demoralizes the mission, it destroys the trust that the Congolese have in the UN's peacekeeping mission in Congo and in the effort of the United Nations.'[639] Haiti and East Timor provide additional examples cases of abuse by armed conflict state security forces—ostensibly present in a protective capacity.[640]

The trauma that people experience during conflict shapes their emotional responses to the police in the post-conflict environment as well. In Timor Leste, for instance, the Judicial System Monitoring Programme report on police treatment of women highlighted reluctance by women to report crime to the reformed

---

638 Irena Cristalis, *Bitter Dawn: East Timor, A People's Story* (London: Zed Books, 2002), 157.

639 Jonathan Wald, "Sex Abuse of Girls in Congo Continues", CNN, 8 Jan. 2005 (at: www.cnn.com/2005/WORLD/africa/01/08/congo.peacekeepers.sex/index.html).

640 Irena Cristalis, *Bitter Dawn: East Timor, A People's Story* (London: Zed Books, 2002), 157; Human Rights Watch, *Global Report on Women's Human Rights* (New York: Human Rights Watch, Women's Rights Project, 1995); Judicial System Monitoring Programme, Police Treatment of Women in East Timor, (Dili: JSMP, 2005).

police service.[641] Undoubtedly, this trend is contingent upon a wide range of factors which includes a history of endemic gender-based discrimination. Yet at the same time the acknowledgement of a multitude of factors should not diminish the case that emotional reactions such as mistrust and fear of the policing institution are likely to have contributed to this reticence by locals.

On the other hand, if policing actions engender the types of emotions that ultimately prove conducive to peace and security, these contributions can go a long way toward achieving necessary milestones for success. Nigel Fielding and Martin Innes argue that 'policing should undertake not only to make people 'objectively' safer but also improve their 'subjective' feelings of security',[642] suggesting that police must consider closely the public perceptions of their actions. However, even signs of improvement must not be interpreted superficially. For example, only after an in-depth analysis of case of the DRC did it come to light that the increase in trust toward peacekeepers by some females was due largely to the fact that peacekeepers were merely treating them better than the non-peacekeeping soldiers which had brutally raped them.[643] A cursory assessment would have overlooked the underlying reason for the 'improvement' and falsely attributed the positive relationship to policing performance, thereby failing to alert supervisors to the practices of 'survival sex' with peacekeepers, into which the women had been effectively impelled. The upshot is that not only will legacy feelings need to be addressed when advancing security sector reform, but they should also be considered in the performance evaluations of these activities.

The emotional engagement of the intervening police themselves with the conflict/post-conflict environment is similarly important. It is not difficult to imagine that a police contingent whose members are marred by disgust, anger or a lack of compassion for either local populations or their indigenous police counterparts is unlikely to conduct itself in the optimum fashion. On a positive note, there is an increasing emphasis on the emotional stability of police. The need for new officers to function appropriately in the face of grotesque death events or extreme grief, for example, is recognised.[644] New police recruits may be engaged in informal desensitization processes conducted by senior officers

---

641 Judicial System Monitoring Programme, Police Treatment of Women in East Timor, (Dili: JSMP, 2005), 13.

642 Nigel Fielding and Martin Innes, "Reassurance Policing, Community Policing and Measuring Police Performance," *Policing and Society: An International Journal of Research and Policy* 16, no. 2 (2006): 130.

643 Refugees International, "Must Boys be Boys? Sexual Exploitation in UN Missions", (Refugees International, 2005) www.refugeesinternational.org/section/publications/pk_exploit.

644 Vincent Henry, *Death Work: Police, Trauma, and the Psychology of Survival* (Oxford: Oxford University Press, 2004), 26.

to build their 'emotional toughness'.[645] However, such preparation designed to build emotional resilience is not the same as acknowledging that emotions (however well-restrained) influence police behaviour, and therefore how the institution of policing is represented then perceived. Hence the feelings of intervening police must be incorporated into assessment frameworks no less so than others, because if they experience the 'wrong' types of emotions at the wrong times, this too can have a devastating effect on success.[646]

The above examination, however brief, highlights the central role played by emotions in peace and policing missions. Richard Rorty, for instance, maintains that feelings, rather than knowledge, determine the respect for human rights. As he expresses it, '[t]he emergence of the human rights culture seems to owe nothing to increased moral knowledge and everything to hearing sad and sentimental stories.'[647] This observation sounds the following warning concerning a conceptually narrow evaluative focus on the activities comprising civilian policing: that technical excellence may matter little to positive outcomes if emotions are left unaccounted for. Similarly, it emphasises the need to consider the feelings of the intervening forces, because it is they who must be counted on to ensure proper behaviour such as upholding human rights. Democratic policing practices and the RoL depend on it. Having summarized the indispensible part emotions play in politics broadly as well as illustrated this point in police missions more narrowly, the discussion now examines how the topic is treated by the mainstream views.

Mainstream Conceptions: Where is the Emotion?

As above, we begin with the macro narratives and then move to a narrower focus on policing since the realm of international policing can be located as a subset of, and informed by, the much wider (western) traditions of examining world politics. Despite the remarkably visible place emotions occupy in human behaviour, and the reality that emotions are a part of all decisions, the dominant conceptualizations of world politics have tended to stay clear of emotions, putting them in the 'too hard basket'. The 'politics of fear' is a rare exception. However, the

---

645 Vincent Henry, *Death Work: Police, Trauma, and the Psychology of Survival* (Oxford: Oxford University Press, 2004), 28–31.

646 For exploration of the many stressors experienced by peacekeepers that generate emotions may adversely affect performance see, Pena Garrido and Maria Muñoz, "Morale as a Protection Factor against Mission Related Stress", in *Human Dimensions in Military Operations—Military Leaders' Strategies for Addressing Stress and Psychological Support*, 10.1–10.2, http://ftp.rta.nato.int/public//PubFullText/RTO/MP/RTO-MP-HFM-134/MP-HFM-134-10.pdf.

647 Richard Rorty, "Human Rights, Rationality, and Sentimentality", in *On Human Rights: The Oxford Amnesty Lectures*, ed. Stephen Shute and Susan Hurley (New York: Basic Books, 1993), 118.

conceptualization of how fear affects mobilization ends almost before it begins; similarly deficient, it fails to engage the myriad other (positive) emotions that may link to collective action.[648] Martha Finnemore and Kathryn Sikkink observe how 'affect and empathy have been swept under the carpet in recent decades.... The result is politics without passion or principles which is hardly the politics of the world in which we live.'[649]

Paradoxically, although most notable political thinkers from the western tradition have given emotion substantial attention, the study of emotions is still in its 'infancy'.[650] At least since James Madison in the eighteenth century, it has been common to treat emotion as something which needs to be minimized to make way for decisions based on reason.[651] This legacy equates thinking with cognition on the one hand and feeling with affect on the other. Western political theory has effectively set apart the emotion of love, for example, relegating it to the private sphere on the basis that it has an irrational or corrupting influence in civil affairs.[652]

A Reliance on 'Rational Humans'

Instead, mainstream political conceptions assume that the key ingredient of cooperation, for instance, 'should be studied from the perspective of egoistic, individual actors responding primarily to external stimuli'.[653] This ontological view of the social world has been imported from micro-economics and is now found across the social sciences.[654] This 'rational actor' paradigm became dominant in the mid-twentieth century as the foundation of social sciences theory. As such, mainstream political theory promulgates the view that 'progress' requires

648 See Neta Crawford, "The Passion of World Politics: Propositions on Emotion and Emotional Relationships," *International Society* 24 no. 4 (2000): 146, who notes that even the terms fear and threat are often left 'dangerously fuzzy'. See also Richard Ned Lebow, "Reason, Emotion, and Cooperation", *International Politics* 42 no. 3 (2008): 305.

649 Martha Finnemore and Kathryn Sikkink, "International Norm Dynamics and Political Change", *International Organization* 52 no. 4 (1998): 916.

650 Andrew Linklater, "Emotion and World Politics", *Aberystwyth Journal of World Affairs* 2 (2004), 71.

651 George Marcus, "Emotions in Politics", *Annual Review of Political Science* 3 no. 1 (2000): 222.

652 Paul Cocoran, "*Liaisons dangereuses*: Friends, Enemies and Others", paper at Australian Political Studies Association Conference, 6–9 July 2008, 2.

653 Richard Ned Lebow, "Reason, Emotion, and Cooperation", *International Politics* 42 no. 3 (2008): 283.

654 Richard Ned Lebow, "Reason, Emotion, and Cooperation", *International Politics* 42 no. 3 (2008): 291.

less emotion and more reason, even though emotions are vital to these so-called rational processes.[655]

The assertion that the 'rational' individual is natural is both historically and conceptually flawed. In ancient Greece, for example, the concept of self-interested individual did not exist, and even today many societies are still likely to define themselves in communal rather than individual terms.[656] The core ingredient of self-interest was not even used as the first principle of economic models until the late nineteenth century.[657] An otherwise staunch proponent of the rational actor paradigm, Kenneth Waltz, strays temporarily from this standpoint to admit that 'one cannot expect political leaders to make the nicely calculated decisions that the word 'rationality' suggests'.[658] Among the numerous unrealistic expectations attached to this conception is the capacity that humans can gain 'full' knowledge of any given circumstance in order for an individual to make so-called rational decisions;[659] and put in stark terms: with the exception of 'sociopaths, the rest of us are embedded in a web of relationships' as opposed to the atomistic egoism which underpins traditional social science views.[660]

Consequently, processes of world politics, such as post-conflict peacebuilding or norm following, are typically considered from the perspective of rationality, despite a compelling case to the contrary. Emotions, more generally, are treated with misgivings or indifference. Innumerable stereotypes, such as 'hysterical women', attach yet go unrecognised as well—each of which can misinform decision making. This state of affairs is not only undesirable but unnecessary. Emotions can be conceptualized in a manner that will shed light onto the critical aspects that are left unexplored by traditional social sciences perspectives.

---

655 George Marcus, "Emotions in Politics", *Annual Review of Political Science* 3 no. 1 (2000): 221; Neta Crawford, "The Passion of World Politics: Propositions on Emotion and Emotional Relationships," *International Society* 24 no. 4 (2000): 145.

656 Richard Ned Lebow, "Reason, Emotion, and Cooperation", *International Politics* 42 no. 3 (2008): 291–2.

657 Amartya Sen, "Rational Fools: A Critique of the Behavioural Foundations of Economic Theory", in *Scientific Models and Men*, ed. H. Harris (Oxford: Oxford University Press, 1978), 321.

658 Kenneth Waltz, "Reflections on *Theory of International Politics*: A Response to My Critics", in *Neorealism and its Critics*, ed. Robert Keohane (New York: Columbia University Press, 1986), 330.

659 Neta Crawford, "The Passion of World Politics: Propositions on Emotion and Emotional Relationships," *International Society* 24 no. 4 (2000): 146.

660 Richard Ned Lebow, "Reason, Emotion, and Cooperation", *International Politics* 42 no. 3 (2008): 296.

Methods and Emotion: Thinking Anew

Admittedly, at first blush there are a number of seemingly insurmountable obstacles to overcome when attempting to integrate the role of emotion into a framework by which to assess peace missions. Its 'mysterious character' may be to blame.[661] How, for instance, can any of us know another's deeply internal experience? As Bleiker and Hutchinson put it, '[o]ne person can never really know what another person's pain feels like.'[662] Further, how do we discern 'real' emotions from contrived expressions intended for instrumental uses—either of which can be employed to mobilize audiences? Can we examine archives to ascertain what persons were actually feeling when they put forward arguments? Similarly, because emotions are socially-constructed and interpreted they will vary across cultures and contexts, how can we be sure that we have avoided cultural misinterpretation?[663]

Current Methods for International Policing

Current endeavours to determine policing performance largely eschew attempts to capture emotion on anything but superficial levels. First, the practitioners who deploy police missions, such as the UN and the EU, have tended to rely on anecdotal accounts of success.[664] Though these accounts often include observations on emotions, no systematic attempts are made to understand, for example, from whence the emotions have come and what they might suggest to the mission performance itself. Second, the bulk of independent experts offer narrowly-scoped arguments addressing particular aspects with no attempt to connect the analysis into an overarching framework.[665] None engage with emotion in the systematic manner outlined here. Third, some experts strive for comprehensiveness by putting forward what amounts to a check-list of relevant considerations and lessons learned closely aligned with recommendations.[666] As pragmatically helpful as

---

661 George Marcus, "Emotions in Politics", *Annual Review of Political Science* 3 no. 1 (2000): 221.

662 Roland Bleiker and Emma Hutchinson, "Fear No More: Emotions and World Politics," *Review of International Studies* 34 (2008): 129.

663 See Neta Crawford, "The Passion of World Politics: Propositions on Emotion and Emotional Relationships," *International Society* 24 no. 4 (2000): 118–19.

664 European Police Mission in Bosnia Herzegovina, *A Review of the First 100 Days of the EU Police Mission in Bosnia and Herzegovina (EUPM)* (Brussels: Council of The European Union, 2003); UN Security Council, *Report of the Secretary-General of the United Nations Civilian Police Mission in Haiti*, UN High Commissioner for Refugees, 28 May 1998 www.unhcr.org/refworld/country, UNSC,,HTI,4562d94e2,3ae6aed10,0.html.

665 Tonita Murray, "Police-Building in Afghanistan: A Case Study of Civil Security Reform", *International Peacekeeping* 14 no. 1 (2007): 108–26.

666 Centre for International Cooperation and Security, *International Post-Conflict Policing Operations: Enhancing Co-Ordination and Effectiveness* (Wilton Park: CICS, 2004); Paul

these guides may be, they do not attempt to systematize emotion as an assessment tool. Lastly, fewer independent experts still have developed sophisticated frameworks organized according to various models or criteria.[667] These too, however, lack any systematic attempt to capture emotion. Therefore, a survey of current approaches to understanding policing performance reveals a basic neglect of emotion. Its capacity to offer insights remains unrecognised.

An Emotional Approach: Conceptual Preconditions

Despite the challenges outlined above, there are ways to gain meaningful insights.[668] Methods for emotion must be reconsidered. Moreover, the time is long overdue to acknowledge and tease out the positive contributions of emotions to reason, order and cooperation. In the following sections I chart ways by which policing performance can be 'assessed' according to emotion. While these ideas are not fully developed—they require more unpacking—they should nevertheless suffice as a basis for a new direction.

This rethinking is informed by the following four points. First, not all legitimate 'knowledge' is objective or measurable or certain.[669] Emotions, such as pain, are an inherently unknowable phenomenon; emotion is part of an unseeable class of objects which are not available to sensory confirmation and thus its existence is destined to remain in doubt to all those not experiencing it.[670] In that sense it can neither be denied nor confirmed; likewise, it cannot be shared.[671] Second, as Bleiker and Hutchinson maintain: representations of emotion are as

F. Diehl, Daniel Druckman, and James Wall, "International Peacekeeping and Conflict Resolution: A Taxonomic Analysis with Implications", *Journal Of Conflict Resolution* 42 no. 1 (1998): 33–55; Alex J. Bellamy, Daniel Druckman, Paul Boreham, Paul F. Diehl and Regan Neal, *Framework for Performance Indicators in Australian Federal Police (AFP) Peace Operations*, Final Report prepared for the AFP (Brisbane: University of Queensland Social Research Centre, 2006).

667 Ylber Bajraktari, Arthur Boutellis, Fatema Gunja, Daniel Harris, James Kapsis, Eva Kaye and Jane Rhee, *The PRIME System: Measuring the Success of Post-Conflict Police Reform*, (Princeton: Princeton University, 2006); Todd Foglesong, Zainab Latif, Cybele Merrick, Janet Miller, James Parsons and Timothy Ross, *Measuring Progress toward Safety and Justice: A Global Guide to the Design of Performance Indicators in the Justice Sector* (New York: Vera Institute, 2003).

668 See, for example, how leaders and audiences react emotionally in George Marcus, "Emotions in Politics", *Annual Review of Political Science* 3 no. 1 (2000).

669 Roland Bleiker and Emma Hutchinson, "Fear No More: Emotions and World Politics," *Review of International Studies* 34 (2008): 127–9.

670 Elaine Scarry, *The Body in Pain: the Making and Unmaking of the World* (New York: Oxford University Press, 1987), 108–26.

671 Elaine Scarry, *The Body in Pain: the Making and Unmaking of the World* (New York: Oxford University Press, 1987), 4.

close as we can come to 'knowing' them.[672] Thus representation analysis can be a surrogate for 'knowing' emotion rather than empirical methods *per se*. Emotions can be understood by how they are communicated (e.g. speeches, protests and visual representation). Representation analysis can help ascertain how the private nature of emotions is channelled into the public sphere whereby they take on collective meaning and in turn influence behaviour. Public mourning is one relevant example.

Third, the element of uncertainty is not unique since all knowledge is 'inherently situated and inevitably ambivalent', being based upon what has been negotiated to be considered 'legitimate'.[673] This contrasts the fiction that knowledge exists based upon *a priori* standards that have merely been discovered. Branches of IR such as critical theory and feminist studies, for instance, have heavily critiqued the marginalization of particular knowledge processes by conventional scientific conceptualisations of knowledge acquisition.[674] Hence, examinations of emotion can yield explanations that would otherwise be obscured by more scientific methods, and therefore alternative approaches can help bridge an important gap in our understanding.

The final point is that cross-disciplinary methods can be employed to ascertain the role and impact of emotions. Consistent with our conception of emotion, inquiries can range from the scientific approaches, such as quantitative surveys to capture how individuals respond to events, to the non-social science approaches embraced in the humanities.[675] This means that mainstream methods do not have to be jettisoned; rather, a comprehensive framework will first include emotion, while also identifying a variety of ways in which they can be accounted for—based upon which methods may be most useful for particular tasks.

Since this chapter's thinking has been inspired by non-traditional perspectives, it will not go back over traditional approaches by which feelings have been recognised. Rather, it concentrates on identifying non-traditional methods that may be developed for these purposes, recalling that an underlying aim of this chapter is to stimulate dialogue.

---

672 For the following ideas on representation analysis see Roland Bleiker and Emma Hutchinson, "Fear No More: Emotions and World Politics," *Review of International Studies* 34 (2008): 128–31.

673 Roland Bleiker and Emma Hutchinson, "Fear No More: Emotions and World Politics," *Review of International Studies* 34 (2008): 128.

674 Marysia Zalewski, "Feminism meets International Relations: Some Methodological Issues", in *Feminist Methodologies for International Relations*, ed. Brooke Ackerly, Maria Stern and Jacqui True (Cambridge: Cambridge University Press, 2006): 45–6.

675 Roland Bleiker and Emma Hutchinson, "Fear No More: Emotions and World Politics," *Review of International Studies* 34 (2008): 134.

An Emotional Approach: Framework for Mapping Performance

Assessment frameworks that are limited to so-called objective evidence (e.g. the number of arrests made or the institutions established) suffer from an over-reliance on superficial, material factors at the expense of evidence of the progress that matters most: namely, the mindsets of key actors. Frameworks would benefit from mapping performance onto emotion by identifying the performance-emotion correspondences. For example, evidence of trust bodes well for the efficacy of performance. This move relies on the view that performance can be understood through the expression of emotion, because feelings reflect beliefs and judgements.

Moreover, the idea hinges on the assumption that key emotions will be widely present in certain phases of peace missions: conflict, transition to peace, and peace. As such, in times of conflict some of the pervasive emotions can include fear, anger, resentment and frustration.[676] In the transition to peace phase, these feelings would begin to give way to sentiments such as remorse, reconciliation, sympathy and hope, whereas trust, confidence and contentment are likely to accompany stable peace.[677] This is merely a sketch of the emotions that could be present in particular phases; its development must go much further.

Evaluations should also consider the level of intensity for each emotion in addition to the insight that because emotion is socially constructed, its expression and understanding may vary across time and space. The capacity to misperceive emotions takes on particular salience in the context of policing interventions because cultural differences can be the main contributor to misperceptions.[678] Local knowledge and expertise must be brought to bear in order to make reasonable interpretations. With these caveats noted, the development of this concept is well situated to augment traditional frameworks, with benefits that include diminishing blind spots by highlighting apparent assessment contradictions (e.g. instances whereby rising official crime rates may be coupled with a growing sense of security due to yet discovered forces).

An Emotional Approach: Methods

Mapping performance onto emotion entails re-thinking underlying methodologies. What sources and sites of data as well as methods can be used? This section identifies responses to this question, which in many cases might appear similar to traditional approaches. For instance, external (as well as local) experts, police

676 Jeffrey Rubin, Dean Pruitt and Sung Hee Kim, *Social Conflict: Escalation, Stalemate and Settlement 2nd Edition* (New York: McGraw Hill, 1994), 212.

677 Jeffrey Rubin, Dean Pruitt and Sung Hee Kim, *Social Conflict: Escalation, Stalemate and Settlement 2nd Edition* (New York: McGraw Hill, 1994), 18, 211–12.

678 Neta Crawford, "The Passion of World Politics: Propositions on Emotion and Emotional Relationships," *International Society* 24 no. 4 (2000): 133.

themselves, and the local population can be sources for data collection and its analysis. Likewise, surveys, interviews and workshops can be suitable methods to collect data.

On the other hand, the data and the manner in which it is gathered may differ fundamentally to the conventional logical framework models which underlie current approaches. For instance, we advocate a participatory evaluation approach which relies on interviews, surveys and workshops across various levels of the community.[679] This means that, in many situations, data should be generated in situ and fed up into measurement systems to inform indicators of success. This also means enabling evaluation processes to take place at a grass roots level, and a comprehensive engagement with agents of emotion is paramount. Trials of participatory evaluation tools in disarmament and small arms and light weapons programmes have shown that engaging with a wide range of local actors is beneficial in capturing complex issues such as emotion.[680] Local workshops, for instance, have highlighted differences in how women and men experience insecurity as fear in different parts of their lives. Practitioners in the UN Institute for Disarmament Research participatory programme in Albania, for example, learned that some women felt afraid even after comprehensive and supposedly successful disarmament programmes because of high levels of domestic violence.[681] Yet conventional approaches may fail to uncover these emotional states due to a lack of participation.

More organic data is also necessary. Participatory methods might involve having participants (police included) keep a visual diary, perhaps using a disposable camera to record what they see. This is not a vehicle for engaging with the subject of such images but the photographer him/herself. Similarly, photo elicitation techniques, or 'seeing through the eyes' of research subjects, can provide unique insights into people's experiences.[682] Ethnographers have used such tools with children to bridge divides in the way different individuals 'know' their own lived realities.[683]

'The pictorial turn' is another widely used tool for reading visual texts that can provide a productive way to ascribe emotion. Visual texts are 'sensate rather than

679 See Jodie Curth-Bibb, *Participatory M & E*, Paper at Oceanic Conference on International Studies, Brisbane, 4 June 2008.

680 Shukuko Koyama, *Comparative Analysis of Evaluation Methodologies in Weapon Collection Programmes* (Geneva: UN Institute for Disarmament Research, 2006), 39–40.

681 Shukuko Koyama, *Comparative Analysis of Evaluation Methodologies in Weapon Collection Programmes* (Geneva: UN Institute for Disarmament Research, 2006), 24.

682 Michael Angrosino, *Doing Cultural Anthropology: Projects for Ethnographic Data Collection 2nd Edition* (Illinois: Waveland, 2007), 130.

683 Jenny Edkins, *Trauma and the Memory of Politics* (Cambridge: Cambridge University Press, 2003), 4–5.

purely intellectual means of communication.'[684] Image, distinct from language, behaves on both conscious and subconscious levels and is 'as concerned with feelings as with sentences and stories'.[685] The pictorial turn method draws on semiotics to allow analysts to signify meaning within a text by engaging with its 'signs'. Notably, 'reading' visual texts is an inherently reflexive process so analysts must be aware of their own subjectivities when attaching meaning.[686]

Anthropologists are increasingly recognizing the benefits of visual research methods. Visual representation has emerged as one of the primary, non-conventional, tools for analysing shifts in, and mobilization of, collective emotion over long periods. The move to employ such methods means traversing a divide not only between 'legitimate' and 'other' forms of knowledge but also 'legitimate' and 'other' forms of knowing. Other methods might include having researchers visit sites of cultural communication and memory—perhaps a painted wall or a shrine, the site of an atrocity, a protest or reconciliation. Here 'knowing' might be defined as getting a sense of the spirit or mood of the site, observing how people interact within that site including the presence of silence. Though only a sprinkling, these examples open space regarding ways to develop unconventional forms of knowing for our purposes.

Importantly, application of such tools needs to be layered in order to combat the limitations inherent to any single 'science' of capturing emotion. That is, due to the immediacy of emotions data is susceptible to manipulation and misinterpretation.[687] If used in isolation, tools can be subverted by participants, used for persuasion and resistance in pursuit of personal goals. Without ignoring this potential for intervening parties, the common mischaracterization of 'locals' as passive recipients obscures their capacity to subvert data; similarly important is whether they trust a practitioner or her specific organisation. This becomes particularly relevant in the case of cross-cultural research where 'the relation between informant and field-worker is be-speckled with mutual misunderstandings, clientelistic interests, power games and cultural proselytising.'[688] Adding

684 Tony Shirato and Jen Webb, *Reading the Visual* (Crows Nest NSW: Allen and Unwin, 2004), 6, 66.

685 Tony Shirato and Jen Webb, *Reading the Visual* (Crows Nest NSW: Allen and Unwin, 2004), 6.

686 Tony Shirato and Jen Webb, *Reading the Visual* (Crows Nest NSW: Allen and Unwin, 2004), 6–7, 17.

687 Antonius Robben, "The Politics of Truth and Emotion among Victims and Perpetrators of Violence", in *Fieldwork under Fire: Contemporary Studies of Violence and Survival*, ed. Carolyn Nordstrom and Antonius Robben (Berkeley: University of California Press, 1995), 85.

688 Clifford Geertz cited in Antonius Robben, "The Politics of Truth and Emotion among Victims and Perpetrators of Violence", in *Fieldwork under Fire: Contemporary Studies of Violence and Survival*, ed. Carolyn Nordstrom and Antonius Robben (Berkeley: University of California Press, 1995), 85.

layers to the data collection process therefore helps mitigate the distortion from these problems. Field researchers may look at, for instance, the production of art (particularly street art), local news sources and political satire to compile emotional indicators. Likewise, engaging indigenous research groups presents the opportunity not only to complement field work conducted internally for reporting but offers the opportunity for a broader scope of data collection and analysis.

Methods Summary

The critique outlined above emphasizes not just the importance of acknowledging emotion but of ensuring the creative and non-conventional methods are a crucial part of this process. Approaches such as surveys and interviews are useful in opening space for conversation about emotions. However, it is the layering of such approaches with humanities contributions, such as visual culture, which reinforces the move toward a new understanding of the role of emotions.

Altogether the information generated from these techniques can feed an ongoing analysis linking actions (by both police and the public) to emotional responses. The aim is to account specifically for how the performance of international police affected those responses. Interpretations can be used to make conclusions such as: that a specific set of activities led to anger and defiance, and therefore that they undermined peace in whatever ways were uncovered by the specific analysis. On the other hand, we may find that certain activities appeared to trigger positive emotions, thus building a case that the activities contributed to peace and security in specific ways. Baselines of emotions can be established in order to determine directions of progress no different to other, more traditional, benchmark indicators. For example, when police deploy is the emotional landscape one of suspicion, fear and trepidation, yet after a month of activities there is a growing sense of security and easing of tensions? Moreover, the use of multiple perspectives offers an opportunity to identify and then explore any contradictions that may arise, such as if traditional sources report improvements which are repudiated by local viewpoints or even ethnographers.

This chapter built the case that emotions must be considered to achieve a fuller understanding of international policing performance in peace operations. An initial task was to demonstrate that emotions are at the core of political behaviour and therefore critical to the actions and reactions that comprise peace missions. Accordingly, their appreciation can shed light where conventional social science assessment methods may falter. If, for instance, crime rates begin to skyrocket yet observations of emotion indicate parallel increases in positive feelings such as safety or optimism among the public, this added perspective could be integral to showing that performance was yielding progress: the paradox may have little to do with better capture of crime statistics but instead a growing confidence in the capacity of intervening or local police forces. The 'fact' of success can never be captured entirely by tangible measures such as a lack of overt violence, particularly since too often such myopic measurements mask feelings of resentment or a desire for vengeance, the exact emotions which fuel slides back into violence.

Moving beyond the limits of our existing imagination, which is informed by the fashionable dichotomy of fact versus fiction,[689] means appreciating other forms of knowledge. An array of methods should be developed in order to achieve the maximum insights. These can continue to include more 'precise' social science approaches stretched to incorporate feelings (e.g. quantitative surveys). At the same time we must countenance 'imprecise' interpretive methods (e.g. tapping aesthetic sources like art). An inter-disciplinary synthesis offers the widest array of tools through which to illuminate the role of emotion in peace and capacity building operations. The move to take emotions seriously, coupled with the move to embrace alternative forms of knowledge, promises a significantly improved capacity to assess performance.

689 Roland Bleiker and Emma Hutchinson, "Fear No More: Emotions and World Politics," *Review of International Studies* 34 (2008): 134.

PART FOUR

EVIDENCE FROM THE FIELD FOR AN UNCONVENTIONAL WISDOM

CHAPTER NINE

THE MARSHALL ISLANDS MICROCOSM: SHOWING THE NEED FOR A 'POLITICAL' LENS

The preceding eight chapters have covered enormous ground, exploring issues and forces as varied as how to use an understanding of emotions to better our understanding of mission success to ensuring we engage with the socio-cultural aspects of a recipient society when becoming involved in security and development operations. The examinations have deliberately striven to remain 'grounded' so that the many theoretical claims have continued to be informed and corroborated directly from real-world situations.

This final section of the book takes the nexus between theory and reality a step further by employing recent (ongoing, in fact) research in the terms of three case studies which have been undertaken with the express purpose of helping to illustrate how an unconventional wisom can, and should, be replacing the conventional wisdom. How might the conceptual arguments made previously translate into day-to-day concrete decisions in order to help the international community improve its part? What can a political consciousness offer to programming by highlighting the multiplicity of crucial perspectives, state as well as non-state, with their potentially vastly different world views? And how might we grapple with all of this, recognizing that it takes place within a fluid, complex social system in which the interactions between the stakeholders are both the key to success and impossible either to isolate or predict far in advance? Both programming and the attendant M&E are of course fully affected by the manner in which the environment is interpreted. With the overarching aim of bringing together the theory to view differently unfolding missions in mind, each case study interrogates a current case of international assistance through our alternative lens. The methodologies and foci purpose-designed for the case studies enable the reader to gain 'lived' examples of how our many above contentions play out on the ground—if only we had the lenses capable of detecting their existence.

The first of three case studies, comprising this chapter, relates to the Republic of Marshall Islands. To be fair, its brevity renders it more of an entrée than a full-fledged case study; its analysis nevertheless sufficiently illustrates how a heightened awareness of complex, political realities would lead to starkly different conclusions—and thus recommendations for mission design and programming. An added point is that while the brevity of this case is due to the short time spent in-country, the silver lining is that it demonstrates how efficiently the genuine circumstances of recipient countries can be grasped, given a complex, political lens approach. The second empirical case, highlighting a community policing initiative within the RAMSI mission in the Solomon Islands, not only underscores how differently mission environment and thus recommendations for programming would be given a complex political lens, but points out how these nuances extend into M&E practices. The third and final case looks at an African context. It delves deeply into current M&E practices, while specifically teasing out the potential that our alternative framework could bring to bear on the learning and implementation of major UN missions.

External Assistance for Police Reform in RMI

This chapter focuses on the ongoing work in the Republic of the Marshall Islands (RMI). Among the various international assistance programs currently in place, the specific focus is the work being conducted by the Australian Federal Police in the public safety sector. The insights are based on field research conducted by two of the book's authors[690] in combination with the AFP. What is notable—given our steadfast belief in the need for practical tools, which therefore are capable of working in the field—is that although the time in-country was comparatively brief, the insights gleaned (from a complex, political lens) in that short of time were remarkable in terms of how well they could begin to inform both the intervention programming as well as its M&E.

In short, we set out recent security and justice sector fieldwork in the Republic of the Marshall Islands (RMI) to begin to show how a conventional, state-centric and technical approach—devoid of such a political consciousness—can miss the mark entirely. The chapter argues that what is needed instead is a sound grasp of the politics that comprise RMI, i.e. not just the intentions of state actors or according to what Westerners may deem their interests to be. First and foremost, the sources related to power, legitimacy and interests of the groups that comprise an environment should begin to be identified as fully as practicable. This endeavour entails recognizing the different values and beliefs of intervening and local actors alike. Furthermore, the fluid relationships and emerging interaction between stakeholders that comprise the social system must remain at the forefront of any thinking about where and how to allocate resources during interventions. Such awareness does not presume to be able to guess the future, but instead recognizes

[690] Charles T. Hunt & Bryn Hughes.

the central importance of stakeholder interaction so that the inevitable reactions can continue to be a chief consideration for program planning and adaptation. As such, identifying the emergence of unforeseen consequences should remain a prominent aim for all concerned. The underlying point is that an appreciation of the above ideas means that avenues for sustainable and context appropriate assistance can start to come into focus. It is the kind of involvement that avoids instilling local resistance due to political disinterest.

It should also be noted that a case as seemingly obscure as RMI features characteristics common to international assistance circumstances but in a microcosm more conducive to gleaning instructive insights. That is, despite the inevitable differences between one case and another, there are perhaps an uncannily high number of similarities across time and space, and accordingly the RMI case can be used to wonderful effect in terms of demonstrating how an unconventional wisdom can offer significant benefits to the international community in their future undertakings.

RMI Overview

The Republic of the Marshall Islands shares a similar history of colonial occupation and conquest as many nations in the Micronesian region. Colonised first by the Spanish in 1874, the Islands changed hands a mere 10 years later after significant German compensation won them the right to claim the territory. The Japanese assumed control at the beginning of World War I only to surrender that control to the United States at the end of World War II. As the occupying power, the US agreed to administer the Marshall Islands as part of the UN's Trust Territory of the Pacific Islands, along with much of Micronesia in 1947. After more than four decades of administration the US recognised the establishment of an RMI Government and Constitution in 1979.[691] In the 1980s, following extensive negotiations, RMI and the US entered into a Compact of Free Association. The Compact recognises RMI as a self-governing nation but gives the responsibility for and authority over security and defence to the US whilst RMI retains control over all other domestic and foreign policy. In return, the Compact allows the US to lease the Kwajalein Atoll, including a US Army missile test site, until 2066 at US$2.3 billion.[692] The two countries negotiated an Amended Compact that came into force in 2004 which commits the US to giving US$57million to RMI annually

691 Federal Information and News Dispatch, *Background Notes: Marshall Islands* (Lanham, United States: FIND, 2012).

692 Shiuh-Shen Chien, Tzu-Po Yang and Yi-Chen Wu, "Taiwan's Foreign Aid and Technical Assistance in the Marshall Islands," *Asian Survey* 50 no. 6 (2010): 1192; Australian Government Department of Foreign and Trade, *Marshall Islands Brief*, (Canberra, DFAT: 2012) http://www.dfat.gov.au/geo/marshall_islands/marshall_islands_brief.html.

including joint contributions to a trust fund until 2023, when the trust fund will begin annual payouts in perpetuity.[693]

US aid and assistance is the mainstay of RMI's economy and it receives the vast majority of its income from aid grants from three main sources; the US, Taiwan and Japan.[694] As part of the Compact and other agreements the US provides, at no cost, the services of more than 40 US government agencies including air safety, weather prediction, postal services, health services, disaster relief assistance and numerous USAID operated or funded programs. The agreement also covers compensation costs for US nuclear testing on the Bikini and Enewetak Atolls from 1946 to 1958.[695] Aside from the US, Taiwan is RMI's second largest aid donor. It contributes directly to the RMI Trust Fund set up by the Amended Compact and provides financial aid for soft and hard infrastructure and technical assistance, particularly in the upgrade of agricultural and rural development.[696]

Regional neighbour, Australia, also offers humanitarian aid to RMI, with an expected contribution of AUD$3.5million in 2011–2012 to provide scholarships, technical assistance and small grants for community organisations. In 2010 the two nations signed a Pacific Partnership for Development which prioritised the development of affordable, accessible and sustainable energy and water.[697] The Australian Federal Police maintains a presence in the region and contributes material resources and skills training through its Law Enforcement Cooperation Program. The AFP has funded the attendance of RMI law enforcement officials at domestic and international training seminars and workshops, provided personnel to train officers in various skill sets such as Disaster Victim Identification (DVI) training and assisted in the capacity building of regional law enforcement agencies to gather evidence against illicit drug traffickers.[698] Perhaps as a reflection of this capacity building, RMI has since 2006 provided two police officers to

---

693 Central Intelligence Agency, *World Factbook: Marshall Islands*, https://www.cia.gov/library/publications/the-world-factbook/geos/rm.html; Australian Government Department of Foreign and Trade, *Marshall Islands Brief*, (Canberra, DFAT: 2012) http://www.dfat.gov.au/geo/marshall_islands/marshall_islands_brief.html.

694 Shiuh-Shen Chien, Tzu-Po Yang and Yi-Chen Wu, "Taiwan's Foreign Aid and Technical Assistance in the Marshall Islands," *Asian Survey* 50 no. 6 (2010): 1192.

695 Australian Government Department of Foreign and Trade, *Marshall Islands Brief*, (Canberra, DFAT: 2012) http://www.dfat.gov.au/geo/marshall_islands/marshall_islands_brief.html; Shiuh-Shen Chien, Tzu-Po Yang and Yi-Chen Wu, "Taiwan's Foreign Aid and Technical Assistance in the Marshall Islands," *Asian Survey* 50 no. 6 (2010): 1193.

696 Shiuh-Shen Chien, Tzu-Po Yang and Yi-Chen Wu, "Taiwan's Foreign Aid and Technical Assistance in the Marshall Islands," *Asian Survey* 50 no. 6 (2010): 1193.

697 Australian Government Department of Foreign and Trade, *Marshall Islands Brief*, (Canberra, DFAT: 2012) http://www.dfat.gov.au/geo/marshall_islands/marshall_islands_brief.html.

698 Australian Federal Police, *Law Enforcement Cooperation Program*, (Canberra: AFP, 2011) http://www.afp.gov.au/policing/international-liaison/law-enforcement-cooperation-program.aspx.

the Regional Assistance Mission to Solomon Islands (which constitutes the case study in the following chapter).[699]

One can see the value of such assistance by examining the issues currently facing RMI's law and justice sector, which is embattled with accusations and evidence of corruption and fraud against government officials and ministers, who have misappropriated hundreds of thousands of dollars of government money. Given that much of this money is in fact US aid, the US government has repeatedly requested to be kept abreast of and involved in the proceedings, a request which does not sit well with a RMI government seeking to be more independent of the US. However, with increasingly high-ranking officials becoming embroiled in this scandal, the question is asked both in RMI and the US as to why the US's Federal Bureau of Investigation has not yet been invited to investigate. The RMI government maintains this would undermine its sovereignty.[700] Clearly, any international policing assistance must be approached with care and take into consideration these significant reservations when addressing issues of crime and corruption in RMI.

Nevertheless, the country is in a difficult situation regarding crime, both local and transnational. Recent years have sent shipments of drugs with or without their traffickers unintentionally wash up on the shores of RMI's many islands, a territory that is particularly hard to monitor.[701] RMI has thus been drawn into the international fight against illicit drug trafficking and its resources and capacity building are necessarily being expanded as a result of that.[702] Closer to home, murder and suicide rates have hit an all time high necessitating an increased police response and the country struggles to deal with what is seen as its imminent surrender to the sea as a result of climate change.[703] Thus it is in this context and with these influences in mind that the case study examined in this chapter was undertaken.

The following analysis is based on viewpoints elicited from a wide spectrum of stakeholders in RMI. Consistent with the chapter's recommendation to gain as comprehensive as possible an awareness of the politics, the net was cast

---

699 Australian Government Department of Foreign and Trade, *Marshall Islands Brief*, (Canberra, DFAT: 2012) http://www.dfat.gov.au/geo/marshall_islands/marshall_islands_brief.html.

700 David W. Kupferman, "Marshall Islands," *The Contemporary Pacific* 24 no. 1 (2012): 150–153.

701 David W. Kupferman, "Marshall Islands," *The Contemporary Pacific* 24 no. 1 (2012): 153.

702 Australian Government Department of Foreign and Trade, *Marshall Islands Brief*, (Canberra, DFAT: 2012) http://www.dfat.gov.au/geo/marshall_islands/marshall_islands_brief.html; Australian Federal Police, *Law Enforcement Cooperation Program*, (Canberra: AFP, 2011) http://www.afp.gov.au/policing/international-liaison/law-enforcement-cooperation-program.aspx.

703 David W. Kupferman, "Marshall Islands," *The Contemporary Pacific* 24 no. 1 (2012): 154.

deliberately wide to gather the diversity of perspectives across community and government alike. At the same time, it was appreciated that the nature of the environment was a complex social systems, and this in turn warranted special focus on how each stakeholder might interact with and perceive the others. The information was gathered through semi-structured interviews conducted in May and June 2010, by four members of the Australian Federal Police's (AFP) Pacific Policing Development Program and two researchers[704] from the Institute for Social Science Research, The University of Queensland (ISSR).

Methodology

The express purpose of the enquiry was to draw a picture of the situation from which planning and monitoring and evaluation for sustainable peace and development could be produced. More than 50 persons from over 30 organizations or government units were asked about issues pertaining to public safety, in general, as well as specific information related to police performance and coverage. Church groups, women's organizations, traditional leaders, local NGOs, educational institutions, and the chamber of commerce were met together with members of the police (RMIP), attorneys general and ministers of government departments.

The broad categories developed to prompt story-telling responses included: identifying current practices and viewpoints together with any concerns; the causality underpinning the current circumstances (a focal point for political considerations); perceptions of the police; and accompanying recommendations linked to what local resources might be brought to bear. Headline findings included: the top public safety concern was alcohol related, anti-social behaviour; and perceptions of the police were divided, perhaps predictably, between community stakeholders and public safety personnel (for example, the police). Recommended solutions varied from creating 'safe houses' for women and limiting alcohol access, to specific ways to improve RMIP's responsiveness. From a methodological point of view, variances to these generalizations stood out clearly, demonstrating the moderating value of triangulation. Concurrently, there were many original additions to the common views which, when put together, offered a robust picture of the multiplicity of Marshallese perspectives on these issues. The varied views also provided myriad options concerning solutions to be pursued or where to allocate resources, irrespective of any contradictions among the perspectives.

The Conventional Interpretation of Complex Realities

Seen through a conventional, state-centric, technical lens, the interpretation would tend to suggest that more and better police training and more government

704 Bryn Hughes and Charles Hunt.

resources (including the right kinds of legislation or formal enhancements to policing or judicial powers) would be advisable in order to redress RMI public safety problems. But more nuanced points came from the interviews, which help to appreciate the politics of RMI public safety (i.e. the way various perspectives converge to influence how Marshallese society functions). These points included:

- Patriarchal cultural norms have contributed to many abuses of women (for example, sexual and domestic violence) yet, these mores are a departure from centuries-old traditions whereby women had authority and respect, and were protected; hence there is precedence for returning to these less problematic cultural norms.
- There is societal stigma associated with abused women, which in turn makes it difficult to prosecute and convict male offenders because it means asking women to be publicly shamed by coming forward.
- Traditional leaders (mainly *Iroij* but also the *Alaps*, who are the 'caretakers' of the land) continue to hold significant albeit informal sway in the community. (*Alaps*, for example, can heavily influence voting by threatening to evict persons from their land and more generally, *Iroij* are able to command significant compliance to their edicts.)
- Numerous forces in recent decades (for example, the increasing influence of Western culture, the availability of alcohol, and movements of persons from one island to another) have seen an erosion of the cultural mechanisms that previously helped to maintain order, with one result being that the younger generation in particular appears to resist traditional power and norms.
- The ethnic Chinese are an important political consideration, since their actions as profit-driven business owners have appeared to contribute significantly to the widespread youth drinking problem.
- Regarding resources to improve the situation, it was consistently pointed out how NGOs and community groups (for example, church groups such as Salvation Army and the Police Wives' Group) could be productive local sources to begin sustainable progress. A variety of vehicles through which to communicate effectively to the community were identified. In addition to conventional sources such as the radio and newspapers, they also include traditional mechanisms such as village meetings (*Weto*) to spread the word in effective and culturally appropriate fashions, i.e. Western institutions and sociotechnologies are not necessarily the best way to convey what peace and development programs are doing.

Adding a Political Interpretation to the Complexity

While underscoring that our understanding of the RMI context is incipient, a political mindset quickly enabled both the authors as well as the AFP to become aware of a sort of 'clash of regimes of truth' between the more traditional

Marshallese socio-cultural value and idea systems and those from the introduced Western. Sources of material, institutional and ideational power—and their impact on agency—are unsurprisingly split down similar lines. In concrete terms this is reflected in the fact that traditional leaders—the Iroij, mainly, but also the Alaps, which are the 'caretakers' of the land—still hold considerable albeit largely informal sway in matters pertaining to security and justice. They draw on informal institutions and traditional ideas for their capacity to control and regulate society, enjoying little sanctioned access to the material resources coming from the donor community.

On the other hand, state actors (some of which are traditional leaders spanning the formal-informal divide as elected politicians) possess considerably greater material power, which is attached to ideational and institutional power from a Western political regime of truth. Theirs is a world of formal, Westphalian government institutions, marked by the notions of separations of powers and formal elections, and from which comes a dependence on civil servants to deliver essential public goods and services. This uncomfortable juxtaposition and blend of traditional and introduced means that members of parliament rely for their agency on forms of knowledge, power, and legitimacy that are still largely foreign to, and thus fail to resonate with, most of the population. This story fits countless places across the globe, and holds numerous ramifications for how to approach a recipient society.

For the limited space herein we have selected a key issue elicited from the interviews in order to illustrate how a political consciousness could inform assistance to the RMI. It provides an opportunity to delve more deeply and in so doing instantiates the vast difference to what the technical approach can offer RMI. The issue is about the near unanimous view (among non-police related interviewees that is) that the RMIP were not enforcing the law equally or effectively. It is a common criticism in peace and capacity development sites. Correspondences to impunity, corruption, and simply inadequate training are frequent superficial diagnoses.

The conventional state-centric, technical approach would likely have proceeded by rather quickly developing some type of 'gap analysis' based around technical problems such as human and financial resourcing issues. Explanations and cures would normally suggest that endemic corruption is part of the 'flawed' condition of local culture and therefore redoubling of the training and 'educating' about how to be good police, coupled with tighter oversight measures to coax more ethical behaviour, is what is needed. That interpretation however fails to consider the political realities encompassing RMI, foremost the divergence of political regimes of truth. As a consequence, it falters in its advice to development assistance.

A political lens, by contrast, goes below the surface to where the heart beats. In this case, the inequitable enforcement of the law stems from the tensions between traditional and Western regimes of truth and their underlying sources of power, not an issue remedied through training. Specifically, interviewees chronicled how police were severely hampered from enforcing the law equally across society because of how powerful members of society were able to draw upon ideational and institutional power from traditional origins to remain above a formal law (supported by Western sources of power). Examples were given whereby police were contacted shortly after detaining 'connected' persons and pressured (including the use of physical threats) to release them. The incisive questions however pertain to the sources of that pressure, with conventional lenses often failing to recognise non-state forms of power and legitimacy and thereby being ill-equipped to answer questions of *why* some persons seem to enjoy impunity whereas others do not.

In this case, members of the RMIP have been caught in a political cross fire. Particularly in close-knit communities like those across the Pacific Islands, police understandably find it hard to ignore the socio-political forces under which they live out their daily lives. In an ideational sense, they have grown up being taught both to respect the authority of traditional leaders and to be suspicious of Western impositions (*e.g.* the vexatious post-WWII relationship with the USA). We cannot expect them to go 'outside' themselves somehow ignoring their life's socialisation in order to follow Western models of best practice policing. Moreover, informal institutions, such as how land tenancy is granted, mean that they or their family members are vulnerable, for example, to expulsion should they dare to challenge traditional leader's wishes. Just as McLeod has warned,[705] their capacity to carry out their formal duties has been impeded by myriad informal political forces. Their political regime of truth does not sync with those of donors such as the AFP. Tacit frustration was apparent along these lines among RMIP interviewees; and continuing to put them into this bind is likely to exacerbate morale and general conduct.

Given the political realities of RMI, questions *should not* be cast narrowly as: How can we better 'educate' state police so that their conduct more exemplifies Western practices? They should instead revolve around: How can we help overcome tensions between political regimes of truth that constrain socially generative outcomes? This means, *inter alia*, working with traditional leaders and their underlying sources of power and legitimacy so that these forces can form a greater part of the solution rather than the problem as has so often been the case. It also implies that intervening actors, such as the AFP, need to develop different strategies as well as personnel skill sets.[706] To their credit, the AFP appears to

705 Abby McLeod, "Police Reform in Papua New Guinea" in *Security and Development in the Pacific Islands: Social Resilience in Emerging States*, ed. M. Anne Brown (Boulder, CO: Lynne Rienner, 2007), 80.

706 Bryn Hughes, "Moving Beyond Rethinking the State of the State: to the Challenge of Reshaping International Contributions to Peace operations," *Conflict Security & Development* 10 no. 3 (2010): 329–352.

recognise these aspects and seems prepared to move in the directions needed to ultimately close these gaps between conventional and unconventional wisdoms.

Additionally, our recommendation to continue to build relationships and cooperation need cost no more than other approaches. What is more, it explicitly embraces the World Bank's aim of being demand-driven. In concrete terms, the political approach promises to generate a grounded accountability, which could help to remove a crippling impediment to RMIP's capacity to enforce the law equally. At the same time, it embraces an awareness of complex social systems, meaning that the RMIP is not seen as existing in a vacuum. Therefore, aid programming must take into consideration the emerging relationships and their changing environment rather than believe that more training will lead to equitable enforcement. Yet another benefit is that the resources that the *Iroij* and other community members could bring to bear for improved peace and security are vital. This is particularly so because, as with the vast majority of recipient societies, available state resources in the RMI conspicuously lack the capacity to provide daily law and order services to the bulk of the population. Therefore, in sum, experience from the RMI has highlighted the ways in which the political either constrains or enables particular courses of action—indicating the promise that a political consciousness possesses toward the practical issues of the daily programming and ongoing management decisions facing the international community.

CHAPTER TEN

HYBRIDITY AND POLICE CAPACITY DEVELOPMENT IN THE SOLOMON ISLANDS

The previous chapter unpacked the ongoing external assistance to the public safety realm of the Marshall Islands in order to offer insights as to the nature of international policing. It directly illustrated many of the contentions we have made throughout the book, with specific emphasis on the need to approach the mission environment through a political lens which refuses to view recipient societies through a Western state and ethno-centric prism. Accordingly, the programming prescriptions generated were starkly different to what the conventional wisdom would have us pursue. Of equal importance, and similarly fundamental departures from extant mainstream practices, were the conceptions and advice surrounding the *processes* by which to glean the most desirable (*i.e.* context-sensitive and sustainable) ways forward. Altogether the analysis served as an entrée indicating how dramatically different missions and their environs can be interpreted when equipped with a complex, political lens. It was however merely a synopsis, based on minimal time in the field compared to the highly involved next two chapter case studies.

The setting for this next interrogation is current day Solomon Islands[707] in the South Pacific, whereby the international community, in the form of the Regional Assistance Mission to the Solomon Islands (RAMSI henceforth) has undertaken to reform and develop the law and justice sector (L&J) corresponding broadly to the Rule of Law system. The chapter[708] aims to demonstrate the complex

[707] It is important to note that things are constantly changing in the Solomon Islands and this chapter draws on case study material from 2010. That said, the focus of this chapter is in fact the processes and the observations regarding process and these points remain relevant.

[708] The research and analysis conducted herein is based solely on the work of Jodie Curth-Bibb.

interconnectedness between formal and informal systems (*i.e.* hybridity), while arguing that these complex realities must be accounted for when seeking to engender locally owned and sustainable capacity development. Vitally, the examination illustrates that the ideal 'end state' in hybrid approaches to capacity development in the Solomon Islands is not clear; and perhaps more to the point, it does not need to be since such goals stem from a flaw in the conventional wisdom that presumes such end states are achievable in the first place. As such, the notion and content of hybridity should not become the next 'pre-packaged' solution to meet the international community's challenge of institution building.

The ensuing exploration is instead concerned with how hybrid relations have emerged, continue to evolve, and—crucially—what this means for capacity development and program management. What is important 'are the relations and processes which generate hybrid order and allowing the space for "hybridity" to emerge and correct itself'.[709] Not to be missed, the analysis also underscores many of the other warnings we make repeatedly of dominant practices, such as: the need to avoid a reliance on hard indicators and stopping at 'outputs' as opposed to using data that is capable of capturing emergence and focusing on impacts; the use of simplistic 'cause and effect' frameworks; and making sure to build from the bottom up on what exist locally rather than imposing 'global' solutions top-down. A more concrete point made, and one that corroborates the insights from the Marshall Islands experience, is that the conventional approach of rolling out generic technical capacity development including training has not only wasted scarce resources but undermined organisational capacity itself as well. Overall, the insights derived from this investigation of the Solomon Islands support our advice for how to improve M&E frameworks used for police capacity development.

Before we continue the exploration itself, however, a note on the importance of methodology to how these case studies are developed is warranted. Great care was taken in setting up the methodology to explore hybridity in the Solomon Islands RoL. This emphasis affords an opportunity to focus briefly on a topic which is indispensible to achieving learning. A continued reliance on popular tools and techniques promises only more of the same misleading advice. Such mainstream methodologies are particularly problematic when considering that to develop a representative picture of hybridity in the RoL space demands a *meaningful* engagement with a diverse range of stakeholders groups. Indeed, the capacity to generate a rich understanding of policy, practice and experience depends on such an engagement.

Consistent with our ongoing recommendation to elicit views from the most diverse spectrum of society practical given circumstantial constraints, data

---

709 Morgan Brigg and Jodie Curth, *Policy Disorder or Evolving Hybridity? Post-conflict Capacity Development in Solomon Islands*, International Peace Research Association Conference, University of Sydney, 6–10 July, 2010.

sources accessed for this examination spanned external and internal, civil society, government and a cross section of local people. The research behind this case study explored how local people, outside the capital area, draw on formal and informal systems to deal with crime, generate conditions of safety and maintain social order.[710] The methodology designed and employed herein ultimately constituted a mixed method approach, which draws on primary source documentation, expert unstructured interviews, semi-structured interviews with local and external police, story-telling, community focus groups and participatory observation.

The story-telling approach employed was useful for avoiding one word answers and gave participants the opportunity to just talk rather than in engage in a stifled question and answer format. This allows the conversation to take its logical path according to the participants—rather than forcing the predetermined logic of the interviewer (a common mistake made by popular methods such as the short-answer surveys currently used by many practitioner organisations). It was important in all the interviews and focus group sessions to use a mix of commonly spoken English and Pijin as appropriate. This too ensured a more relaxed approach.[711] As is highlighted throughout previous chapters it is this difference in the approach to engagement and participation that generates meaningful contributions.[712]

Having highlighted the integral role of methodology to the learning process, the chapter proceeds by briefly recounting the historical backdrop, after which it moves to explore the current state of hybridity in RoL in the Solomon Islands, which is marked by the ongoing dependence of local people on informal

710 The research was conducted in five different sites: Maul'u, in North Malaita; Savo a small island off of Guadalcanal; AvuAvu a remote region on the weather coast of Guadalcanal; Kakabona, just outside the national capital; and Sigana in Isabel Province. These locations were selected for their strategic importance and diversity. Maul'u and AvuAvu were selected as they are both conflict related sites as well as pilot sites for the Community Officer pilot. Savo and Sigana were selected in contrast for their relative absence of violence and because they were not directly involved in the tension. Kakabona is a peri-urban site on the fringe of Honiara, bringing a different perspective again. The relevance of kastom and the effectiveness of traditional practice it has been argued is less than in other sites as the settlement is a product of urban drift. Together these sites provide a diverse perspective on kastom, traditional justice, gender relations and social norms. This particular aspect of the research was largely funded by the Asia Pacific Centre for the Responsibility to Protect.

711 This also has some interesting effects on power relations.

712 Solomon Islanders are known for giving responses that they feel are polite or agreeable—there is a tendency in a capacity development setting for there to be a power imbalance which is likely to skew the results as it impacts upon what people feel they can and cannot say. Importantly this interview approach achieved a level of informality to encourage, and generally achieve, a much more open and relaxed interaction, therefore to some extent, avoiding this pitfall.

mechanisms and systems. Rather than being pre-occupied with the notion of an ideal balance and complementarity between the 'local' or traditional practice and state-based institutions, the chapter begins with the matter of fact acknowledgement that hybridity in the Solomon Islands does indeed exist, and accordingly the real point is to strive to understand its characteristic processes and how best to work within those dynamics to deliver the optimal outcome for Solomon Islanders. To that end, the next section briefly examines the Solomon Islands' Government (SIG) policy towards traditional justice mechanisms, setting out its continuing move towards the formal incorporation of informal approaches to order. With an understanding of the status quo, there is then an inquiry into how RAMSI has attempted to incorporate these demands for local approaches into their state-based institutional capacity development, followed by an important section on the challenges to doing so. Of particular relevance to these developments is that 'knowledge barriers' continue to hamper efforts to integrate the informal with the formal, in short because official ways of 'knowing' have the unwitting effect of undermining local ownership and capacity to participate. This 'rational policy' approach to hybridity is a theme echoed amongst the key insights from Chapter 9's interrogation on emotion which pointed out how mainstream, 'rational' social science fails to accept knowledge based on other traditions. Importantly, this section contains a significant look into how women fair in this space. Having explored the problems associated with hybridity the chapter then contemplates good practice ways to move forward. This entails examining new approaches currently underway which show promise for embracing the concepts to do with complexity unpacked in Chapter 8—particularly interconnectedness, local interaction producing the global, emergence, complex adaptive agents and non-linearity. The focus is on the recent establishment of the 'Community Officers Pilot Program' pertaining to community policing. Hence, the final part of the chapter concentrates on this unfolding capacity development initiative and the learning value it may generate for other such situations.

Background Context

Solomon Islands is a former British protectorate.[713] It is a young and inexperienced state,[714] having achieved full independence as recently as 1978.[715] The

[713] Michael Fullilove, *The Testament of Solomons: RAMSI and International State-building* (Sydney: Lowy Institute For International Policy, 2006), 5.

[714] Michael Fullilove, *The Testament of Solomons: RAMSI and International State-building* (Sydney: Lowy Institute For International Policy, 2006), 5.

[715] 'Timeline: Solomon Islands—A chronology of key events', *BBC News*, 9 August 2007 http://news.bbc.co.uk/1/hi/world/asia-pacific/country_profiles/1249397.stm accessed 3 September 2007.

majority of the small population (estimated to be somewhere over 550,000)[716] are Melanesians (94.5%)[717] but many other identity groupings exist amongst this population. Such 'ethnic division' has continued to cause serious problems between some groups and 'arbitrarily imposed colonial borders' are often cited as a contributing factor to instability.[718] Solomon Islands has been described as 'a nation of villages'[719] with the vast majority of the diverse Islanders living in remote and widely dispersed communities.[720]

Social organisation in the Solomon Islands traditionally comprised of (and to varying degrees still does) relatively flat, or at least non-hierarchical, groups formed along family and tribal lines. These groups are generally made up of small communities and whilst chiefs and other authorities do enjoy an elevated position in society they are usually reliant on the consent of the group which enables them to act. This authority is regulated through socially flux systems of conditional legitimacy.

Whilst the state has developed formal institutions, traditional forms of customary law and social practice were not replaced. Rather they continue to exist, sometimes through their absorption and 'upward migration' into the formal system, sometimes through ad hoc arrangements of recognition and cooperation and often as a parallel (and sometimes competing) system of power and legitimacy. The state has never replaced the wantok system and loyalty to kin remains the basis of the social system.[721] This is particularly the case in relation to policing.[722] The country's population is spread across 300–400 islands[723] with

716 Australian Government Department of Foreign Affairs and Trade, *Solomon Islands Country Brief*, Canberra: DFAT, 2012) http://www.dfat.gov.au/geo/solomon_islands/solomon_islands_brief.html accessed 29 May 2012.

717 *Foreign Affairs & International Trade—Canada*, 03/09/07.

718 Anna Powles, "Mission Creep: Statebuilding from Honiara to Dili" *Security Challenges* 2 no. 2 (2006): 9.

719 Peter Morgan, *RAMSI and Capacity Development: Report on a field trip to the Solomon Islands (Revised)*, Report Commissioned by AusAID (Canberra: AusAID, 2007).

720 Solomon Islands Government, *Report On The 1999 Population And Housing Census: Analysis* (Honiara: SIG Statistics Office, 2002), 3.

721 James Watson, *A Model Pacific Solution?: A Study of the Deployment of the Regional Assistance Mission to the Solomon Islands*, Working Paper 126 (Duntroon, ACT: Land Warfare Studies Centre, 2005), 18; Peter Larmour and Manuhuia Barcham, "National Integrity Systems", in *Transparency International Country Report—Solomon Islands 2004* (Blackburn: Transparency International Australia, 2004), 4, 9, 12, 14, 56.

722 Australian National University, *People's Survey Pilot 2006: Solomon Islands*, (Canberra: The Australian National University (ANU) Enterprise P/L on behalf of RAMSI, 2006), 57.

723 Sources range from stating 'less than' to 'over' a thousand islands—for number of *populated* islands see *Solomon Islands Government—UNDP—Provincial Governance Strengthening Program—Preparatory Assistance Document—DRAFT* (UNDP, no publishing date—implementation 2007), 4.

the most dominant groups being those from the islands of Guadalcanal and Malaita—the source of recent conflict.[724]

'The Tensions'[725] between the people of Guadalcanal and Malaitans are not new, however, over the past 50 years they have intensified.[726] Honiara attracted migrants from Malaita and over time they have moved into the rural areas of Guadalcanal. Tensions over Malaitan land acquisition and domination of paid employment have caused widespread resentment.[727] In 1998 violent conflict erupted[728] when the militant group of Guadalcanal, Isatabu Freedom Movement (IFM),[729] forced Malaitans off traditional land. Malaitan elites granted compensation payments, further fuelling claims of corruption and the Malaita Eagle Force (MEF) formed, resulting in the escalation of violence.[730] Several requests for Australian intervention were denied until and the state began to collapse.[731] Politicians and public servants were drawn into the clash, with RSIPF becoming deeply entrenched in the conflict.[732] In June 2000 the MEF, supported by RSIPF officers, forced the Prime Minister to resign at gunpoint.[733]

---

724 Michael Fullilove, *The Testament of Solomons: RAMSI and International State-building* (Sydney: Lowy Institute For International Policy, 2006), 5.

725 The conflict in the Solomon Islands or small scale civil war is generally referred to by local people as the *tensions.*

726 James Watson, *A Model Pacific Solution?: A Study of the Deployment of the Regional Assistance Mission to the Solomon Islands,* Working Paper 126 (Duntroon, ACT: Land Warfare Studies Centre, 2005), 3–4.

727 Resentment was further flamed by the marital arrangements between Malaitan men and Guadalcanal women resulting in the transfer of land entitlements to Malaitans. People of Guadalcanal pass their land through matrilineal lines—transferred through marriage. Malaitan tradition is on the other hand patriarchal and this has been continued.

728 Michael Fullilove, *The Testament of Solomons: RAMSI and International State-building* (Sydney: Lowy Institute For International Policy, 2006), 5.

729 SIG papers refer to the Guadalcanal Revolutionary Army (GRA)—see *Community Engagement In Post Conflict Situation: The Case of Solomon Islands,* http://www.pmc.gov.sb/files/ENGAGEcommunitiesPAPER.doc accessed 18 August 2007.

730 Michael Fullilove, *The Testament of Solomons: RAMSI and International State-building* (Sydney: Lowy Institute For International Policy, 2006), 5–6.

731 Michael Fullilove, *The Testament of Solomons: RAMSI and International State-building* (Sydney: Lowy Institute For International Policy, 2006), 5–7.; M. O'Callaghan, 5 May 2006.

732 Elsina Wainwright, "Responding to State Failure—the case of Australia and the Solomon Islands", *Australian Journal of International Affairs* 57, no. 3, (2003): 20.

733 It is important to note the conflict was, and is, far more complex than this, involving splinter groups within ethnic and village groups—see Ben McDevitt, "Operation Helpem Fren: A personal Perspective," *Australian Army Journal (based on presentation delivered 23/06/05),* (2005): 3–4, 12–13.

All out civil war was narrowly averted when Australia and New Zealand[734] finally intervened, facilitating the Townsville Peace Accord in October.[735] Despite comprehensive instructions for fostering enduring peace and reconciliation[736] the support to enforce and monitor such peace failed and criminal gangs took over.[737] By early 2003 the state was again on the brink of failure. The State apparatus ceased to function, as police were compromised by their connections and unable to prevent, and too often participated in, the violence and social upheaval. Treasury was victim to armed robbery and extortion generally drained public finances.[738] Theft, assault, murder, rape, kidnapping, torture and intimidation became common place in the conflict affected areas and widespread fear spread through large sections of the Solomon Islands population.[739]

It is important to acknowledge that the common representation of this conflict as being primarily ethnically motivated between groups from Guadalcanal and Malaita can certainly account for a great deal of the *tension* events but is an overly simplistic analysis of a far more complex reality. Other contributing resentments were fuelled by Government corruption and general impotence in handling migration issues, development and land ownership.[740] Factions and alliances within Government were complex and did not divide evenly along ethnic lines. Politicians and other political actors manipulated the *tension* issues and mobilised young people for their often dubious causes. The lines of conflict were in the end difficult to describe from the outside—with violent conflict occurring within these ethnic groups.[741]

In April 2003 the then Prime Minister, Kemakeza, appealed again to Australia for help. A face-to-face meeting with the Australian Prime Minister, prompted the 'Framework for Strengthened Assistance to Solomon Islands',[742] outlining the

---

734 Michael Fullilove, *The Testament of Solomons: RAMSI and International State-building* (Sydney: Lowy Institute For International Policy, 2006), 6.

735 Solomon Islands Government, *The Townsville Peace Agreement*, (Honiara: SIG, 15 October 2000).

736 Solomon Islands Government, *The Townsville Peace Agreement*, (Honiara: SIG, 15 October 2000).

737 Ben McDevitt, "Operation Helpem Fren: A personal Perspective," *Australian Army Journal (based on presentation delivered 23/06/05)*, (2005): 4–6.

738 Michael Fullilove, *The Testament of Solomons: RAMSI and International State-building* (Sydney: Lowy Institute For International Policy, 2006), 6.

739 Michael Fullilove, *The Testament of Solomons: RAMSI and International State-building* (Sydney: Lowy Institute For International Policy, 2006), 6.

740 Morgan Brigg and Jodie Curth, *Policy Disorder or Evolving Hybridity? Post-conflict Capacity Development in Solomon Islands,* International Peace Research Association Conference, University of Sydney, 6–10 July, 2010.

741 This term is used here in line with the common analyses of the situation albeit problematic.

742 Michael Fullilove, *The Testament of Solomons: RAMSI and International State-building* (Sydney: Lowy Institute For International Policy, 2006), 7.

provisions for an Australian-led intervention. Following further official requests from the Solomon Islands,[743] The Ministers of Foreign Affairs of the Pacific Islands Forum,[744] agreed to enact commitments made in the Biketawa Declaration,[745] accepting the Australian designed assistance package.[746] The 'Facilitation of International Assistance Act 2003' (FIAA) was passed by the Solomon Islands Parliament on the 17th of July.[747] The Act provides the legal framework for the virtual free range of the armed forces and policing contingents. The provisions included the appointment of visiting police officers to executive policing roles and the jurisdiction to take over policing powers. Together with the wide-ranging powers, immunity from legal proceedings under Solomon Islands law was granted.[748] Further provisions were made placing the 'Command and Control of the Visiting Contingent' exclusively in Australian hands.[749]

A watershed development has been the RAMSI intervention. RAMSI is a police led mission with military support and whilst this approach is unusual, it has been suggested it will become increasingly utilised.[750] The policing aspect of RAMSI had been considered its strength.[751] This contingent is known as the Participating Police Force (PPF), operating under the control of the Australian Federal Police's (AFP) International Deployment Group (IDG). It is comprised of AFP members, Australian State Police and officers from New Zealand and 13 Pacific Island countries. The objectives and priorities of the operation were broken down into a phased approach whereby the first phase aimed for stabilisation in the area of

[743] Australian Government Department of Foreign Affairs & Trade, "Agreement between: Solomon Islands, Australia, New Zealand, Fiji, Papua New Guinea, Samoa and Tonga concerning the operations and status of the police and armed forces and other personnel deployed to Solomon Islands to assist in the restoration of law and order and security", *Australian Treaty Series 17*, (Townsville: DFAT, 24 July 2003).

[744] *Outcome Statement*, Forum Foreign Affairs Ministers Meeting, Sydney, 30 June 2003.

[745] *Biketawa Declaration*, 15 October 2000.

[746] Forum Foreign Affairs Ministers Meeting, Sydney, 30 June 2003.

[747] *Facilitation of International Assistance Act 2003*, Solomon Islands National Parliament, 17 July 2003.

[748] *Facilitation of International Assistance Act 2003.*

[749] Australian Government Department of Foreign Affairs & Trade, "Agreement between: Solomon Islands, Australia, New Zealand, Fiji, Papua New Guinea, Samoa and Tonga concerning the operations and status of the police and armed forces and other personnel deployed to Solomon Islands to assist in the restoration of law and order and security", *Australian Treaty Series 17*, (Townsville: DFAT, 24 July 2003), articles 4 and 5.

[750] James Watson, *A Model Pacific Solution?: A Study of the Deployment of the Regional Assistance Mission to the Solomon Islands*, Working Paper 126 (Duntroon, ACT: Land Warfare Studies Centre, 2005), vii–1; Ben McDevitt, "Operation Helpem Fren: A personal Perspective," *Australian Army Journal (based on presentation delivered 23/06/05)*, (2005): 1, 6.

[751] Australian Federal Police, "Rocks and Renewal—A new phase for the Solomon Islands," *Platypus Magazine: the Journal of the AFP* (June 2006): 4.

law and order, the second was envisaged to consolidate and normalise, and the final phase sought to build the capacity of the RSIPF.

The first phase was remarkably successful, with the mass apprehension of criminals, violent group members and militants, as well as the confiscation of weapons.[752] The initial strategy addressed areas of lawlessness through increased police presence and a wider distribution of forces. The PPF quickly established police posts throughout the islands.[753] Seventy-four RSIPF officers were prosecuted for corruption related offences and significantly more were dismissed (approximately 400).[754] A new recruitment program was introduced in the interests of establishing a culturally, ethnically and gender[755] diverse and representative force.[756] The operation is now in phase three, albeit overlap between phases is obviously necessary.[757] As the PPF move through the phases success is increasingly difficult to achieve and define.[758] Whilst RAMSI's presence in the Solomon Islands is generally supported, the commonly held view that its departure would see the country revert to a state of lawlessness says little for the sustainability of its capacity building so far.[759]

Capacity building is again proving itself to be a long-term and convoluted endeavour, emerging within a complex system, which means it cannot be counted on to follow a linear path toward some desired end goal (no matter how precisely articulated or tirelessly planned by 'experts'). The existence of complex systems and, in particular, struggling with how to develop hybrid law and justice systems going forward to achieve optimum capacity building comprises the chapter's focus.

---

752 *Platypus Magazine*, June 2006, p. 5; B. McDevitt, June 2005, pp. 3–4 & 12–13; PIFEPG, May 2005, p. 8.

753 Ben McDevitt, "Operation Helpem Fren: A personal Perspective," *Australian Army Journal* (*based on presentation delivered 23/06/05*), (2005): 11.

754 Ben McDevitt, "Operation Helpem Fren: A personal Perspective," *Australian Army Journal* (*based on presentation delivered 23/06/05*), (2005): 16.

755 Australian Federal Police, "Assessing New Age Policing," *Platypus Magazine: the Journal of the AFP* (June 2006): 7.

756 Australian Federal Police, "Assessing New Age Policing," *Platypus Magazine: the Journal of the AFP* (June 2006): 7.

757 Elsina Wainwright, "How is RAMSI Faring?: Progress, Challenges and Lessons Learnt," *Australian Strategic Policy Institute Insight 14* (2005): 3.

758 Peter Morgan, *RAMSI and Capacity Development: Report on a field trip to the Solomon Islands* (*Revised*), Report Commissioned by AusAID (Canberra: AusAID, 2007); Elsina Wainwright, "How is RAMSI Faring?: Progress, Challenges and Lessons Learnt," *Australian Strategic Policy Institute Insight 14* (2005): 5.

759 Australian National University, *People's Survey 2007: Solomon Islands*, (Canberra: The Australian National University (ANU) Enterprise P/L on behalf of RAMSI, 2007), 57, p. 8 "Survey finds strong support for RAMSI," *Solomon Star Newspaper*, 26 September 2007.

The Solomon Islands Government and Hybridity

Traditional approaches to justice in the Solomon Islands have evolved and changed over time, but forms of social order and processes of dispute resolution have always existed.[760] Colonisation brought with it state based mechanisms for the delivery of justice—with mixed results—and local informal institutions have adjusted and responded continually. As aforementioned however, manifestations of hybridity in the Solomon Islands are not new. The so-called modern era has seen the imperfect ad hoc manifestation of hybridity as people on the ground draw on the systems available to them in the interests of maintaining social order and a basic level of safety.

A succession of Solomon Islands governments have ostensibly acknowledged the importance of local approaches to justice and the need for government to recognise these systems formally—in the interests of drawing on these locally embedded capacities and ensuring widespread access to justice. In particular informal systems of dispute resolution are recognised as legitimate mechanisms for maintaining order, providing a level of safety, and ensuring culturally appropriate applications of 'the'[761] law. Whilst informal and 'traditional'[762] justice; maintenance of social order; dispute resolution; and the provision of safety/security, manifest themselves in different systems, through different sources of legitimacy and authority and draw on a range of different 'local'[763] actors, traditional justice primarily includes decision making and reconciliation practices associated with chiefs, elders and church leaders.[764]

The motivations for drawing on and formally recognising informal and traditional approaches to justice and order are varied and they are not all benign. It is fair to say however that the most obvious and frequently cited reasons include the cultural sensitivity and appropriateness of informal justice, in addition to the acknowledgement of the State's inability to service the vast majority of the people

---

760 Ministry of Justice and Legal Affairs Solomon Islands & The World Bank, *Justice Delivered Locally: Draft Concept Note*, (Honiara: The Ministry of Justice and Legal Affairs Solomon Islands & The World Bank, 2009).

761 Whilst it is commonly referred to as 'the law' (as in the Rule of Law)—this is clearly a *small* 'the' as it is applied differently across the country and in some cases it is not applied at all.

762 The word 'traditional' is no doubt problematic. For our purposes here it is acknowledge that systems do not exist in some 'pre-modern' state unchanged over time. But rather kastom based practices absorb influences and are fluid and changing. The term traditional here refers to those practices which are commonly referred to as being 'traditional' by SIG, and donor organisations—such practices and informal institutions generally draw on 'culture' for both their legitimacy and internal logic or are seen as evolving (that is to say 'they have always been there' but are nevertheless a product of change over time).

763 The term 'local' refers to community level actors unless otherwise specified.

764 Ministry of Justice and Legal Affairs Solomon Islands & The World Bank, *Justice Delivered Locally: Draft Concept Note*, (Honiara: The Ministry of Justice and Legal Affairs Solomon Islands & The World Bank, 2009).

of the Solomon Islands. It is also true that official state institutions have limited legitimacy in some geographical areas as well as with some groups, a point we have made earnestly throughout, but most specifically in Chapter 6. Similarly there are instances where the legitimacy of the state apparatus is actively contested. The formal State reach of the Solomon Island's Rule of Law institutions is limited to the capital and major provincial centres. Whilst RAMSI no doubt supplements the State's capacity to police outside of Honiara, in reality police contact is more the exception than the norm. In most areas where police activity and response to crime has increased it is heavily reliant on the logistical support of the PPF. This arrangement is clearly unsustainable. Of course these characteristics mark most of the 'majority world' in which international missions take place, yet again highlighting a false assumption of the conventional wisdom.

Working with the World Bank, the Ministry for Justice and Legal Affairs has concerned itself with gaining a greater understanding of the current informal capacities on the ground in the Solomons in the interests of integrating these systems into the Government's approach to the delivery of justice. This project, 'Justice Delivered Locally' is one of several attempts to account for and include informal systems in formal policy and practice. The priorities of this project are focused on strengthening hybrid solutions to the justice challenges the people and institutions of the Solomon Islands face. The project has a range of objectives including the assessment of the capacities and functions of both informal and formal justice mechanisms and institutions. It aims to find out how these myriad of institutions function and what it is that local people expect of them. Crucially they are looking to understand what 'justice' means to people and how supporting and linking with informal practice may help to satisfy these needs. The work explicitly acknowledges that the majority of the population rely on bodies other than 'state controlled organs' for the provision of 'public order and [to] assist in the resolution of disputes'. Consequently it makes sense to work with this reality.

In 2010 SIG policy made provisions for: recognizing, strengthening and respecting the role of chiefs in the administration of justice at the local level; recognizing just and humane traditional values and customs; reviving the native/local court system;[765] and other hybrid approaches to governing and decision-making are underway in other areas including the Tribal Lands Dispute Resolution Panels.[766]

765 The following sections concerning SIG and RAMSI policy towards the incorporation of traditional practice draw on a mixture of primary source material for documentary analysis and unstructured expert interviews. Expert interviews were conducted with senior RAMSI officials on the ground in the interests of clarifying official information and exploring the complexities of implementing policies surrounding issues to do with hybridity. Such officials include RAMSI Law & Justice personnel and PPF as well as local officials involved in RAMSI planning.

766 Ministry of Justice and Legal Affairs Solomon Islands & The World Bank, *Justice Delivered Locally: Draft Concept Note*, (Honiara: The Ministry of Justice and Legal Affairs Solomon Islands & The World Bank, 2009).

In the 2010 election the influential parties all had a strong focus on strengths-based reform with an emphasis on the importance of culture and traditional approaches to strengthening service delivery and decision-making. Statements include the intention to invite 'traditional and community leaders in each province to establish a council of leaders to meet and discuss matters of mutual interest'—'with the aim for eventual institutionalisation of traditional leadership'.[767] Influential member, Manasseh Sogavare's party asserted a 'narrative [that] builds on the philosophy of the bottom up approach' there is a focus on decentralisation, and they call to 'legislate for the recognition of the authority of Chiefs and other traditional leaders for the administration of justice over custom matters at the local level'.[768] The Democratic Party led by Steve Abana (who was narrowly defeated in the post election scramble to form collations) have stated their intentions to 'strengthen and empower traditional decision making process'.[769] Danny Phillip's party 'Reform Democratic Party', which in the end took government, were also committed to constitutional reform.[770]

There has been ongoing pressure in the Solomon Islands for constitutional reform including the introduction of a federal system. In such a system provinces would become states and the incorporation of traditional approaches to justice would therefore fall under state jurisdiction.[771] It is uncertain when (and if) constitutional reform will go ahead and how long it will take to go through the process of decentralising. Given this uncertainty it is important that national reforms remain mindful of the uncertainty around this issue and implement changes which can absorb such reforms. The draft Federal Constitution too has an emphasis on the importance of traditional justice and explicitly makes provisions for the maintenance of diverse and culturally appropriate systems. Under the heading of 'Traditional Law Practice' it permits:

> *(1) To the extent compatible with this Constitution, clan or tribal communities shall exercise authority to administer their own system of justice according to their distinctive juridical customs, tradition and procedures... (2) Traditional justice shall decide or resolve a matter or punish in accordance with methods customarily practised by the people concerned for dealing with offences. (3) State legislature must enact law to give effect to this section.*[772]

---

767 Solomon Islands Party for Rural Advancement Party Platform, Website, http://www.pacificpolicy.org/ 2010.

768 Ownership, Unity & Responsibility Party—Party Platform, Pacific Institute of Public Policy, Website, http://www.pacificpolicy.org/blog/2010/07/19/our/.

769 Democratic Party—Party Statement, 2010.

770 Danny Phillip stepped down in November 2011 when 12 members of his collation defected (Solomon Star, November 11, 2011).

771 Draft Federal Constitution of Solomon Islands, 2011 http://www.sicr.gov.sb/.

772 Draft Federal Constitution of Solomon Islands, 2011 http://www.sicr.gov.sb/.

The extent to which SIG have pursued hybridity in practice is debatable; but they have at various times acknowledged the possibility and attempted to grapple with developing a hybrid law and justice system, reflecting the complexity concepts of how adaptive agents can co-evolve.

RAMSI and Hybridity

RAMSI predictably focused on the interruption of violence and the following maintenance of order in the initial stages. After a period of relative stability the mission was then meant to transition to capacity development in the interests of creating a sustainable institutionally embedded solution to the country's 'fragility'. What is interesting is the diagnosis of state failure and consequent focus on institutional capacity development ignored some rather obvious realities: foremost among these was that the state had never been effective, insofar as living up to characteristics of the Westphalian state ideal which rests at the heart of the conventional wisdom. In other words, not only is there little question that the failure of SIG to respond to the mounting concerns of its local people was a key factor in the conflict, and that state agents themselves were perpetrators of the ensuing violence, but the *state itself* lacked the capacity to restore or maintain order. What is more, SIG's lack of capacity is emblematic of recipient countries, a characteristic highlighted in other chapters which in turn goes a long way to invalidating key mainstream assumptions.

Initially this reality appeared to be overlooked, generally, particularly by RAMSI.[773] Over time however individuals within RAMSI appear to have become increasingly aware of the need to look beyond the state and this issue has been pushed by several other bodies supporting SIG sentiment.[774] In hindsight it appears that the question should have been: if it was not an effective state that delivered relative peace and stability before the 'tension', then what combination of factors had been responsible? The thornier question (for the international community perennially) became one of whether RAMSI should help restore whatever had been working adequately before.

The response, in short, has continued to be in the affirmative for an acceptance of hybrid approaches. Interviews with senior RAMSI figures in the PPF and Law & Justice arena confirm a shift towards placing greater emphasis on informal processes and traditional practice.[775] At the same time, the increasing emphasis

---

773 This is not a criticism as such, or at least not a criticism of those RAMSI actors on the ground. State reform was the mandate, so the institutional emphasis was arguably inevitable.

774 It is important not to overstate SIG commitment to hybridity. Whilst the provisions for allowing this do exist the commitment to achieving it is uneven and debatable.

775 The commitment to this fluctuates—it is important to note that these observations were drawn from interviews conducted in 2010.

on drawing on informal capacities in state-building is not limited to working with traditional systems, per se. Rather, the space has opened up to draw on community strengths generally and this is seen as an avenue for linking with traditional approaches as part of a broader connection with 'the local'. RAMSI policy documents began to reflect those of SIG and the assertions of party platforms. Elements of this change are also evident in the SIG-RAMSI Partnership framework which not only recognises the role of traditional values and customs but talks about strengthening traditional justice mechanisms.[776] Further, the framework makes provisions for the establishment of crime prevention committees based upon a decentralised approach to safety and justice at the village level. The important point for our purposes is that these provisions for the decentralisation of decision-making in relation to law and justice are not only to enable community based decision-making but to enable the formal system to draw on the informal. As such, support for chiefs and traditional systems is explicit—but so too are the caveats regarding Constitutional Laws and the assertion that this remains the decision of SIG and not donors.[777]

The RAMSI Law & Justice Design Team were charged with developing the planning document that would inform the next phase of RAMSI in this area. This process included a wide ranging scoping exercise that ventured well beyond the bounds of institution building. The team was involved in what has been described as a survey of capacities on the ground, looking for opportunities to strengthen links between the formal and informal systems. The result was a design document that paid considerable attention to informal systems in the appendix, but was ultimately unable to carve out of defined path for hybridisation and rather reasserted that this is a decision for SIG.[778]

In preparing for future planning the Design Team essentially toured through rural and remote communities speaking to local people to gain a sense of the existing informal capacities, the current state of informal justice and to gauge community sentiment—with a view to find out what local people would like

---

776 Partnership Framework between Solomon Islands Government and Regional Assistance Mission to Solomon Islands, April 2009.

777 LAW & JUSTICE Strategy: 1.52 Chiefs and traditional leaders are recognized at the local level together with the revival of the native/local court systems in villages, which also sees the establishment of a Tribal Land Dispute Resolution Panel.

SIG/RAMSI TARGET: 1.52.1 Traditional Justice is recognized within the Court System.

ASSUMPTIONS/IMPLICATIONS: The Traditional Justice systems must conform to the Constitution and National Laws. Different components of SIG strategy in this area may require different donor assistance. SIG intent is to strengthen chiefs rather than just local courts. Important that whatever is implemented is driven from the Solomon Islands rather than donors. Donors could assist with research and drafting instructions on possible legislation.

778 Interview with Senior Australian Development Official, 20 April 2010, Ministry for Justice & Legal Affairs, Honiara.

to see happen in this space. What they found was a strong support for the formal acknowledgement of informal systems and a clear desire to link the two to improve service delivery and ensure the state works with and supports local processes. According to a senior RAMSI L&J official, by definition the above finding means the state *does* matter and therefore a great deal of resources will need to continue to flow to the building of state capacity if it is to become an effective actor in meeting people's expectations in linking with the informal.[779]

The pragmatic move by RAMSI to working expressly with hybridity is a view shared by others. For instance, in 2004 the UNDP reported:

> *It appears that higher levels of violence have occurred in areas where traditional mechanisms have weakened or broken down. Managing the nexus between traditional and non-traditional systems is critical to ensuring Solomon Islanders accept and implement good governance.*[780]

From a regional perspective, the Pacific Islands Forum Secretariat (PIF-S) and the PIF Eminent Persons Group (PIFEPG) have also encouraged the inclusion of informal systems and actors in the formal systems of justice. Importantly this has meant the inclusion of such in the approach to state-building. In fact there has been a growing consensus within program management and practitioner circles that, due to budget and capacity constraints, state based institutions may never be capable of delivering broader access to justice and for this reason capacity development focused solely on institutions are destined to achieve only modest gains—a point we made variously in Chapters 4, 5 and 6. Hence, in the interests of finding a sustainable solution hybrid approaches are gaining traction.

Challenges with Hybridity

According to accounts of community perspectives on informal and formal justice, the two systems can and do work together with some success, some of the time. The uneasy embrace of hybridity, however, is far from sorted. The following (unpublished) quote excerpt concerns how RAMSI has struggled with hybridity. It is a product of collaboration between one of this book's authors[781] and the Inspector of Prisons for Correctional Services Solomon Islands. Not only does it support key points of critique we make throughout this book, more specifically it highlights the tensions the international community should address as it better learns how to approach the fluid nexus between Western and endogenous (*i.e.* the matter of hybridity).

---

[779] Interview with Senior Australian Development Official, 20 April 2010, Ministry for Justice & Legal Affairs, Honiara.

[780] Kenneth Bush and Sue Le Mesurier, *Solomon Islands Peace and Conflict Development Analysis: Emerging Priorities in Preventing Future Violent Conflict* (New York: United Nations Development Programme, 2004), http://www.kmcgovern.com/wp-content/uploads/2010/04/undp_2004.pdf.

[781] Jodie Curth-Bibb.

> *At first there was an inability to see the existing systems or understand the nature of local process and living conventions of practice... the (ensuing) importation of managerial processes and the disempowerment of local people and personnel... means that a large number of local people become swamped by, and withdraw from, a new order that they are no longer equipped to 'know'. Rather than build capacity, this effectively blocks local participation in any meaningful way.*

The full quotation, which summarises key forces at play between local and introduced ways of thinking about the Rule of Law sector, goes on to argue that even though RAMSI eventually has been attempting to incorporate local knowledge and systems alongside state-based solutions, that path too is fraught with problems. These problems stem from, *inter alia*, the contrasting systems of 'knowing' between introduced Western and endogenous—as we have highlighted frequently in previous chapters. As such, there are undoubtedly some serious obstacles to strengthening informal systems and in turn supporting hybridity in the Solomon Islands' RoL sphere.

Senior RAMSI L&J actors[782] described this current landscape: that while there is significant 'philosophical interest' in traditional justice from all the important players and certainly a rhetorical commitment from SIG, at this stage the resolve to officially incorporate non state actors in the RAMSI program is lacking. A general inclination to stall on these matters exists for at least two main reasons. Firstly, there is still a great deal of uncertainty around the current state of traditional and informal justice and the existent capacities of non-state actors. Delivery of such services and the manner of provision is extremely inconsistent across the country and there certainly is not the possibility to roll out any wide ranging laws or standard approaches to justice given the varying degrees of legitimacy, the lack of clarity around jurisdiction and the wide ranging levels of capacity.[783] It has been reported that SIG want to wait for the findings of the JDL project and even then only reluctant and gradual action is anticipated from some informants. It is acknowledged that this is an extremely sensitive issue which no one wants to get wrong. At the same time, it was suggested that lurking beneath this hesitation is the fact that some SIG actors have other motivations for delay tactics. The key political issue, not surprisingly, is funding: namely, some SIG actors are apparently losing interest in a hybrid approach *if* it means aid money is to be diverted from state-based capacity development and moved into supporting non-state actors; in other words, some SIG actors have an interest in preventing a diversion of funding away from their ambit.[784]

---

782 Interviews with RAMSI Senior Officials, 2010.

783 Interview with Senior Australian Development Official, 20 April 2010, Ministry for Justice & Legal Affairs, Honiara.

784 Interview with Senior Australian Development Official, 20 April 2010, Ministry for Justice & Legal Affairs, Honiara.

A second impairment has to do with the fact that despite the policy goals highlighted in the partnership agreement and the 'in principle' commitment to working with informal justice and local strengths, it has been argued by Senior Law & Justice program officials in SIG that 'RAMSI has no mandate to jump into this space'. They must, it seems, wait for definitive SIG policy on such matters. This is one of the double-edged sword consequences of the progress in international thinking registered by documents, such as the Paris Accord and Accra Agenda, which recognise the need for countries to make their own futures. Given the potential to delay action until exhaustive research has been conducted, analysed, discussed and debated the opportunity for RAMSI to fund and support informal actors in any meaningful way may be lost. This is clearly frustrating for some who feel that continued state focussed capacity development is likely to be unsustainable, and that RAMSI efforts, if not linked to and supported by the informal capacities of Solomon Islanders, will therefore be wasted. It is also incredibly frustrating (as revealed through community focus groups) for those on the ground who are working to resolve conflict and maintain order and cannot understand why the SIG seemingly does nothing to support them.

The longstanding objection to the incorporation of traditional and informal practice on the grounds of human rights violations is yet another obstacle to hybridity, one that extends beyond RAMSI's role. The Solomon Islands are no exception to this sticking point. The issue of women's rights in particular is often seen to be incompatible with customary law, and in the context of the Solomon Islands women's rights warrants the considerable attention we now give it. In Jalal's report *Harmful Practice Against Women in Pacific Island Countries: Customary and Conventional Laws*, a scathing critique on the formal recognition of customary law is put forward drawing many of its disturbing examples from the Solomon Islands context. The paper argues that customary law and practices in the Pacific Island region are based largely on patriarchal systems which either implicitly or actively undermine gender equality and the rights of women. Moreover, the paper argues that "These parallel legal regimes scrutinize and control community norms and practices, which often means legitimising male power over women and sanctioning violence against them."[785]

These criticisms are certainly relevant to many parts of the Solomon Islands and are particularly true of some cultural groups and customary practice. Whilst the validity of the claims the paper makes about the ongoing complaints of women in the region regarding customary law is not questioned here, the specific research undertaken herein would suggest that the position of women regarding informal justice is Solomon Islands is more complicated. For instance, some women acknowledge that informal justice is the only mechanism for maintaining

[785] I. Jalal, *Harmful Practices Against Women in Pacific Island Countries: Customary and Conventional Laws*, (Suva: Pacific Regional Rights Resource Team, 2009).

order. They maintain that through these social controls women are indeed afforded a level of safety, and that there are indeed chiefs, elders and church leaders who encourage and promote respect. That being noted, there are serious tensions elsewhere.[786]

As the Permanent Secretary for the Ministry for Women, Youths and Children Affairs, Ethel Sigimanu, pointed out there is a real conflict between SIG's growing emphasis on rights based protection of women and children and customary and communal practices. Ms Sigimanu was supportive of drawing on local strengths but was very wary about the potential abuses this approach might fail to address adequately. In particular she was concerned with both (1) the rights of the individual and the deeper human experience and (2) the assumption that traditional approaches have meaning and legitimacy to everyone,[787] aspects which she contends customary practice *can* fail to take account of. In her words:

> *Before going to do any reconciliation [one should ask] how meaningful is this to this person? Because we generalise a lot of things and it's also an issue we find with women themselves. You know how culture can reconcile between tribes, but we forget about the victim. If you have a girl who has been raped for instance and so when we reconcile, the reconciliation is really to make peace between tribes... but we do not go deeper as to looking at how the victim sees this and whether it's meaningful to the victim because it brings shame to the family, how she is then going to get on with life.*[788]

The following quote from a Solomon Islands Magistrate's decision regarding a sexual assault similarly highlights that there continues to be serious problems in this awkward hybrid arrangement of reciprocal recognition when it comes to the rights of women:

> *I think the most that can be done is to call the parties involved, maybe the chief can do it in a chief's hearing—he will take a walk over to the house of the man, and ask him to pay compensation to her or to the family (usually not her). The payment is to prevent a payback against him, maybe to rape his daughter.*[789]

The above quotes illustrate how social norms and traditional practices can result in a prioritisation of communal harmony over the rights of the individual, and more specifically the rights of women. These concerns to do with human rights violations and the problems associated with taking a communal order approach

---

786 In fact the Community Officers pilot itself, as discussed below, has revealed some highly problematic treatment of women which has come about through some aspects of culture surviving and other aspects not—resulting in a perverse interpretation of cultural norms which leaves women in highly vulnerable and sometimes dangerous position.

787 Interview with Permanent Secretary for the Ministry of Women, Youth & Children's Affairs, Honiara, January 2010.

788 Interview with Permanent Secretary for the Ministry of Women, Youth & Children's Affairs, Honiara, January 2010.

789 I. Jalal, *Harmful Practices Against Women in Pacific Island Countries: Customary and Conventional Laws,* (Suva: Pacific Regional Rights Resource Team, 2009).

to justice are serious, and no one is suggesting they should be ignored (at least not in formal or public discussions). Concern with communal order is not in itself problematic and is in fact critical for crime prevention and to avoid further suffering.

Working Through the Challenges of Hybridity

Given the circumstances highlighted above, many, such as the Permanent Secretary, have acknowledged that more needs to be done. Yet there is an understandable hesitation to move forward. Many working in this space are attempting to reconcile the contradictions and fully understand how informal practices work before they plan a way to formally incorporate them. Others have argued that such an endeavour is an exercise in futility and it is time to work it out through practice and engagement. A senior Solomon Islander, with a great deal of experience in government and working with donors (RAMSI in particular), put it this way:

> *There is no need to do more surveys or to consult with everyone on the ground as seems to be the pattern at the moment... there are plenty of Solomon Islanders who have knowledge of how things work on the ground so that programs can get moving/happening if they are asked and involved.*[790]

Regardless of that particular disagreement, what is important to the overall debate is the need to let go of the illusion that any directions taken are a matter of choosing between formal law, which is based on human rights, and customary law which clearly is not. It is instead crucial to accept that this will be a process of social change, fostered by actors from both the formal and informal sectors, through processes that should themselves be acknowledged as hybrid.

On the one hand, though it is appropriate to draw upon customary approaches to justice and reconciliation, the formal law should also be allowed to take its course.[791] For instance, it is imperative that the legal environment enables the rights of women and human rights generally. The good news is that such legislation does exist and is being improved.[792]

---

790 Email correspondece with Senior Solomon Island Government Official, July 2010.

791 Interview with Permanent Secretary for the Ministry of Women, Youth & Children's Affairs, Honiara, January 2010; Interview with Senior RSIPF Officer, Rove, Honiara, June 2010.

792 See J. Corrin Care, "Customary law and women's rights in Solomon Islands," *Development Bulletin* 51 (2000): 20–22 regarding the legislative framework for human rights and tensions between customary law and legislation. See also Jalal regarding proposed changes to the Draft Constitution including the following proposed provision: "*Where there is a conflict between customary laws or practices and women's right to equality under this Constitution or any other law, women's right to equality shall prevail.*" I. Jalal, *Harmful Practices Against Women in Pacific Island Countries: Customary and Conventional Laws*, (Suva: Pacific Regional Rights Resource Team, 2009).

However, a top-down, state-driven approach to this will not work on its own—particularly in an environment lacking capacity and resources for enforcement to such an extent. Even if there were consensus on human rights in the Solomon Islands as well as the political will to pursue such a rights-based approach to justice, it is folly to suggest that the State can or will have the capacity to enforce it. Solomon Islanders outside of the capital, including women, cannot rely on the State; they do not have access to formal justice and they consequently draw on a grossly inadequate ad hoc hybrid arrangement. The inability to access formal RoL institutions means there remains a need for improved treatment of women and recognition of basic human rights in informal approaches as well as the formal.

Fortunately there appears to be a growing consensus that human rights can be part of the dialogue around strengthening informal capacities. As it has been clear in SIG policy the Government has been interested in 'recognising just and human traditional values and customs'.[793] Furthermore, drawing on informal capacities and appealing to the aspects of culture that do promote 'positive principles, practices and behaviours, and... that foster respect for women and girls, condemn violence against women, and facilitate equality between women and men'[794] is a deliberate component of the women's rights strategy.

Community Officers and Crime Prevention Committees: *Evolving Intentions*

With that contextual landscape in mind, both SIG and RAMSI have been looking for opportunities to make incremental improvements on the ground. What follows is an example of a recent foray into this space: the Community Officers and Crime Prevention Committees, which is basically a community policing initiative meant to marry up formal models of policing with locally-appropriate practices. The work so far affords us with a unique opportunity to peer inside innovative approaches to grappling with the challenges of hybridity and capacity development operations.

The Community Crime Prevention Committees, for the most part are comprised of local community members who are responsible for maintaining social order with the assistance of RSIPF. The Committees are different in each area but where intended to include local chiefs, church leaders, women's groups and youth and to draw on the existing processes for resolving conflict and disputes and managing crime and violence. The idea was that each local community would

---

[793] Coalition for Natioinal Unity and Rural Advancement Government Policy Statement, Honiara, 2008.

[794] Secretariat of the Pacific Community for the Ministry of Women, Youth & Children's Affairs, *Solomon Islands Family Health and Safety Study: A study on violence against women and children* (Honiara: Secretariat of the Pacific Community for the Ministry of Women, Youth & Children's Affairs, 2009).

make its own decisions around Committee membership and activities.[795] Their role was designed essentially to pro-actively prevent crime and to work with SIG and RSIPF to maintain safe and ordered communities. Whilst the details remain unclear at this stage there has been some concern about the sustainability of creating new bodies and arguments are being made to instead draw on existing functioning forums of community engagement—ensuring such forum agendas explicitly address crime prevention issues and invite other community members to participate.[796]

It should be noted, however, that these community level committees are not a new implant as such (or at least not implanted by PPF). The concept has derived from previously running programs instigated and supported by the NGO, Save the Children. Save the Children had been supporting crime prevention committees scattered throughout regional areas of the Solomon Islands. The program 'fell over' because its funding ended. RAMSI L&J and PPF have seen this as a vehicle to get into the informal/community space in an uncontroversial way and in some sense side-step the highly political issues outlined above.[797] Together they are funding the continuation and expansion of this project to ensure it meets the needs of community policing and crime prevention more broadly throughout the Islands. From the PPF perspective this is seen as enabling them to 'cover off' on two key objectives: (1) Improve public demand for better rule of law outcomes across the Solomon Islands; and (2) Establish and maintain support for traditional justice processes which maintain order and accountability inaccessible areas of the Solomon Islands.[798]

Whilst there is still some uncertainty surrounding these fora, with no guarantee that new governments will provide the support and policy framework to enable these initiatives—community crime prevention committees have gone ahead in at least some manifestation through the funding of Save the Children's now expanded program. These locally embedded and to varying degrees community owned[799] approaches to crime-prevention are seen as a platform for steering the activities of the Community Officer (COs) program, explored in detail below, in the future. The reason we have included its story is that it outlines an approach considered to have the potential to allow for new hybrid solutions to emerge, ensure local accountability, help manage fluidity, and cater to the unique and culturally specific needs of the different communities throughout the Solomon Islands.

795 Interview with Senior RSIPF Officer, 14 June, 2010 at Police Headquarters, Rove, Honiara Solomon Island.

796 Interview with Senior RSIPF Officer, 14 June, 2010 at Police Headquarters, Rove, Honiara Solomon Island.

797 Interview with Senior Australian Development Official, Honiara, 2010

798 Interview with PPF Capacity Development Program Management, June 2010.

799 How community owned these committees are varies between villages and people give greatly differing accounts as to their effectiveness.

Closely affiliated to the Community Crime Prevention Committees is the Community Officer (CO) pilot currently being trialled. This is a different and innovative approach to community policing in a post-conflict environment. The primary purpose of this Community Officer's project is to move past the formal/informal dichotomy and begin to work with community strengths, including traditional approaches to justice, to support and strengthen access to justice and ensure some level of police presence and support to all areas—including remote and rural locations. The work is still being done on defining exactly what this program will look like. It was decided that the Community Officer would be an elected community member whose job it is to be the link between the police and community. It was to be an unpaid role, but like many aspects of this approach this was to be reviewed and may change. It was possible the position would in the future be funded and/or the associated expenses of the role would be reimbursed.

The motivation for this pilot project is largely driven by the geography of the Solomon Islands and often-related logistical constraints. Police posts have been left to cover vast areas of the country with few officers and even fewer resources. The remote parts of the country are isolated by either distance or terrain and are often quite literally not policed at all. Whilst the CO would not police these areas as such, the idea was that they provide a policing presence. The COs are required to undertake a number of duties, these were always intended to be negotiated depending on the needs of the community, but it was envisaged the role would include reporting to the police on issues to do with low level crime, keeping a record of how these 'disputes' are settled and ensuring the police are informed of serious matters, preferably before they become serious.

The COs do not wear uniforms, instead they are allocated with T-Shirts displaying an emblem identifying them as the local CO. They do not have any particular powers for enforcement, so in formal terms at least, there is no serious interruption in terms of local authority. Of course the legitimacy afforded to the CO through their appointment (however informal the role may be) still has the potential to impact upon local systems of legitimacy and hierarchy.

The ownership over the COs program is not a straight forward external imposition or a wholly locally owned proposition. Rather it is a complex mixture of PPF intervention, RSIPF support, local ideas and a colonial legacy. It is, in short, the emergence of a new-hybridity. There appears to be a lack of consensus about whose idea this was—but this might be a good thing, with all involved taking at least some credit for the approach. Based on early planning and concept documents and consequent correspondence regarding the initial proposals it would appear that the idea stems from former approaches to community policing and what has been referred to as the 'Village Constable'.[800] The Village Constable

800 Phil Norris, *Community Policing in the Solomon Islands—Scoping Document*, A response to Foreign Relation Committee Comments, (unpublished, March, 2009).

or 'Headman' were appointments made during colonial administration by the High Commissioner. The District Headman, supported by Assistant Headmen (depending on circumstances), acted as a link between the community and the Government as well as enforcing Council by-laws. More recently Area Constables have worked in similar roles (up until 1998). A 'revisiting [of] the old system of having a government official in the communities who acts as a link up with the Government in terms of effective policing in the communities' was endorsed by the then Chairman of the Law Reform Commission (and now Solomon Islands Governor General), Frank Kabui.[801] It is fair to say that those involved from the PPF side of the house were wary of introducing new structures and sources of power and they were also keen to build on existing norms.[802] As a senior PPF Officer in program management explained, the PPF support for this approach was at least partly due to local support for, and familiarity with, the concept:

> *I had concerns at first because you had the legitimate authority by legislation of the police and Constitution, you had the legitimate authority through traditional customary law in terms of the chiefs and alike and I was originally concerned about having something in the middle... but before independence the headman was an appointment that was voted by the villagers... so the history of this and its significance in the context of this culture, or multiple cultures... is actually in existence, so we're not creating something [entirely] new.*[803]

It was explained by both RSIPF and PPF members responsible for the implementation of this program that ideally the CO would respond to the community. How responsive this role would be and to what extent the instructions for COs would be centralised was at this stage unclear. It was hoped however, that both the national level and community level crime prevention bodies would be functioning in order to support and mould the role of the CO.

What is particularly interesting about this approach to the COs program is that specific design, planning and policy all appeared to be undecided at the stage of staggered implementation. Whilst most involved did have answers to design and planning questions—they were inconsistent. Despite this there were already several community officers on the ground. Even the rolling out of the pilot had been uneven at this stage. It has been confusing for those involved on the ground and the lack of precise planning meant the COs were unclear of their roles and complained that they were scarcely supported. When we interviewed COs, police and community leaders in the immediate region of the COs' responsibility we found mixed understandings as to their role and the expectations, with no clear

---

801 Written correspondence from the Solomon Islands Law Reform Commission to the Commander of the PPF dated 19 March 2009.

802 Personal contact with Commander PPF in Honiara in 2009; Personel contact with the Comissioner of the Solomon Islands Police Force in Honiara in 2009.

803 Interview with PPF Capacity Development Program Management, June 2010.

sense of when this might be cleared up or how the RSIPF or Government intended to support the efforts.

Learning to Learn despite 'Uncertainty'

The official intention was to have at least 20 or more community officers in the field in the immediate period. Once these positions were filled the actual trial would begin. Again details were unclear and accounts conflicting but it would seem the trial would be in place for six to eight months. The intention was to have these COs in place and then to bring them in to Honiara for initial training. After a period of time in the field they would come together again for further workshops and to discuss their experiences, identify needs and to work out a way forward. As far as could be determined through interviews with those driving the project, what would constitute a successful pilot had not yet been articulated.

There was a lack of clarity around all of these issues and from a conventional perspective this may all seem somewhat *disordered*.[804] What is important here is that those involved seemed to be prepared to do a little bit of feeling their way through—rather than planning everything from a conference room miles from the context and well in advance. In this case the implementation, design and planning appeared to be coinciding and moving backwards and forwards—rather than in a linear fashion.

In stark contrast to the rational conventional approach to policy, planning, objective setting, predicting and measurement—the uncertainty in this space presented some promising potential. In fact, key personnel involved in the implementation of this pilot appeared to be well aware of the benefits of allowing for fluidity and very wary of prescribing outcomes. Whilst it seems that most donor supported activities that are attempting to marry the formal with the informal are busily gathering information about what exists 'out there' in an attempt to carefully formalise a neat welding together of approaches and capacities, a more fluid approach was emerging in the COs project. It appeared that the idea was that the CO's mandate could be to adapt and respond to community demands and contributions rather than to codify a division of responsibilities and service provision between the formal and informal. The idea being to embed processes for relations and the inherent productive value of dialogue and dynamic interaction

804 Having said that, there is a planning and design team set to work on these issues. It is important not to overemphasise the uncertainty as this has evolved in a roundabout way. In fact those responsible for the planning the details of implementation bring a wealth of experience—including a PPF officer that has worked with similar approaches in Bougainville and there is no suggestion that there is a lack of attention to detail at this early stage.

was explicitly understood as reflected by the both the view of senior PPF and in this explanation provided by a key Senior RSIPF Officer.

> *... I think it's about the RSIPF getting down to the community and understanding their systems and their processes... how do they handle issues... and as you know a lot of these systems are not written... they exist... and they are passed on... and they stored in somebody's brains... they are adjusted to the situation... I am aware that we will not come up with a standard system at the end of the day... systems will vary as you go through the communities... I think... It is understanding the community, how people deal with their issues... it is important also to get what they expect... what do they expect? Where do they want the RSIPF to come in... where do they want to be left alone and deal with these issues themselves? If we go down that track, my view is that we are empowering them, to deal with their own business... as locals (the RSIPF) we still have a lot to learn from the various communities and the cultures that we have in the country... it's just so many that we cannot just apply one set of rules in one community and then transplant them... my view is that it's getting down to each individual community, understanding them properly... not taking away our powers and authority in terms of law and order... but... recognising their strengths, recognising what they can provide and them recognising what we can do to assist them... it is sort of a two way thing...*[805]

There was a keen awareness that there are indeed many instances of where the state would put 'down on the table' what it can realistically offer and the community does the same and there are no obvious solutions for the still gaping holes in capacity. In an interview with the Deputy Commissioner of RSIPF[806] the following scenario was put to him:

> *In Maul'u there have been instances where the community have in fact gone to the police and reported a matter they felt was beyond their control... according to the local police they pursue such matters, but they lay charges, perpetrators are given automatic bail or left out on open bail and await a hearing... the local court never sits, the offender is therefore never dealt with by the legal system and the community think the police haven't done anything... what do you do in such circumstances... how can this approach really overcome this?*

The Deputy Commissioner responded by acknowledging that such capacity shortfalls would continue to undermine the work of police and compromise the safety of community. But he reinforced the need to talk, the need for inclusion and to ensure that the community at least understands how these situations come about.

> *It's a challenge... but I think the more we interact with the community the more we speak with them... we'll come up with something... that both community and the RSIPF are happy to go with... without actually breaking the law... we need to find a mid-point*

805 Interview with Senior RSIPF Officer, 14 June, 2010 at Police Headquarters, Rove, Honiara Solomon Island.

806 Interview with Deputy Commissioner RSIPF, 14 June, 2010 at Police Headquarters, Rove, Honiara Solomon Islands.

> *that all of us are willing to contribute to... it's about what we will bring to the table and what they can bring to the table... how much they can participate and how much we can participate....*[807]

He went on to explain (in contrast to the rational stock-take approach of component parts)... that it's more than the sum of its parts... if parties come together without the collective resources to deal with a situation that's not the end of it... the process of communication itself changes the nature of the problem and moves the dynamics... it's not an assessment that can be made separately from the interaction.[808]

Whilst formal planning and M&E processes were yet to take shape, there was an implicit caution towards promising any particular outcomes, or using any strict measurement tools to demonstrate success. It is understood by those involved that this would need to evolve and will be very difficult if not impossible to pre-empt meaningful indicators of success. Some mentioned that they would like to see the trial take place and to learn from that what outcomes might be reasonably expected.[809] PPF Management have acknowledge that some of the CO appointments would be politically initiated, some would be taken by chiefs or other senior people of the social hierarchy others would continue to have an existing Headman of sorts and they would be the natural 'choice'. Given the anticipated variance of circumstances and manifestations of these CO roles there was an inclination to gather data, bring in academics to work with local Senior RSIPF and attempt to collaboratively analyse how this was 'tracking on the ground'. Such an analysis it was hoped may then form the basis for a public dialogue about the way forward.[810] When pushed to describe what success might look a Senior PPF Program Manager responded:

> *What does success look like? Success looks like—some form of cohesion between the State through the police force and community at the traditional level, someone who can engage in a dialogue...*[811]

Dialogue works well when the international community sees its role as one of facilitating local responses to local challenges rather than the conventional external impositions—a point we make repeatedly throughout. In this specific context, it is noteworthy that from the many interviews of both RSIPF and PPF, two PPF advisers stood out as being particularly well thought of. It was felt generally

807 Interview with Deputy Commissioner RSIPF, 14 June, 2010 at Police Headquarters, Rove, Honiara Solomon Islands.

808 Interview with Deputy Commissioner RSIPF, 14 June, 2010 at Police Headquarters, Rove, Honiara Solomon Islands. This is a paraphrasing of the response.

809 Interview with Senior RSIPF Officer, 14 June, 2010 at Police Headquarters, Rove, Honiara Solomon Island.

810 Interview with PPF Capacity Development Program Management, June 2010.

811 Interview with PPF Capacity Development Program Management, June 2010.

that these advisers had achieved quite a lot through their capacity development activities and approach. What did they have in common that was seen to affect this success? Both of these advisers are known for repeatedly asking the basic input questions of their local policing counterparts: 'What do you need?', and 'How can capacity development help you?'

The importance of local knowledge in planning and problem diagnosis cannot be overstated. Both RSIPF and PPF respondents were quick to point out the benefits of consulting local personnel on capacity development issues with social and/or cultural implications. This includes gaining an understanding of the initial conditions and context, comprised by the interrelatedness between systems and within subsystems, upon the international community entering a new environment—a philosophy of approach we argued for earnestly in the conceptual part of the book. In support of that view, all RSIPF and most PPF respondents agreed that it is beneficial for capacity development efforts to include a wide variety of stakeholders, where possible, as this allows police and other agencies and society to work together. An added benefit is that this approach improves police creditability and ensures the widespread dissemination of police messages and goals. Several RSIPF members explained how such relationships worked to improve policing, including the use of chiefs, church leaders and respected community members to circulate information on behalf of police as this ensures appropriate use of language and mode of communication as well as the benefit of endorsement.

Local police consistently offered examples illustrating why it is important to engage local personnel as well as members on the community about the tricky questions surrounding culture, values and social issues—in the same manner highlighted in the Marshall Islands case to appreciate 'the political'. For example, the problem of wantok (clan) obligations affecting everyday policing is rife in the RSIPF. Family put pressure on police officers for special treatment as a matter of course and it is expected that criminal matters will be overlooked in cases where family members are involved. Many external experts have wrestled with the ethical challenges faced by the RSIPF and their wantok obligations—which are seen by many as just simple corruption. In the hope of solving this problem professional ethics are pushed, promoted and repeated ad nauseam, but according to several interview participants surprisingly few RSIPF have been asked for *their* advice on how to handle these issues—much less the community. All RSIPF interviewed had an opinion on this subject and many had thoughtful and practical solutions. In one case a local member recounted an incident involving a sexual assault within her family. She explained how she handled the pressure from wantok to drop the charges and insisted that such an approach would work for others, which augurs well for a future in which local voices genuinely—not just rhetorically—contribute to the development of their own directions.

Interestingly, while the COs program outlined above may not at first glance look like a Western concept of community policing, the principles at work here do in fact correlate strongly with concepts such as partnership policing and community-led intelligence. Furthermore, there is evidence to suggest that community policing might work better (albeit differently) in such a setting. Unlike in Western countries, it is not just your average 'busy body' that considers safety and crime prevention to be their business. In a setting such as the Solomon Island community members are usually engaged and have a strong interest in maintaining public order.

Summary Insights

In a general sense, the Solomon Islands case illustrates how the incorporation of local knowledge, strengths and traditional and informal practice in capacity development is a highly political and complex process. Distinct and not infrequently divergent perspectives about what is legitimate, reasonable, preferred, and so forth abound from across the formal and informal sectors. Hybridity underpins the Solomon Islands not only in the practices through which law and justice are prosecuted but also the ideas that rest behind those practices. The practices that continually emerge, importantly, do so as a result of the interactions among these many stakeholders and segments of society. Nothing is a foregone conclusion, and nothing can be expected to play out in any conventional notion of linearity.

All this is significant to our interrogation herein because it means that mainstream approaches to program management, planning and M&E are largely incapable of allowing the space for the emergence of hybrid solutions to the capacity gaps of the state. Put another way, the imposition of so-called 'rational' planning and evaluation process as well as standard operating procedures would almost certainly destroy the potential for innovation and undermine practitioners and local counterparts alike in their efforts to explore the possibilities, reflect on impacts and respond accordingly.

In contrast to conventional wisdom, the systems approach to which we subscribe points out that during program implementation one impact that we need to monitor are the many relational understandings between stakeholders of what is occurring and what should occur. The Solomon Islands' experience offers hope that this can be done in a manner which is accountable and transparent without being prescriptive. Importantly, a complex systems approach ensures the measurements of success are not limited to an arbitrary output or an external assessment of outcome—but rather are embedded in the grounded experienced realities of those whom capacity development ought to be benefiting. Such an approach can absorb the political, account for and value the relational, and perhaps most importantly accommodate difference—both in practice and in knowing. All together, the insights from the Solomon Islands therefore constitute the essence of learning from complex, political realities. Such epiphanies are at the heart of the need to overturn the conventional wisdom.

CHAPTER ELEVEN

THE UN IN LIBERIA: ARTICULATING THE UNARTICULATED CONSENSUS FOR CHANGE

Introduction

The previous chapter examined hybridity in the context of ongoing developments pertaining to the recent international intervention in the Solomon Islands, and more specifically, the policing sector. The emphasis placed on the community policing foray produced insights as to the hybrid, complex nature of international policing programs. The upshot of the examination directly illustrated many of the contentions we have made throughout, not least of which was the need to make central the local voices with their inimitable knowledge of the local, political. Without an awareness of the political, coupled with the mechanisms to monitor the complex relationships among the myriad stakeholders as they inexorably evolve, international missions are truly flying blindly through a labyrinth and thus destined to fair badly.

This chapter offers another in-depth field study, this time the experience of the United Nations Mission in Liberia (UNMIL), to buttress the case for recasting the conventional wisdom. We have chosen to include UNMIL because it contains many of the issues germane to the challenge of M&E in peace operations deployed to conflict-affected settings, insofar as both the environment and the mission type display many of the characteristics that make M&E in peace operations uniquely difficult. It comprises a situation in which a UN peace operation was deployed to stem a protracted civil conflict. The decaying security sector prompted the United Nations Police (UNPOL) to become a central part of the UN response. The fact that the UNPOL mandate is broadly representative of police peacekeeping in contemporary UN missions makes it especially beneficial for our purposes herein. That is, its representative characteristics make it an ideal case to examine the unconventional claims encompassing international policing made in the book's conceptual section. What is more, the insights concerning

UNPOL in Africa nicely complement the previous two case studies, which were 1) a small, cutting-edge bilateral policing relationship in a remote Pacific Island (RMIPF) and 2) a comparatively large, regional multi-lateral arrangement close to Australia (RAMSI).

As with the other cases, this examination reflects research designed expressly to probe the merits of our unconventional ideas vis-à-vis helping to overcome the myriad practical challenges that present themselves to those in the field. To a much greater extent than the previous two chapters, this chapter engages directly with the issues and aspects pertaining to M&E. Its underlying method asks a wide variety of stakeholders how conventional M&E is done today within UNMIL and what they think about these designs and practices vis-à-vis our beliefs/approaches. In so doing, one of the authors[812] manages to elicit the views of a truly rare and impressive array of practitioners within and concerned with the mission.[813]

That the interrogation has been designed expressly to flesh out how our conceptual developments could operate in the field is a major strength of this chapter, with its interrogation featuring stakeholder responses to the specific concerns raised throughout the book, including: the treatment of attribution, context-sensitivity, outcome versus output focus, degree and forms of participation, inclusivity of non-state actors and local ownership, embedding of M&E within management processes, and learning focus coupled with deliberate iterative and reflexive qualities. The upshot is that the practitioner responses chronicled in great detail below further establish a powerful case for how deficient conventional approaches should be supplemented—if not supplanted altogether—by those we advocate. The clear implication is that the international community is far better served by adopting such lenses and processes based on complex, political realities when conceiving the M&E of international policing.

The chapter proceeds in two parts. The first briefly accounts for the M&E frameworks and approaches currently employed in UNMIL. This includes strategic frameworks as well as operational or tactical level tools. The second identifies the comparative advantages of a framework based upon our standpoints vis-à-vis current orthodoxy. It brings a weight of evidence—from whence it matters most, namely in the minds of those involved in the day to day of interventions—to bear on the kinds of characteristics needed to improve on current practice and deliver on the promise of effective M&E.

---

812 Charles T. Hunt.

813 Unlike the previous chapter, interview references for this chapter have been deliberately depersonalised to adhere to the ethical considerations that authorise the author (Charles T. Hunt) to gather and utilise this information.

Extant M&E Architecture for UN Presence in Liberia

In order to compare mainstream tenets with our many alternative propositions, it is first necessary to identify the M&E processes and tools that are employed today in UNMIL. This section therefore introduces the main M&E instruments that will be compared and contrasted in subsequent sections. It is not intended to be an exhaustive review, but rather a primer to foreground what follows. Based on a review of publicly available reporting, documents provided to one of the authors by mission officials, and the responses of interviewees in the field, there are a range of provisions and requirements that govern M&E in UNMIL. These can be categorised as either *strategic frameworks* or *operational/tactical tools*.

In terms of strategic-level frameworks, these are positioned at the nation or mission-wide level. In Liberian context, there are a number of tools employed by the UN and the government of Liberia to monitor and evaluate its progress towards post-conflict recovery. The first such tool was the 'Results-Focused Transitional Framework' (RFTF).[814] It was produced in February 2004 by the National Transitional Government of Liberia (NTGL), along with the UN and the World Bank. The RFTF was the core framework guiding the implementation of the Comprehensive Peace Agreement (CPA) until it was replaced by the 'interim Poverty Reduction Strategy' (iPRS) in late-2006, later to be replaced by its sequel the 'Poverty Reduction Strategy' (PRS), developed under Ellen Johnson-Sirleaf's elected government, released in April 2008. In its own words, the PRS "articulates the Government's overall vision and major strategies for moving toward rapid, inclusive and sustainable growth and development during the period 2008–2011."[815] The final strategic framework of note is the 'United Nations Development Assistance Framework' (UNDAF), originally launched in 2003 updated in 2007 for the period 2008–2012; it constitutes the UN system's joined-up response to the Liberian government's goals as laid out in the PRS.[816]

These strategic frameworks are holistic in nature insofar as they are comprised of all the pillars deemed central to the effective transition from war to peace and from internationally underwritten security to Liberian owned and self-sustaining peace and poverty-reduction. Each contains a focus on the objectives of UNPOL

---

814 "Results Focused Transitional Framework (RFTF)," (Monrovia: National Transitional Government of Liberia / United Nations / World Bank, 2005).

815 "Liberia Poverty Reduction Strategy," (Monrovia: Republic of Liberia, 2008), 13, 45–47. This version was perceived to be 'home-grown' and more locally owned than its predecessors in that, whilst it was still developed collaboratively by the government of Liberia, the UN and international partners/donors, it was based on extensive participatory and broad-based consultative approach.

816 "United Nations Development Assistance Framework Liberia 2008–2012: Consolidating Peace and National Recovery for Sustainable Development," (Monrovia: Government of Liberia & United Nations 2007).

and broader security sector reform, falling under pillars relating to 'security' or 'governance and the rule of law'. Importantly, each also contains its own M&E provisions largely predicated on broad targets such as the Millennium Development Goals (MDGs) or those that form the basis of the UN's benchmarking approach.[817]

Notwithstanding the plethora of design considerations ostensibly incorporated, the UN's strategic M&E arrangements have been ineffective at capturing progress towards outcomes and impacts associated with the various outcome pillars. As the mid-term review—relevant to both the PRS and the UNDAF—noted, "One of the major challenges for the UN system has been the absence of a fit-for-purpose M&E framework including baselines and indicators."[818] In response, the UN system established a 'monitoring and evaluation support unit' in March 2011 to assist its 'delivering as one' approach and to complement the planning for the envisaged 'one programme' framework and road-map which is intended to align with the Liberian government's forthcoming national visioning and growth and development processes—'Liberia Rising 2030'.

UNMIL and UNPOL are only one part of the overall international community approach with a unique context and objectives. Yet, according to the viewpoints we have put forward throughout this book, these facets are some of the most critical not only to ensuring buy-in from intervening practitioners but also to better understanding how their activities have affected the relationships, dynamics, and thus conditions on the ground—the latter of which are the express purposes and value of M&E.

There are also a number of M&E tools focused on assessments at the *operational/tactical levels*, circulating well beneath any national or mission-wide realm. Most M&E mechanisms employed by UNMIL at this level can be depicted as fragmented, insofar as that each invariably has its own reporting, monitoring and self-evaluation approaches, focusing on different components of the mission.[819] A number of these ad hoc approaches have offered some flexibility and context-specific development; however their lack of systemisation and formalisation affords only limited learning potential beyond the individual managers and their units.[820] Still other M&E tools are *intended* to be cross-cutting and mission-wide. The two approaches pervasive in all UN peace operations, and entrenched in UNMIL, are Results Based Budgeting (RBB) and Benchmarking.

The most task-oriented, micro-management tool used to track progress in-mission is without doubt the RBB system. RBB has been present in UNMIL since

---

817 Michael Dalton, *Mid-Term Review of the United Nations Development Assistance Framework 2008–2012*, (Monrovia: United Nations, 2010), 42–44.

818 Michael Dalton, *Mid-Term Review of the United Nations Development Assistance Framework 2008–2012*, (Monrovia: United Nations, 2010).

819 Interview: UNMIL Senior Management—Monrovia, Liberia, September 2010.

820 Interview: UNMIL Senior Management—Monrovia, Liberia, September 2010.

its inception. The primary objectives of RBB are twofold: first, to provide demonstrable accounting for activity and the use of resources in the preceding financial period; and second, to propose and defend sustained or increased budgetary needs for the subsequent financial period. One official heavily involved in the process described RBB as "a management tool, focused on tactical level activities conducted on a daily basis—e.g. meetings held, nature of joint-programming with government."[821] At the beginning of each financial year, mission managers are required to disaggregate their particular mandated objectives into actionable programmes, set associated targets and then report back against these at the end of the reporting period. The process sometimes involves auditors from HQ who come to check back against RBB submissions.[822]

The second approach, Benchmarking, is a technocratic means of monitoring mandate implementation gauging progress towards peace consolidation, drawdown and eventual transition and withdrawal of the mission. It has existed in UNMIL since 2006.[823] An off-shoot of the overarching benchmarking approach is the Integrated Mission Priorities and Implementation Plan (IMPIP) and associated Mandate Implementation Plan (MIP). These were established in UNMIL in late 2006, including benchmarks for all parts of an integrated UN endeavour, purported to be a tool for joint-programming and monitoring the efforts of UN integrated missions.[824] All three manifestations use benchmarks for regular comparison between planned and actual achievements to track progress. Whilst these are seen as an "essential management tool" that can "enable monitoring of the progress in achieving the mission's mandate", in relation to UNPOL, the lack of clarity regarding the format and procedures for following MIPs has undermined their utility for M&E purposes. This conclusion was supported by an Office of Internal Oversight Services (OIOS) report assessing the management of UNPOL operations.[825]

Other noteworthy elements of the UNMIL M&E architecture are those associated with 'Knowledge Management' implemented incrementally since 2006.[826] These include the 'Knowledge Management Toolkit' comprising four tools for

---

821 Interview: UNMIL Senior Management—Monrovia, Liberia, September 2010.

822 Interview: UNMIL Senior Management—Monrovia, Liberia, September 2010.

823 See: "Sixteenth Progress Report of the Secretary-General on the United Nations Mission in Liberia," (New York: United Nations, 2008), 14–20.

824 Till Blume, "Implementing the Rule of Law in Integrated Missions: Security and Justice in the UN Mission in Liberia," *Journal of Security Sector Management* 6, no. 3 (2008): 6.

825 United Nations Office of Internal Oversight Services, "Management of UN Police Operations," in *Audit Report* (New York: UN OIOS, 2008), 4–5.

826 Interview: UNMIL Official—Monrovia, Liberia, September 2010.

capturing experiences[827] and a Best Practices Officer.[828] In addition, the complementary but *ad hoc* OIOS Evaluations (up to four per year) have been a fixture of UNMIL's evaluation culture.[829]

All together, the above collection of tools and processes constitute the M&E architecture that overlays and occupies those in UNPOL when it comes to assessing 'progress' and determining the impact of mission activities. The M&E tools and instruments specific to the police component are few and far between, but since UNMIL initially deployed, performance appraisals of UNPOL personnel have become obligatory. Whilst it is significant that such M&E tasks are being undertaken, these approaches rarely stray from the conventional and thus gather a deeply imperfect view of the situation in Liberia. Although it is impossible to understand and capture all the complexities underlying any situation, certainly more can be done in this case to carry out effective and collaborative M&E. The important questions revolve around the issue of where and how these conventional approaches may falter—critically, in the eyes of those charged with their implementation and use. This next section chronicles the field research findings in each of the areas of overall design, internal field-level M&E process, and importantly the facilitation of organisational learning.

Flaws of Conventional Approaches: UNMIL's Overarching Design

There were two main flaws identified in the overarching design: 1) the lack of circularity (meaning iterative and continual M&E processes and hence the findings that ensue); as well as 2) the failure of the many discrete mechanisms to cohere in a systemic way. In terms of circularity, the frustration with conventional M&E most consistently flagged by mission officials was the issue of inconsistent or inappropriate implementation timeframes. For example, a number of peacekeepers experienced in RBB stated that the annual time-horizons associated with RBB were too elongated to offer much real-time value to decision-makers on a day-to-day basis.[830] Moreover, some contended that the corollary demands for precise forecasting of programme objectives and likely indicators of their attainment ahead of time (i.e. one full year) were inappropriate for and ill-suited to objectives where outcomes are inherently unpredictable.[831] In the opinion of many respondents, this further reduced the utility of RBB for accurate

[827] These four mechanisms are the: after action review; survey of practice; end of assignment report; and handover note.

[828] In UNMIL, up until the time of the field research, this has not been a dedicated position, but additional responsibility for an existing staff member.

[829] Interview: UNMIL Senior Management—Monrovia, Liberia, September 2010.

[830] Interviews: UNMIL Officials—Monrovia, Liberia, September 2010.

[831] Interviews: UNMIL Officials—Monrovia, Liberia, September 2010.

real-time assessments and these timeframes became stringent pre-commitments to report against.

Similarly, many of those interviewed highlighted the lag problems associated with infrequent evaluations conducted by a visiting team from the OIOS or Department of Peacekeeping Operations' (DPKO) Division of Policy Evaluation and Training (DPET) Evaluation Unit. For example, a 2010 OIOS evaluation on 'UNMIL mandate implementation effectiveness' identified a lack of focus on reform of the RoL elements as a system.[832] However, according to respondents this finding only really served to formalise a conclusion that had been recognised within the mission years earlier: namely, the need for a more integrated or comprehensive approach to SSR,[833] in addition to legitimating steps already undertaken to address this problem (e.g. adjusted structure of mission creating Deputy Special Representative to the Secretary General (DSRSG) pillar to reflect the centrality of holistic RoL approach and created of position of 'SSR Advisor to the SRSG').[834] In this case, the OIOS evaluation was not deemed to be timely enough for its results to feed back to the mission to inform adjustments—albeit this can be understood as making a contribution to 2nd-level learning.[835] This view was reinforced by others referring to the questionable wisdom of the timing of current M&E undertakings. One respondent, for instance, explained that in addition to the above concerns the "urgency of arbitrary timelines for progress reporting incentivizes people to massage the data even more" to meet objectives.[836] This led to discussions about a perceived lack of effective linkages between M&E findings and their application.[837] Furthermore, it highlights the problem of how objectives that are not owned by practitioners will lend themselves to being populated by fudged or false data merely to appear successful.

By contrast, a circular—i.e. iterative—character was deemed to hold great potential to mitigate the problems and risks associated with ad hoc and inconsistent timeframes synonymous with the extant orthodoxy. Respondents highlighted the benefits of moving beyond from intermittent assessments—intended to meet the periodic reporting requirements of the status quo approaches—towards dedicated and wider analysis that could provide more useful information for

---

832 United Nations Office of Internal Oversight Services, "Programme Evaluation of the Performance and the Achievement of Results by the United Nations Mission in Liberia," in *Report of the Office of Internal Oversight Services* (New York: UN OIOS, 2010), 12–13.

833 Despite UNMIL's SSR mandate being initially disaggregated between US government, UN and Liberian government responsibilities. Nevertheless, there was little mention of judicial and legal reform in the CPA.

834 Interview: UNMIL Senior Management—Monrovia, Liberia, September 2010.

835 Albeit some respondents suggested that the process may have encouraged the pre-emptive moves.

836 Interview: UNMIL Senior Management—Monrovia, Liberia, September 2010.

837 For further discussion, see section below on 'Learning Focus'.

adjustments to tactics and programming in real-time. Additionally, it was suggested that these qualities could help overcome some of the resistance to M&E associated with unexpected/impromptu evaluations. For example, one interviewee said, "if operatives know that M&E is taking place as a continuous process then they will be better able to reconcile the perceived threat it poses and potentially even go on to embrace it as a supportive management tool."[838]

Beyond the problems brought about by a lack of circularity, there were equally troublesome problems that have resulted from the fact that M&E remains largely ad hoc rather than being systemized. That is, it became clear during field research that the numerous M&E reporting procedures and frameworks in and around UNMIL that are intent upon assessing the state of the security sector and RoL reform[839] did not cohere well. Similarly, these mechanisms lacked clearly identified channels for feeding back into on-going planning or strategic decision-making. As one respondent insisted, "they are of an ad hoc nature with little or no systemization."[840] Another pointed out that multiple reporting chains from the local/sub-national level tended to overwhelm the capacity of any centralised mechanism to analyse and synthesise this real-time information flow.[841]

Whilst some interviewees claimed that strategic planning has reached a level of coherence, they were quick to highlight that this planning coherence did *not* translate into implementation coherence, which was deemed to be a much harder goal indeed to realise.[842] In other words, whilst overarching post-conflict recovery frameworks are designed to complement each other and avoid duplication of efforts, there remains a significant degree dissonance in their implementation beset by unclear sequencing and lop-sided focus. A number of interviewees felt that the dearth of cross-cutting or at least complementary M&E was a decisive factor in the creation of these types of problems. For example, an SSR advisor emphasised the importance of M&E in reconciling this disconnect, explaining how:

> *One of the problems with M&E is it always comes across as an after-thought. If you ever read a book it's always in an Annex, or 'Chapter 10, the M&E chapter!' So, the only way we're going to resolve the coherence deficit in implementation, is by having stronger monitoring and evaluation from the outset so that we ensure we're coherent. It means that…, in terms of the programme cycle, [M&E] must be the programme cycle.*[843]

M&E must be, in other words, systemic and embedded from the outset, rather than bolted-on. He and others believed, therefore, that the focus on ensuring systemic awareness of and coherence with the rest of the M&E architecture was

838 Interview: UNMIL Official—Monrovia, Liberia, September 2010.
839 For example PRS, UNDAF, benchmarking, RBB, etc.
840 Interview: UNMIL Senior Management—Monrovia, Liberia, September 2010.
841 Interview: UNMIL Senior Management—Montserrado County, Liberia, September 2010.
842 Interview: UNMIL Senior Management—Monrovia, Liberia, September 2010.
843 Interview: UNMIL Senior Management—Monrovia, Liberia, September 2010.

not only important for more effective impact assessments, but moreover, could have positive knock-on effects for better implementation coordination and policy harmonization.

In the same vein, one official claimed that the lack of feedback from existing approaches into on-going planning processes was in part due to the fact that M&E is not entrenched in the day-to-day practice of peace operations.[844] Another respondent captured the organisational challenge underlying this, saying that "[existing] M&E elements are not continuous... they are more like a snap-shot assessment of a particular issue area based on urgent need. The immediate needs supersede the holistic and systematic—people are constantly putting out fires."[845] This reactive posture and lack of attention to process and continuity in M&E was repeatedly identified as a major cause of dysfunctional feedback mechanisms between M&E and mission planning and consequently a contributing factor to variance witnessed in meeting mission objectives. For instance, numerous interviewees pointed to uneven progress in the reform of the various criminal justice institutions as a prime example of this.[846]

The above insights echo the findings of others that UNMIL needs to link planning processes to qualitative assessments of progress on the ground.[847] Therefore, a more holistically conceived framework that embeds M&E in overall mission management, avoiding the 'afterthought-ism' typical of extant approaches, would be better placed to support enhanced congruency in planning and implementation. Importantly, participants also generally believed that a heightened awareness of the complex systemic environment, explicit linkages between field M&E and multi-tiered organisational learning as well as entrenched feedback loops to planning and implementation hold considerable promise for addressing these systemic issues. Overcoming the ad hoc, inconsistent and un-systemic nature of current orthodoxy represents genuine, if simple, value-add in this domain.

Flaws in the Field-Level M&E Process: Context-Sensitive Foregrounding/ Baselines

A recurrent criticism of M&E in UNMIL concerned the extent to which analyses failed to be situated in the specific operating context, with common practice relying on generic, imported approaches. Many interviewed pointed to insufficient attention to the specific and historically contingent conditions that constituted UNMIL's operating environment. Regarding UNPOL, the Police Commissioner

844 Interview: UNMIL Senior Management—Monrovia, Liberia, September 2010.
845 Interview: UNMIL Senior Management—Monrovia, Liberia, September 2010.
846 Interview: UNMIL Senior Management—Monrovia, Liberia, September 2010.
847 See, for example: Till Blume, "Implementing the Rule of Law in Integrated Missions: Security and Justice in the UN Mission in Liberia," *Journal of Security Sector Management* 6, no. 3 (2008): 12.

(POLCOM) emphasised the "huge importance of contextual considerations" and was adamant that M&E "should not and cannot generalize!"[848] This notion was supported by another senior UNPOL official who explained that "... we have to understand the cultural factors and ... the working environment which impact on your ability to achieve change."[849] The 'political', in other words. A major associated issue highlighted concerned the resources available to not only implement police reform programmes but also to sustain the new entities thereafter. As one respondent noted, "we can't do these assessments without also looking at the state of the economy they have to operate in—and every post-conflict economy is weak. So, that is a chicken and egg problem."[850]

It was agreed that the contextual assessments proposed in our framework principles would go a long way towards improving this predicament. Furthermore, it was noted that dedicated foregrounding would importantly allow for an accounting of key facets of the mission environment commonly omitted/side-lined in current M&E orthodoxy. One frequently cited example was the prevalence of non-state providers of policing type services.[851] Whilst incorporating an awareness of these stakeholders will provide a clearer and fuller picture of the providers of public safety, it was also believed to be a precursor to determining preferences amongst the population for their use and a vital element of understanding the extent to which the state police are (or are not) the first port of call for matters of protection and criminal justice. It was believed that this, in turn, could be used to provide insight into changing perceptions of the Liberian National Police (LNP).

A corollary shortcoming identified repeatedly concerned baseline assessments. When asked about the existence and reliability of baselines for tracking change and gauging impact in M&E, the most common response was that there was little or no accurate and useful baseline data collected or assessments made.[852] This, many concluded, left assessments lacking a 'how things were' measurement against which relative improvements could be gauged.[853] Indeed, in relation to UNPOL undertakings, one official went as far as to say that "most of these things we're doing, there has never been a baseline taken."[854]

One possibility for plugging the baseline gap identified by a number of interviewees across the RoL components was the fledgling Rule of Law Indicators Project (RoLIP).[855] Many believed this was a positive development given its focus on

848 Interview: UNMIL UNPOL Senior Management—Monrovia, Liberia, September 2010.
849 Interview: UNMIL UNPOL Official—Monrovia, Liberia, September 2010.
850 Interview: UNMIL Senior Management—Monrovia, Liberia, September 2010.
851 Interviews: UNMIL Officials—Monrovia, Liberia, September 2010.
852 Interviews: UNMIL Officials—Monrovia, Liberia, September 2010.
853 Interviews: UNMIL Officials—Monrovia, Liberia, September 2010.
854 Interview: UNMIL UNPOL Senior Management—Monrovia, Liberia, September 2010.
855 The RoLIP was being piloted in UNMIL at time of field research, the project has since been completed. See: "The United Nations Rule of Law Indicators: Implementation

producing an appraisal of current capacities across the RoL institutions. However, there remained some doubts about the suitability of the indicators proposed for the RoLIP. One official pointed to a lack of cultural and context sensitivity in the selection of some indicators included in final drafts for RoLIP, giving the example of standards for daily costs per prisoner to assess whether or not these institutions were functioning effectively and satisfactorily. In this official's opinion, these standards were alien to the realities of Liberia in terms of welfare available to any citizen, let alone those who had committed serious crime. The related concern was that these indicators may hold UNPOL efforts to standards that are simply not realistic or sustainable in the context of post-conflict environments such as Liberia.[856] Perhaps worse, one official explained how these targets can serve to dictate reform efforts and in doing so produce perverse consequences such as, "making going to prison attractive to people who would otherwise try and stay out of it."[857] Ultimately, some in the police component claimed that even if it could ascertain accurate baseline studies and subsequent snap-shot analyses, RoLIP's shortcoming in this regard emphasised the need for context-sensitive design and implementation of all M&E elements. Our proposed development of indicators of change through participatory approaches was believed to hold promise in mitigating the risk of inappropriate—a-political—measures.[858]

Notwithstanding these challenges, a large proportion of those interviewed argued that it was important to have baseline data to work against. Furthermore, given the unique state of incapacity of the LNP at the inception of the UNMIL reform programme, it was stressed that baselines must accurately reflect the realities of the particular context to be useful.[859] In addition, it was regularly cited that as the process unfolded it was especially important that baselines are updated in an iterative way; but this was rarely the case with existing instruments.[860] These alternatives to the mainstream, such as the imperative of context-sensitivity, the construction of relevant baselines, and an iterative inbuilt modality, are at the core of the advice offered in this book. Many respondents believed that these alternative approaches have the potential to overcome fundamental problems identified with existing modalities, with the capacity to build the foundations for more precise and reliable findings.

Guide and Project Tools," (New York: United Nations Department of Peacekeeping Operations / Office of the High Commissioner for Human Rights, 2011).

856 Interview: UNMIL Senior Management—Monrovia, Liberia, September 2010.

857 Interview: UNMIL Senior Management—Monrovia, Liberia, September 2010.

858 See section below on 'Inclusive/Participatory Approach'.

859 Interview: Liberian Government Minister—Monrovia, Liberia, September 2010.

860 Interview: UNMIL UNPOL Senior Management—Monrovia, Liberia, September 2010.

Flaws in the Field-Level M&E Process: Impact/Outcome Focus

The targeting baselines and enhanced context-awareness we espouse also relates to the next suggestion: the need to focus on assessing impact. Senior mission staff interviewed argued that gauging the impact of UNMIL activities was the focus of *ad hoc* evaluations commissioned by Headquarters (HQ) or the UNMIL Senior Mission Leadership Group (SMLG).[861] However, most respondents agreed that the absence of an impact-focus in on-going M&E within the mission was conspicuous. Regarding focus, many of those interviewed—irrespective of their place in the operation's hierarchy—lamented the fact that the majority of current practice was preoccupied with demonstrating accountability rather than ascertaining the impact of action. A senior official summarised the current state-of-play in this regard, explaining that:

> *I think there are two issues at stake: The first is that program officers on the ground have to be accountable for the money they spend—so there's an accountability issue. The other issue of course relates to impact—whether what we're doing is actually making a difference. And I think impact and accountability are actually two completely different things and we somehow have conflated both into one with this M&E stuff—to be accountable to our financiers and show that the money has been spent but at the same time to show that there is value in spending that money.*[862]

As a result of accountability eliding impact motivations, extant approaches were not highly thought of as a modality for reporting on the actual impact of actions or enabling learning from findings. Many respondents highlighted that the techniques employed in benchmarking and RBB struggled to get at the issue of impact due to their overdependence on output level and quantitative measures synonymous with accountability audits.[863] This is the point we make in a number of places in the book, not least Chapter 7's critique of conventional M&E. The perspective of one civil society organisation typified these sentiments noting that, "The UN may focus on the numbers, but in doing so the actual challenges on the ground are not captured."[864] As one senior staff officer said, "RBB is very good at counting things, but not so good at getting at the associated impacts of the activities we do."[865] Another official concurred, describing current orthodoxy as "limited" because it is "using predominantly quantitative indicators to demonstrate productivity without much attention paid to the effect or impact of those activities."[866] According to mission officials, benchmarking and derivative Inter-

---

861 Interview: UNMIL Senior Management—Monrovia, Liberia, September 2010.
862 Interview: UNMIL Senior Management—Monrovia, Liberia, September.
863 Interview: UNMIL Senior Management—Monrovia, Liberia, September 2010.
864 Interview: West African Network for Peacebuilding (WANEP) Senior Official—Liberia Chapter—Monrovia, Liberia, September 2010.
865 Interview: UNMIL Senior Management—Monrovia, Liberia, September 2010.
866 Interview: UNMIL Senior Management—Monrovia, Liberia, September 2010.

grated Mission Priorities and Implementation Plan (IMPIP)/Mandate Implementation Plan (MIP) are beset by similar problems given that they generally employ the same predominantly quantitative metrics found in the other instruments to assess progress on mandate implementation.[867] Some claimed that conventional approaches were particularly inappropriate for demonstrating impact in some instances. For example, measuring success of the Political, Policy and Planning Section towards elections involved counting the number of meetings held with political parties. The official referred to the metrics employed as "absolute nonsense" adding that "it is not the number, but the substance of those meetings that matters."[868] He continued that these measures "might make some sense to those demanding [them], but not to people on the ground," further adding that "... in the political realm these approaches are not only insufficient, but also risk distorting the work of our departments to meet these targets."[869]

Senior members of UNPOL dismissed the output-orientation of current M&E approaches, or what one called "wooden numbers",[870] asserting in relation to police reform, "we may have ten nice new police stations but whether anybody bothers to go and make a report is a separate question altogether and if they don't bother to make a report, then you want to know why... It's easy to count how many buildings you have put up; but not so easy to assess the impact [of doing so]."[871] An example of inappropriate measures given numerous times was the UNPOL Quick Impact Projects (QIPs) to construct Women and Children Protection Centres (WCPCs) as part of LNP infrastructure where the indicator of success was simply the number of centres built. The isolated output-focus missed the reality that, despite having a new building, staff had too few vehicles to transfer perpetrators and victims of sexual violence separately and no money to buy food for the women and children once at the centre.[872] That is, the existence of the building alone was not enough to facilitate better services to women/child victims of crime—a nuance absent in the measure used.[873] This example is indicative of the wider challenges with output metrics employed under current M&E orthodoxy.

The need to replace the de facto outputs obsession with a focus on patterns of behaviour was widely held. One senior mission leader asserted that, contrary to current approaches, it was important for M&E to tease out the 'quality' of

867 Interview: UNMIL Official—Monrovia, Liberia, September 2010.
868 Interview: UNMIL Senior Management—Monrovia, Liberia, September 2010.
869 Interview: UNMIL Senior Management—Monrovia, Liberia, September 2010.
870 Interview: UNMIL Senior Management—Monrovia, Liberia, September 2010.
871 Interview: UNMIL Senior Management—Monrovia, Liberia, September 2010.
872 Interview: Liberian Government Minister—Monrovia, Liberia, September 2010.
873 Interview: West African Network for Peacebuilding (WANEP) Senior Official—Liberia Chapter—Monrovia, Liberia, September 2010; Interview: UNMIL Senior Management—Monrovia, Liberia, September 2010.

police performance.[874] This is a view firmly supported by the Governance Reform Commission (GRC) that has repeatedly emphasised the need to measure police performance rather than training output.[875] Others in the UNPOL establishment agreed that there was a need to gain better clarity on what is being measured, why and what it can tell us, stressing that, "We need to be clear about the differences between inputs, outputs, outcomes and impacts."[876] In relation to police reform objectives in particular, one senior mission leader agreed that going deeper and broader when attempting to assess impact was critical, stating that "M&E is crucial to the issue of sustainability. Getting at 'impact' is the only way to get an idea of how sustainable productivity has been."[877]

When asked to explain why current practice failed to address impact, many replied that it was simply too difficult to produce meaningful impact assessments with the existing tools at their disposal. For instance, one official stated that, "Contextual accounts or 'thick descriptions' are hard to construct and harder to justify and substantiate to 'bosses' than simple metrics. In this way, non-quantifiable attributes are left unattended to—the focus is elsewhere."[878] Respondents also gave examples where even qualitative benchmarks were tracked and measured using quantitative metrics. For instance, the overriding benchmark for the reform of the LNP uses the term 'operational' to be indicative of successful attainment of standing up the new LNP. However, as the POLCOM stated, "Practices and procedures are what makes the LNP operational, not numbers... Concepts like 'operational' are qualitative, subjective and intangible and cannot be quantified and measured in the ways we are required to under these systems."[879]

Despite this recognition, a criticism that figured prominently was the lack of methods, tools, policies and procedures available to those in the field for doing so.[880] One official was forthright in proclaiming that the mission environment is beset by a "complete lack of sophisticated methodologies for measuring impact"[881] and stated that in reality UNMIL personnel had to use their individual acumen to draw on models and templates developed in other UN peace operations, not to mention different contexts (in this case United Nations Assistance Mission in Afghanistan UNAMA), due to a lack of in-mission options.[882] The POLCOM similarly lamented the paucity of suitable M&E models, stating that, "I don't

---

[874] Interview: UNMIL Senior Management—Monrovia, Liberia, September 2010.
[875] Interview: GRC Official—Monrovia, Liberia, September 2010; Amos Sawyer cited in Mark Malan, "Security Sector Reform in Liberia: Mixed Results from Humble Beginnings," (Strategic Studies Institute, 2008), 52.
[876] Interview: UNMIL Official—Monrovia, Liberia, September 2010.
[877] Interview: UNMIL UNPOL Official—Monrovia, Liberia, September 2010.
[878] Interview: UNMIL Senior Management—Monrovia, Liberia, September 2010.
[879] Interview: UNMIL UNPOL Senior Management—Monrovia, Liberia, September 2010.
[880] Interviews: UNMIL Staff—Monrovia, Liberia, September 2010.
[881] Interview: UNMIL Senior Management—Monrovia, Liberia, September 2010.
[882] Interview: UNMIL Senior Management—Monrovia, Liberia, September 2010.

think there are currently any ready-made mechanisms or tools that can measure the things UNPOL would like to measure—that being the impact of UNPOL activities."[883]

This is not to suggest that these dominant practices were dismissed as useless. On the contrary, mission personnel were at pains to highlight when primarily quantitative output measures could be useful. Almost without fail, interviewees stated that any M&E architecture for a mission needed a modality for tracking implementation of project outputs, if only as a basic management and reporting tool.[884] That noted, the majority of those questioned believed that although this was a necessary element of M&E, it was nevertheless entirely inadequate. Consequently, despite the difficulties identified in terms of conducting and 'selling' impact-focused M&E there was a widespread acceptance within the mission that the impact of activities needed to be the focus of M&E to make it more effective. One respondent epitomized this, noting, "There is clearly a need to move beyond reporting outputs and target the outcomes and impact associated with those outputs."[885] Summarising the challenge, the UNMIL Chief of Staff noted that, "As a mission, we need to be sure that, beyond the numbers and the buildings, that the impact is being understood and reacted upon."[886]

When asked about the most pertinent means of understanding the impact of UNPOL, many were of the opinion that, given the stage of the mission, it was necessary to focus on the extent to which the LNP and other law enforcement agencies had improved and developed. In addition to looking at the quality as well as the quantity of human resources in the LNP, there was a general belief that the best way of determining improvements in the LNP was by getting a handle on how Liberians experiences of the police were changing.[887] For example, the Deputy-POLCOM noted that, "Given that UNMIL are now primarily here to develop the LNP it is important that public perceptions of how the LNP is improving are used as the indicator of 'success'."[888] As many emphasised, this sits in stark contrast to current convention which does not focus on eliciting public perceptions but remains heavily output-centric—both in terms of the targets and 'expected accomplishments' identified as well as the indicators used to demonstrate this. Whilst these are often employed as proxies for improved perceptions, as a senior mission official asserted, "Public confidence is not built by doing one

883 Interview: UNMIL UNPOL Senior Management—Monrovia, Liberia, September 2010.
884 For example, one senior mission manager said that in relation to disarmament, counting the number of AK-47s collected makes perfect sense as an empirical measure of successful disarmament.
885 Interview: UNMIL Senior Management—Monrovia, Liberia, September 2010.
886 Interview: UNMIL Senior Management—Monrovia, Liberia, September 2010.
887 Interview: UNMIL Senior Management—Monrovia, Liberia, September 2010.
888 Interview: UNMIL UNPOL Senior Management– Monrovia, Liberia, September 2010.

act, or doing one act well; but series of activities done well simultaneously and over time."[889]

For these reasons, and as others have shown, UNMIL demonstrates the need to "think beyond short-term goals and quantitative indicators for benchmark evaluations."[890] This is increasingly recognised in rhetorical statements and internal audit reports,[891] but the evidence from the field is unequivocally that the practice lags significantly behind. The priority focus on impacts and outcomes whilst simultaneously contextualising outputs when necessary is therefore the paradigm to adopt. Furthermore, the participatory methods for doing so were deemed particularly better suited to ascertaining a valuable picture of progress and impact by how these approaches elicited public perceptions.

Exogenous Factors and Unintended Consequences

Related to this issue of broader impact, mission experts appreciated the capacity of our framework to incorporate the effect of external influences while seeking out the unexpected—looking for 'known unknowns' or unintended consequences, that is. Interviews frequently revealed that current M&E is not good at revealing and incorporating the presence and effect of exogenous factors and unintended consequences. In relation to external influences respondents highlighted two major considerations. Firstly, there was a widespread agreement that UNMIL was just one actor amongst many who contribute towards change in Liberia and that this should be better reflected in M&E. As one senior official admitted, "Ultimately, we—the mission—are not in control of all the factors."[892] In particular, the centrality of the Liberian government as a partner in post-conflict reconstruction was singled out as an important variable insufficiently captured in existing practice.[893] For instance, one respondent noted that "at this stage of the mission, partnership with the government is crucial. After all, UNMIL's mission is to support and assist the government. M&E needs to get at that."[894]

This is an equally salient concern for UNPOL, particularly when engaging in a political process like law enforcement reform. UNPOL, after all, is just one of many influencing agents in producing change in the Liberian criminal justice

---

889 Interview: UNMIL Senior Management—Monrovia, Liberia, September 2010.

890 Till Blume, "Implementing the Rule of Law in Integrated Missions: Security and Justice in the UN Mission in Liberia," *Journal of Security Sector Management* 6, no. 3 (2008): 12.

891 See, for example: United Nations Office of Internal Oversight Services, "Audit of United Nations Police in UNMIL," ed. Internal Audit Division (New York: UN OIOS, 2009), 3; United Nations Office of Internal Oversight Services, "Management of UN Police Operations," in *Audit Report* (New York: UN OIOS, 2008), 4–5.

892 Interview: UNMIL Senior Management—Monrovia, Liberia, September 2010.

893 Interview: UNMIL Senior Management—Monrovia, Liberia, September 2010.

894 Interview: UNMIL Senior Management—Monrovia, Liberia, September 2010.

architecture given the involvement of bilateral donor governments and private companies in security system reform. In line with emerging consensus, mission personnel pointed to the importance of understanding police effectiveness in the context of an interdependent RoL system, as we emphasised in Chapter 5. On this point, one official explained that, "There is a sense in which the reputation of the police is really in the hands of the courts ... such that, the arrests don't become a revolving door."[895] She further asserted that, "if the courts are not functioning then what confidence do people have that people they report won't come back and threaten them, if they go in and come back right out again and come and beat them on the head for having made the report to begin with."[896] In this sense, interviewees argued that the dysfunction of other parts of the criminal justice system should be conceptualised as negative exogenous factors in the outcomes of police reform.

However, it was commonly remarked that the recognition of multiple external influences was not sufficiently reflected in the design and findings of current M&E in the field. Despite rhetorical commitments and organisational arrangements to integrate thematic RoL efforts, interviewees stated that UNPOL M&E remained siloed and isolated from UNMIL assistance to the broader criminal justice system, not to mention a deeper-seated security and justice landscape.[897] For example, some argued that understanding non-state actors as exogenous actors with significant influence was vital to overall impact assessments.[898] One official emphasised that examples such as these reflect the lack of appreciation of the systemic nature of change in this domain more generally.[899] This insight underscores a point we make throughout about the importance of accepting complex systems as the conceptual backdrop for missions. Many described how the M&E tools at their disposal were unable to include forces and variables beyond the strict remit of their section or programme—as one interviewee lamented, "We are trapped in a bureaucratic straitjacket."[900] In this regard, a number of interviewees also questioned the indicators employed under extant M&E regimes. A mission RoL expert, by way of illustration, explained how indicators such as 'number of arrests' can become "a faulty measurement of how we are doing."[901] In reference to the lack of a systemic focus in extant M&E, one interviewee declared that, "Any attempt to assess the performance of the police alone—that fails to see

895 Interview: UNMIL Senior Management—Monrovia, Liberia, September 2010.
896 Interview: UNMIL Senior Management—Monrovia, Liberia, September 2010.
897 Interviews: UNMIL Officials—Monrovia, Liberia, September 2010.
898 Interview: UNMIL Official—Monrovia, Liberia, September 2010.
899 Interview: UNMIL Official—Monrovia, Liberia, September 2010.
900 Interview: UNMIL Senior Management—Monrovia, Liberia, September 2010.
901 Interview: UNMIL Senior Management—Monrovia, Liberia, September 2010.

how things trickle further down the line—are less valuable. Without all of those things working, the police will never inspire confidence."[902]

When asked about unintended consequences, common responses coalesced around the belief that extant M&E only reports what it is looking for and generally fails to include an account of the externalities associated with UNMIL implementation—be they positive or negative.[903] The example given above of Women and Children Protection Centres (WCPCs) provides further insight into the limitations of current M&E in this regard. The simple metric utilised to count the number of WCPCs built neglects the unintended consequences of producing new buildings, whereby in one case, the WCPC was commandeered by the LNP as it was a much better facility than the local LNP station.[904] This perverse effect of producing not just a WCPC but rather an entirely new building that could be misappropriated by others is missing from the account, which wrongly assumes creating WCPCs will have an automatic and exclusively positive intended effect. In regard to follow-up M&E of these QIPs that might pick-up these contextual factors and externalities, an UNMIL official admitted that, "this is just not happening."[905] This exemplifies the lack M&E that reveals negative consequences associated with UNPOL activities as and when they occur.

In trying to gain a clearer picture of what change is taking place and why, or indeed why not, one official noted that, "We must be able to recognize the existence of external factors and influences on outcomes in such endeavours. It is vital that we acknowledge the context within which these developments are taking place."[906] Another senior staffer was clear about the importance of having a complete picture when conducting assessments, noting that, "The existence of exogenous factors and unintended consequences means it is vital that UN peacekeeping develops a way of incorporating these phenomena into its M&E approach."[907] This was indicative of a widespread agreement amongst interviewees that for M&E to be more useful for all stakeholders it needs to be able to present a more systemic picture of what is happening and why.[908] A systemic approach, plus the focus and methods proposed to reveal and seek out the unexpected was said by many to offer great advantage in ways that can overcome the shortcoming of existing approaches in relation to external forces and unintended consequences. The comments and examples add further weight to the argument

902 Interview: UNMIL Official—Monrovia, Liberia, September 2010.
903 Interviews: UNMIL Officials—Monrovia, Liberia, September 2010.
904 Interview: UNMIL Senior Management—Monrovia, Liberia, September 2010; Interview: West African Network for Peacebuilding (WANEP) Official—Liberia Chapter—Monrovia, Liberia, September 2010.
905 Interview: UNMIL Senior Management—Monrovia, Liberia, September 2010.
906 Interview: UNMIL Senior Management—Monrovia, Liberia, September 2010.
907 Interview: UNMIL Senior Management—Monrovia, Liberia, September 2010.
908 Interview: UNMIL Senior Management—Monrovia, Liberia, September 2010.

for the iterative and on-going assessments of impact embedded in M&E frameworks.

Attribution: Causality vs. Contribution

Issues of impact, external influences and externalities were further believed to have important ramifications for the challenge of attribution. When asked about the question of attribution—i.e. what achievements can be attributed to the work of UNPOL and to what extent?—many stated that the way M&E is currently designed means that it lacks humility when claiming causality for certain outcomes and prevailing conditions. Numerous respondents stated that they believed extant M&E over-claims what UNMIL components have achieved collectively or individually without acknowledging the influence of other actors and factors.[909] Many identified the aforementioned beliefs—i.e. M&E largely absent the influence of exogenous factors and the unintended consequences of action—as a major reason for the lack of convincing attribution of accomplishments, particularly those at the most macro level (i.e. 'peace writ large'). Furthermore, it was often said that ambiguous understandings of cause-and-effect curtailed M&E's utility for learning.[910]

One long-serving senior official pointed to, "methodological inelegance regarding the attribution question."[911] UNPOL officers concurred, describing how extant approaches lack the methodological leverage to construct a compelling case for cause-and-effect between UNPOL programming and observable outcomes, rendering such claims as largely inferential and contingent on the validity of assumptions in the theories of change underpinning assessments.[912] For example, referring to the reality that outcomes are the product of multiple influences, a mission official in the political affairs section said that, "... we are part of a multi-actor implementing team ... in these circumstances there can be no single causal agent and M&E should not be trying to assert otherwise."[913]

As a result, most respondents advocated for an M&E approach that produced more humble findings, focusing on explaining potential influence on strategic goals as opposed to attempting to demonstrate, or at least intimate, a direct cause-and-effect relationship between the actions of UNPOL and the changes taking place in the security sector. In this regard, one official simply implored that any approach used "needs to be underpinned by a sense of realism."[914] Another

909 Interviews: UNMIL Staff—Monrovia, Liberia, September 2010.
910 See section below—'Learning Focus'—for further discussion.
911 Interview: UNMIL Senior Management—Monrovia, Liberia, September 2010.
912 Interviews: UNMIL UNPOL Senior Management and Officials—Monrovia, Liberia, September 2010.
913 Interview: UNMIL Senior Management—Monrovia, Liberia, September 2010.
914 Interview: UNMIL Senior Management—Monrovia, Liberia, September 2010.

respondent emphasised the importance of getting at how things had changed—i.e. what has the peace operation actually done to influence outcomes and impacts—rather than rudimentary indications that something had indeed happened.[915] These findings suggest that our alternative approaches to measuring the impact of mission activities focused on unexpected emergent outcomes as well as greater humility in what can be attributed to UNPOL and other elements of the mission offer significant potential advantages over current orthodoxy.

Regarding contribution analysis techniques in league with other methods capable of mapping and constructing narratives about change reflects this consensus and it was strongly believed that such an approach could add genuine value in this regard. The framework's multi-method character appears to better reflect the changing needs on the ground whilst remaining appropriate such that the approach is uncomplicated and practical yet careful and insightful. Many experts interviewed believed that such an approach held promise for providing the necessary focus on the realities of change on the ground as well as the avoidance of distorting practice or pandering to political masters unnecessarily.[916] A large part of these methods pertains to broadening the scope of what constitutes 'good enough' data.

Multiple Data Sources

In this regard, the overwhelming majority of those interviewed identified the framework's focus on multiplying and diversifying the sites and sources of data for M&E as a key strength. Many attested to the fact that government statistics are not readily available or particularly trustworthy in Liberia.[917] The Liberian government has focused on building the capacity of formal information gathering and analysing entities,[918] however, when asked whether or not this had garnered positive improvements in the type and quality of information available for assessment of UNPOL and the LNP, most suggested that it had not.[919] For instance, it

---

915 Interview: UNMIL Senior Management—Monrovia, Liberia, September 2010.

916 Interview: UNMIL UNPOL Official—Monrovia, Liberia, September 2010.

917 For instance, whilst the first National Population & Housing census since 1984 was conducted in 2008, a number of those interviewed during this field research explained how the fidelity of its outcomes was debated in some quarters. Interview: UNMIL UNPOL Official—Monrovia, Liberia, September 2010; Interview: West African Network for Peacebuilding (WANEP) Official—Liberia Chapter—Monrovia, Liberia, September 2010.

918 For example, the Liberia Institute for Statistics and Geo-Information Services (LISGIS) has been an explicitly part of the PRS and the National Strategy for the Development of Statistics (NSDS) [The NSDS is the government strategy aimed at creating a coordinated and efficient statistical system for Liberia by 2012]. Interview: UNMIL UNPOL Senior Management—Monrovia, Liberia, September 2010.

919 At the time of this research the general perception was that there had been little notable progress with government statistics emanating from this and other complementary

was remarked upon that there are few, if any, sources of authoritative statistics to measure rates or trends in crime.[920] Ultimately, according to the overwhelming majority of respondents, the lack of conventional data availability should not detract from the important realisation that statistics—however trustworthy—are not the panacea to M&E in these settings.

Furthermore, it was frequently said that attempts to substitute this type of information through existing M&E had proven to be inadequate. For example, one previous employee of the monitoring unit of the Legal/Judicial Unit explained how, despite having dedicated monitors in all areas of the field, the low quality of reporting left analysts at headquarters level with primarily anecdotal evidence and little reliable information to work with in producing their own assessments. The lack of a systematic approach to credible data collection and analysis was perceived as a "serious circuit-breaker in planning, monitoring and evaluation",[921] and a major stumbling block to effective interpretation and utilisation of field-level experiences.

These findings suggest that due to a dearth of adequate conventional sources of data, a peace operation may need to look elsewhere, and be innovative in doing so, in order to construct a nuanced but reliable picture of what is happening. The framework's focus on identifying and utilising alternative data sources was highlighted as a major strength in this regard. For instance, one interviewee claimed that, "there is a need to seek out and cultivate sites of information and networks through which data can be harvested."[922] As mentioned above, many interviewees highlighted the fact that this needs to include a range of both quantitative and qualitative sources.[923] The framework's call for being more creative when deciding what constitutes 'good enough' data or indicators of progress was also emphasised as a positive development. For example, a senior official in the Ministry of Justice stated that things like the ability of money-changers to operate on the streets, the attendance of children in schools, and even the presence of foreign researchers like myself, could be understood as indicative of progress in re-establishing the RoL and improved community perceptions of police.[924] Another official highlighted that UNPOL and LNP officers themselves were a rich source of information and feedback for M&E—particularly given their privileged vantage point to observe and experience changes in organisational behaviour.[925]

institutions. Interviews: UNMIL UNPOL Senior Management and Officials—Monrovia, Liberia, September 2010.

920 Interviews: UNMIL UNPOL Senior Management and Officials—Monrovia, Liberia, September 2010.

921 Interview: UNMIL Senior Management—Monrovia, Liberia, September 2010.

922 Interview: UNMIL Official—Monrovia, Liberia, September 2010.

923 Interview: UNMIL UNPOL Official—Monrovia, Liberia, September 2010.

924 Interview: Liberian Government Official—Monrovia, Liberia, September 2010.

925 Interview: UNMIL UNPOL Official—Monrovia, Liberia, September 2010.

In addition, a number of interviewees identified a myriad of community-based actors and networks that present a rich source of information about local perceptions of the public security system as well as a means of tracking change over time.[926] For example, one interviewee spoke about the role of hybrid arrangements such as the Community Policing Forums.[927] Similarly, another official pointed to the fledgling County Security Mechanisms (CSM) as a potential site of valuable input given their local level location and composition that includes stakeholders from both formal (e.g. head of the LNP, the local district attorney, prosecutor) and informal (e.g. the Paramount, local, clan chiefs, religious leaders and respected and influential CSOs) spheres.[928] Another representative of civil society spoke about the latent value of the multiplicity of other community-based forums across the counties such as the County Peace Councils and Country Development Committees as rich sources of information.[929] It is, however, important to note that the same interviewee highlighted that despite the burgeoning of committees and mechanisms, those serving on them were often fewer insofar as the same individual often represented a particular community on many of these different arrangements.[930] Other pointed to the role of the media, in particular the example of a daily 'Crimewatch' programme on privately owned local radio (Truth F.M. 96.1) between the hours of 2 and 4am where the general public can call in to report crime, directly linked to LNP, but also creating a forum for discussions and sharing perceptions of the LNP.[931]

However, it is clear from the field research that these sites and sources of information are not systemically utilised in extant M&E. For example, the measures synonymous with RBB/benchmarking do not tap into informal data sources. Similarly, qualitative evaluations undertaken rarely interview or survey host populations as a means of ascertaining their perceptions about impact and change. Ultimately, however trustworthy and abundant conventional sources of statistical information, insights from the field research emphasised that the peace operations environment dictates that alternative sources of data are both available to mission M&E and vital in producing a textured picture of what is happening. As one senior UNMIL official asserted, "It makes sense—in addition to the traditional form of information gathering—to use this alternative approach of working with

---

926 Interview: Truth and Reconciliation Commission Official—Monrovia, Liberia, September 2010.

927 Interview: Liberian Government Official—Monrovia, Liberia, September 2010.

928 Interview: UNMIL Official—Monrovia, Liberia, September 2010.

929 Interview: West African Network for Peacebuilding (WANEP) Official—Liberia Chapter—Monrovia, Liberia, September 2010.

930 Interview: West African Network for Peacebuilding (WANEP) Official—Liberia Chapter—Monrovia, Liberia, September 2010.

931 Interviews: UNMIL Senior Management, Liberian Government Officials Monrovia, Liberia, September 2010. See also: "UN Development Assistance Framework 2008–2012: Joint Annual Review Report 2008," (Monrovia: United Nations Liberia, 2008), 17.

local organisations, community groups, chiefs, etc, to get information."[932] There was agreement that M&E needs to be more malleable in terms of what constitute 'good enough' data sources and types. These empirical findings emphasise how the framework therefore promises to add value by broadening the criteria for what constitutes good enough data to inform M&E.

Flexibility

Another key issue described by many respondents concerned the rigidity of current M&E approaches in the mission. It was often stated that mission phases are important and—as one senior official put it—"there is a need for different types of M&E for different stages of a mission."[933] However, the general consensus was that current orthodoxy was inflexible such that it was lethargic and rendered incapable of responding effectively to inevitable changes to mission circumstances and objectives.

This was deemed to be the case at both the macro and micro level. For instance, whilst initially in partnership with the transitional government, police reform programs were significantly re-jigged following the election of President Johnson-Sirleaf and her government.[934] UNPOL officials regularly noted that the inability of extant M&E to adjust to changing objectives led to disconnect between expected accomplishments and the focus of altered programming. At the operational level, UNPOL officials intimated that the strict targets embedded in extant M&E are problematic when there is a strict definition attached to a benchmark but it is misguided. The POLCOM gave the example of the ERU creation, whereby a benchmark of '500 members trained' was set in stone by the powers that be, explaining that it was only when his office insisted that it was an operational imperative to shift focus towards up-skilling the Police Support Unit (PSU) that a reduction of the Emergency Response Unit (ERU) target/benchmark to its current strength was accepted.[935] As it was described, this required an extremely adamant stance by senior UNPOL figures to "break the sanctity of the benchmark."[936] In addition to losing relevance to changing objectives and activities, a number of interviewees warned that the inflexibility of mechanisms for tracking mission implementation also risked distorting the action of peacekeepers on the ground in line with prescriptive instruments.[937] For example, some described how resources were increasingly ear-marked to meet particular targets rather

932 Interview: UNMIL Official—Monrovia, Liberia, September.
933 Interview: UNMIL UNPOL Senior Management—Monrovia, Liberia, September 2010.
934 Interview: UNMIL Senior Management—Monrovia, Liberia, September 2010.
935 Interview: UNMIL UNPOL Senior Management—Monrovia, Liberia, September 2010.
936 Interview: UNMIL UNPOL Senior Management—Monrovia, Liberia, September 2010.
937 Interviews: UNMIL UNPOL Senior Management and Officials—Monrovia, Liberia, September 2010.

than to fund holistic operations and programming. One official explained how in this case, the demand to report on particular targets can, at times, alter the original intent of the reporting process, adding that, "The framework [for M&E] has essentially become a series of numbers that dictates what is collected in the field," in effect flip-siding the M&E process such that "the data comes last!"[938]

Similarly, it was lamented that—rare as it might be—good data from the ground cannot influence benchmarks or prevent the perverse diversion of work towards attaining them.[939] This dysfunction in the transmission of meaningful information from and back into the M&E process were identified as a major breakdown in feedback loops that could enable learning.[940] This perception was corroborated by another official who said, "It is important in the peace operations setting that M&E has the built-in flexibility to adapt to changing objectives over time."[941] Furthermore, there was a general belief that changes in missions and their operating environment are not necessarily discrete or self-evident, and therefore M&E would be most useful if it was designed in such a way that allowed for recursive adaptation to these unpredictable circumstances.[942] As the POLCOM asserted, "There is a need for greater flexibility and adaptability to be built in to [M&E] so that it can be calibrated along the way as the mission progresses."[943]

It was emphasised that the proposed framework was potentially more capable of dealing with this dynamical change. The insights in this domain therefore suggest that the framework's design to be adaptive to the realities of post-conflict environments and UNPOL idiosyncrasies is not only worthwhile and desirable, but also achievable. Built-in flexibility promises a more responsive approach to assessment, allowing for those with awareness of the situation to select the most appropriate approach and methods to match the circumstances at any given time. This is further buttressed by the embedded reflexivity which also presents an opportunity to continuously revisit elements of the M&E process to ensure its currency.[944] A number of respondents pointed to these advantages as a way of substantiating attempts to mitigate the pressure from above to fit a corporate accountability model and the prescriptive and distortive tendencies of existing approaches that are governed more by political objectives than operational realities.

---

938 Interview: UNMIL Senior Management—Monrovia, Liberia, September 2010.
939 Interview: UNMIL Senior Management—Monrovia, Liberia, September 2010.
940 Interviews: UNMIL Staff—Monrovia, Liberia, September 2010.
941 Interview: UNMIL Senior Management—Monrovia, Liberia, September 2010.
942 Interviews: UNMIL Staff—Monrovia, Liberia, September 2010.
943 Interview: UNMIL UNPOL Senior Management—Monrovia, Liberia, September 2010.
944 See section below on 'Interpretation and Response'.

Inclusive/Participatory Approach

As touched on above, insights and examples from UNMIL point to advantages of an inclusive nature, embedding participatory approaches and the spin-off benefits for ownership that come with both. This was deemed to be the case for the value added in relation to setting objectives, carrying out the process for measuring against them and inculcating a sense of ownership and cooperation in the implementation of M&E. Regarding objective-setting, when asked about the value of the benchmarks and targets used in current approaches, respondents regularly disputed the wisdom of the selection of these milestone targets. For example, many questioned what criteria were used to guide the design process and what factors were considered in setting the targets in the first place.[945] Similarly, a number of officials in UNPOL highlighted issues relating to the 'framing' of the benchmarks and queried whether or not the prescribed target/benchmark for number of LNP personnel was sufficient to meet the real needs of public security throughout Liberia—before any questions about its sustainability in the longer term.[946] One official stated that this was indicative of the reality that, "There exists a huge gap between the 'imposed benchmarks' set elsewhere and the emergent challenges and associated targets which arise from on-the-ground knowledge and experience."[947] It was said that enhanced participation would constitute valuable feedback opportunities from a broad-based constituency to inform the generation of locally grounded and realistic objectives and a "collaborative way of driving the process forward."[948]

As such, many identified the narrow participation in extant approaches as an inhibiting factor that had ramifications for both the utility and the credibility of the findings.[949] In direct support for our exhortation to identify then elicit as many perspectives from across society as practicable, members of government interviewed stated their displeasure with program management and M&E that was overly mission-centric, failed to adequately incorporate national and local perspectives and thus led to unilateral decision-making. For instance, a former Deputy Inspector-General of the LNP pointed to the initial vetting of former LNP officers as a prime example of a "non-consultative and non-participatory approach that was ill-conceived and failed to appreciate local concerns."[950] She went on to explain that she firmly believed that this deficit was a major factor in the significant problems encountered in early LNP reform efforts. One example given was the reluctance of people in the leeward counties to come forward and testify

---

945 Interview: UNMIL Senior Management—Monrovia, Liberia, September 2010.
946 Cf. Chapter 5
947 Interview: UNMIL UNPOL Senior Management—Monrovia, Liberia, September 2010.
948 Interview: UNMIL UNPOL Official—Monrovia, Liberia, September 2010.
949 Interview: UNMIL Senior Management—Monrovia, Liberia, September 2010.
950 Interview: Liberian Government Official—Monrovia, Liberia, September 2010.

against the war-time activities of candidates for the new LNP for fear of retribution. This, she said, severely limited the effectiveness of that component of the vetting procedure.[951] She, and others, added that when subsequent improvements occurred they were largely due to enhanced collaboration between the UN, the LNP and local communities in the implementation and tracking of reform and restructuring activities.[952]

Regarding execution of M&E, it was commonly stated that the majority of existing M&E instruments lack any significant level of participation in information gathering and analysis beyond a small number of formal mission personnel. Even then, the involvement and input of mission personnel is filtered through the stringent orthodoxy. On this point, many respondents claimed that they saw first-hand when progress, or indeed regression, occurred but felt that the mission did not have appropriate tools to capture these developments. The conventional M&E, in other words, was not deemed flexible, inclusive or participatory enough to capture these insights in a way that fed into on-going processes of impact assessment. One official echoed this conviction in saying that, "The challenge is formalizing what is usually individual intuition and sensitivity based on contextual knowledge: 'we know it when we see it!' "[953]

This lack of participation in M&E was further emphasised as an issue at the sub-national level where partnership with government heralded at the national level was not reflected at the local level.[954] Many of those interviewed felt strongly about the potential value-add of the framework for expanding this pool of participants. In addition to discussion above about community-based organisations as sources of data, many respondents believed non-governmental and community-based actors had much value to add as potential contributors and collaborators in conducting M&E. For example, one NGO official pointed out that, "Community-based networks for feeding into M&E and disseminating M&E findings do exist and have the potential to broaden the perspective."[955] However, challenges remain in regard to sustainable funding for their continued work over the long-haul.[956] Civil society organisations and local community members also stated that they have a lot to offer to M&E processes, due to their 'on-the-ground' knowledge and intuitive sense of progress as well as a clearer sense and experience of the unintended consequences of action as well as the exogenous factors

---

951 Interview: Liberian Government Official—Monrovia, Liberia, September 2010.

952 Interview: Liberian Government Official—Monrovia, Liberia, September 2010.

953 Interview: UNMIL Senior Management—Monrovia, Liberia, September 2010.

954 Interview: UNMIL Senior Management—Monrovia, Liberia, September 2010.

955 Interview: West African Network for Peacebuilding (WANEP) Official—Liberia Chapter—Monrovia, Liberia, September 2010.

956 Interview: West African Network for Peacebuilding (WANEP) Official—Liberia Chapter—Monrovia, Liberia, September 2010.

inhibiting progress.[957] These opinions were repeated by others, for example, the Minister for Justice implored that the valuable contributions of ordinary Liberians "... should be harnessed by the UN and others in their assessments of impact."[958]

In addition, many emphasised that the conspicuous absence of non-state actors in conceptualising and implementing SSR and its M&E belies the importance of informal provision of public safety and justice to large populations in Liberia.[959] How an appreciation of this reality feeds into M&E is largely without precedent in the peace operations setting and interviews revealed strongly held views on how the issue of non-state providers should be addressed and/or incorporated. Nevertheless, respondents were broadly agreed that M&E tools available to them are generally blinkered to the existence and effect of non-statutory policing actors in relation to the impact of UNPOL activities.[960] Notwithstanding disparate perspectives on their rightful role, as important stakeholders in SSR, it was widely agreed that non-state providers are well-placed and have both capacity and knowledge to provide unique information and feedback into the M&E process. The POLCOM explained that, "In Liberia, there is no precedent for the state—specifically the police—as conceived by UNMIL."[961] Consequently, what cannot be ignored is that public perceptions of the LNP are not only on a relative scale including their own historical legacy, but on a comparative scale vis-à-vis alternative sources of protection and security. As another senior official explained, "[Liberians] have been used to looking elsewhere. Getting them to look at the state is, in itself, an exercise in reorientation, so they had better get something concrete from it, or they aren't ever going to have confidence in it."[962] These findings suggest that M&E has a lot of distance to travel if it is to incorporate and appreciate the importance of the pluralistic nature of security and justice provision in the Liberian context. Nevertheless, it was remarked that the inclusivity and systemic awareness built-in to this framework presented the opportunity to bring important contributions to the process as well as much-needed balance to the state-centrism of extant approaches.

---

957 Interview: West African Network for Peacebuilding (WANEP) Official—Liberia Chapter—Monrovia, Liberia, September 2010.

958 Interview: Liberian Government Minister—Monrovia, Liberia, September 2010.

959 The challenge of understanding the relevance of informal provision of security and justice services to post-conflict SSR has been identified in previous chapters as important. Non-state provision is a characteristic of most peace operations environments. Indeed, large portions of the Liberian population have never really experienced the presence of the formal state in providing for their day-to-day personal safety.

960 Interviews: UNMIL UNPOL Senior Management and Officials—Monrovia, Liberia, September 2010.

961 Interview: UNMIL UNPOL Senior Management—Monrovia, Liberia, September 2010.

962 Interview: UNMIL Senior Management—Monrovia, Liberia, September 2010.

Importantly, many respondents pointed out that the framework's participatory approach to M&E would not be a radical proposition as Liberia has been a crucible for innovative approaches to consultative and participatory reform, in particular through initiatives of the GRC as well as nationwide consultations on developing a national security strategy and the PRS.[963] It was regularly noted that a major perceived benefit of this participatory modality was enhanced local ownership of the processes underway. Insights from the field supported the argument that this framework's focus on shared, 'transitional' and local ownership has the potential to facilitate these aims. For instance, a senior UNPOL official claimed that the example of the performance management system developed to track the implementation of the LNP Strategic Plan demonstrated the advantages of formalising transitional ownership of M&E as police reform priorities are increasingly deemed to be the responsibility of the host government.[964]

It was suggested that an enhanced sense of ownership amongst relevant stakeholders promises to facilitate better relations and trust between communities and security actors (international and/or domestic) through improved interaction, cooperation and building of mutual trust and confidence between police and those they serve. This potentially has corollary added value of facilitating successful community policing philosophies/initiatives. Many interviewees emphasised that at the local level, where much of UNPOL programming was targeted, relationships with community-based stakeholders and civil society organisations such as the Rotary Club, religious leaders and institutions and familial/informal networks were vital to eliciting information to inform M&E.[965] The framework's ability to (semi-)formalise these relationships and take them out of the remit of individuals was universally deemed to be a comparative advantage of the framework.[966] Ultimately, the case of UNMIL points to the value in embedding shared ownership of M&E and with it the broad-based participation and cooperation of a wide range of stakeholders in a process that will eventually become their responsibility.

This framework's focus—where practicable—on broad-based stakeholder participation in the design, implementation and utilisation of M&E was believed to constitute an effective antidote to the inhibitive exclusivity and associated tunnel-vision of extant M&E in UNMIL. Furthermore, the privileging of consensus-derived notions of success and the most appropriate means of assessing progress towards them, offers an alternative way of increasing relevance that is intrinsically more grounded in local perspectives and understanding of the challenges

963 Interview: ICTJ Liberia Senior Management—Monrovia, Liberia, September 2010; Interview: Truth and Reconciliation Commission Official,—Monrovia, Liberia, September 2010.

964 Interview: UNMIL UNPOL Official—Monrovia, Liberia, September 2010.

965 Interview: UNMIL Senior Management—Monrovia, Liberia, September 2010.

966 Interview: UNMIL Senior Management—Monrovia, Liberia, September 2010.

and opportunities at play. The framework provides the means of entrenching these governance and monitoring mechanisms and promoting shared ownership to ensure that they do not erode and fall away but instead become an integral part of a sustainable and on-going process of reform.[967] Consequently, many pointed to the foreseeable utility for many different stakeholders at all levels of operation and hierarchy as one of the major benefits of the proposed framework.

Interpretation and Response

Whilst implicit in some of the discussion above, it is important to note that findings from the field research reinforce the framework's dedicated focus on interpretation and acting on findings as critical to the relevance and value of M&E. Drawing meaning from information collated was said to be particularly important in the peace operations setting due to the causal ambiguity at play. The specifics of interpretation and making sense of data was said to be the even more important in the realm of policing and public safety, particularly where public perceptions were involved.[968] Emphasising this challenge, a senior mission manager underscored that, "First of all, we have to admit that in no country in the world are the citizens entirely happy with the police."[969]

Consequently, some interviewees applauded the design of the framework for its use of multiple perspectives to validate insights in the interpretation of information. That is, increasing the data pool and diversifying participation allows for triangulation to verify and/or repudiate particular perspectives. Given the paucity of reliable traditional sources of data discussed above, a number of those interviewed highlighted the shortage of cross-referencing of indicators and lack of verification and/or triangulating data-sources as adding to the problems with current M&E such as the RBB and benchmarking.[970] As one respondent asserted, "You can collect [information] from within, but you always need something like a check—an alternative source."[971] Most of those interviewed extolled the importance of having multiple, and even competing, perspectives to form a textured picture of what is happening and why that might be the case.[972] The framework's focus on developing narratives about change based on broad stakeholder participation was generally deemed to be an important facilitator of this. Contribution stories that are the synthesis of multiple perspectives and portray a textured

967 Interview: UNMIL UNPOL Official—Monrovia, Liberia, September 2010.
968 Interviews: UNMIL UNPOL Senior Management and Officials—Monrovia, Liberia, September 2010.
969 Interview: UNMIL Senior Management—Monrovia, Liberia, September 2010.
970 Interview: UNMIL UNPOL Official—Monrovia, Liberia, September 2010.
971 Interview: UNMIL Senior Management—Monrovia, Liberia, September 2010.
972 Interview: UNMIL Senior Management—Monrovia, Liberia, September 2010.

account of what is happening as well as the possible reasons why were universally deemed to be a useful way of augmenting current modes of conducting M&E.

Many respondents lamented what they perceived to be a lack of reflection in any of the current M&E approaches used in the mission. It was emphasised that this shortage of critical introspection related to the strategic approach taken, as well as the derivative operational concepts and tactical level activities conducted in pursuit of this. Many believed that in effect current M&E was preoccupied with validating prescriptive intervention logic rather than reflecting upon and interrogating the strength of assumptions undergirding the day-to-day activities of the mission/UNPOL.[973] In other words, a number of respondents identified that extant M&E is concerned with demonstrating and reporting on 'planned' change at the expense of emergent and unforeseen change.[974]

Many participants therefore welcomed the idea of more reflexive process inherent in this framework. A number of section heads and senior managers pointed out that it was particularly advantageous to have this reflexivity built-in to the system given the limited time, space and freedom afforded to them to reflect on these 'bigger questions' when preoccupied with pressing day-to-day operational tasks and problem-solving.[975] Others concurred, highlighting that it was precisely these reflective insights they felt were missing in much of the extant practice.[976] Similarly, at the operational level, many remarked that even simple reflections would help to identify areas of issue, counter-intuitive developments or reasons for unpredicted lack of progress in key areas. For instance, one senior official described an example where entrenched cultural perceptions of the police were running against the grain of what the UNPOL efforts were hoping to produce in terms of behavioural change. She described how:

> *The average Liberian behaves in the exact manner of someone who has been subjected to years of abuse. They have been used to being hammered on the head by heavily armed police who shoot if provoked, and so on. Now we are forcing them to get used to the notion that a police officer need not be armed to do police duties. And we have a lot of the crisis of confidence founded on this disconnect, between what they consider to be an effective police officer—one who is heavily armed and who 'brokes' no nonsense and who will break a head or two... or the officer imbued with human rights principles who is not necessarily armed. But you can tell by the way that they hail the [militarised police] that it has nothing to do with the fact that they are more effective on the job than the other police, but they just look more impressive and more like the American type, macho, heavily armed, police officer on the street who swaggers and puts fear into everybody. We are trying to get them to accept this other image of the gentler version and it's not easy.*[977]

---

973 Interviews: UNMIL Officials—Monrovia, Liberia, September 2010.
974 Interviews: UNMIL Officials—Monrovia, Liberia, September 2010.
975 Interviews: UNMIL UNPOL Senior Management—Monrovia, Liberia, September 2010; UNMIL Senior Management—Monrovia, Liberia, September 2010.
976 Interview: UNMIL Senior Management—Monrovia, Liberia, September 2010.
977 Interview: UNMIL Senior Management—Monrovia, Liberia, September 2010.

In this case, a number of UNPOL officials said that the ability to identify this phenomenon and feed realisations such as these into planning might have facilitated more suitable restructuring and ongoing capacity-development of the LNP and its specialised agencies.[978] Examples such as these demonstrate that a more reflexive modality would constitute a significant breakthrough compared to existing practice. The framework's focus on continual reflection and using information analysis and interpretation to seek out the unexpected as a way of informing adaptation of operational concepts and tactical activities appears to constitute a positive development in that direction.

The framework's focus on *response* and in particular the dissemination of M&E findings further reflects the belief of many in the field that results need to be widely shared in suitable forms for learning to occur. UNPOL interviewees emphasised that this was particularly important in regard to police reform due to the dependency on improving public perceptions and both meeting and managing expectations about change in this domain. It was remarked that the format used in current orthodoxy was a major issue in communicating what was happening, many pointing to the simplified 'traffic lights' system as a problematic approach due to its bluntness,[979] and the POLCOM stating that, "there is a preoccupation with painting pictures—the UN is very good at it—but they don't tell us much."[980] These findings reflect the recommendations for more targeted dissemination in recent UN self-evaluation such as an OIOS report stated that the "compilation and dissemination of lessons learned through chief of staff bulletins, magazines and flyers, UNMIL broadcasts and the intranet"[981] was an area that warranted attention.

Ensuring that M&E findings elicit a suitable response is another advantage of the framework evidenced by insights from the field. Many in the mission gave examples of how existing approaches tend to induce reactions when it comes to controversial issues but less so in regard to the seemingly mundane. For instance, one official spoke of how monitoring of issues such as corruption and human rights abuses by the LNP and accusations of sexual abuse by peacekeepers tended to preoccupy the reactions of section heads.[982] Whilst these are obviously important to the mission's image and that of reforming security apparatus, it was suggested that this focus was to the detriment of other issues that were not making headlines. Furthermore, some emphasised how this tendency contributed to the distortion of M&E towards searching out evidence of criminal activity at the

978 Respondents were also at pains to point out that the level of US influence over SSR in Liberia also factored into the penchant for armed policing units.

979 Interview: UNMIL Official—Monrovia, Liberia, September 2010.

980 Interview: UNMIL Senior Management—Monrovia, Liberia, September 2010.

981 United Nations Office of Internal Oversight Services, "Audit of United Nations Police in UNMIL," ed. Internal Audit Division (New York: UN OIOS, 2009), 4.

982 Interview: UNMIL Senior Management—Monrovia, Liberia, September 2010.

expense of other information also useful to overall M&E of mission progress.[983] It was noted that the framework's provisions for broadening the scope for response to M&E findings promised to facilitate larger quantities and better quality of feedback to inform future cycles of the M&E process.

Learning Focus

The final major area of comparative advantage of the framework identified during the field research relates to its focus on and facilitation of organisational learning. Whilst a recent internal assessment of UNPOL in UNMIL pointed to effective reporting structures between UNPOL and senior mission management, as well as between the mission and headquarters level,[984] many of those interviewed for this research identified a number of fragilities and blockages in information exchange when it comes to the transition of information leading to institutional learning within the mission as well as at HQ. Indeed, when asked about the relationship between impact assessment and organisational learning, most agreed that learning, both within the mission (i.e. 1st-level learning) and for the peace operations apparatus more generally (i.e. 2nd-level learning), was the primary un-optimised benefit of an effectual field-level M&E system focused on measuring impact.[985]

Respondents described how they perceived extant mission M&E to be ineffective learning tools. As one official stressed, "good auditing does not always enable the most innovative and effective response because sometimes effective auditing will end up curtailing an innovative risky approach that may yield more dividends."[986] Many highlighted the potential for M&E to play an integral role in learning, but were also quick to emphasise how current M&E did not and that on the contrary it had the tendency to "cement bad plans" and risked institutionalising misguided programming due to its veneration in a benchmark or indicator. One official captured these frustrations, summarising that, "Sometimes the M&E tools employed are largely self-serving, predominantly attend to bureaucratic needs and do little to further the strategic goals of the organisation or mission beyond sustaining the funding to perpetuate its existence."[987] Many believed that the linkages between M&E and the learning infrastructure within the mission as well as at HQ were inadequate and consequently the learning cycle invariably breaks down. For example, some pointed to enduring cultural rigidities within the military vis-à-vis the police and uniformed vis-à-vis civilian sections as resist-

983 Interview: UNMIL Senior Management—Monrovia, Liberia, September 2010.
984 United Nations Office of Internal Oversight Services, "Audit of United Nations Police in UNMIL," ed. Internal Audit Division (New York: UN OIOS, 2009), 3.
985 Interview: UNMIL Senior Management—Monrovia, Liberia, September 2010.
986 Interview: UNMIL Official—Monrovia, Liberia, September 2010.
987 Interview: UNMIL Senior Management—Monrovia, Liberia, September 2010.

ing cross-mission learning through existing M&E mechanisms.[988] Furthermore, an evaluation of the strategic frameworks introduced above suggested that whilst decision-makers knew of their existence they do not appear to use the M&E findings emanating from them to inform their own engagement.[989] For instance, even the M&E provisions in Strategic Frameworks (e.g. PRS and UNDAF) were perceived to be heavily focused on tracking progress through tangible indicators and as a result offering little by way of reflection on the validity of overall political strategies, despite the pre-planned written-in (bi-)annual evaluations. Therefore, these tools and frameworks and the reporting upon them do not appear to be guiding strategic policy-making as intended.

Notwithstanding the inefficiencies of extant practice, most agreed that the potential benefits of doing so implored a shift towards a learning focus. For example, regarding 1st-level learning, referring to the UNPOL objectives, respondents emphasised the central importance of learning on the go due to the 'newness' of this work to these particular people, in this peculiar context. One official noted that, "this is organisational learning both for UNPOL—don't forget there are 39 different police cultures in the mission—and also the LNP."[990] Interviewees across the mission stressed that, for UN peace operations in general, the wholesale reform of security sectors from scratch is also a nascent practice and constitutes "not just a cultural shift, it's a paradigm shift."[991] Summing up the potential value-add of M&E in identifying and capturing good practices in this regard, a senior UNPOL policy advisor described how the whole endeavour should be understood as the "business of learning" adding that a learning focus for field-level M&E was vital, "because you're never 'there'—you recognise that you've got to continually improve this process. Pick at it and say: how can we improve it and what are the weak spots?"[992] This need was deemed to be accentuated in light of the short rotations synonymous with UNPOL personnel and the need to furnish arriving personnel with the learning of their predecessors. In general, it was emphasised that credible and reliable information informing real-time learning would be a huge 'force multiplier' to the existing arrangements for capturing 'best practices' at the field level.

Regarding 2nd-level learning, the extent to which extant M&E tools are feeding into second level organisational learning is unclear. Although some respondents remarked upon recent innovations such as the increasing use of knowledge management tools, including online aids such as communities of practice and

988 Interview: UNMIL Senior Management, Liberia, September 2010.
989 Michael Dalton, *Mid-Term Review of the United Nations Development Assistance Framework 2008–2012*, (Monrovia: United Nations, 2010).
990 Interview: UNMIL UNPOL Official—Monrovia, Liberia, September 2010.
991 Interview: UNMIL UNPOL Official—Monrovia, Liberia, September 2010.
992 Interview: UNMIL UNPOL Official—Monrovia, Liberia, September 2010.

regular sharing of experiences between missions,[993] there remained a general sense of dissatisfaction with the way UNPOL experiences in the field had fed back into organisational knowledge management processes at headquarters level.[994] Interviewees across the mission highlighted the framework's focus on learning as a positive development in this regard. For instance, numerous interviewees emphasised UNMIL's pioneering experience including the deployment of all-female FPUs and breakthroughs on police-military division of labour and interoperability as important opportunities for organisational learning that were being missed. Another example of the value of learning related to the early identification of any mismatch between the activities undertaken and the human resources at the mission's disposal, particularly regarding reform and capacity-building activities. For example, a member of the senior leadership team emphasised that reflective M&E might have brought to their attention earlier that, "what UNPOL needs are not police on the beat, but rather civilian specialists on management, forensics, pathology, and suchlike."[995] As one senior mission manager noted, "If we have the ability to measure impact and identify gaps, maybe we can use this information to address through advocacy to member states/GA [General Assembly] about the need for different capacities within missions—particularly in the area of UNPOL."[996]

One of the most commonly cited benefits of the learning orientation of the framework related to the issue of non-state policing entities. In addition to challenges of a technical nature (e.g. resources, recruiting, training and retaining UNPOL) learning more about how to address and deal with non-state actors—what works and what doesn't—was deemed to be one of the most pressing challenges for UNPOL today—both within ongoing missions and as an organisation. As the POLCOM said, "although the plans are ad hoc and characterised by impromptu decision-making, the reality is that UNMIL and UNPOL in particular are about creating new systems and social orders. They are extremely state-centric at that, so we need to keep asking ourselves whether our approach is the right one or not."[997] UNMIL demonstrates that a major part of M&E utility is capturing how the shoots of engagement with non-state actors in law and justice domain—rare in UN peace operations—play out and what this means for future strategy and operational concepts. In addition, and more generally, some respondents suggested that insightful assessments from the ground would be better placed

---

993 Interview: UNMIL Senior Management—Monrovia, Liberia, September 2010.

994 Interviews: UNMIL UNPOL Senior Management and Officials—Monrovia, Liberia, September 2010.

995 Interview: UNMIL Senior Management—Monrovia, Liberia, September 2010.

996 Interview: UNMIL Senior Management—Monrovia, Liberia, September 2010 See also paragraph above in 'Reflexivity' section: "what UNPOL needs are not police on the beat, but rather civilian specialists on management, forensics, pathology, and suchlike".

997 Interview: UNMIL UNPOL Senior Management—Monrovia, Liberia, September 2010.

to populate periodic reporting to the Security Council such that, in keeping with recommendations of the Brahimi Report, the peace operations apparatus stresses to the Council "what it needs to know and not what it wants to hear."[998] As one senior mission leader explained that, "If we can find a way to assess the effect of our actions, so we can take corrective measures, perhaps it also gives the latitude for future missions to learn from the experience of other missions."[999]

The framework's focus on clarifying and developing the linkages between the field and HQ such that pragmatic and innovative solutions in the field can feed up into the organisational learning infrastructure of the peace operations bureaucracy was said to constitute real value add to the overall endeavour of M&E. These reflections from the field lend significant support and advocacy for the framework's proposed shift from 'fear of failure' to 'hunger for learning'.

Conclusions

Despite a bewildering array of M&E frameworks, tools and demands at multiple levels aimed at disparate audiences, the impact of UNPOL in UNMIL thus far has primarily been measured by indications of productivity such as the number of patrolling hours clocked up, quantity of material resources deployed, and in particular by the number of graduates from the police training academy who have become LNP officers and members of the various specialised units and agencies. This latter focus on training output as the barometer of police reform, rebuilding and restructuring—in the same manner as the RMIP and RSIPF cases—has neglected to address the issue of performance whether through the appraisal of LNP conduct or through measurement of changes in public perceptions of their service. Furthermore, this approach offers little insight to into the impact of UNPOL in providing assistance in the reform, restructuring and capacity-building of the Liberian law enforcement entities—let alone uncovering the effect of exogenous factors on the process or the unintended consequences of these intrusive interventions. Of particular note, it is has done little to assess the extent to which the reformed LNP have contributed to positive change in wider RoL experiences of which they are a critical component and broader issues of peace and security in Liberia. Finally, these approaches have offered little in terms of learning for UNMIL as it has progressed or to the peace operations apparatus as a whole. In short, UNPOL in UNMIL has lacked an effective means of monitoring and evaluating the impact of its work or contributing to institutional learning from these efforts since it deployed eight years ago.

This is not to underestimate the challenge. It is extremely difficult to monitor and evaluate change in policing services where there was no police service

[998] Interview: UNMIL Official—Monrovia, Liberia, September 2010.
[999] Interview: UNMIL Senior Management—Monrovia, Liberia, September 2010.

to speak of a mere six years ago; where the process of recruitment, training and equipping the new corps is on-going; where there is a paucity of trustworthy data from which to analyse crime and victimization patterns; and where until recently there has been no clearly articulated national security strategy and architecture nor national visions and polices for crime prevention.[1000] Furthermore, enduring ambiguity around where the responsibilities of UNMIL end and where those of the government of Liberia begin regarding the resurrection of the RoL dictate that measuring progress against the objectives of UNPOL endeavours will remain an imperfect and difficult task. The realistic expectations for what UNPOL can achieve and expect to attribute to themselves need to be placed in the context of the lengthy time horizon for behavioural and organisational change implicit in SSR processes. However, this has left mission managers and political decision-makers with little evidence when striving to: be responsive, adjust their practices on the ground, calibrate the Consolidation, Drawdown and Withdrawal plan (CDW), and ultimately move towards UNMIL transitioning out of Liberia.

In terms of looking beyond conventional practices in order to mitigate the challenges identified above, the extensive primary research findings presented in this chapter make evident a number of ways in which the M&E framework principles proposed throughout this book offer enhancements when compared to the mainstream approaches currently in use in UNMIL. In the first instance, the above analysis clearly supports the view for a need that the overall design trait of *embedding* M&E in a framework which in turn privileges a recursive and systemic modality promises to be more responsive to the dynamics and uncertainties at play. Next, an internal, field-level M&E process has the potential to enhance M&E by fostering the following: context-sensitivity; an impact—rather than outputs—focus; flexibility; participation from those in the know and whom matter most; retention of multiple perspectives; and creating the space for critical and reflective feedback and responses. Finally, by developing linkages between field-level impact assessments and institutional learning, the alternative principles of the framework present comparative advantages for facilitating a learning focus through an embedded organisational learning cycle. In doing so, this clears the way for a number of issues that have heretofore constituted significant stumbling blocks or simply been omitted in the approaches of current convention. These have implications for the way in which peace operations, and more specifically international policing efforts, should be conceived, designed, assessed and ultimately managed. The point of this emphasis on learning is so that the knowledge generated can in turn lead to advancements in the way M&E is designed and implemented, better reflecting the complexity and other factors of the environment.

1000 Mark Malan, "Security Sector Reform in Liberia: Mixed Results from Humble Beginnings," (Strategic Studies Institute, 2008), 52.; Interview: Liberian Government Official—Monrovia, Liberia, September 2010.

WHERE TO FROM HERE?
GETTING BEYOND TODAY'S CONVENTIONAL WISDOM

The investigations carried out herein have covered enormous conceptual and empirical ground to be sure. To begin to understand international policing, one must appreciate the wider context in which police operate—hence the need to include the many facets overlapping peace and capacity development operations. In plain terms, this overlap relates to the notion of complex systems, a facet to which we dedicated significant discussion. In concrete terms, this means that the role and activities of international police are affected by—and affect—myriad other stakeholders, not least the multiple segments with divergent perspectives and goals that comprise recipient country populations. These divergent perspectives (held by the many international community stakeholders as well as the many stakeholders within the formal and informal segments of endogenous people) relate to our notion of the 'political' in which each group should be expected to respond according to their unique socio-cultural belief systems. The three case study chapters helped illustrate just how divergent cultures can be, and in turn what this means to mission programming when we begin to truly listen to local voices. The 'majority world' does not necessarily share the perceptions of the powerful in far away Anglo-European capitals. Progress in how the international community addresses peace and capacity development depends on its capacity to learn from such complex, political realities.

Therefore, if 'learning' continues to occur based on flawed assumptions, processes and thus interpretations, then the price will be more of the same underachieving missions. Blind spots pertaining to the panoply of ideas and resources that exist beyond the formal state, for instance, will persistently hamper sustainable solutions but we will continue to be none the wiser. The underlying purpose of the book therefore has been to challenge the conventional wisdom comprising international policing. To readers with vast experience on the issues, the content may have at times confirmed long held viewpoints while at other times been entirely at odds with what one had come to believe over the years. Our ultimate aim therefore has been twofold: to make a case so compelling as to prompt orthodox mindsets to probe their own ideas further, in order to end the cycle of passing on flawed views that have merely been passed on uncritically; and to help legitimise viewpoints which are pervasive among those on the ground but have yet to inform official doctrine.

But there is much more to superseding conventional wisdom than a contest over which argument presents the more compelling evidence. The technical and intellectual struggle is only the first of two daunting obstacles. We have, in a comparative sense, taken on the easy job: of exposing the many fallacies that undergird today's conventional wisdom while also developing alternatives needed to begin to understand the true nature of mission environments[1001] and the processes that hold the potential to engender locally-owned and driven changes. In so doing, we have put forward many—albeit forever unfinalised—innovative ideas and conceptual tools pertaining to the big themes occupying this space, including the role and capacity of the state, how to engender local owndership and navigate among the fluid, multiple political perspectives—all with an eye to learning continuously in order to improve the contributions of the international community.

The hard part, to be sure, is the second task: that of shifting the inertia of today's conventional wisdom in new directions for what we do on a day-to-day basis, in practice. Even though history is replete with examples of commonly accepted notions that were eventually seen as ill-begotten, such as that certain races are inherently more or less intelligent than others, history is also filled with examples whereby supremacy of logic and evidence failed to change dominant practices. The knowledge-power nexus underpinning human perception applies to international policing just the same. The seismic shifts we propose require changes to whole institutions, including the many formalised organisational institutions such as the UN but also many informal patterns of behaviour and the belief systems upon which they rest. Someone with ample experience in this area, Gordon Peake, summarises the current situation thusly: "A dappled mix of politics, bureaucratic conservatism and ability of indivduals means that the aperture for introducing and instantiating change in the organisations working on international policing is much smaller than that imagined by the global peace studies community."[1002] Soberly put, to realise the new form of conventional wisdom we recount herein will be a difficult task indeed.

1001 To reiterate, the use of the terms 'true' and 'nature' are not to be confused with essentialising environments. To the contrary, our arguments consistently decry the prospect of reducing any facet of any mission environment to one, and only one, truth or essential quality, and instead insist that there will forever be many perspectives on what constitutes the 'realworld'. This means we consider the environment to be contested, fluid, and mult-perspective—inexorably; that is its true nature.

1002 Gordon Peake, "Understanding International Police Organisations: What the Researchers do not See" in *Making Sense of Peace and Capacity Building Operations:*

Though the scope of the book does not explicitly extend to an examination of how to effect the fundamental shift we advocate, we felt our accumulated contributions would be incomplete without at least musing about this daunting goal. Hence, the following comments sketch out possible paths going forward in response to the question: Where to from here?

The starting point is to recognise that the nexus between knowledge and power is how we have come to current mainstream views in the first place. This recognition leads to questions about what has enabled the creation and maintenance of today's conventional wisdom. In a general sense, we would argue that three segments have contributed in their own peculiar way: 1) those in positions of power pursuing socio-political agendas such as state-centricism; 2) those providing the intellectual inputs that—intentionally or not—support such agendas; and 3) those at the coal face in a position to do little more than pass on such beliefs and practices, and in the process ensuring the broad reproduction of dominant viewpoints. Although we can only ponder aloud about the possible paths forward that may eventuate in a tipping point (of first ideas then practice), a framework of strategies based on those three segments is as good a place as any to begin, particularly when recognising that each segement will utimately need to accept new ideas in order for the changes to take root and flourish. Patience and persistence will be required in substantial amounts regardless of how each of the three levels are approached.

Starting with the group listed second above, there are those intellectually engaged with this space in positions of policymakers, managers and M&E experts cum researchers. While there is much ground to be made, a growing portion of those within this sector now make arguments against—rather than in support of—conventional wisdom. There have in fact been enormous strides in simultaneously exposing the flawed assumption while constructing a more accurate view of what is happening in this space. Luminaries such as Bruce Baker, Alice Hills, and more recently the likes of Gordon Peake, Eric Scheye and Abby Mcleod have been increasingly successful at getting the word out. Persons such as Peake and Mcleod, who have come from research backgrounds but then become staff of international policing organisations (e.g. AFP) possess particular promise to act as catalysts for change because of how they inject their new ideas directly into the mainstream practitioner bodies.

It is from within the practitioner bodies at the coal face however that those with scant opportunity to conceptualise this area due to the frenetic and even life-threatening character of their days dwell. Out of necessity they either pass on uncritically mainstream practices or know better, but lack the fora to express their dissenting insights—even though more are beginning to question and speak

---

Rethinking Policing and Beyond, ed. Bryn Hughes and Charles Hunt (Boston: Martinus Nijhoff Publishers, 2010): 213–233.

up. The link between those responsible for the intellectual facets of this space and those charged with implementation is therefore strong, meaning that strategies to move them on from antiquated wisdom should be closely linked.

Despite the mere existence of the practitioner-academics having helped bridge the divide between academic research and practice, thereby allowing the conditions on the ground to inform a more accurate and grounded theoretical composition, there is still a long way to go in terms of having the link between research and practice impact upon what is considered fact or fiction, this direction is vital by how it erodes the intellectual pillars supporting misinformed policy and practice. The goal then is to grow these elements of practice-orientated academics whereby critical analyses are undertaken by greater numbers to the point where, like climate change science now enjoys today, there are only a few outlayers who insist on holding out on the overwhelming weight of evidence.

One tactic to realise this goal is to make the research more accessible to practitioners. As an innovative article from Peake[1003] points out, the current manner of academic production does not lend itself to being useful to those in the field. For example, the typical publication cycle entails the time-consuming process of research, draft development, peer review, revision, then ultimately publication, rendering its content often times outdated to those in the field[1004] (with re-usable frameworks, processes and timeless principles being notable exceptions to this rule). Moreover, academic output commonly has characteristics that make it far too lengthy and beholden to theory to prove useful to practitioner communities, with access for these vital audiences effectively blocked behind copyrighted journal websites attached to universities.

Hence, if we work to alter the format and access of academic outputs to better suit those in the field, the learning produced would increase dramatically, so too the opportunity for the insights to help create a new conventional wisdom. Peake[1005] argues for 'action-oriented' writing, and we would suggest this approach entail that all research include an executive summary style format, plain language, and somehow be made accessible in short-time. Less is indeed more. Perhaps publish-

---

1003 Gordon Peake, "Understanding International Police Organisations: What the Researchers do not See" in *Making Sense of Peace and Capacity Building Operations: Rethinking Policing and Beyond*, ed. Bryn Hughes and Charles Hunt (Boston: Martinus Nijhoff Publishers, 2010): 229.

1004 Gordon Peake, "Understanding International Police Organisations: What the Researchers do not See" in *Making Sense of Peace and Capacity Building Operations: Rethinking Policing and Beyond*, ed. Bryn Hughes and Charles Hunt (Boston: Martinus Nijhoff Publishers, 2010): 229.

1005 Gordon Peake, "Understanding International Police Organisations: What the Researchers do not See" in *Making Sense of Peace and Capacity Building Operations: Rethinking Policing and Beyond*, ed. Bryn Hughes and Charles Hunt (Boston: Martinus Nijhoff Publishers, 2010): 229.

ers could evolve their product offerings to include blog-style media from noted field academics, linking up with practitioner networks able to reach UN, EU, and other major peace operation staff. Many of those interviewed in Chapters 12 and 13, whether working for UNMIL or the associated NGO community, or RAMSI would seem all too eager to hear more about the kinds of M&E innovations they, themselves, were helping to articluate when given the chance. The end effect would be a redoubling of the efforts to dispel the many myths propping up the conventional wisdom, such as the AFP figure cited above that 85% of Solomon Islanders have no meaningful daily interaction with the state. In so doing make it increasingly untenable for organisations to continue with their currently misinformed policies.

The flipside is to make practice more accessible to academia. That direction requires a further shift in convention—one taking place already in educational institutions such as the University of Queensland—whereby research and degrees in related peace and capacity development fields are increasingly accepted, and even expected, to contain sizeable portions of fieldwork. A corrollary could entail pushing for more funding by government bodies such as the Australian Research Council (ARC) earmarked for interdisciplinary work and more specificallly for projects which deliberately put together academics and practitioners. This could also mean shifting convention by encouraging practioner organisations, such as the AFP, to continue down the innovative path they have already started by augmenting traditional policing career persons with non-traditional skill sets, such as anthroplogist Abby McLeod or researcher Gordon Peake as highlighted above. At the end of the day, it is about offering access to practitioners in order to allow a more meaningful sharing of ideas between the vast wealth of academic and practitioner knowledge.

The 'elephant in the room', at least for those of us who recognise how little local voices currently influence mission design and implementation, is the role of local stakeholders. For the specific purpose of facilitating a shift in conventional wisdom, the question is one of: How could local stakeholders help convince both leading intellectuals and line staff and managers that we need to change our thinking? The challenge is to find vehicles to give their insights a platform to be aired. In our experience, it usually takes only a few minutes perusal of the typical program design or evaluation report to spot how ostensible local ownership or input remains marginalised, disempowerd: it merely takes looking beneath the surface in order to discern who makes the key decisions on everything from resourcing to what constitutes so-called legitimate knowledge. The same tendency applies to the mainstream literature.[1006] Without delving too deeply, our

---

1006 See, for example, Diehl, Paul and Daniel Druckman. *Evaluating Peace Operations,* (Boulder, CO: Lynne Rienner, 2010).

response has to do with the adoption of the processes and overall approach of our Democratising and Collaborative M&E framework. If put into widespread practice, the learning engendered will produce overwhelming evidence for those yet convinced of the flaws in today's conventional wisdom.

The above suggestions are intended to help alter the thinking—and subsequently the practice—of both the intellectual and practitioner segments supporting conventional wisdom. It may very well be that a groundswell of belief needs to be present in order to win over the most trenchant of the three segments identified above as responsible for the continuation of conventional wisdom: those in powerful positions with socio-political agendas. A germane saying not infrequently invoked to help rein in military responses is that "to a hammer everything looks like a nail". It applies here insofar as the biggest obstacle to evolving beyond the current conventional wisdom may very well be the state-based nature of the international community. That is, representatives of states logically see problems and thus solutions through a state-based prism. The state-centricism to which we have devoted significant time problematising, unsurprisingly has its strong roots in the state-based institutions that dominate this realm, from the United Nations and the European Union down to the individual states themselves which both finance and orchestrate peace and capacity development operations. The modern state is pervasive, and therefore it is asking a lot to eliminate the Western assumptions and institutions to which the state ideal is a core ingredient. In one sense, the conventional wisdom is beholden to the knowledge-power nexus that constitutes these elements. They will be the most difficult to convince, the most difficult to dislodge.

Yet on this front there are promising signs as well. Albeit insufficient from the lack of genuine enforcement mechanisms, a number of influential world-wide accords have been propagated in recent years. The 2005 Paris Declaration, the 2008 Accra Agenda for Action,[1007] and most lately the 2011 Bussan Partnership for Effective Development Co-operation,[1008] are high profile agreements that offer hope in two senses: first, by how they demonstrate a significant move towards

1007 The five core principles initiated with the Paris Accord reflect an intention to listen to local voices and begin to place endogenous stakeholders in the key decision making and management roles: 1. Ownership: Developing countries set their own strategies for poverty reduction, improve their institutions and tackle corruption. 2. Alignment: Donor countries align behind these objectives and use local systems. 3. Harmonisation: Donor countries coordinate, simplify procedures and share information to avoid duplication. 4. Results: Developing countries and donors shift focus to development results and results get measured. 5. Mutual accountability Donors and partners are accountable for development results. See Organisation for Economic Cooperation and Development, Website, http://www.oecd.org/document/18/0,3746,en_2649_3236398_35401554_1_1_1_1,00.html.

1008 Organisation for Economic Cooperation and Development, Website, http://www.oecd.org/document/12/0,3746,en_2649_3236398_46057868_1_1_1_1,00.html.

appreciating the political, the interconnectedness and complexity of local societies, as well as pushing back on much of the early Western, state and ethnic centrism that has plagued the programs in this space heretofore; and second, by how they erode old ideas and in the process help build a new conventional wisdom. Added to these manifest swings in thinking are developments of the kind of transparency that hold promise to make those in power more accountable by broadcasting beyond their control the conditions and outcomes on the ground. The recently functioning Swedish aid transparancy guarantee is one example of this.[1009] Because these types of developments derive from the loci of state-based power, they have the potential to go a greater distance toward restructuring the imagination of what the international community should do than developments coming from peripheral sources easily dismissed by those in powerful positions.

Although it may seem imperceptible at times, the tide is shifting against those advocating the many strands of fallacious status quo thinking and practice. When searching for optimism concerning the pace of progress, we should remind ourselves that in historical terms the current modalities of international assistance are only in their adolescence. It is therefore not implausible to posit that future generations could look back on this period's conventional wisdom of international operations as astronomy's equivalent of the Middle Ages. That is, if we cast our minds back to Europe in the Middle Ages, we would find ourselves in a place and time whereby conventional wisdom posits that the earth resides at the centre of the universe. It is a belief supported by the technical findings of leading intellectuals, passed on uncritically by less erudite segments of society, and propped up by powerful elements in pursuit of socio-political goals. In that instance, the Catholic Church—in conjunction with myriad other sources of authority and expertise from both contemporaneous and bygone eras—managed for more than a millennium to maintain a widely held view of reality that we now consider utterly false. In the case of international policing, the sources of authority and expertise include international organisations such as the United Nations and the European Union, various national policing bodies, as well as a supporting troupe of consultants and researchers. Although these many entities are seldom in total alignment, nonetheless, together their mutually reinforcing stances about the what, why and how have proven a formidable barrier indeed to the introduction of fundamentally contrasting ideas—no different, in that regard, to the challenge faced by Copernicus those many centuries ago when suggesting the sun may be at the centre. It is a plainly drawn analogy—wherein the normally vital distinction between natural and 'social fact' does not apply—yet which powerfully reminds us how unfounded knowledge can nevertheless become deeply entrenched.

1009 Government of Sweden, Website, http://www.sweden.gov.se/sb/d/13179/a/145626.

Removing ourselves from the immediacy of current contexts—by taking that same long term perspective—may be exactly what is needed to gain clarity and perspective. If those of us who have come to see a very different story than the conventional wisdom would have us believe continue to press our case, the day may come when the peoples of Liberia, the Solomon Islands, the Marshall Islands and beyond, can work together with an international community which has learned to learn from complex, political realities.

APPENDIX ONE

CHANGE THEORY COMPENDIUM

Peacebuilding Change Theories[1010]

The Individual Change Theory: Peace comes through transformative change of a critical mass of individuals, their consciousness, attitudes, behaviours, and skills. Methods include investment in individual change through training, personal transformation/ consciousness-raising workshops or processes; dialogues and encounter groups; trauma healing.

The Healthy Relationships and Connections Theory: Peace emerges out of a process of breaking down isolation, polarization, division, prejudice and stereotypes between/ among groups. Strong relationships are a necessary ingredient for peacebuilding. Methods include processes of inter-group dialogue; networking; relationship-building processes; joint efforts and practical programs on substantive problems.

The withdrawal of the resources for war theory: Wars require vast amounts of material (weapons, supplies, transport, etc.) and human capital. If we can interrupt the supply of people and goods to the war-making system, it will collapse and peace will break out. Methods include anti-war campaigns to cut off funds/ national budgets; conscientious objection and/or resistance to military service; international arms control; arms embargoes and boycotts. (Also other embargos)

The reduction of violence theory: Peace will result as we reduce the levels of violence perpetrated by combatants or their representatives. Methods include cease-fires, creation of zones of peace, withdrawal/retreat from direct engagement,

1010 All peacebuilding change theories are taken from Cheyanne Church and Mark M. Rogers, 'Understanding Change', in *Designing for Results*, (Washington D.C.: Search for Common Ground, 2006), http://www.sfcg.org/Documents/dmechapter2.pdf, 14 5.

introduction of peacekeeping forces/interposition, observation missions, accompaniment efforts, promotion of nonviolent methods for achieving political/social/economic ends.

The root causes/justice theory: We can achieve peace by addressing the underlying issues of injustice, oppression/ exploitation, threats to identity and security, and people's sense of injury/victimization. [Methods: long-term campaigns for social and structural change, truth and reconciliation; changes in social institutions, laws, regulations, and economic systems.]

The institutional development theory: Peace is secured by establishing stable/reliable social institutions that guarantee democracy, equity, justice, and fair allocation of resources. Methods include new constitutional and governance arrangements/entities; development of human rights, RoL, anti-corruption; establishment of democratic/equitable economic structures; economic development; democratization.

The Political Elites theory: Peace comes when it is in the interest of political (and other) leaders to take the necessary steps. Peacebuilding efforts must change the political calculus of key leaders and groups. Methods include raising the costs and reducing the benefits for political elites of continuing war while increasing the incentives for peace; engaging active and influential constituencies in favour of peace; withdrawing international support/funding for warring parties.

The grassroots mobilization theory: "When the people lead, the leaders will follow." If we mobilize enough opposition to war, political leaders will have to pay attention. Methods include mobilizing grassroots groups to either oppose war or to advocate for positive action; nonviolent direct action campaigns; use of the media; education/mobilization efforts; organizing advocacy groups; dramatic events to raise consciousness.

The Economics Theory: As a politician once said, "It's the economy, stupid!" People make personal decisions and decision makers make policy decisions based on a system of rewards/ incentives and punishments/sanctions that are essentially economic in nature. If we can change the economies associated with war making, we can bring peace. Methods include the use of government or financial institutions to change supply and demand dynamics; control incentive and reward systems; boycotts.

The Public Attitudes theory: War and violence are partly motivated by prejudice, misperceptions, and intolerance of difference. We can promote peace by using the media (television and radio) to change public attitudes and build greater tolerance in society. Methods include TV and radio programs that promote tolerance; modelling tolerant behaviour; symbolic acts of solidarity/unity; dialogues among groups in conflict—with subsequent publicity.

Additional Peacebuilding Theories[1011]

Peace agreements/accords*:* Some form of political settlement is a prerequisite to peace—we must support a negotiation process among key parties to the conflict and violence. Examples include: official negotiations among representatives of key parties; "track 1½" and "track 2" dialogues among influential persons; civil society dialogues in support of negotiations.

Transitional justice: Societies that have experienced deep trauma and social dislocation need a process for handling grievances, identifying what happened, and holding perpetrators accountable. Addressing these issues will enable people to move on to reconstruct a peaceful and prosperous society. Examples include: Truth and reconciliation commissions; criminal prosecutions and war crimes tribunals; reparations; community reconciliation processes; traditional rites and ceremonies; institutional reforms.

Community reintegration: If we enable displaced people (IDPs/refugees) to return to their homes and live in relative harmony with their neighbours, we will contribute to security and economic recovery. Examples include: negotiation and problem solving to enable returns; intergroup dialogue; ex-combatant-community engagement; processes for handling land claims; trauma healing.

Economic action: People make personal decisions, and decision makers make policy decisions based on a system of rewards/incentives and punishment/sanctions that are essentially economic in nature. If we can change the economies associated with war-making, we can bring peace. Examples include: use of government or financial institutions to change supply and demand dynamics; control incentive and reward systems; boycotts and embargoes.

Social justice: If we address the underlying issues of injustice, oppression/exploitation, threats to identity and security, and peoples' sense of injury/victimisation, it will reduce the drivers of conflict and open up space for peace. Examples include: long-term campaigns for social and structural change; truth and reconciliation processes; changes in social institutions, laws, regulations, and economic systems.

Culture of peace*:* If we transform cultural and societal norms, values and behaviours to reject violence, support dialogue and negotiation, and address the fundamental causes of the conflict, we can develop the long-term conditions for peace. Examples include: peace education; poverty eradication; reduction of social inequalities; promotion of human rights; ensuring gender equality; fostering

1011 Taken from Organisation for Economic Cooperation and Development (b), *Guidance on Evaluating Conflict Prevention and Peacebuilding Activities*, (Paris: France: OECD, 2008) http://www.oecd.org/secure/pdfDocument/0,2834,en_21571361_34047972_39774574_1_1_1_1,00.pdf, 82–4.

democratic participation; advancing tolerance; enhancing the free flow of information/knowledge; reducing the production of and traffic in arms.

Security Sector Reform Change Theories[1012]

Capacity building: National security and justice institutions will perform with greater success if they have greater resources. This theory places substantial focus on providing training and equipment, often in the absence of institutional reform, safeguards or reference to accountability and governance.

Capacity building is hitherto the most commonly employed theory underpinning donor SSR work, however has known limitations and sometimes unintended negative results.

Professionalisation: Improving standards of professional conduct, self-image and esprit de corps will lead to better behaviour by staff and enhanced service delivery; through a sense of pride and public service that in time breeds accountability. This theory places a strong focus on codes, training, conditions of service, exchanges and learning from outsiders; though surprisingly little on monitoring actual behaviour through methods such as observation, surveys and user groups. Professionalisation is favoured by both progressive senior personnel in unreformed institutions and foreign advisers and has strong personal appeal for staff interested in career progression and meritocracy. It is often informed, for better or worse, by specific views on the suitability of systems and principles applied consistently elsewhere.

Good governance and accountability: Introducing mechanisms and structures for internal or external accountability over institutions will enhance accountability through the prospect of negative sanctions against rule-breakers. In time, effective accountability mechanisms can channel public or civil society demand for further reform or better delivery. Attention is paid to the existence, setup and functioning of internal and external accountability mechanisms; to their handling of exemplary or high-profile cases; to the legal framework and application of the law in these areas; and to the political independence of security and justice institutions at operational level. Attention is also paid to higher-level security sector policy development as a contribution to improved governance. The good governance and accountability theory is an approach favoured by current OECD DAC policy but employed only by a minority of programmes. Emphasis on external mechanisms such as parliaments, civil society and ombudsperson's offices is particularly lacking, making this theory often less attractive to partner governments.

1012 Organisation for Economic Cooperation and Development (a), *INCAF Task Team on Peacebuilding, Statebuilding, Security—Room Document 5: Draft Justice and Security Monitoring and Evaluation Toolkit*, (Paris, France: OECD, 2009), 9.

Institutional reform/restructuring: Given the right institutional set-up (laws, procedures, management and recruitment systems and tools), security and justice institutions and those working within them will begin to function more rationally and effectively. Strong focus is placed on re-designing institutional structures and their operating procedures in line with perceived models of best practice. This theory is particularly common with regard to creating operational separation between MOD/Armed Forces or Interior Ministry/Police. It may achieve little, however, if the institutional setup is changed without reforming the attitudes and behaviour of the politicians and managers that run them and the staff that work for them.

Enhance national security: The main threats to security and justice are from external/international factors such as regional conflicts, terrorism, weapons proliferation, etc. Strengthening the capacity of national actors to combat these threats will increase security for everyone. Under this theory, significant resources are spent on training and equipment for national security forces, particularly armed forces, policing and intelligence services. Often the aim is only to strengthen capacity (see above) with little thought given to whether this capacity will be used effectively and accountably. It is the most prevalent form of donor assistance to security actors in recent years, though often not considered by donors as 'SSR' or related to SSR principles and standards. A critique of this theory is that strong donor emphasis on counter-terrorism may distort national perceptions of security or redirect resources away from other pressing local needs.

Enhance community security: Many security and justice concerns are essentially local in nature. Addressing security at the community level will thus have the biggest impact for improving security and justice and can reduce the risk of violent conflict. Emphasis is placed on training police to employ a 'community policing' approach, often with resources for new equipment and facilities. Also involved are community safety plans, based on local perception surveys, that encourage local state and non- governmental actors to work together to improve security. Community policing has been popular for several years, while the broader approach to community security is more recent. It is important to note, however, that under this theory the relation to and impact on state/national security and conflict dynamics is sometimes unclear.

Comprehensive approach: Different elements of the security system influence each other and reform in one sector may fail if not supported by reform in an adjacent sector; therefore a comprehensive approach is needed which links reforms together across the security system. This theory emphasizes a system-wide approach to reform, with an overarching SSR strategy to which specific reforms of sectors and sub-sectors are subordinate. It often aims to build capacity of an overarching body such as a national security council to promote joined-up thinking. OECD DAC policy emphasizes the importance of comprehensive and whole-of-government approaches to SSR. However, a genuinely comprehensive approach would be highly complex and it is unclear how far or how effectively such approaches have been employed in practice.

Enhance service delivery: Security and justice are public goods like health and education. The public are seen as service users who are entitled to security and justice. National security and justice institutions should be reformed with a focus on those issues and mechanisms most likely to meet demand in the near term. Opinion surveys, workshops, and the like are used to identify key public demands and expectations of security and justice. This is a rights-based approach that emphasizes links to constitutional and legislative provisions; specific interventions for reform and support. Capacity building is then designed on this basis with public participation and support. This approach is relatively new and has recently been enshrined in the UK Department for International Development's White Paper. It is important to note that this theory raises various dilemmas about how to treat security and justice as basic services in fragile and conflict-affected countries.

APPENDIX TWO

COLLABORATIVE M&E FRAMEWORK

We have referred to this attached Appendix on numerous instances throughout the book. It comprises a standalone framework by which to approach M&E in peace and capacity development operations. It is a vital addition to our exploration because it provides a viable alternative to conventional wisdom M&E, and thus a paradigmatic shift to learning—featuring process rather than pre-determined content and techniques. As will be elaborated upon further in its own Introduction, it employs the principles for which we have built the case to challenge conventional wisdom. Its development owes an enormous debt of gratitude to the AFP; and as a tribute to their support, our hope is that its guidance may someday begin to make meaningful differences not only to the manner in which the AFP prosecute their sizeable assistance to the world's most vulnerable people, but that its advice spills over more broadly to the way the international community approaches its assistance.

COLLABORATIVE POLICING, MONITORING & EVALUATION: PROGRAM MANAGEMENT FRAMEWORK

INTRODUCTORY MANUAL

Authors: Bryn Hughes, Project Manager; Jodie Curth-Bibb[1013] & Charles Hunt, Senior Researchers

June 2011

Prepared for:
The International Deployment Group, Australian Federal Police

1013 The M&E methodology is based on the conceptual framework developed by Jodie Curth-Bibb.

Contents

Introduction

Monitoring and Evaluation (M&E) processes for international police stabilisation and capacity development operations have traditionally heavily emphasised the need to develop specific performance indicators at the expense of broader methodological considerations. The AFP International Deployment Group engaged the University of Queensland to develop a means of performance measurement for international police operations that considers not only the measures of progress that are most relevant to the work undertaken by police, but also the most effective way to capture this information. Reviews of methodologies used by a variety of international development practitioners clearly reinforced an emerging view that collaborative processes, that is those processes that involve the widest practicable consultation with all groups concerned in and about the outcome of development efforts, had the best chance of providing meaningful feedback about progress. Given international police stabilisation and capacity development operations are most effective when police have the opportunity for direct community engagement across a broad range of groups, a collaborative framework builds upon activities already undertaken by police in the field.

On the basis of the understanding that collaborative processes of this type are best placed to deliver the best outcomes for performance measurement of international police missions, the University of Queensland developed the framework described in abridged form in this document. This introductory document offers both a detailed overview of the process as well as practical step-by-step guidance for field practitioners using this recently developed collaborative framework. As such this document must strike a delicate balance between providing detailed enough instruction that all elements of the process can be understood and properly utilised without overwhelming the practitioner or management team members seeking to understand the framework.

M&E which appears impressively sophisticated regularly fails to live up to its promises when attempted in practice, leading instead to haphazard execution and flawed data with findings packaged in the type of long or complicated formats that make them inaccessible. In order to avoid these pitfalls, only the information needed to conduct and convey the framework's core facets is included. This streamlined design means the vast majority of the framework's potential can be realised with little specialised knowledge. For those who become proficient with the content contained in this document, over time or with training, a comprehensive operational manual has been created with considerably greater detail, tool options, and demonstrative examples. A third document exists for those interested in a comprehensive explanation of the framework's conceptual developments and the debates from whence they have come.

Overview

Although the purpose of this document is not to elaborate on the framework features or surrounding conceptual debates, a summary of its main characteristics and points of departure from conventional M&E nevertheless enhances a working knowledge. Firstly, this collaborative framework can be used for M&E across the entire spectrum of peace and capacity development operations. It is designed so that each particular mission environment and mandate determines how it is used. For instance, specific tools and processes are applicable if your mission deploys into a hot conflict as a minor part of a much bigger operation, whereas other elements should be used if your mission were operating independently in a stable environment with a development mandate. Further, in circumstances where your organisation has significant influence on planning and M&E, the framework tools can be employed to their maximum extent; conversely, scant influence or capacity means a dramatically scaled-back version which nevertheless continues to provide valuable guidance. This in-built flexibility avoids the 'one-size-fits all' problematic by the way its M&E processes and content adapt to each specific context.

Who does the M&E? In a break from conventional approaches, the practitioners and local stakeholders themselves integrate M&E into their normal operational duties. Apart from assuring actual local ownership *and* capacity development, this 'democratisation' of M&E eliminates much of the opportunity cost and waste that inadvertently accompanies mainstream methodologies. For example, typically practitioners have been made to interrupt their already hectic workloads in order to compile input for M&E reports, and they can become frustrated then resist M&E because they deem it to be intrusive and inaccurate rather than beneficial. Rather than having 'experts'—be they internal from a mission's staff or flown in from external sources—drive M&E, this framework puts in charge those most familiar with what matters on the ground. This paradigm shift underscores the usefulness of a practical, un-specialised design.

Why is M&E done? Accountability and learning (for tactical adaptations or future design) have been the ostensible motivations heretofore. While these reasons are crucial to this framework, there are additional similarly important benefits that otherwise go uncultivated when M&E is handled by small groups of experts. Specifically, these are (1) enabling local ownership (2) developing local (as well as intervening) actor capacity and, perhaps most vital to sustainable peace, (3) fostering dialogue and relationships among the local stakeholders who are ultimately responsible for self-sustaining peace and development outcomes. This latter quality is why the term 'collaborative' features in the framework's title.

How is M&E done? Practical and inexpensive qualitative methods such as interviews and focus groups are relied upon not only for information pertaining to M&E but also to build relationships, engender cooperation, and resolve conflicts. In the process, those conducting M&E activities come to serve as positive 'agents of change'. These methods can produce quantitative data if needs be. Broad surveys or 'official' statistics are not enough, however, due to the superficial picture they provide. Further, unlike stable Western countries, peace mission environments often render these conventional sources entirely impractical not to mention expensive. A main advantage of this framework is that in circumstances marked by an absence of reliable conventional sources of information (e.g. government statistics) the methods proposed herein can generate a rich and multi-perspective understanding of cause-and-effect as well as existing resources. The veracity of stakeholder input can be moderated by 'triangulating' responses against others. What is more, the framework's methods are largely conducted through activities that should already be part and parcel of mission-critical operations. This dual-purpose efficiency extends further to allow the framework to double as project management guidance rather than having M&E conducted in isolation, or even in contradiction, to other mission activities. For instance, time spent identifying and engaging with the multiplicity of stakeholders that makes up a conflict environment is not only as vital for stable peace as it is to this framework's M&E, but those activities can be situated in relation to other program processes to keep track of what has been done. On the other hand, effective M&E cannot be rushed. Although there are many efficiencies afforded, this framework's approach nevertheless does not countenance 'quick fixes' such as one-off benchmarking survey exercises. In the same sense that practitioners should re-calibrate their temporal expectations concerning peace and development goals, they should recognise that patience and persistence are needed when it comes to genuinely collaborative M&E.

Rule of law (RoL) forms the backdrop against which M&E is mapped. It is the necessary platform from which just and sustainable improvements to security and development can derive. That noted, it must be defined in a manner that not only provides a degree of clarity that ensures actors can be made accountable but also in such a way that can be translated across culture and time. Vague, Western or state-centric conceptions often overlook what matters most and thus fail to operationalise RoL to a point whereby it can be used for M&E. The delineation provided (in a subsequent section) aims to satisfy these criteria. Lastly, the framework emphasises an 'outcomes' focus. Outputs focused M&E fails to appreciate what is most important: how the myriad forces interact to produce the outcomes of patterns of behaviour. This is critical since each mission environment is an ever-changing product of a complex social system of interacting forces. It is not, as conventional reductionist political science would suggest, an aggregate of isolated phenomena. On the contrary, interactions matter integrally to the behaviour of each actor and the system as a whole. The recommended format by which to assess a program therefore begins with outcomes and then asks for the case to be built about how activities *contributed* to each outcome.

Framework Methodology Stage Summary

Mission Context
Involves identifying and understanding the context into which missions deploy, including its own capacity and mandate.

Stakeholders
Involves the identification of key stakeholders and the determination of how these stakeholders can best interact.

Situation Analysis
Involves determining benchmarks—what is happening *now*, and why? May also include **Visions of Success** goals.

Planning
Change-processes are planned so as to move from benchmarks generated in the Situation Analysis down the agreed upon paths.

Monitoring Loops
An ongoing monitoring process is designed for collating data on the deliverance of work plans set out in the Planning stage, and monitoring change.

Community Communications
Strategies are devised to keep the broadest circle of stakeholders informed. This includes those stakeholders not already involved (such as the broader community).

Unintended Consequences
This stage looks specifically for information not previously targeted, or unplanned/unintended effects.

Evaluation Reporting
Information is adapted to feed into various donor and performance management reporting systems.

After Action Review
Lessons learned and ways to adapt going forward are explored through joint reviews and/or feedback.

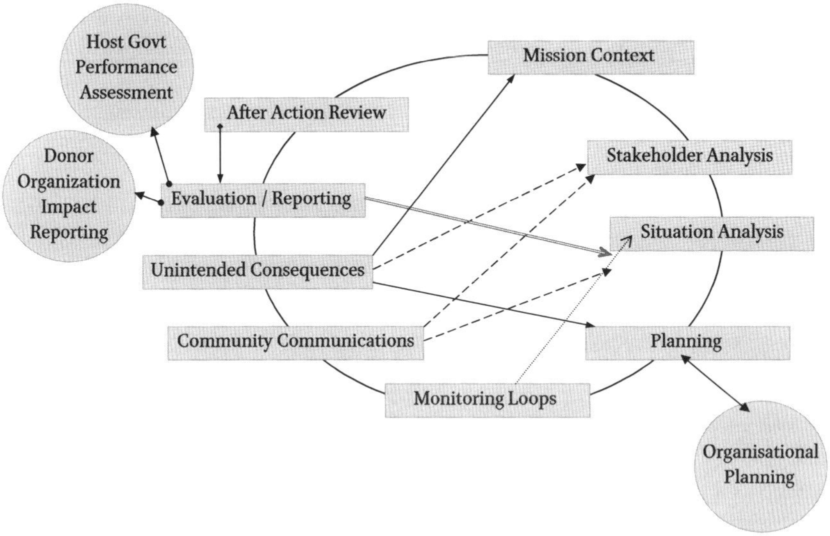

Framework Diagram

Methodology Stages in Detail

The following stages enable M&E information to be generated in ways that build stakeholder collaboration and learning, as well as serve as a program management framework that can be used to guide planning. They are designed to be used in a flexible and iterative fashion so that data collected for one stage can be shared across the others. Information gathered during the stage known as 'Unintended Consequences', for instance, should be fed back into a number of the other stages, in particular the 'Situation Analysis' step. Information generated from each stage can be adapted to basically any manner of report document to satisfy various organisations' conventions. Lastly, because the real world is in constant flux, previously developed plans should be capable of adjusting to incoming information, adapting to the inevitable changes; these stages have been designed accordingly to contain such mechanisms.

Mission Context

The first step is to scope the mission or program. This means understanding the **mission type/mandate** and its **environment** in order to contextualise the activities of external agents (e.g. police). Is your mission a minor part of a much larger and more complex mission or is it in a highly influential or independent position? Does it have executive policing powers or a merely observatory capacity? Is the environment relatively stable with a development focus or is there widespread violence? It is important to establish these characteristics because they will affect which aspects of the framework are used and in what manner.

Being comparatively straightforward this stage requires little elaboration beyond what is outlined below other than to note that the information will directly inform the stages that follow. An initial 'Terms of Reference' document can also be generated from this step, while emphasising that it should be used only to initiate the engagement rather than a fixed view incapable of evolving to fit changing circumstances and needs.[1014]

Mission Type: Establish the mandate, initial change theory assumptions, scope and resources of the mission/program. Locate it in relation to other introduced actors as well as the RoL system (defined further below). Importantly, the capacities of mission staff will determine which elements of the framework are advisable to undertake, since some depend on relevant experience whereas others do not. In general, this framework's approach requires staff with good listening skills, as well as a high capacity for empathy and cultural sensitivity.

Mission Environment: Establish the country's form of governance (e.g. democratic or authoritarian) and its capacity and legitimacy. Include the economic situation and, in general terms, appreciate the degree of stability (i.e. in a *crisis* phase with a mandate to enforce law and order, or relatively *stable* thus focussing on capacity development).

Stakeholders

The next step ensures that stakeholders are identified as well as understood. Stakeholders are seen as 'individuals, groups, and organisations who have an interest (stake) and the potential to influence the actions and aims of an organisation, project, or policy direction'.[1015] This means not only the spectrum of practitioners but non-state and quasi-state actors as well. Hence Australian, international state-based organisations and host-country government agencies

---

1014 **Terms of Reference** are an ideal entry point for any assistance because they establish the basis upon which cooperation is to begin. This document should include: **Broad** scope of assistance (e.g. in the case of the Marshall Islands, PDPP, it concerns delivery and capacity for the Department of Public Safety), including what AFP's contributions might look like (e.g. personnel hours and money anticipated); **Key stakeholders** at the outset, whereby the initial aim is highlighted as being to identify those stakeholders to gain approval to start mission/program, a list which will almost certainly expand and be refined; and finally, a **Process** section featured to provide an outline of the framework stages and how they would be pursued in general terms. For example, it will likely say that, given the framework processes, the activities will entail: 1) contact and identify interested stakeholders; 2) ask them what is currently happening in the nominated space/domains; 3) gain suggestions for improvements; 4) determine who is well placed to offer feedback concerning what is happening (i.e. monitor); and 5) possibly more steps should be listed at this point if appropriate.

1015 Brugha and Varvasovszky (2000: 239).

will not be the only stakeholders considered. When making decisions about which stakeholders to include, it is important to consider your organisation's operational influence in the environment, boundaries of responsibility, resources at your disposal to carry out this process, lines of accountability, and whom you need to win over, satisfy, and mobilise to accomplish your mission goals (as set out in the Mission Context stage above). These considerations could mean as little as a single stakeholder in situations whereby a mission is extremely limited in its scope and capacity. See procedural steps and example diagram below.

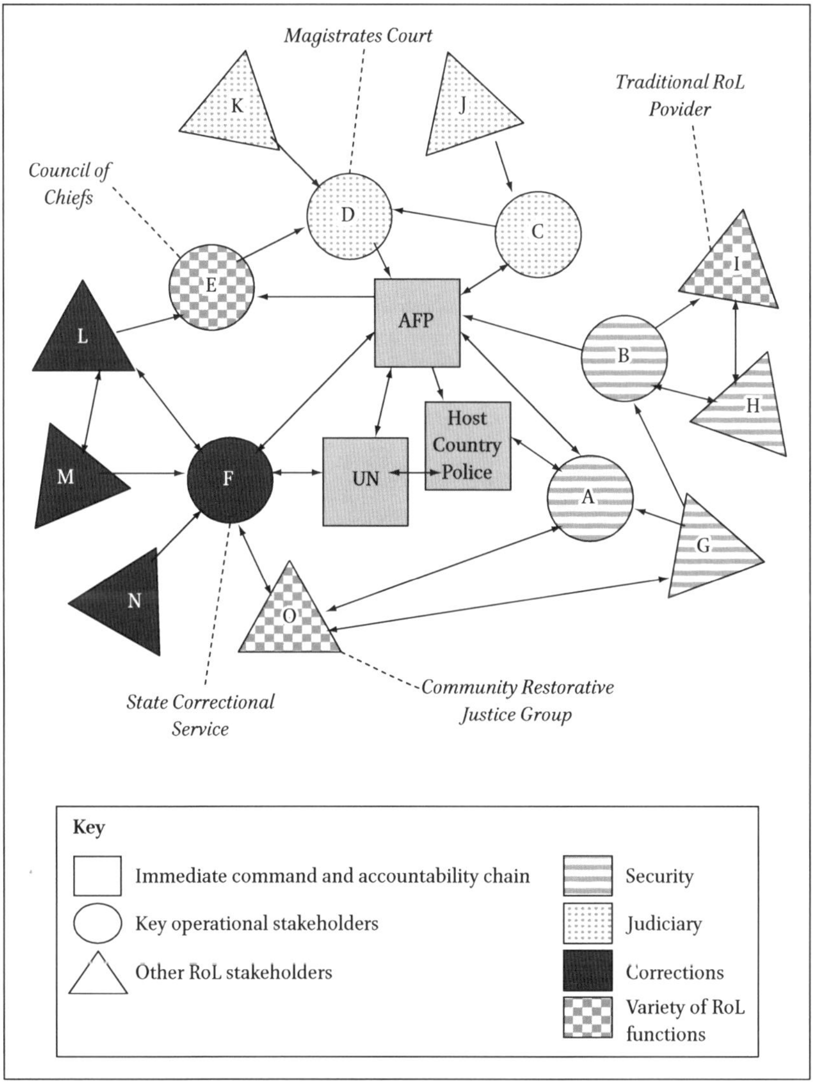

Identify Stakeholders

1) Place your organisation (or the focus of M&E) in the centre of the map;
2) Map immediate domestic command and accountability chains (arrows indicate direction of relationship);
3) Map other key operational stakeholders;
4) Begin to identify then map the broader context of RoL stakeholders according to how they may provide any of the three functional categories (i.e. security, judiciary, corrections)—see example below;
5) Where practicable, contact those identified in step 4 and ask them to do likewise (in workshops or interviews) to expand the pool of potential stakeholders.
6) NB: there may be utility in dividing stakeholders into 'internal' (meaning state-based) and 'external' (denoting the broader community beyond formal state) since there may be need to approach these broad categories differently

Analysis of Stakeholder Engagement

Once stakeholders have begun to be identified, it is important to understand how they might engage with each other within the RoL system. Equally crucial is to consider how they may interact with you, acknowledging the likelihood of a notable power imbalance due to your influence and resourcing potentials. The iterative nature of this framework means that this analysis should be ongoing and continually unfolding so that future versions are fuller and more precise. Following on from step 5 above:

7) Seek information about and from stakeholders regarding their existing relationships by asking the below cache of questions relating to *risk and power relations, capacity*, and *logistics and preference*. You may need to solicit advice from persons outside your organisation as to appropriate modes of engagement. Almost certainly you will need to engage the services of trustworthy persons to help bridge the cultural and linguistic divides.

Questions to consider:

Risk and Power Relations

1. Do these stakeholders normally communicate? How so, and what forces influence these modes (historical, social, institutional)?
2. Are these stakeholders normally in the same space (room, community, etc.)?
3. Do any of these stakeholders feel threatened or intimidated and, if so, by what or whom specifically (physically, politically, economically, socially etc.)?
4. Are you asking for input which would compromise stakeholders in the presence of others?
5. Would stakeholders prefer to contribute via a proxy?
6. Are other stakeholders higher in the formal or informal hierarchy?

7. Is it disrespectful or culturally inappropriate for certain stakeholders to question or contradict other stakeholders? (e.g. Would young people be able to disagree with elders or women disagree with men?)
8. What are stakeholders' motivations for sharing information? Is the information likely to increase risk, and how might this affect or reflect power relations?
9. Are there some things that some stakeholders cannot know?

Capacity and Preference

1. What might their socialisation suggest in terms of how/when/even if at all to communicate/engage?
2. How do these capacities and cultural preferences differ from *ours* or others—and what does that mean for the ways through which we should engage local stakeholders?
3. What language is commonly spoken?
4. Can security and development issues be addressed within their forums—and can you be involved in that process?
5. Are stakeholders in close physical proximity and/or do they have affordable access to transportation?
6. Do these stakeholders normally keep records or receive written documentation or is preference to distribute information verbally or informally?
7. Do stakeholders have the capacity, and are they inclined, to use communication technology?
8. Are these stakeholders in regular contact with someone who can communicate on their behalf?

Situation Analysis

The collaborative processes get underway substantively when stakeholders are asked what currently exists. The purpose of this stage is to learn about the current situation, which may include today's: strengths, weaknesses, opportunities and threats, in addition to what dynamics are perceived as causing these realities. Information gathered from this stage informs planning and its corresponding M&E (baselines in particular).

Key Questions:

- What is happening now—and why?
- What needs to change—and how?

These straightforward questions can be pursued in a number of ways (dependent upon the findings from the Stakeholder stage as well as staff capacity). Practitioners who are more experienced at group facilitation techniques should refer to the **Comprehensive** Operational Manual version for a variety of more sophisticated tools. This version, however, assumes practitioners have minimal experience not only with this framework but also with stakeholder engagement techniques. In this case, semi-structured interviews are recommended as the most pragmatic and effective tool. 'Storytelling' techniques feature in these interviews. This means coming into the interview with a topic or 'domain' (e.g. public security) and then asking stakeholders to talk about that domain (prompted by the key questions set out above). Importantly, the selection and articulation of a domain should be carefully considered due to its central influence on their responses by, among other aspects, framing the discussion itself. During the interview: avoid 'leading' questions; exercise patience for sufficient response time; and allow wide latitude to chronicle what is important and 'real'. *Perceived* cause and effect links can be drawn from the narratives that unfold, specifically after the interviewer asks 'why is something happening?' Moreover, be prepared to adapt the lines of questioning should subsequent interviews begin to reveal issues or aspects unknown at the outset.

Throughout this process, there is no need to deny the 'subjectiveness' of information gained in this analysis, since humans cannot help but see the world based upon what we have come to understand as real. Importantly this unavoidable subjectivity can be turned into an asset by harnessing local perceptions as well as recognising that it reflects the various stakeholder perspectives that comprise their complex social system. Triangulating the various viewpoints can ensure information does not become misleading. In other words, the stakeholder forum that should be put in place, manifestly, by this framework's processes will help *manage* questionable claims for change by providing a platform for counter-claims. For example, if there is a vested interest in reinvigorating the power and legitimacy of traditional RoL actors *at the expense of* women, practitioners should not assume that such claims represent *the* local perspective, as there will be *many*. In such cases practitioners could, first, highlight the inconsistency with their own values and policy imperatives (as they too are legitimate stakeholders), while also ensuring that local stakeholders with counterclaims (e.g. women's groups) are afforded a negotiating platform from which to strive to overcome repressive conventions.

From this stage onward, practitioners should be prepared to take on an active, conflict resolution and change agent role rather than a passive/observer role, which wrongly presumes 'neutrality' in the first place. This will entail continually looking for opportunities to 'mend fences' between various stakeholders. A key goal is to help set up the stakeholder forum mentioned above so that local actors can begin to solve their own challenges rather than constantly relying on external assistance. External actors must avoid doing the 'heavy lifting' and key decision making as happens all too often currently. Apart from facilitating the concrete emergence of a stakeholder forum, a good initial step is to send out summaries of their responses (at first only their own, but with the view to ultimately sending all responses to all). Related to this goal is the need to identify and enable local change agents. Problematically, the most willing local change agents may be the least 'local' due, for instance, to time spent and/or education received abroad. This tension between competing legitimacies (i.e. foreign notions of what is legitimate versus local notions) should be watched to ensure the positive efforts of any change agents are not undermined.

It may be possible to gain a sense of stakeholders' **'Visions of Success'** towards the end of these interviews. In other words, gaining a sense of what it looks like to them when sustainable peace and development endeavours (from both external and internal sources) succeed? The point is to identify the desired conditions and outcomes of as many stakeholders as practicable, and then to prioritise goals. While these visions may not neatly track from the 'desired changes' and thus 'suggested solutions' drawn out from the above questions to put into the planning stage, they can nevertheless serve as powerful beacons symbolising what is important. It is also likely that many stakeholders will present overlapping visions which opens space to build relationships and common goals. Group facilitation techniques, described in the **Comprehensive** version, can be used to bring groups together and work through their visions to gain consensus and focus on action plans—but again, only for those with experience in these activities. Any commonality developed can potentially serve as a powerful source for conflict resolution.

In addition to enquiring about Visions of Success, these interviews will also be prime opportunities to learn what types of vehicles are best situated to communicate to the broader community. While this realm is taken up fully in the subsequent stage **'Community Communications'**, a **Situation Analysis** interview may afford the chance to begin to build that information for later use.

The RoL system continues to form the backdrop for this collaborative M&E framework. If resources permit, baselines of the broader RoL system can provide more than just useful context for narrower M&E priorities; they can uncover sites of concern that may in fact be impacting on your current focus. **RoL is conceived** herein as a complex 'system' comprising both the practices *and* the underpinning beliefs put forward by formal as well as informal actors in the areas of **security, judiciary, corrections**, and **laws**. The ongoing interactions are vital to how each other and the whole behave; as such, the system should not be understood as isolated parts. 'Security' refers to physical safety and those who provide it (e.g. policing, counter-insurgency, and/or direct measures to prevent violence). 'Judiciary' denotes the systems of rules and practices used to settle matters of justice. 'Corrections' refers to mechanisms of internment, rehabilitation and restoration of social balance. Finally, 'Laws' comprises the rules that govern society in general (distinct therefore from carrying out the provision of security, judiciary, and corrections). These functional areas are the key organs which *work together* to enable RoL; they cannot be treated as isolated or unconnected. Depending on the cultural context, many may even be provided by the same entity, whereby separation is not seen as integral to the achievement of RoL. What security, judiciary, and corrections 'look like' on the ground are thus notions which must be elicited from the broadest possible spectrum of local voices.

The *ideal* of RoL is realised when the functions of security, judiciary, corrections, and laws (in whatever manifestations they may take) adhere to the following four principles: 1) participation, 2) lack of bias, 3) accountability, and 4) transparency (or PLAT, as defined below). The contributions of international policing, as with other RoL components, should therefore be located in this broader systemic context.

Participation can be understood in conventional terms as a public which can influence state legislation in ways such as town meetings, or in unconventional ways conceived as the general public's ability to influence norms, conventions and practices—regardless of whether these are formalised and codified in a Western sense. As such, it is about members of a society having the capacity to participate in deciding how their RoL affairs are formulated and conducted.

Lack of Bias denotes an absence of discrimination or unequal treatment, which may be based (deliberately) on any criteria such as ethnicity or gender. Beyond discriminatory tendencies it is also about equal access to provision, which then asks if certain segments of society have lesser access based upon, for example, financial wherewithal or geographic location.

Accountability means that each one of the functional areas (including non-state mechanisms) must be accountable for their actions, whereby the point is to ensure that those delivering RoL do not operate with impunity. Accountability for actions includes a second aspect, that of ensuring the delivery of what the populace wants and in an effective manner.

Transparency refers to the public having a sound understanding of RoL functions, and the way in which they are enacted and developed.

Ask the following questions in regards to: 1) security 2) judiciary 3) corrections and 4) laws—either for each realm as a whole, and/or for specific actors and processes:

1) How well can the public influence provision? (participation)
2) How unbiased and equitably is it provided? (lack of bias)
3) How well does provision match what people want and conducted without impunity? (accountability)
4) How transparent is provision? (transparency)

The table below offers a tool by which to structure an assessment of, and therefore benchmark, the RoL system (or a narrower segment as needed). It shows how RoL *functions* are to be assessed against RoL *principles*, pointing out priority areas that may benefit from assistance. Use a scale from 1 (ideal condition) to 5

Rule of Law System	Functional Areas			
Principles (PLAT)	(1) Security	(2) Judiciary	(3) Corrections	(4) Laws
(1) Participation	Specific Evaluations (1–5): Provider #1 (e.g. state military or police) Provider #2 (e.g. local chief system) Provider #3 (e.g. vigilante gangs) Overall Evaluation (1–5)	Specific Evaluations (1–5): Provider #1 (e.g. state courts) Provider #2 (e.g. local customary system) Overall Evaluation (1–5)	Specific Evaluations (1–5): Provider #1 (e.g. state prison system) Provider #2 (e.g. local customary restorative system) Overall Evaluation (1–5)	Specific Evaluations(1–5): Provider #1 (e.g. state legislation) Provider #2 (e.g. local customary system rules) Overall Evaluation (1–5)
(2) Lack of bias	Specific Evaluations (1–5) Overall Evaluation (1–5)	Specific Evaluations (1–5) Overall Evaluation (1–5)	Specific Evaluations (1–5) Overall Evaluation (1–5)	Specific Evaluations (1–5) Overall Evaluation (1–5)
(3) Accountability	Specific Evaluations (1–5) Overall Evaluation (1–5)	Specific Evaluations (1–5) Overall Evaluation (1–5)	Specific Evaluations (1–5) Overall Evaluation (1–5)	Specific Evaluations (1–5) Overall Evaluation (1–5)
(4) Transparency	Specific Evaluations (1–5) Overall Evaluation (1–5)	Specific Evaluations (1–5) Overall Evaluation (1–5)	Specific Evaluations (1–5) Overall Evaluation (1–5)	Specific Evaluations (1–5) Overall Evaluation (1–5)

(poorest possible condition to score each functional area, based upon the above questions as they relate to each of the PLAT principles. ('Word pictures' describing each of these areas can be found in the Comprehensive version.)

Planning

After having identified and prioritised what is wanted (possibly including **'Visions of Success'**) and what is currently happening (baselines from the Situation Analysis), the aim of the next step is to describe the path forward for change. What activities might help achieve identified areas of change? This will involve determining what needs to change in the environment in a broad sense and how such change can be achieved in more specific terms. The change sought in the environment needs to be in line with the agreed upon visions, capacity, and organisational imperatives of engaged actors (including the AFP).

Steps for developing work plans:

- Break down the previously collated information into plans for action (include intervening police plans).
- Develop processes for change in consultation with stakeholders based on the cause and effect conclusions generated in the Situation Analysis stage (i.e. home-grown change theories).
- These plans for action will require consideration of human resources, activities, physical resources and material support (Who does what? What do we need? Where do we get it from?).
- Identify participants/actors for change (from the Situation and Stakeholder analyses).
- It will be necessary to formulate step by step processes for change (in cases of institutional change, this might include breaking down job descriptions or standard operating procedures).
- Identify activities for addressing the attitudes and relationships of those noted above.
- Planning should systematically consider risk including issues of sustainability and dependency.

Monitoring Loops

Not only should M&E derive explicitly from the above Planning stage, but it should also feed continuously into program management processes. In this sense M&E should be *embedded* not bolted-on. The aim of this stage is to design and initiate uncomplicated, ongoing processes for monitoring the implementation of work plans. Monitoring of current conditions generates a wealth of information to inform performance reporting, organisational learning, capacity development, and program adaptation. The establishment of these 'monitoring loops' includes the selection of indicators and their data sources, while formalised evaluation reports are generated in a subsequent stage.

It is important that these data collation processes are: simple, sustainable, context-specific and relevant to those on the ground, and transparent to those on the ground. Stakeholders should therefore be involved in the design as well as the ongoing data collection, ensuring this approach remains 'demand driven'. Those stakeholders who nominate particular visions of success will be generally best placed to observe and report on change. This empowerment of local people to report on the change processes and impacts important to them not only develops local capacity and cooperation but it increases access to information for intervening actors (e.g. intelligence gathering).

A major differentiation of this framework is that a highly effective form of *accountability* stems from the transparent communication engendered by the ongoing feedback loops developed from this stage. That is, it bypasses the unrealistic expectation that systemic accountability will come from the often lengthy and complicated formal evaluation reports. Rather than relying on written reports being widely read by local stakeholders and practitioners alike, actors are continuously held accountable since transgressions or ineptitude are transparently communicated throughout the stakeholder/practitioner forum. The upshot is that the monitoring transforms from an internal management function known only to a relatively small number. In so doing, it becomes 1) shared as widely as is appropriate, and 2) a *de facto* evaluation function because it informs stakeholders about the progress and cause-effect related to the key issues.

This is very straightforward in practice, flowing from previous stages as summarised here:

> informed by mission context parameters → highlight problems → identify change process → plans are made to address these issues → action is taken → stakeholders remain informed → and stakeholders monitor the situation and report back through the broader stakeholder forum mechanisms

The process is inherently transparent. There is genuine grounded accountability and local people are informed and in turn disseminate information to their social/professional spheres. Moreover, no different to each of the elements herein, it must remain simple and direct because making it complicated promises myriad problems.

Consider the following questions when establishing monitoring loops:

- How will we know we have achieved the visions?
- What will it look like?
- What changes will be happening along the way (i.e. planning steps)?
- What are the indicators of having achieved steps in the work plan?
- How can we know when things are going wrong (i.e. process for being continually informed)?
- How can we gain valuable insights from the 'emotional' landscape (e.g. from fear to hope)?
- What data do we need for these indicators and how can we collect and collate it?
- Who is best placed to collect this data?
- Will this data be reliable; has it been triangulated sufficiently, or can we improve its validity by getting information from further sources?

Community Communications

This step develops the means by which to communicate to the broadest audience (i.e. those not already aware) the plans and goals generated throughout the previous stages. Issues already identified—such as power, risk, capacity, logistics and preferred modes of communication—will be crucial to this endeavour, which seeks to inform the largest number of people in the most engaging, relevant and efficient manner.

While the main purpose is to inform, some opportunity for participant input will be beneficial toward the goal of broader ownership. Accordingly, the process may need to be flexible to allow feedback and participation where necessary. Anonymous drop-in boxes are useful for this purpose as well, while providing an additional tool for complaint mechanisms, thus adding to accountability.

This step is crucial for accountability and legitimacy. Informing the broader community ensures that reasonable expectations evolve and are managed. If the community is informed about the changes being initiated they can offer support as well as apply reasonable pressure to deliver (strengthening demand side reform). It is critical this stage be undertaken prior to exploring the unintended consequences as it will increase the chance of valuable feedback.[1016]

Unintended Consequences

Prior to formal evaluation and reporting, it is important to explore unintended consequences (both positive and negative) in order to incorporate these insights into future planning and M&E design. Ideally this step will entail an open forum to allow a broad range of views and experiences to emerge. Avoiding the blind spots which typically accompany tunnel vision is the most important aim of this stage.

Stakeholders and practitioners should be engaged in open-ended questions that reveal otherwise concealed issues. In short, we must acknowledge that those implementing M&E cannot always know what they are looking for in advance. For example:

- What is the most significant change (around a selected domain such as policing or security) you have witnessed in the last (specific period of time)?[1017]

Answers to questions such as this can be abstracted, grouped and prioritised to gain inductive insights identifying disabling and enabling factors and producing evidence of cause and effect relationships.

Evaluation Reporting

The aims of the previous stages have been to generate information and provide ongoing feedback to *broad* audiences, while simultaneously developing capacity and fostering relationships. Accountability is an important side effect. These aims are either missing or left largely unfulfilled by mainstream models. This

---

1016 A common problem with engaging the community in evaluation processes (as per the following stage) is they are often not well informed about donor ToRs or activities, nor are they aware of the specific changes happening within their own institutions. As a consequence expectations tend to be inflated—this results in critical feedback which is ill informed and often useless for informing program adaptation and reports.

1017 Refer to 'Most Significant Change Technique'—see Comprehensive version.

stage is about transferring and translating this wealth of information into more formalised evaluation reports for managerial or accountability purposes. Practitioners will therefore refer to the data they have already generated in the various practical documents compiled along the way. Baseline data should be sufficiently established by this point.

Evaluation reporting may take two forms, depending on the purpose and thus recipients: 1) those for mainly **external** consumption (e.g. donors/funders), being driven by accountability imperatives foremost on top of learning; and 2) those developed principally for **internal** learning concerned with program or M&E adaptation.

'**External Reports**' can be used to fulfill accountability mechanisms in many instances such as: the overarching operational commanding organisation (e.g. AFP, UN etc); the in-country partner agency; and domestic reporting requirements (i.e. donor Government reporting). For these reports, the requirements of the external agency's reporting template will determine how the data collated from previous stages can be used and how it should be presented. The basic donor reporting process will follow these steps:

1) Map the most current iterations of information/data you already have (e.g. use cause and effect mapping to plot the myriad of enabling and disabling factors as reported by stakeholders).
   - The primary purpose of this exercise is to generate a visual representation to understand how the data fits into the changing environment and to demonstrate that it is all accounted for in this process (transparency).
   - Ensure that it is in a manner accessible to those who can assist and/or have an interest (i.e. participating stakeholders). Whatever form this takes, it should become standardised for the operation.
   - Organise this data in a manner that can be transferred to the relevant reporting framework.
   - Identify the data which needs to be further verified, standardised, ranked or condensed (abstracted).
2) Transfer data to the report format
   - Ideally the format of this external document will be able to account for all your information—even if in a heavily reduced form (i.e. inputs, activities, outputs, outcomes, (vision) impacts, indicators, and findings in relation to indicators and key learning and actionable information).
   - Sections of the report could include successes, challenges, lessons learnt, action plans and monitoring loops, recommendations for change, and sustainability assessment/capacity status.

Regarding the '**Internal Reports**' over which those in the stakeholder forum such as yourselves have control, the following characteristics are recommended. Firstly, because questions pertaining to cause and effect are central to evaluation, the distinction between 'attribution' and 'contribution' should be clearly spelled out. That is, what effect did our program have in particular timeframes? Although practitioners commonly speak in terms that imply programs 'cause' outcomes (e.g. improved policing practices), outcomes result from a combination of many forces, one of which will have been mission programming activities. The portrayal of cause and effect should be understood as follows. Claims of causation beyond outputs (e.g. number of police having completed a training course) must be altered to reflect the *contribution* that specific activities or programs may have had at the outcome level. (See below graph adapted from Channel Research.)

Moreover, since 'reality' is never seen identically across the spectrum of stakeholders it rings false to speak of a singular outcome. The set of conditions that comprise an outcome will be perceived differently according to stakeholder perspective and therefore it is accurate only to speak of outcomes in the plural, even though the topic focus is singular (e.g. police conduct). This articulation will reflect the multiplicity of perspectives held by each stakeholder group as already elicited from the data collation processes. For example, increased school attendance by girls is an outcome that may be viewed positively by many while negatively by some.

Secondly, reports should maintain this 'outcomes' focus rather than feature outputs. Outputs may occasionally need to suffice as a measure of success but, generally speaking, they are at best a partial indicator of short-term productivity and it will be important to avoid the pitfalls associated with an 'outputs' focus. In spite of the relative ease with which to 'attribute' outputs to activities, and the similarly high degree of control over outputs, such a focus nevertheless risks missing the point by ignoring how policing outputs combine with other forces/factors to produce that which truly matters: namely, the outcomes and impacts relating to the visions of success developed in the early process stages. This approach entails rejecting conventional reductionist thinking which operates as though

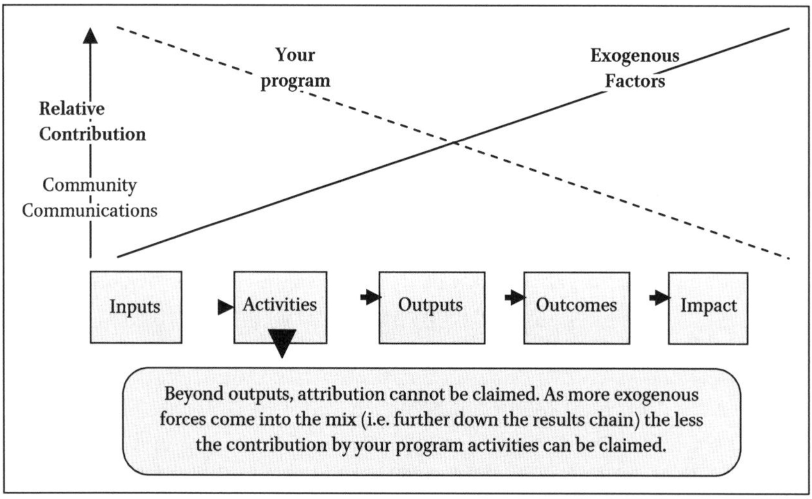

any system can be understood by analysing its component parts in isolation. An outcomes focus instead recognises that complex systems science is suited to this space by emphasising that the interaction between component parts is what matters to emergent patterns of behaviour.

The diagram illustrated below remains straightforward so that it can be used in the real world. Once specific indicators have been developed through the processes set out in above stages, the data used to populate findings can be made to consider the following forms of aggregation: 'geographic levels' (e.g. national, provincial, village); 'spatial phenomena' (which cut across geographic levels—such as natural resource boundaries or transportation routes); 'units of analysis' (social organisations/groups such as women or government agencies). For instance, how has security changed for different provinces, or for women as opposed to men, or around areas of natural resource abundance (e.g. diamond mines)? Asking how indicators might differ according to these forms of disaggregation promises incisive rather than misleading analyses ensue. The vital caveat however is to consider these facets through the 'stakeholder forum' rather than only by those outside of the collaborative processes espoused in this framework.

Example of recommended reporting format (for external reports too if possible):

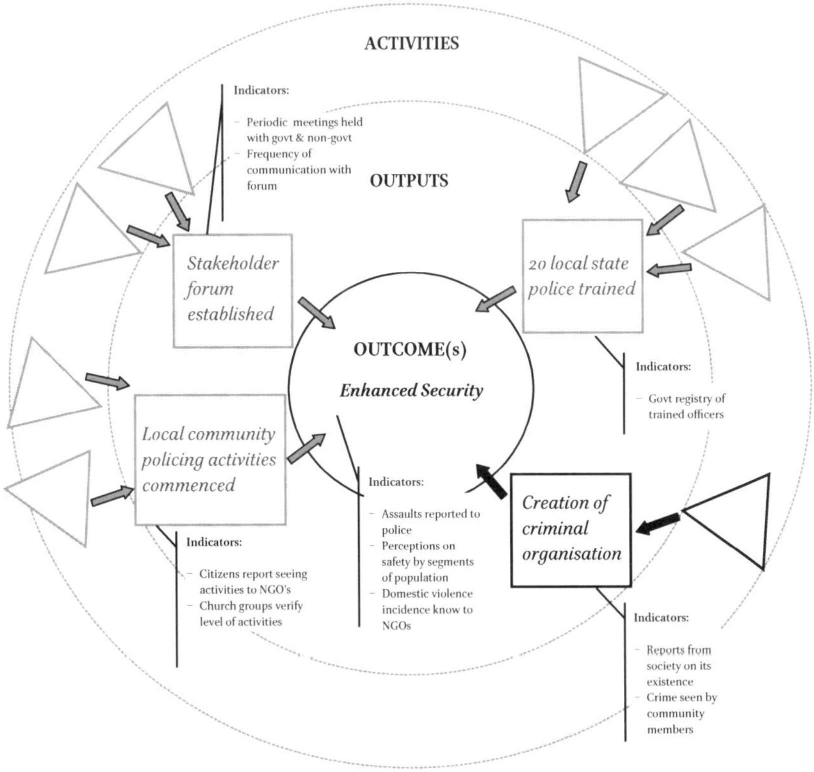

While retaining the focus on outcomes or impact indicators, and ensuring that indicators have been developed as much as practicable by stakeholders, the following criteria (consistent with OECD/DAC—albeit with added elements) can ensure important aspects have been considered.

- How have activities contributed to sustainable outcomes? For instance, if external aid were to stop, could the systems in place be financed (or resourced more generally) by the host country or community?
- How relevant to the desired outcomes were the activities? In other words were they aligned demonstrably?
- How efficient were they? Could they have made similar contributions to the outcomes with fewer resources?
- How significant were they in relation to other factors? Mildly or substantially?
- How extensive were the changes that came about as a result of program contributions? That is, were the changes quite narrow in their effect or touch a much wider base of the community?
- Has the 'emotional' landscape been considered? Do we see, for instance, a reduction in fear?
- Have outcomes been considered based upon the following forms of aggregation: 1) 'geographic levels' (e.g. national versus local); 2) 'spatial phenomena' (e.g. along supply lines); 3) 'units of analysis' (e.g. women or ethnicity)?

The best results from the above questions, for instance, might be a policing program for which activities aligned closely with the desired changes, yielding sustainable systems, done with minimal resources and maximum significance, having penetrated the widest possible cross section of stakeholders.

Finally, reports must remain straightforward and succinct, thereby accessible to the widest practicable audience. Historically, complicated and/or lengthy reports have failed to reach anything but the smallest audiences. Regardless of the particular formatting, the information derived from a broad spectrum of stakeholder engagement will have the benefits of maximizing buy-in while minimizing resistance.

After Action Review

The main purpose of this stage is to identify lessons learnt and ensure this information is used and retained. This is an opportunity for collaborative reflection. During the After Action Review, valuable evaluation data will emerge and can be further explored and analysed as appropriate. Further, it offers an excellent opportunity to meet with stakeholders, including other agencies (whole-of-government) and operational partners as well as international organisations working in the environment (i.e. multinational bodies, other donor governments and NGOs). This joint review should reflect on what went wrong, what went right and what needs to change. Reference to process and therefore the process indicators (see attached 'Process Appraisal' table) may also be useful in these discussions.

It will depend on what you need to achieve as to the number and type of stakeholders you consult in this process. Refer to the Stakeholders stage for determining an appropriate forum and format for communication based on the desired participants.

Steps for a Joint After-Action Review:

1) Identify the end of a particular action, program or era. This may be anything from an actual activity or event to a periodic review time;
2) Identify participants—try to include those involved in implementation as well as those in the environment who may have experienced the consequences of activities;
3) Agree upon an agenda with participants and a forum/format for discussion.

Exit interviews are a way of retaining information in an organisation when someone leaves. They are a relatively quick and inexpensive way of shortening the learning curve of newcomers, and retaining vital information. If feedback about the way the organisation functions is also sought from those leaving, exit interviews can be a source of evaluation data that can help with richer program adaptation. Often the end of an employment period provides an opportune time to seek honest and open feedback. Information from exit interviews can also form a new baseline from which we gauge changes within the new deployment period.

It is beneficial to begin planning how to capture the leaver's knowledge as early as realistically possible. Face-to-face interviews are ideal when the focus is on (tacit) knowledge retention. In terms of performance feedback—strengths and weaknesses of the organisation, and what can be done better in the future—surveys and telephone interviews are appropriate.

Process Appraisal

		Which process phases have been completed,			
		Mission Context	Stakeholders	Situation Analysis	Planning
Toolbox	Interviews by Proxy				
	Single Text Docs				
	Citizen Councils				
	Dynamic Facilitation and Choice Creating				
	Participatory Social Mapping				
	Force Field Analysis				
	Storytelling Interviews				
	Community Focus Groups				
	Dialogue Interveiws				
	Learning Journey				
	Appreciative Inquiry				
	Spheres of Influence				
	Historical Narratives				
	Local Spokesperson				
	Cook Ups				
	Wish List				
	Card Techniques				
	Affinity Analysis				
	Matrix Analysis				
	Adaptation of the 21st Century Town Meeting				
	Story Telling Workshops				
	Participatory Cause and Effect Mapping				
	Fishbone Analysis				
	Six Thinking Hats				
	Overcoming Power and Difference				
	Community Interactive Theatre				
	Chat Shows				
	Pass It On (Utilising Informal Networks)				
	Drop in Boxes				
	Most Significant Change				
	Success Case Method (SCM)				
	Storytelling as a Building Block in Strategic Evaluation				
	Critical Moments Reflection Methodology				
	Exit Calendar/Diary and Exit Interviews				

using which tools, and to what degree?				
Monitoring Loops	Community Comm'tions	Unintended Conseq'nces	Evaluation Reporting	After Action Review

INDEX